THE
HANDY
CHRISTIANITY
ANSWER
BOOK

Stephen A. Werner, Ph.D.

VISIBLE INK PRESS

Detroit

About the Author

Stephen Werner has a doctorate in the historical study of Christian theology. He has taught as an adjunct instructor at several universities in the St. Louis area for over twenty-eight years. In addition to Christian history; he has taught courses on world religions, religion and art, mythology, and creative thinking. His book *How to Study Religion* (Cognella Academic Publishing, 2019) provides a highly readable and easy-to-understand introduction to religion for college students or for those who are curious about religion.

Werner has also taught courses on American culture covering such figures as Frank Sinatra and Elvis Presley. His research area has been on important American Catholic Jesuits from the St. Louis area such as his biography on the influential Daniel Lord: *Daniel Lord, S.J.: The Restless Flame: Thinking Big in a Parochial World*. (The website is daniellordsj.com.) Dr. Werner has also written about Dismas Clark, S.J., who set up the first halfway house to support men coming out of prison. Clark was portrayed in the 1961 movie *The Hoodlum Priest*.

Werner is also the writer of plays, musicals, and an opera. His song "Irish Farewell" has been popular on YouTube.

Acknowledgments

Many thanks to John Waide and James T. Fisher, who have been the biggest supporters and believers in my research and writings. Many thanks to Terry Cooper, Dan Finucane, and Ed Lisson, S.J., who have been the biggest believers in my work as a teacher. Frank Cleary, S.J., was a great inspiration and model as to how to teach.

Lastly, many thanks to the staff of Visible Ink Press: publisher Roger Jänecke and managing editor Kevin Hile.

PHOTO SOURCES

Art Renewal Center: p. 266.

Balliol College, University of Oxford: p. 219.

Basillica of Santa Maria Novella: p. 337.

Bibliothèque de Genève: p. 228.

British Library: p. 207.

Bureau of Public Affairs: p. 271.

Adam Carr: p. 225.

CBS Television: p. 360.

Didier Descouens: p. 53.

Dnalor 01 (Wikicommons): p. 182.

Farragutful (Wikicommons): p. 6.

Manfredo Ferrari: p. 254.

Bernard Gagnon: p. 256.

Kanu Gandhi: p. 294.

Gemäldegalerie, Berlin: pp. 305, 317.

Georges Jansoone: pp. 155, 195.

Library of Congress, Carl Van Vechten collection: p. 359.

Los Angeles County Museum of Art: p. 345.

Louvre-Lens: p. 171.

Metropolitan Museum of Art: p. 102.

Musée Thomas-Henry: p. 189.

Museum Boijmans Van Beuningen: p. 144.

National Gallery of Art, Washington, D.C.: p. 339.

National Museum Kraków: p. 181.

National Portrait Gallery, London: p. 244.

Marie-Lan Nguyen: pp. 122, 137.

Odescalchi Balbi Collection, Rome: p. 167.

Ohara Museum of Art: p. 29.

Oro2 (Wikicommons): p. 4.

Palace of Versailles: p. 211.

Paradiso (Wikicommons): p. 96.

Philadelphia Museum of Art: p. 184.

Pinacoteca di Brera: p. 209.

Pinocoteca Vaticana: p. 38.

Peter Schmelzle: p. 204.

Rheinisches Landesmuseum Bonn: p. 215.

Scrovegni Chapel: p. 111.

Shutterstock: pp. 2, 8, 10, 12, 14, 16, 22, 30, 33, 36, 44, 46, 49, 51, 57, 60, 63, 66, 70, 71, 73, 77, 80, 82, 84, 86, 88, 90, 95, 99, 104, 107, 108, 113, 120, 123, 126, 131, 139, 142, 145, 150, 153, 157, 160, 162, 173, 187, 193, 198, 199, 218, 230, 233, 236, 246, 275, 276, 279, 281, 284, 289, 292, 297, 299, 301, 308, 312, 314, 324, 327, 328, 331, 347, 353, 380, 382.

Eric Stoltz: p. 322.

Swarthmore College: p. 243.

Antoine Taveneaux: p. 342.

Pete Unseth: p. 136.

Unterlinden Museum: p. 19.

Valyag (Wikicommons): p. 385.

Steve Werner: p. 152.

Wrongkind707 (Wikicommons): p. 24.

Zeromancer44 (Wikicommons): p. 177.

Public domain: pp. 40, 42, 55, 63, 127, 147, 213, 240, 247, 251, 260, 261, 264, 269, 355, 365, 367, 371.

ALSO FROM VISIBLE INK PRESS

PLEASE VISIT THE "HANDY ANSWERS" SERIES WEBSITE AT WWW.HANDYANSWERS.COM.

THE HANDY CHRISTIANITY ANSWER BOOK

Visible Ink Press®
43311 Joy Rd., #414
Canton, MI 48187–2075

Visible Ink Press is a registered trademark of Visible Ink Press LLC.

Most Visible Ink Press books are available at special quantity discounts when purchased in bulk by corporations, organizations, or groups. Customized printings, special imprints, messages, and excerpts can be produced to meet your needs. For more information, contact Special Markets Director, Visible Ink Press, www.visibleink.com, or 734–667–3211.

Managing Editor: Kevin S. Hile
Art Director: Mary Claire Krzewinski
Typesetting: Marco Divita
Proofreaders: Larry Baker and Shoshana Hurwitz
Indexer: Larry Baker

Cover images: Shutterstock.

ISBN: 978-1-57859-686-7

Cataloging-in-Publication data is on file at the Library of Congress.

10 9 8 7 6 5 4 3 2 1

Printed in the United States of America

Table of Contents

Timeline

This is a timeline of some of the major events and significant people in Christian history. Because so much has happened in the Christian world the past two thousand years, not every important event and person is listed.

Year	Event
c. 6–4 B.C.E. to 27–30 C.E.	Jesus of Nazareth
c. 5 B.C.E. to 67 C.E.	Paul of Tarsus, tireless missionary who wrote many of the letters in the New Testament and shaped the basic theology of Christianity
c. 34	Stoning of Stephen
c. 35–c. 107	Ignatius, early Christian writer and bishop
37–68	Emperor Nero, first Roman emperor to persecute Christians
c. 50	The Council of Jerusalem
69–155	Polycarp, early Christian writer and bishop.
70	The destruction of the Temple in Jerusalem by the Romans
Date unknown	Writing of the *Didache*
c. 70–c. 100	Writing of the Christian gospels
c. 100	Writing of the Book of Revelation
100–165	Justin the Martyr, early Christian apologist
121–180	Marcus Aurelius, emperor who persecuted Christians. He also wrote the *Meditations* on Stoic philosophy.
c. 155–c. 240	Tertullian, early Christian writer called "the father of Latin Christianity." He coined the term "Trinity."
d. 160	Marcion, denied the Old Testament and its image of God. His teaching would be called Marcionism and were seen as heretical.
c. 184–c. 253	Origen, writer and biblical scholar
201–251	Decius, Roman emperor who persecuted Christians
d. c. 202	Irenaeus, writer of *Against Heresies*.

Date unknown	List of the twenty-seven books in the New Testament accepted by most Christian communities
244–312	Diocletian, launched The Great Persecution of Christians
c. 250–c. 325	Lactantius, writer of *Divine Institutes*
c. 256–336	Arius, denied the divinity of Jesus. His teaching would be called Arianism and be seen as heresy
c. 260–c. 339	Eusebius, writer of *History of the Church,* the first history of Christianity
272–337	Constantine, Roman emperor who legalized Christianity
296–373	Athanasius of Alexandria, led a tireless fight against Arianism
313	Edict of Toleration (also called the Edict of Milan), legalized Christianity
325	Council of Nicaea, created the Nicene Creed defining the essential beliefs of Christians
c. 329–370	Basil the Great, theologian and bishop. He is known as the Father of Eastern Monasticism.
c. 329–390	Gregory of Nazianzus, important theologian and writer
c. 340–397	Ambrose, influential bishop of Milan
347–395	Theodosius, Roman emperor who made Christianity the official religion of the Roman Empire
347–420	Jerome, scholar who wrote the Latin translation of the Bible
c. 349–407	John Chrysostom, Archbishop of Constantinople who created the *Divine Liturgy of Saint John Chrysostom*
354–430	Augustine, prolific Christian writer who wrote the *Confessions*
381	Council of Constantinople I
431	Council of Ephesus
451	Council of Chalcedon
Late 400s	Patrick, brought Christianity to Ireland
c. 466–511	Clovis I, who became the first king of the Franks. He converted to Christianity
480–543 or 547	Benedict, wrote the *Rule of St. Benedict* and is known as the Founder of Western Monasticism
c. 482–565	Emperor Justinian, built the Hagia Sophia and created a uniform code of laws, the *Corpus Juris Civilis*
537	Hagia Sophia completed in Constantinople
540–604	Gregory the Great, influential and powerful bishop of Rome
553	Council of Constantinople II
570–632	Muhammad, the final prophet of Islam
d. 604	Augustine of Canterbury, missionary who brought Christianity to England
622	The Hijrah, the flight of Muhammad from Mecca
675–754	Boniface, Christian missionary to the Germanic tribes
680–681	Council of Constantinople III
732	The Battle of Tours in which Charles Martel, leading Christian forces, defeated Muslim forces under Abdul Rahman al Ghafiqi
787	Council of Nicaea II
800	Charlemagne crowned as the Holy Roman Emperor by Pope Leo III
826–869	The missionary Cyril, who, along with Methodius (815–885), brought Christianity to the Slavic people
869	Council of Constantinople IV

c. 1033–1086	Anselm of Canterbury, theologian who proposed the ontological argument for the existence of God
c. 1042–1099	Urban II, influential medieval pope
1054	The Great Schism, the break between the Orthodox Church and the Roman Catholic Church
1079–1142	Peter Abelard, theologian and writer, also known for his relationship with Héloïse
1095–1099	The First Crusade called by Pope Urban II
c. 1096–1160	Peter Lombard, theologian who wrote *Four Books of the Sentences*
1099	Fall of Jerusalem to the Crusaders
1123	Council of Lateran I
1139	Council of Lateran II
1147–1149	Second Crusade preached by Bernard of Clairvaux
1160–1216	Innocent III, influential medieval pope
1170–1221	Dominic de Guzmán, created a new religious order, the Order of Preachers, known as the Dominicans
1179	Council of Lateran III
1182–1226	Francis of Assisi, founder of the Franciscans. He became one of the most popular Catholic saints
1187	Saladin retook Jerusalem and then destroyed much of the Crusader States
1187–1192	Third Crusade, which included King Richard the Lionheart of England
c. 1200–1280	Albert the Great, wrote extensively on theology, philosophy, astrology, music, and science
1202–1204	Fourth Crusade, the Crusaders attacked and looted the Christian city of Constantinople
1212	Children's Crusade (much uncertainty exists over what actually happened)
1215	Council of Lateran IV
1217–1221	Fifth Crusade called by Pope Innocent III
1224–1274	Thomas Aquinas, important medieval theologian and author of the *Summa theologiae*
c. 1234–1303	Boniface VIII, influential medieval Pope
1245	Council of Lyons I
1248–1254	Seventh Crusade, led by King Louis IX of France
1265–1321	Dante Alighieri, author of *The Divine Comedy*
1270	Eighth Crusade; King Louis IX died on this crusade
1271–1272	Ninth Crusade
1274	Council of Lyons II
c. 1287–1347	William of Ockham, theologian and philosopher who proposed the philosophy of nominalism
1291	Acre, the last Crusader city, fell to Muslim armies
1309–1376	The Avignon Papacy, a period when the pope moved to Avignon, France
1311–1313	Council of Vienne
c. 1320–1384	John Wycliffe, theologian who called for reform in the Catholic Church
c. 1343–1400	Geoffrey Chaucer, author of *The Canterbury Tales*
1347–1351	The worst outbreak of the bubonic plague: The Black Death
c. 1347–1380	Catherine of Siena, theologian, philosopher, and a mystic who had great influence

Introduction

Welcome to the exploration of Christianity! Christianity is the largest religion in the world. Over two billion people identify themselves as Christians. Christianity begins with the life and teachings of Jesus. Over the past two thousand years, Christianity has spread throughout the world to become the religious faith giving meaning to the lives of countless people. Christianity has also had enormous influence on global culture.

This book explores the beliefs, practices, and influence of Christianity. It is written both for Christians who want a deeper understanding of their own tradition and for non-Christians and nonbelievers who want to understand the influence of Jesus, the history of Christianity, and all the diverse expressions of Christianity in the modern world.

This book is written in a clear and straightforward style. Although much detail is given, information is presented in such a way as to be understandable to readers who are new to the study of Christianity and to readers who are already knowledgeable about the Christian tradition. All the important topics of Christianity are covered: the life of Jesus, Christian beliefs about Jesus, how Christians live out their faith, the major figures and events in the history of Christianity, and the influence of Christianity on human culture. However, lots of small, interesting details are added to enrich the fascinating world of Christianity.

As you will see, Christianity is very diverse. If you are a believing and practicing Christian, you may discover practices and beliefs that are different from yours. Keep an open mind and understand that, from the beginning, different ways to live out the Christian message have existed. Hopefully, this book will give you an understanding of how different Christians think and the richness of the Christian tradition. On many points you may be reaffirmed in your understanding of your beliefs. On other points you may see things in a different way.

The first chapters explore Jesus: what we know about Jesus, what happened during his life, his teachings, other people in his story, Christian beliefs about Jesus, and the

Bible. A detailed overview of Christian history follows. If you have never learned about Christian history, you may discover it to be fascinating. Knowing Christian history helps people understand the shape of modern Christianity and the origins of various Christian denominations. The book then goes on to investigate how Christians live out their faith today. Topics covered include Christian celebrations and rituals, Christian beliefs about life after death, and Christian beliefs about angels and the devil. Since the Catholic Church is the largest denomination, it is described in detail. Finally, we will explore the influence of Christianity on culture in the arts of painting, sculpture, architecture, music, and film.

Note: quotes from the Bible are drawn from two commonly used, modern translations: the New Revised Standard Version (NRSV) and the New American Bible Revised Edition (NABRE).

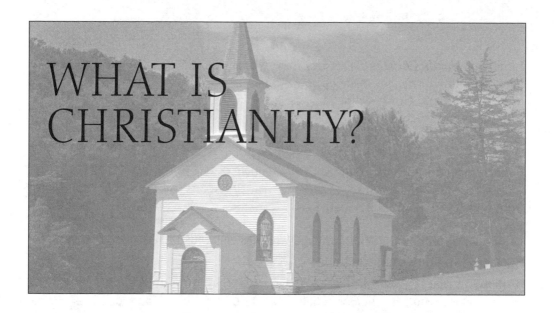

WHAT IS CHRISTIANITY?

THE DEFINITION AND SIZE OF CHRISTIANITY

Who is a Christian?

There is no simple, agreed-upon definition of what a Christian is. Many Christians hold different views on how to define the term "Christian." A simple and very broad definition states that a Christian is anyone who has religious beliefs about Jesus of Nazareth, who lived in the first century.

There are many people who believe that Jesus existed and that he had interesting and/or influential teachings. If these people hold no religious beliefs about Jesus, then they typically would not be called Christians. Religious beliefs about Jesus would include ideas such as the belief that his teachings were divinely inspired, or that he was a person specially chosen by God, or that he was more than simply a wise, human teacher, or that he rose from the dead.

Most Christians believe that the teachings of Jesus are uniquely special and that he was a uniquely special being. In later chapters, more details will be given on these beliefs.

Why are there so many different kinds of Christians?

Because no agreed-upon definition exists for the term "Christian," over the past two thousand years, a wide variety of groups have arisen who call themselves "Christians" yet have different beliefs.

Is it hopeless trying to study Christianity if there is no definition of what is a Christian?

No, not at all. All one has to do in studying Christianity is to keep track of which group of Christians one is describing. For example, after describing the life and teachings of

1

Jesus, this *Handy Christianity Answer Book* will explore the beliefs of mainline Christians. Mainline Christians make up some of the largest Christian denominations with long histories and clearly defined beliefs. Later in the book, other groups with divergent views will be explored.

What does the term "true Christian" mean?

Because of all the different groups with different views who call themselves "Christians," some Christians define themselves as being "true Christians" to differentiate themselves from others who hold different views.

Is the definition of a Christian "anyone who has religious beliefs about Jesus of Nazareth" an adequate definition?

It turns out that a qualification needs to be added to improve this definition. A Christian is "anyone who has religious beliefs about Jesus of Nazareth and identifies himself or herself as a Christian."

Why does the definition need to be clarified?

Studying religion is tricky even in trying to define "What is a Christian?" Islam is the second largest faith after Christianity. Muslims have religious beliefs about Jesus: they believe that Jesus was one of the prophets chosen by God. Therefore, it is helpful to add the qualification to the definition.

This definition of a Christian as "anyone who has religious beliefs about Jesus of Nazareth and identifies himself or herself as a Christian" is not a perfect one, but it is good enough to get started in exploring Christian belief down through the centuries. At some point, the reader might want to develop his or her own definition of what is a Christian.

I heard someone say that to be a Christian, one has to "accept Jesus as your Lord and Savior." Why can't that be the definition of who is a Christian?

For some people, that is the definition of a Christian: one who has accepted Jesus as his or her Lord and Savior. Some want to insist on this narrow definition. However, there are many people who call themselves Christians, who are very devout and regular churchgoers yet do not use that language as their definition of what it means

A Christian is "anyone who has religious beliefs about Jesus of Nazareth and identifies himself or herself as a Christian."

to be a Christian. In this book, which will explore all the various forms of Christianity, a broader definition is needed.

How many Christians are there?

There are about 2.3 billion Christians in the world, making it the largest religion. Islam is the next largest religion with about 1.8 billion followers. Hinduism has over one billion followers. In the United States, about 280 million people identify themselves as Christians.

However, counting the number of Christians is a bit tricky. The studies that give us these numbers simply try to estimate the number of people who identify themselves as Christians. The studies do not try to separate active Christians from nonactive Christians. Many of the people counted as Christians do not go to church regularly, do not belong to a church, nor do they have any sort of prayer life.

What do you mean by the term "religion"?

In this context, the term "religion" refers to the various religions of the world. The most important world religions are Buddhism, Christianity, Hinduism, Islam, Jainism, Judaism, Shintoism, Sikhism, and Taoism (listed alphabetically). There are also large numbers of people who practice traditional tribal religions and ethnic religions. Lastly, there are many people in the world who are not religious. (*The Handy Religion Answer Book,* second edition, provides a thorough introduction to the various religions of the world.)

Studying the various world religions can be complicated because there are different divisions within each religion, such as Theravada and Mahayana Buddhists and the Reform, Conservative, and Orthodox branches of Judaism. Christianity is particularly difficult to understand because in Christianity, there are more different groups than any other religion.

How many Christian groups are there?

There are somewhere between thirty thousand and forty thousand different Christian groups or denominations in the world.

However, note that Christians do not use the same language to describe their own groups. Some call their communities a church, while others call it a denomination. Others call their churches "nondenominational," which means they are not part of any traditional denomination.

One aid to try to understand the diversity of Christianity is to identify five major divisions within Christianity.

What are the five major divisions of Christianity?

Here are the five major Christian divisions. Numbers 1 and 2 are the oldest traditions going back to the early centuries of Christianity. The denominations in number 3 developed in the 1500s. The American-born denominations developed in the last several centuries.

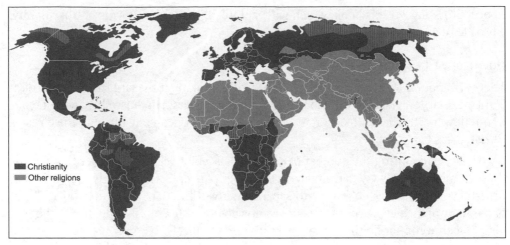

A somewhat simplified map of the distribution of Christian-faith populations throughout the world. The dark-grey regions are where Christianity is prominent, though not the only religion practiced.

1. The Christian Orthodox Churches; these churches are typically identified by nationality, such as "Greek Orthodox" and "Russian Orthodox."
2. The Roman Catholic Church.
3. Denominations that came from the Protestant Reformation in Europe; a few examples would be the Lutheran Church, the Presbyterian Church, and the Anglican Church.
4. American-born Christian denominations; a few examples would be the Disciples of the Christ and the Pentecostal churches.
5. American-born Christian denominations that reject the ideas of the Nicene Creed; the three most significant examples are the Church of Jesus Christ of Latter-day Saints (the Mormons), the Church of Christ, Scientist (the Christian Scientists), and the Jehovah's Witnesses.

In later chapters, *The Handy Christianity Answer Book* will explore in detail these five major divisions of Christian churches. There are also a few groups that do not fit within these divisions and will not be covered in this book.

THE CULTURAL INFLUENCE OF CHRISTIANITY

Why is it important to know about Christianity?

Christianity has had an immense influence on global culture. In particular, it played an important role in shaping Mediterranean, European, American, Canadian, Central American, and South American cultures. It is essential that Christians understand this influence but also important that non-Christians and nonbelievers also understand the significant influence of Christianity.

The influence of Christianity in America is most easily seen by driving on major streets where one encounters churches of many different denominations. Many cities in America have Christian names such as St. Louis, St. Paul, San Antonio, and Ste. Augustine. All the city names in California starting with "San" and "Santa" are the names of Christian saints.

Christianity has had a huge influence on art and architecture. Although museums of modern art have little or no Christian art, museums that cover longer periods have numerous paintings based on Christian themes. In the 1400s through the 1700s, many artists painted many significant and famous Christian paintings.

Some of the most famous pieces of architecture are Christian cathedrals such as the Hagia Sophia in Istanbul, Turkey; Notre Dame in Paris, France; the Chartres Cathedral in Chartres, France; and St. Peter's Basilica in Rome, Italy.

Christianity has also influenced our calendar. For example, Jesus lived two thousand years ago, and our system for numbering years counts from his life. Many people call the years "A.D." for *Anno Domini*, which means "Year of our Lord," which is based on the belief of Christians that Jesus is the Lord. Other people call the years "C.E.," which means "Common Era," but the years still count from the life of Jesus.

Christianity is the largest religion in America. For many Christians, their faith influences how they think and how they live. Many Christians believe in shaping their lives around Christian values. Christianity has a large impact on how many people live in American society. Some Christians vote according to their Christian values.

IMPORTANT VOCABULARY FOR STUDYING CHRISTIANITY

It is important to define and explain several key words to help in the study of Christian history and Christianity today.

What does the word "theology" mean?

"Theology" is made of the two Greek words *theos*, which means "God," and *logos*, which means "word." "Theology" is "words about God," or "the study of God." The Greek word *logos* gives the English root "ology," which means "the study of," so "geology" is the study of the earth since "geo" is the Greek word for "earth."

Although the word "theology" literally means "the study of God," there is no way to study God directly. God cannot be seen, and most believers do not think that God speaks to them directly. (Occasionally, people do claim to have messages directly from God.

5

However, smart people are very cautious about such messages since there are numerous examples in Christian history of people claiming to be guided by God who did very un-Christian things.) One definition describes theology as the critical study of the divine. The word "critical" means to take a serious look at something. Theology can also be defined as the critical reflection on the human experience of God. Yet another definition is that theology is the effort to understand religious faith and apply it to the current situations that people face.

As you can see, there are several different understandings of the term. Christian theology has to do with expressing and explaining the religious beliefs of Christianity. Theology can also be about exploring Christian faith and trying to figure out how to live out that faith. Theology is not limited to Christianity. Theology is part of all major religions. For example, one can speak of Islamic theology or Hindu theology.

Two other words derive from the word "theology": the adjective "theological" and the word for a person who does theology in a serious way: a "theologian." There are many Christian theologians today and many important theologians of the past such as Augustine, Thomas Aquinas, and Martin Luther.

What do the words "doctrine" and "dogma" mean?

"Doctrine" and "dogma" are two words that refer to the teachings and beliefs of a denomination or a church. To some people, the word "dogma" has a negative feel to it, implying a rigidity of thought. However, the word can also simply mean the teachings of a Christian group.

Christian denominations disagree on the need to spell out their doctrine in detail. Some groups, relying on the Bible, do not have written documents laying out their teachings. Other churches have documents such as Martin Luther's *Large Catechism* (1529) and *Small Catechism* (1529) that give the basics of the Lutheran Church's doctrine. The Roman Catholic Church has given its doctrine in great detail in the *Catechism of the Catholic Church*, which can be viewed online.

What does the word "catechism" mean?

A catechism is a book that presents and explains the teachings of a denomination or church. A very famous example was *The Baltimore Catechism*, used by millions of American Roman Catholics up until the 1960s. Some denominations have special

On the exterior of the Cathedral of Mary our Queen in Baltimore, Maryland, is a relief that commemorates the famous *Baltimore Catechism* that was used by millions of American Catholics until the 1960s.

programs to teach their faith. A person in the program is often called a "catechumen," and the material being taught is called "catechesis."

What does the word "apologetics" mean?

"Apologetics" is the term for writings that explain or defend Christian faith. The word comes from early Christianity when writers defended their faith in works called "apologies." For example, Justin Martyr, who lived in the second century, wrote his *First Apology* and *Second Apology* to defend Christianity. (There are also non-Christian examples, such as Plato's *Apology*, where Socrates defended himself against the charge that he was corrupting youth with his philosophical questions.) "Apologetics" is writing or speaking to defend one's religious beliefs from people who disagree with it or who do not understand it. "Apologetics" is not about saying "I'm sorry."

What do the words "heresy" and "orthodoxy" mean?

To put it simply, heresy is wrong belief and orthodoxy is right belief. A person who believes in heresy is called a "heretic," and his or her views are labeled as "heretical." A person who believes in orthodoxy has views that are "orthodox."

Some Christian denominations use the word "orthodox" in their names, such as the Greek Orthodox and the Russian Orthodox. One branch of the Jewish religion is called "Orthodox Judaism," and its followers are called "Orthodox Jews."

However, it is important to remember that the words "heresy" and "orthodox" are words of judgment. The terms are used as judgments of people's religious views. Thus in using these terms, one must clarify who is making the judgment. One man's orthodoxy is another man's heresy. One woman's heresy is another woman's orthodoxy. These terms are relative, which means they depend on who is making the judgment. Note that whether a place is east or west depends on where you are standing. The judgments of heresy and orthodoxy depend on who is making the judgment.

What does the word "denomination" mean?

The word "denomination" is helpful in labeling many Christian groups that have some type of organization or share a common history. For example, many people speak of the Methodist, Lutheran, and Baptist denominations. There are many more denominations. In many places. one can drive around and see numerous church buildings that represent different denominations.

The word "denomination" is based on the Latin word *nomen*, which is the word for "name," so "denominations" are simply the names given to different Christian groups. However, there is some imprecision in how the term is used. It can be used to describe an organized religious group, such as the United Methodist Church, or it can be used more broadly to identify groups with a common history, such as to designate the Methodist denomination as different from the Baptist denomination.

In America, some Christian groups have reacted to the term "denomination." Some groups see themselves as the true Christians and not just one group among many. Thus, they call themselves "nondenominational," which means that they are not part of a traditional denomination such as Presbyterian, Methodist, or Baptist. Also, many nondenominational churches are independent congregations unconnected to other congregations.

What does the word "sect" mean?

The word "sect" is harder to pin down than the word "denomination." There is no agreed-upon definition of the word. It is often used for a religious group that is not recognized as its own denomination. The word can also be used for a faction within a denomination.

The word "sect" sometimes seems to have a negative feel. Some people use it to refer to those groups they think have the wrong beliefs. Some other people might be offended if someone called their religious group a "sect." *The Handy Christianity Answer Book* avoids using the term.

Are there churches that are not part of denominations?

There are many independent churches that are not part of any denomination.

What is the meaning of the word "church"?

The English word "church" is derived from words in older forms of English and German. The Greek word used in the New Testament is *ekklēsia*, which is the word for an assembly. Several English words are based on *ekklēsia*. A group of church leaders could be called an ecclesiastical body. A church minister could be called an ecclesiastic. The word "church" has several different meanings. Christian denominations often have different understandings of the word that reflect different theological views.

The word can mean a building, a local church community, or the entire denomination. A person might say, "My church meets in an old church built in 1874, and we are members of the Presbyterian Church." The word is used in three different ways. The first meaning is the local community of believers, the second is the building, and the third meaning is the denomination.

Over the centuries, Christians have often argued over the meaning of the word and use of the word "church." When a Protestant says the word "church," often he or she is describing the people of a congregation coming together to pray and worship. When a Catholic uses the term, he or she often means the institution of the Catholic Church, which is headed by the pope in Rome.

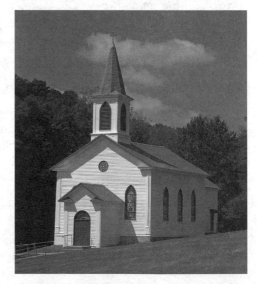

The word "church" can refer to the physical building in which services are held, but it can also refer to a local community attending a church, a denomination, or to the Roman Catholic Church.

WHO IS JESUS?

SOURCES ON JESUS

What are our sources for information about Jesus?

There are seven sources of information about Jesus that can be grouped as biblical sources—information in the Bible—and nonbiblical sources—information not in the Bible:

Biblical sources

The three synoptic gospels: Matthew, Mark, and Luke
The Gospel of John
Information about Jesus found in the rest of the New Testament
Old Testament prophecies

Nonbiblical sources

Roman and Jewish sources from the time of Jesus
Apocryphal writings (early Christian writings not in the Bible)
Later Christian tradition

What are the biblical sources of information about Jesus?

The gospels provide our main source of information on the life on Jesus: Matthew, Mark, Luke, and John. Three gospels provide the most detail: Matthew, Mark, and Luke. These are called the synoptic gospels since they share many passages that are the same or similar. The Gospel of John, however, includes a number of different details and stories about the public ministry of Jesus. The Gospel of John also includes long, theological discourses by Jesus on the meaning of his life and mission. Christians have different views on how the Gospel of John relates to the three synoptic gospels.

9

The gospels are four of the twenty-seven books in the New Testament. However, the other New Testament writings, such as the letters of Paul, give very little information on the life of Jesus. (The New Testament book Acts of the Apostles does describe the Ascension of Jesus in the first chapter.) These other New Testament writings present the early Christian beliefs about Jesus and the vision of early Christians as to how to live out their faith, but they add little to our knowledge of the facts about Jesus. It is likely that most of these other New Testament writings were written by people who were not eyewitnesses of Jesus.

The Old Testament contains many passages that Christians see as prophecies or texts that foreshadow Jesus. For example, Psalm 22:18–19 states, "They stare at me and gloat; they divide my garments among them; for my clothing they cast lots." Many Christians believe this is prophecy of the details of the Crucifixion of Jesus.

The book of Isaiah describes the Servant of the Lord:

He grew up like a sapling before him, like a shoot from the parched earth; He had no majestic bearing to catch our eye, no beauty to draw us to him. He was

A fresco at St. Nicholas Church in Trnava, Slovakia, depicts the authors of the four gospels: Mark, Luke, Matthew, and John.

spurned and avoided by men, a man of suffering, knowing pain, like one from whom you turn your face, spurned, and we held him in no esteem. Yet it was our pain that he bore, our sufferings he endured. We thought of him as stricken, struck down by God and afflicted, but he was pierced for our sins, crushed for our iniquity. He bore the punishment that makes us whole, by his wounds we were healed. (53:2–5)

Most Christians see this as a prophecy or a prefiguring of Jesus. However, Christians disagree over whether or not this passage gives specific information about Jesus, such as the idea that Jesus was not physically attractive.

What is the best way to read the gospels?

If you have the time, the best approach is to read all four gospels. One might start with Mark since it is the shortest gospel, then read Matthew, Luke, and finally John.

If a person only has interest in reading one gospel, the Gospel of Luke is often the best choice. Even better, while reading Luke, is to also read Matthew, Chapters 1 and 2, for both versions of the infancy stories. Then read Matthew, Chapters 5 and 6, along with Luke, Chapter 6, to get both versions of the beatitudes and the key teachings of Jesus.

The Gospel of John is the most challenging to read because it includes long, theological teachings by Jesus. John's gospel is best read after one has some familiarity with the other gospels and some knowledge of Christian belief.

What are the nonbiblical sources of information about Jesus?

There are three nonbiblical sources of information about Jesus: Roman and Jewish sources from the time of Jesus, apocryphal writings (early Christian writings not in the Bible), and later Christian tradition.

What are the Roman and Jewish sources from the time of Jesus?

There are few Roman writings that mention Jesus. Although a census is described in the Gospel of Luke, no public records on Jesus exist. Writing around the year 116 C.E., the Roman historian and senator Tacitus, in a discussion of Christians being persecuted by the Emperor Nero, does mention that Jesus was executed by Pontius Pilate. The Roman writer Pliny the Elder wrote a letter to the Roman emperor Trajan, around the year 112 C.E., discussing the problem of how to handle Christians being persecuted by the Romans.

Jesus is mentioned briefly in the writings of Josephus, a Jewish historian who wrote *Antiquities of the Jews*. Jesus is also mentioned in the Jewish Talmud, a collection of writings that contains commentaries on the Jewish Scriptures and in particular the Jewish Law. The Talmud contains reference to Jesus. (There is debate whether these references refer to Jesus of Nazareth or some other person.) Scholars debate over what these references of Josephus and the Talmud tell us about Jesus. However, neither source adds much to our knowledge of Jesus.

What are the Dead Sea Scrolls?

The Dead Sea Scrolls are manuscripts found in the Qumran Caves near the Dead Sea in the 1940s and 1950s in what is today the country of Israel and the Palestinian Territory. About 40 percent of the manuscripts are copies of writings from the Hebrew Scriptures. (The Jewish Bible is called the Hebrew Scriptures. The texts of the Jewish Bible became the Christian Old Testament.) Another 30 percent are copies of known texts that did not make it into the Hebrew Scriptures. The final 30 percent are previously unknown writings of Jewish religious groups.

Scholars debate over who assembled these writings and why they were buried in the caves. Were they assembled by the Jewish Dead Sea community called the Essenes who lived near the Dead Sea or by the priests in Jerusalem, the Sadducees? Very possibly, these manuscripts were hidden in the caves to protect them from destruction by the Romans, who laid siege and then destroyed Jerusalem and the Temple in the year 70 c.e.

Do the Dead Sea Scrolls tell us anything about Jesus?

The Dead Sea Scrolls do not mention Jesus. Did the people who wrote them know about Jesus? There is no way to know whether they did or not. Although the Scrolls do not add anything to our knowledge of Jesus, they help us to understand the complex religious world of Jesus. Judaism at the time of Jesus had many different competing groups with very different understandings of how to live out being the People of God.

What are the apocryphal writings about Jesus?

There are dozens of early Christian writings, such as the Gospel of Thomas, that did not make it into the Bible. Down through the centuries, Christians have debated whether or not these writings add to our knowledge of Jesus.

The Dead Sea Scrolls are on display at a museum in Qumran, Israel, where they were discovered about seventy years ago. They include texts from the Hebrew Scriptures and related writings.

What is the Gospel of Thomas?

The Gospel of Thomas contains 114 sayings of Jesus. Many of the sayings are the same as the sayings of Jesus in the traditional gospels. Some other sayings are similar to sayings in the four gospels. Finally, some sayings are different from what is in the other gospels. The question is whether these last sayings are more authentic sayings from Jesus or less authentic. Do they add to our knowledge of Jesus, or are they distortions of the original message of Jesus? (More will be said on the Gospel of Thomas in the Appendix.)

What about later Christian tradition?

Later Christian tradition has filled in many details about Jesus. However, it is hard to know whether these details are accurate facts passed down or made up. In some cases, later Christian tradition has distorted the facts. For example, it was a later Christian idea that Mary Magdalene, one of the followers of Jesus, was a former prostitute. Many people believe this, even though there is no evidence for it in the gospels. Mary Magdalene is also identified with the woman caught in adultery in the Gospel of John; however, in the Gospel of John, the woman is not named.

BACKGROUND ON JESUS

What was the name of Jesus?

Although many people refer to him as "Jesus Christ," his name was Jesus. In his time, he would have been called "Jesus, son of Joseph" or "Jesus of Nazareth." "Christ" is not the last name of Jesus but rather a title that means "Messiah." Jesus avoided the title Christ and often referred to himself as the Son of Man. For centuries, Christians have argued over the enigmatic title "Son of Man," which seems to emphasize humility, but to many readers of the gospels, it is not clear what Jesus meant by it.

What are some of the unanswered questions about Jesus?

Unfortunately, our sources of information about Jesus are limited. All kinds of questions have been asked about Jesus that have no definitive answers. Is it certain that Jesus was not married? When exactly did he live? What did Jesus look like? What happened to Joseph, the father of Jesus, who does not appear in the later gospel stories? Could Jesus read and write? Most likely, Jesus spoke Aramaic, but did he know other languages? Over the centuries, many fanciful stories have been created about a love or marriage relationship between Jesus and Mary Magdalene. Exactly what was the relationship between Jesus and Mary Magdalene?

Why do the gospels lack so many details about the life of Jesus?

The gospels were written thirty or more years after the life of Jesus. Although based on stories passed down from eyewitnesses, the gospels were not written by eyewitnesses.

This gets a little confusing because several of the gospels, such as John, are named after eyewitnesses. However, it is unlikely that the Apostle John—an eyewitness—wrote the Gospel of John. (Whether the follower of Jesus named John lived long enough to actually write the gospel named after him is one of many points over which Christians have different opinions.)

Also, Jesus lived at a time when the vast majority of people could not read or write. Written records did not exist for most people. This is very different from the situation today, where the details of our lives are recorded in countless places. It is easy today to find out information about your deceased great-grandparents because of modern record keeping. No records were kept on ordinary people during the time of Jesus.

We also do not know the thoughts of ordinary people of this time period. Only when we have lots of ordinary people leaving behind letters and journals can we know many details of their lives. Beginning from the time of the American Civil War, many such writings have survived. A few centuries prior, no such writings existed.

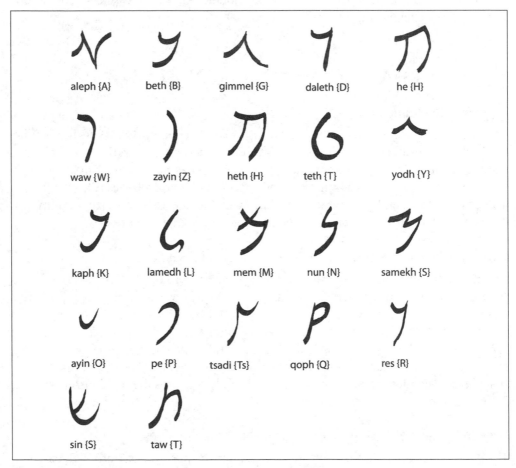

aleph {A} beth {B} gimmel {G} daleth {D} he {H}

waw {W} zayin {Z} heth {H} teth {T} yodh {Y}

kaph {K} lamedh {L} mem {M} nun {N} samekh {S}

ayin {O} pe {P} tsadi {Ts} qoph {Q} res {R}

sin {S} taw {T}

Jesus most likely spoke the common tongue of his time and place, Aramaic, the letters of which are shown here. Aramaic is a language related to both Hebrew and Arabic.

Lastly, the decades after Jesus were a time of trauma and destruction for the land where he lived, called Judaea and Galilee. Many of the Jews of the time resented their occupation by the Romans. These Jews rose up in revolt and drove out the Romans. However, the Romans brought in a larger army and laid waste to the city of Jerusalem, the Temple in Jerusalem, and countless villages and communities in the environs. There is no way to know how much information about Jesus that would have survived under more stable conditions was lost because of the devastation brought about by the Jewish revolt and the Roman response.

What language did Jesus speak?

Most likely, Jesus spoke Aramaic, which is related to both Hebrew and Arabic. Aramaic was the language of the common people of the time in that part of the world. Jesus lived in a province of the vast Roman Empire. Although Latin was the language of the Romans, Greek was an important language in the Empire for business and literature.

We do not know if Jesus knew any Greek or Latin. Very likely he did not since he probably did not receive an education. At the time, very few people received any education. Very few people were literate. After the death of Jesus, the Christian New Testament was written in Greek.

Did Jesus know any Hebrew? Again, we do not know. In recent centuries, most Jewish boys have been educated in reading and writing Hebrew. Such practices were rare at the time of Jesus. Chapter 4 of the Gospel of Luke describes Jesus in the synagogue in Nazareth on the Sabbath reading a passage from the prophet Isaiah. Some Christians use this passage as proof that Jesus did read Hebrew.

Although Jesus grew up Jewish, no details have survived about his religious exposure as a child. However, Jesus was Jewish and never rejected his Jewish background, although he had numerous disagreements with the Jewish leaders and teachers of the time in their understanding of what God demands of people. All of the followers of Jesus were also Jewish. In the gospels, the only non-Jewish figures are the Romans.

What do we know of the early life of Jesus?

Our only sources on the early life of Jesus are the first two chapters of the Gospel of Matthew and the first two chapters of the Gospel of Luke. These chapters are called the Infancy Narratives. Christians disagree on how to understand these stories.

What was the political environment of the world of Jesus?

Jesus lived in the area that today is Israel and the Palestinian Territory. At the time, the area was under the control of the Romans and divided into two regions: Judaea and Galilee. Although Judaea and Galilee were under Roman control, the Romans kept Jewish kings in power, such as Herod the Great and Herod Antipas. The Roman governor, Pontius Pilate, made the decision to execute Jesus.

Some Christians, who take the Bible literally, insist that every detail is historically accurate. Others think that some details of the stories might not be historical; rather, they were created by the authors to make theological points. For example, did the Magi—the Wise Men—actually visit Jesus, or was this detail added by the writer of Matthew's gospel to make the point that Jesus came for the whole world?

Also, keep in mind that the gospels were written some seventy years after the birth of Jesus. In addition, as noted above, no written records existed for the early life of Jesus. The Gospel of Luke tells the only story of Jesus as a young boy, when at age twelve, he was left behind on his family's visit to Jerusalem. His parents find him in the Temple impressing the religious teachers with his knowledge.

A document called the Infancy Gospel of Thomas was written in the early centuries of Christianity. It includes many fanciful stories about Jesus, including the story of Jesus making birds out of clay, and when he claps his hands, the clay birds become real birds and fly away. Several early Christian writers rejected the Infancy Gospel of Thomas. Most Christians today also reject it.

THE PUBLIC MINISTRY OF JESUS

What do we know of the public ministry of Jesus?

According to the Gospel of Luke, Jesus started his public ministry at about the age of thirty. The three synoptic gospels describe the baptism of Jesus at the beginning of his public ministry.

There are three main elements of what Jesus did: he gathered followers, he taught people, and he healed the sick. Jesus chose an inner circle of twelve men. They are called the "Twelve Apostles," the "Twelve Disciples," or "The Twelve." The choice of twelve was symbolic of the twelve tribes of ancient Israel. However, Jesus had other followers, including women.

Three gospels—Matthew, Mark, and Luke—give us a picture of how Jesus taught. Jesus taught by telling stories or giving short sayings. One of the themes of the preaching of Jesus was to describe God as "father." Jesus used the word "abba" for God, which means "father" or "daddy."

The most important theme of the preaching of Jesus was the Kingdom of

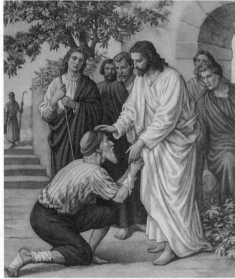

There are many stories in the Gospels about Jesus healing the sick, the lame, and the blind, which some interpret as His driving out of demons.

16

God. In Matthew's gospel, it is called the Kingdom of Heaven. It is not totally clear what Jesus meant by the "Kingdom of God," and Christians down through the centuries have argued over the meaning of the term. However, a careful reading of the statements of Jesus seems to indicate that he was not talking about Heaven after death. Nor was he talking about some interior religious experience. Jesus seemed to be talking about the present with a changed set of relations between people and a changed relationship with God the Father.

In his vision of the Kingdom of God, Jesus rejected the values of the world, such as wealth and power. Jesus spoke about loving enemies, and he taught: "Blessed are the poor" and "Blessed are the meek."

The last element of the ministry of Jesus was that he healed people. Stories of Jesus healing sick, blind, and crippled people are found in all the gospels. Christians have different views on how Jesus healed and what to call his healings. Some call them "miracles" or "signs." In some cases, the healings are described as Jesus driving out demons. In the ancient world, long before medical science, demons were often seen as the cause of physical and psychological illnesses.

THE CRUCIFIXION OF JESUS

Jesus died by crucifixion. The Romans used crucifixion because it produced a horrible and drawn-out death. Crucified victims could live for days before dying. It was used throughout the Roman Empire on non-Roman citizens as a slow and very torturous way to die. If you were a Roman citizen and had to be executed, you got the much better option of being beheaded. Although both were horrible ways to die, a beheading was much quicker.

What was the scourging of Jesus?

Three gospels describe Jesus being scourged before his crucifixion (Mark 14:65, Matthew 27:26, and John 19:1). Scourging before crucifixion was a frequent Roman practice, although it was also used as a punishment on its own. The Romans used whips with metal tips to tear the flesh of the victims. Mel Gibson's 2004 movie *The Passion of the Christ* has a very graphic and disturbing scene of the scourging of Jesus. Scourging is also called flagellation. Many artists have painted the scourging of Jesus.

I am confused about several words regarding crucifixion. Can these be clarified?

The process of being killed on a cross is called "crucifixion." The verb is to "crucify" someone. Most Christian churches have a wooden symbol of this called a "cross." Many Christians even wear a cross symbol on a chain around their necks. Many churches have crosses displayed in the front of the church or on top of the church. Some churches put statues of Jesus on their crosses. Such a cross and statue combination is called a "crucifix." A number of Christians wear crucifixes around their necks.

Why was Jesus crucified?

Although all four gospels describe the crucifixion of Jesus, many questions remain about why he was executed. The simplest explanation is that Jesus got in trouble with the Jewish religious authorities, who turned him over to the Romans to be crucified. Very likely the action of Jesus in going into the Temple area and driving out the money changers was one of the key reasons he got in trouble with both the religious and political authorities.

Another possibility is that the Romans saw Jesus as a potential leader of an uprising against Roman authority. In the years before and after Jesus, there were a number of Jewish figures called "messiahs," who wanted to free Israel from Roman rule and establish a Jewish kingdom. Perhaps the Romans saw Jesus as another messiah who wanted to drive out the Romans.

However, the Romans misunderstood the message of Jesus, for Jesus preached a kingdom of "Blessed are the meek" and "Turn the other cheek." In the Gospels of Matthew and Luke, Jesus rejects political power as a temptation from the Devil (Matthew 4:1–11, Luke 4:1–13). The Devil offered Jesus the kingdoms of the world if Jesus would bow down and worship the Devil. Jesus rejected the Devil's offer of political power.

In the years after the crucifixion, the early followers of Jesus totally changed the meaning of the word "messiah" and removed all its political connotations.

Many paintings and statues of Jesus on the cross show a sign above his head. Why is there such a sign?

It was the Roman practice to nail a board above the person crucified stating the crimes of which he was convicted. The four gospels describe such a sign being on the cross with Jesus. According to the synoptic gospels, the sign read "The King of the Jews" or "This is Jesus, the King of the Jews." In the Gospel of John, it read "Jesus the Nazarene, the king of the Jews." In Christian art, the sign is often depicted as reading "I.N.R.I."

What does I.N.R.I. on the sign mean?

The sign I.N.R.I. stands for the Latin phrase "Iesvs Nazarenvs Rex Ivdæorvm," which means "Jesus Christ, King of the Jews." In Latin, there is no letter "J," so an "I" is used for both "Jesus" and "Jews." The Latin word for "king" is "rex."

The sign charged Jesus with the political crime of being a messiah. At the time of Jesus, there were a number of messiahs who intended to lead the people in uprisings against the Romans. Although the gospels tell us that Jesus had no such political and revolutionary motivations, it is likely that the Romans could not distinguish the message of Jesus from the other messiahs.

Why does Jesus say "My God, my God, why have you forsaken me?" when he is dying?

It turns out that Jesus is quoting the first line of Psalm 22. Perhaps Jesus is just using the first line to express his own despair. However, it is also likely that Jesus is referring to the entire psalm, which ends with an expression of hope in God.

Why don't we know more about crucifixion?

There is much we do not know about the Roman practice of crucifixion. The Romans left no detailed descriptions of it, although it is frequently mentioned in Roman writings, and it is known that many thousands of people were crucified by the Romans. Many old paintings of Jesus on the cross have survived, but these tell us little about the actual practice of crucifixion because in the early centuries, Christians did not depict Jesus in art on the cross. When the image of a crucified Jesus started appearing in paintings and stained glass windows, the actual practice of crucifixion had been stopped centuries before.

What are some of the unanswered questions about crucifixion?

Did the Romans use a T-shaped cross that is the typical Christian image of the cross? Did the person to be executed carry the entire cross? Or did he carry just the cross beam,

The Isenheim Altarpiece includes the center work of art, *Crucifixion,* by Matthias Grünewald.

which was then attached to a stationary pole? Did the Romans nail victims to the cross, or tie them, or both? How did the victim die: asphyxiation, blood loss, shock, or a combination of these? No standard procedure existed on crucifixions, so likely, they were done in different ways. To speed up a person's death, the Romans would break the legs of that person. Crucifixion was very brutal.

Although Christian art always shows Jesus with a loincloth, the Romans typically crucified victims who were totally naked.

There is a famous painting (see page 19) of the Crucifixion by Matthias Grünewald (1475–1528), which is part of the Isenheim Altarpiece, which is on display at the Unterlinden Museum in Colmar, France. Who are the figures? Mary Magdalene is the kneeling figure. The woman in white is Mary, the mother of Jesus, who is being held by John, one of the disciples of Jesus.

The painting is filled with symbolism. The figure on the right is John the Baptist. He was dead by the time they crucified Jesus; however, in the gospels, he pointed the way to Jesus. Notice the right hand of John. The lamb symbolizes Jesus. Just as lambs were slain as sacrifices for sin, so Jesus was sacrificed for human sin. Also, notice that the blood of the lamb is flowing into the cup. Christians believe that the cup of wine (some Christians use grape juice) at Communion either represents or becomes the blood of Jesus.

What happened after the crucifixion of Jesus?

Believers and nonbelievers disagree on what happened after the crucifixion of Jesus. Nonbelievers typically hold that after the death of Jesus, his message and example so inspired his followers that they created a religious movement. That movement would grow to be the largest religion in the world.

Believers hold that Jesus rose from the dead and appeared to his followers. Belief in the Resurrection of Jesus is at the core of Christian faith. The experience of the risen Jesus led his followers to go forth and preach and create the Christian church.

THE JEWISH WORLD OF JESUS

What is the religious background of Jesus?

Jesus was Jewish. Jesus grew up in the Jewish faith and tradition. He had many questions and criticism of how the faith was lived out at the time, but other Jews had similar criticisms. All the followers in the immediate circle of Jesus were Jewish. Although Jesus rejected the teachings and practices of the Jewish leaders of his time, he never rejected the Jewish faith.

Several groups existed within Judaism at the time of Jesus. It was a very diverse religion. The four most important groups were the Sadducees, the Pharisees, the Essenes, and the Zealots. However, the vast majority of Jews—poor people just trying to survive—did not belong to these groups.

Who were the Sadducees?

The Sadducees came from the families of the priests who ran the Temple in Jerusalem. The Sadducees were the social elites of Jewish society. Many were pro-Roman and did well financially under Roman occupation. They owned much of the land, and some people of the time believed that they took advantage of the lower classes. The Sadducees were religious conservatives and rejected new ideas. They insisted that only the written Law of Moses was binding. At that time, an extensive oral tradition had developed on how to interpret the written law. The Sadducees rejected this oral law, which would eventually be written down as the Talmud.

Who were the Pharisees?

The Pharisees were deeply interested in religion yet not part of the leadership of the Temple. The Pharisees accepted the oral law as well as the written law, the Torah—the first five books of the Bible. The Pharisees also embraced new ideas of the time such as a belief in angels and a belief in the resurrection of the dead.

In the gospels, the Pharisees are the key opponents of Jesus. He has several disputes with them about how to interpret the Law of Moses. Jesus also accuses them of hypocrisy.

For I tell you, unless your righteousness exceeds that of the scribes and Pharisees, you will never enter the kingdom of Heaven.

—Matthew 5:20, NRSV

Woe to you, scribes and Pharisees, you hypocrites. You lock the kingdom of Heaven before human beings. You do not enter yourselves, nor do you allow entrance to those trying to enter. Woe to you, scribes and Pharisees, you hypocrites. You traverse sea and land to make one convert, and when that happens you make him a child of Gehenna twice as much as yourselves.

—Matthew 23:13–15, NABRE

Ironically, Jesus shared characteristics with the Pharisees. Like the Pharisees, he was not connected to the Temple priesthood and gathered followers to discuss how to interpret the Law of Moses.

It might be that the friction between Jesus and the Pharisees described in the gospels reflects the antagonism between early Christians and Jews at the time the gospels were written. After the destruction of Jerusalem, the Sadducees and the Essenes disappeared. Very likely, the Pharisees were the only religious competition, which was why they received so much criticism in the gospels. In time, the Judaism of the Pharisees would become Rabbinic Judaism.

Who were the Essenes?

The Essenes were a small group very dedicated to their religious faith. There is much we do not know about them. Many lived in the cities, but small communities also existed where the members lived monastic lives of celibacy, no possessions, and intense prayer. They also practiced some kind of ritual bathing. The Essenes were possibly the ones who compiled the library of documents called the Dead Sea Scrolls. The term "Essenes" refers to a number of different groups with similar beliefs.

Who were the Zealots?

The revolutionary Zealots wanted to drive the Romans out of the land of Israel and set up an independent kingdom. They were driven by both religious and political motives. For almost two hundred years, various groups of revolutionaries existed. These revolutionaries are sometimes called Zealots, for their zeal for their faith. However, the term "Zealot" was actually only used long after the time of Jesus. Many of these revolutionaries hoped for a Messiah who would free the people and then rule over an independent kingdom.

What went on at the Temple at the time of Jesus?

At the time of Jesus, the center of Jerusalem was the Temple. Although the Temple complex was massive, the Temple itself was not big. It did not have to be large because people did not go inside. The crowds gathered in the outside courtyards. Jews believed that God dwelled in the Temple in the innermost room called the Holy of Holies. No one went into the Temple except the high priest, once a year. He had a rope tied around him

The Second Temple in Jerusalem replaced Solomon's Temple and lasted from 516 B.C.E. until it was destroyed by the Romans in 70 C.E. The model shown here is what archeologists believed it looked like in Jesus' time. The actual Temple is the small structure in the center of a large courtyard.

in case he was struck dead by God, in which case the other priests could pull him out by the rope.

An important practice at the Temple was animal sacrifice. People regularly made offerings to God of bulls, goats, sheep, and doves. If one had sinned against God, typically a sacrifice of an animal was required to atone for one's sins and receive forgiveness from God. Numerous animals would be sacrificed most days. One can imagine the stench of blood, entrails, and burnt flesh. However, the entire animal was not burned. The meat and skin were kept for the priests.

It is important to understand the Jewish beliefs about animal sacrifice to understand the Christian view that Jesus is the final sacrifice to God. Jews at the time believed that blood sacrifice was necessary to atone (make up for) one's sins. They believed that God demanded such animal sacrifice.

Pilgrims came from many miles around to offer sacrifice. Due to the inconvenience of bringing animals from long distances, many people bought animals at the Temple. Roman money could not be used to buy animals for sacrifice. Roman money often had the image of Caesar as a god on it. Considered unclean money, it could not be used for buying a sacrificial animal. Thus, money changers were available at the Temple to convert Roman money into Temple money to buy an animal for sacrifice.

The size of the animal depended on one's wealth and how badly one had sinned. Doves or pigeons were the sacrifice of the poor. This is an important detail in the Gospel of Luke.

About forty years after the crucifixion of Jesus, the Temple in Jerusalem was destroyed by the Romans. In the gospels, Jesus seems to predict that fate for the Temple but seems unconcerned about it.

> As he came out of the temple, one of his disciples said to him, "Look, Teacher, what large stones and what large buildings!" Then Jesus asked him, "Do you see these great buildings? Not one stone will be left here upon another; all will be thrown down."

> —Mark 13:1–2, NRSV

The site of the Temple in Jerusalem is a popular place visited by tourists and religious pilgrims. The Islamic shrine the Dome of the Rock sits in the area where the Temple once stood.

What role did the Jews play in the crucifixion of Jesus?

All four gospels describe the arrest of Jesus, his trials, and the decision to execute him. However, the gospels do not agree on the exact details of these events. There is some variation in the four accounts. Also, historians who are not biblical literalists raise questions about how the actual events would have transpired given what is known about ancient Jewish and Roman legal customs. For example, the gospels describe Jesus being arrested on a Thursday evening, then tried by both the Jewish Sanhedrin—the Jewish high council—and the Roman governor Pontius Pilate, and then taken to be crucified

23

The Sanhedrin were a council found in each Israeli city, including Jerusalem, of course. It seems clear that the Sanhedrin turned Jesus over to the Roman governor Pontius Pilate.

on Friday morning. From what we know of the period, it is hard to imagine these events happening so quickly.

However, it is clear that the Jewish Sanhedrin was involved in the decision to punish Jesus by execution and to turn him over to the Romans, so a small number of Jews and Romans were involved in the execution of Jesus.

Down through the centuries, from time to time, some Christians have accused Jews of being responsible for killing Jesus. The Jews have sometimes been called "Christ-killers." Although Jews were involved in the decision to execute Jesus, there were only a handful. It is wrong to hold a whole people responsible for the actions of a few people many centuries before. Also, blaming the Jews goes against the teachings of Jesus. While on the cross, he spoke of those who crucified him—which included the Romans—and said, "Forgive them Father, for they know not what they do" (Luke 23:34, NABRE).

In 1965 the Roman Catholic Church released the document *Nostra Aetate: The Declaration on the Relation of the Church to Non-Christian Religions*. This document called for a respectful attitude toward the Jewish faith and rejected blaming the Jews as a people for the crucifixion of Jesus. The document stated:

> True, the Jewish authorities and those who followed their lead pressed for the death of Christ; still, what happened in His passion cannot be charged against all the Jews, without distinction, then alive, nor against the Jews of today.
>
> —*Nostra Aetate*, 4

Finally, as many Christians have recognized, blaming later Jews for the death of Jesus is very un-Christian.

Is there anti-Semitism in the Gospel of John?

In the Gospel of John, there are several references to the Jews as the opponents of Jesus. Some have claimed that there is an anti-Semitic tone to the Gospel of John. However, several points need to be made. Although the opponents of Jesus were called "the Jews," everyone else in the gospel, except the Romans, were also Jewish. Also, the Gospel of John was the last gospel written, somewhere around the year 90 C.E. At that time, the Christian movement was breaking away from the Jewish religion in which it had started. There was great tension between Christians and Jews and many arguments over who was Jesus and what was Jesus. Was Jesus the long-expected messiah or not? Was Jesus a true prophet or not? Was Jesus the fulfillment of the Hebrew Scriptures or not?

The Gospel of John reflects this polemical atmosphere from the time it was written and not the time when the events described in the gospel happened. Thus, in the Gospel of John, "the Jews" who were the opponents of Jesus symbolize the Jews at the time of the writing of the Gospel of John, who rejected the new Christian teachings.

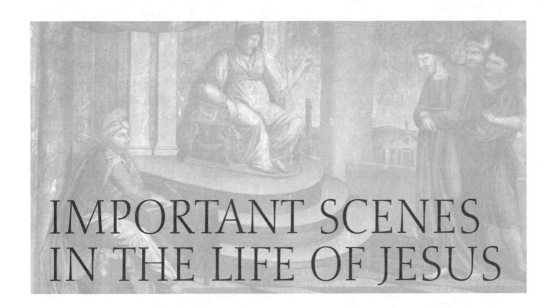

IMPORTANT SCENES IN THE LIFE OF JESUS

EARLY GOSPEL STORIES

What are the Infancy Narratives?

The Infancy Narratives are the stories about the birth of Jesus that are found in the first two chapters of the Gospel of Matthew and the first two chapters of Luke. The Gospels of Mark and John start with Jesus as an adult and do not have the narratives. The stories surrounding the birth of Jesus in Matthew and Luke are very popular and are very well known. However, the accounts in Matthew and Luke have significant differences. What many people know as the Christmas Story is based on combining the details from both gospels. For example, a typical children's play of the Christmas Story includes both the shepherds and the Wise Men. However, the shepherds are in the Gospel of Luke and the Wise Men in the Gospel of Matthew.

To get a better understanding of these infancy narratives, if you have never done so, it might be of value to read the first two chapters of both gospels: Matthew and Luke.

Can you describe the angels who appear in the Infancy Narratives?

In the Gospel of Matthew, an unnamed angel appears to Joseph. Joseph, who was betrothed to Mary, had found out that she had become pregnant, and he knew he was not the father. He had planned on divorcing her quietly. A public divorce could lead to Mary being stoned for adultery.

> But just when he had resolved to do this, an angel of the Lord appeared to him in a dream and said, "Joseph, son of David, do not be afraid to take Mary as your wife, for the child conceived in her is from the Holy Spirit. She will bear a son, and you are to name him Jesus, for he will save his people from their sins."

> —Matthew 1:20–21, NRSV

Some interpreters of the above passage note that it states that "the angel of the Lord appeared." In the Old Testament/Hebrew Scriptures, such language implies that God appeared rather than an angel sent by God. Very likely the Old Testament writers were reluctant to describe God as appearing and interacting with people, so they instead used the term "Angel of the Lord." See, for example, such passages as Genesis 16:7, 22:11, and 31:11.

The Gospel of Luke states that the Angel Gabriel appeared to Mary.

The angel said to her, "Do not be afraid, Mary, for you have found favor with God. And now, you will conceive in your womb and bear a son, and you will name him Jesus. He will be great, and will be called the Son of the Most High, and the Lord God will give to him the throne of his ancestor David. He will reign over the house of Jacob forever, and of his kingdom there will be no end."

—Luke 1:30–33, NRSV

However, Mary questions the news, and Gabriel answers:

Mary said to the angel, "How can this be, since I am a virgin?" The angel said to her, "The Holy Spirit will come upon you, and the power of the Most High will overshadow you; therefore the child to be born will be holy; he will be called Son of God. And now, your relative Elizabeth in her old age has also conceived a son; and this is the sixth month for her who was said to be barren. For nothing will be impossible with God." Then Mary said, "Here am I, the servant of the Lord; let it be with me according to your word." Then the angel departed from her.

—Luke 1:34–38, NRSV

Is this scene called the Annunciation?

Yes, this important scene is called the Annunciation, when the Angel Gabriel announces to Mary that she will carry and give birth to Jesus. The Annunciation has been the subject of many famous paintings from the Renaissance onward. Such paintings usually include a lily. The lily symbolizes purity—that Mary is a virgin. Also, a dove is usually found in Annunciation paintings, representing the Holy Spirit.

Why are the stories in Matthew and Luke describing the appearance of the angel so important?

In the Matthew version, Joseph learns that Mary has become pregnant through the action of the Holy Spirit. In the Luke version, Mary learns that she will become pregnant: "The Holy Spirit will come upon you, and the power of the Most High will overshadow you." She will become pregnant, not in the normal way but by a miraculous conception by the power of God. This means that Mary was a virgin when she became pregnant and when she gave birth.

This becomes an important belief for most Christians: that Jesus was born of the Virgin Mary. This belief affirms the other Christian belief that Jesus was both God and human. He was not simply a normal human chosen by God.

The Gospel of Matthew states: "All this took place to fulfill what the Lord had said through the prophet: 'Behold, the virgin shall be with child and bear a son, and they shall name Him Emmanuel,' which means 'God is with us'" (Matthew 1:22–23, NABRE). Matthew is quoting Isaiah 7:14. Biblical scholars have pointed out that in the original Hebrew of the book of Isaiah, it speaks of a young woman with child and not specifically a virgin.

Is the story of Mary becoming pregnant, though still a virgin, the Immaculate Conception?

No. Most Christians believe that Mary conceived Jesus as a virgin and gave birth to Jesus as a virgin. The conception of Jesus is seen as a miracle. However, this is not the Immaculate Conception, which is a Roman Catholic teaching about Mary. The Immaculate Conception is about the conception of Mary and holds that she was conceived by her parents without Original Sin.

There have been numerous masterpieces about the angel Gabriel appearing before Mary to tell her she will be the mother of Jesus (the Annunciation), including this c. 1600 painting by the master El Greco.

Some people are confused by this and think the Immaculate Conception is about the conception of Jesus, which it is not. The teaching of most denominations that are not Catholic is to believe in the miraculous conception of Jesus by the Virgin Mary and to reject the Catholic belief in the Immaculate Conception.

What is the Visitation of Mary?

The Visitation is when Mary, after receiving the news from Gabriel, goes to visit Elizabeth, her relative, who is already six months pregnant with John the Baptist. The story is only found in the Gospel of Luke (1:39–56).

> When Elizabeth heard Mary's greeting, the infant leaped in her womb, and Elizabeth, filled with the Holy Spirit, cried out in a loud voice and said, "Most blessed are you among women, and blessed is the fruit of your womb. And how does this happen to me, that the mother of my Lord should come to me? For at the moment the sound of your greeting reached my ears, the infant in my womb leaped for joy. Blessed are you who believed that what was spoken to you by the Lord would be fulfilled."

—Luke 1:41–45, NABRE

29

Several famous painters have depicted this scene. Also, a number of Roman Catholic churches and schools have been named for the Visitation.

THE BIRTH OF JESUS

The birth of Jesus has been depicted in countless paintings. At Christmas, many people create a nativity scene of small statues. The word "nativity" refers to birth. You are a native of the country in which you were born.

Where are the stories of the birth of Jesus found?

Only Matthew and Luke describe the birth of Jesus. In both versions, Jesus was born in the small town of Bethlehem just south of Jerusalem. Today, Bethlehem is a town in the West Bank under the jurisdiction of the Palestinian Authority. The Church of the Nativity marks the traditional place honored as the birthplace of Jesus, although there is no way to know for certain if this is the correct place.

An Old Testament/Hebrew Scriptures prophecy describing the importance of Bethlehem as the birthplace of the Messiah is quoted in the Gospel of Matthew: "And you, Bethlehem, land of Judah, are by no means least among the rulers of Judah; since from

The Church of the Nativity in Bethlehem, Israel, is traditionally seen as the location where Jesus was born. In 2017, 3.6 million tourists visited the church, a fact that has become quite a headache for the local government to manage.

you shall come a ruler, who is to shepherd my people Israel" (Micah 5:1, NABRE). In Matthew, Jesus is visited by the Wise Men, and in Luke, Jesus is visited by shepherds.

The Gospel of Luke adds an important detail: "She [Mary] wrapped him in swaddling clothes and laid him in a manger, because there was no room for them in the inn." Most paintings, theater presentations, and nativity scenes show Jesus being born in a stable and laid in a manger, a box, or frame holding hay for the livestock. Often, animals such as a donkey and ox are included in the scene.

What happened next in the Gospel of Matthew?

Several details surrounding the birth of Jesus are only found in the Gospel of Matthew in Chapter 2. Magi, or visitors from the East, come bearing gifts of gold, frankincense, and myrrh. On their way to find Jesus, the Magi visit King Herod and tell him of their search to find the "newborn king of the Jews." Threatened, Herod decides to kill Jesus.

An angel of the Lord appeared to Joseph in a dream and said, "Get up, take the child and his mother, and flee to Egypt, and remain there until I tell you; for Herod is about to search for the child, to destroy him." Then Joseph got up, took the child and his mother by night, and went to Egypt, and remained there until the death of Herod. This was to fulfill what had been spoken by the Lord through the prophet, "Out of Egypt I have called my son."

—Matthew 2:13–15, NRSV

Herod then decides to kill all baby boys two years and younger in the vicinity of Bethlehem. This event is known as the Massacre of the Innocents. (There is no reference to this event outside the Gospel of Matthew.) However, Jesus and his parents have escaped to Egypt, where they live for a number of years before returning and settling in the town of Nazareth.

These details in the Gospel of Matthew show Jesus fulfilling several Old Testament prophecies. They also depict the early life of Jesus as parallel to the early life of Moses. Moses survived despite the efforts of the Pharaoh to kill all the baby boys. Also, just as Moses came out of Egypt, so did Jesus.

What happened next in the Gospel of Luke?

In the Gospel of Luke, the parents of Jesus follow several Jewish traditions surrounding birth, such as circumcision of boys. "When eight days were completed for his circumcision, he was named Jesus, the name given him by the angel before he was conceived in the womb" (Luke 2:21, NABRE).

A scene called the Presentation in the Temple follows:

When the time came for their purification according to the law of Moses, they brought him up to Jerusalem to present him to the Lord (as it is written in the law of the Lord, "Every firstborn male shall be designated as holy to the Lord")....

—Luke 2:22–23, NRSV

Two Jewish customs are being observed here. The first is a ritual purification for a woman after childbirth, which is done forty days after the birth of the child. The second is the redemption of the firstborn son. These customs are described in the Old Testament/Hebrew Scriptures in Leviticus 12:1–7 and Exodus 13:11–15.

During these rituals, Joseph and Mary offer a pair of turtledoves or young pigeons, which indicates that they are poor. People with money would have offered a lamb. The writer of Luke wants to show that Jesus came for the poor and needy and was one of them. While in the Temple, a religious man named Simeon offers a prayer, blessing, and a prediction about Jesus and Mary. A prophetess named Anna also gives thanks for the child.

Some Christians celebrate the Presentation in a religious holiday called Candlemas on February 2 to mark the end of the Christmas season. Candlemas is celebrated by many Christians in Europe and also Central and South America. In the United States, it has been replaced by Groundhog Day.

THE BAPTISM OF JESUS

When does the baptism of Jesus take place in the story of Jesus?

This key event in the life of Jesus marks the beginning of his public ministry. It is described in the beginning chapters of the Gospels of Matthew and Luke after the Infancy Narratives. In Mark, the baptism is the first appearance of Jesus. There is no baptism described in the Gospel of John.

How is the baptism of Jesus described in the gospels?

Here is the account from the Gospel of Matthew:

> Then Jesus came from Galilee to John at the Jordan to be baptized by him. John tried to prevent him, saying, "I need to be baptized by you, and yet you are coming to me?" Jesus said to him in reply, "Allow it now, for thus it is fitting for us to fulfill all righteousness." Then he allowed him. After Jesus was baptized, he came up from the water and behold, the Heavens were opened [for him], and he saw the Spirit of God descending like a dove [and] coming upon him. And a voice came from the Heavens, saying, "This is my beloved Son, with whom I am well pleased."
>
> —Matthew 3:13–17, NABRE

The baptism is also described in Mark 1:9–11 and Luke 3:21–22. These accounts of the scene are very similar to Matthew's account. Interestingly, although John the Baptist appears in the Gospel of John, there is no description of the baptism of Jesus and no reference to it. Very possibly, according to the theology of the writer of the Gospel of John, Jesus would not need to be baptized.

It is important to note that the Gospels of Matthew, Mark, and Luke say that Jesus was baptized yet give no details about how the baptism was done. Did John pour water

Betania, on the Jordan River, is considered to be the place where Jesus was baptized. Unfortunately, the Jordan has been drying up, mostly because so much of its water has been drained for use by the local population.

over the head of Jesus? Did Jesus stand in the river? Was Jesus dunked or immersed in the water? Down through the centuries, Christians have imagined the baptism of Jesus in different ways, and that has reflected how they themselves do baptisms.

What does the scene of the baptism of Jesus tell us about Jesus?

Particularly important is the last part of this story when the Spirit of God descends and a voice declares, "This is my beloved Son." Christians see this passage as the first description of the nature of Jesus. Jesus is the Son of God, which means that the voice speaking must be God the Father. Christians see the dove as representing the Holy Spirit, so for Christians, God is the Father, Son, and Holy Spirit. Most Christians use the "Trinity" label to describe this understanding of God. However, even though Christians speak of God as being Father, Son, and Holy Spirit, Christians still believe in monotheism: one God.

Can you tell me more about the dove that appears?

Based on these baptism stories, the dove as a symbol of the Holy Spirit became a very important image in Christian art. There are numerous paintings of the Annunciation. For instance, there is a scene in the Gospel of Luke when the Angel Gabriel visits Mary and tells her: "The Holy Spirit will come upon you, and the power of the Most High will overshadow you; therefore the child to be born will be holy; he will be called Son of God" (Luke 1:35, NRSV). Somewhere, in almost all of these paintings, a dove representing the Holy Spirit can be seen. Paintings of the baptism of Jesus include the dove.

In paintings representing the Trinity, such as Masaccio's famous fresco *The Holy Trinity*, the dove represents the Holy Spirit. The fresco is found in the church of Santa Maria Novella in Florence, Italy. The white dove is seen between God the Father and Jesus on the cross, who is God the Son. Look carefully as the dove at first glance looks like a collar on the tunic of God the Father.

What are some of the questions Christians have raised about the baptism of Jesus?

Down through the centuries, the baptism of Jesus has raised some interesting questions that have troubled some Christians. For example, if baptism takes away sins, then why would Jesus need to be baptized if he was sinless? If Jesus is the greater figure, why does John baptize Jesus and not vice versa? This second question even bothered John the Baptist. (See Matthew 3:14–15. Perhaps this question of John the Baptist in the gospels reflects the questions of early Christians about the baptism of Jesus.)

Can you clarify that there is no baptism described in the Gospel of John?

Here is the key passage in John:

> The next day he [John the Baptist] saw Jesus coming towards him and declared, "Here is the Lamb of God who takes away the sin of the world! This is he of whom I said, 'After me comes a man who ranks ahead of me because he was before me.' I myself did not know him; but I came baptizing with water for this reason, that he might be revealed to Israel." And John testified, "I saw the Spirit descending from Heaven like a dove, and it remained on him. I myself did not know him, but the one who sent me to baptize with water said to me, 'He on whom you see the Spirit descend and remain is the one who baptizes with the Holy Spirit.' And I myself have seen and have testified that this is the Son of God."
>
> —John 1:29–34, NRSV

Although John describes the Spirit coming down like a dove in the other gospels, there is no mention that John baptized Jesus.

Why is there no mention of the baptism of Jesus in the Gospel of John?

Some Christians would answer that although the baptism is not mentioned in the Gospel of John, it is implied in the story, which is close to the baptismal accounts in the other gospels. Other Christians answer that the baptism was left out of the Gospel of John. Why? The writer of the Gospel of John does not include any of the details from the other gospels that show any weakness or need on the part of Jesus, so there is no baptism in John because according to the theology of John, Jesus would not need a baptism as ordinary humans do.

THE TEMPTATIONS OF JESUS

What are the temptations of Jesus?

The Gospels of Matthew, Mark, and Luke describe Jesus being tempted in the desert by the Devil just after his baptism. Here is the account from the Gospel of Matthew:

> Then Jesus was led by the Spirit into the desert to be tempted by the Devil. He fasted for forty days and forty nights, and afterwards he was hungry. The tempter approached and said to him, "If you are the Son of God, command that these stones become loaves of bread." He said in reply, "It is written: 'One does not live by bread alone, but by every word that comes forth from the mouth of God.'"
>
> Then the Devil took him to the holy city, and made him stand on the parapet of the Temple, and said to him, "If you are the Son of God, throw yourself down. For it is written: 'He will command his angels concerning you' and 'with their hands they will support you, lest you dash your foot against a stone.'"
>
> Jesus answered him, "Again it is written, 'You shall not put the Lord, your God, to the test.'" Then the Devil took him up to a very high mountain, and showed him all the kingdoms of the world in their magnificence, and he said to him, "All these I shall give to you, if you will prostrate yourself and worship me." At this, Jesus said to him, "Get away, Satan! It is written: 'The Lord, your God, shall you worship and him alone shall you serve.'" Then the Devil left him and, behold, angels came and ministered to him.
>
> —Matthew 4:1–11, NABRE (see also Luke 4:1–13)

The version in the Gospel of Luke is similar except that the order of the last two temptations is switched.

The Gospel of Mark (Mark 1:2–13) mentions the scene briefly, saying that Jesus went into the desert for forty days and was tempted by the Devil. The Gospel of John does not mention the scene at all, which is not surprising since John does not depict any weakness on the part of Jesus or even Jesus having to deal with temptation.

What is the symbolism of Jesus being in the desert for forty days after his baptism?

The forty days of Jesus in the desert parallel the forty years the Hebrews wandered in the desert after the Exodus from Egypt. The number forty also appears in the Noah story, where it rains for forty days and forty nights.

Christians recall this period of prayer and fasting by Jesus in their tradition of the forty days of Lent before Easter. For many Christians, Lent is a time for more prayer and religious devotion. Also, over the centuries, many Christians have included fasting or avoiding certain foods as part of Lent.

An 1866 illustration by the famous engraver Gustave Doré showing the temptation of Christ by the Devil in the wilderness.

Did the Devil or Satan really tempt Jesus?

Different Christians answer this question differently. Some Christians understand this scene literally and believe that the Devil, called Satan, appeared to Jesus and spoke these temptations and somehow took him to the parapet of the Temple and to a high mountain. For such Christians, it is typically assumed that Jesus and the Devil did not walk to and then climb up the wall of the Temple and then the mountain, but rather, they were able to instantly move to these places as spiritual beings such as angels are capable of doing. Other Christians imagine that Satan appeared to Jesus and was able to create scenes before him.

Yet other Christians see the story in metaphoric or symbolic terms. For these Christians, the temptations represent inner struggles within Jesus about what was the right thing to do in terms of using his powers and in terms of what kind of Messiah he would be. Such Christians often do not believe in an active Devil leading others to do evil. This leads to the broader questions on which Christians disagree: whether or not the Devil exists and whether or not the Devil is active in trying to lead people astray.

Was Jesus really tempted?

Since a temptation is a desire to do something that is wrong to do, and many Christians see Jesus as not doing anything wrong, was Jesus truly tempted to do something wrong? Was Jesus truly tempted, and did he struggle over what to do? Or was he more or less going through the motions of struggling with temptations as ordinary humans do? What do you think?

What were the wrong things that tempted Jesus?

One possibility is that these temptations had to do with what kind of Messiah Jesus was going to be. As each gospel shows, in the end, Jesus was a Messiah who was rejected and then suffered a brutal death. Could Jesus have been tempted to be a different kind of Messiah? Is the Devil offering Jesus three different temptations to be a different kind of Messiah?

> ## What does the word "temptation" mean?
>
> **A** temptation is an urge to do something that one should not do or that is wrong to do. If you are on a diet, a piece of cake is a temptation. To an alcoholic, another drink can be a very strong temptation.

The first temptation is to turn stones to bread. Since Jesus was out in the desert with little food, this would be an obvious temptation to feed himself. However, if Jesus could turn stones to bread—and any picture of the Holy Land shows an abundance of stones— then he could become a Messiah, giving bread to the hungry masses, and create a great following.

In the second temptation, the Devil suggests that Jesus throw himself down, not from a cliff out in the desert but from the parapet—the top of the wall—of the Temple. At first, this seems like a temptation to test God the Father to see if angels will catch Jesus. However, maybe the temptation is to do some demonstration of the power of Jesus in some place where there would be large crowds, such as at the Temple. Jesus could be a Messiah with a large following of people who were impressed by such a spectacular miracle.

The third temptation seems to be the promise of political power: that Jesus would have all the kingdoms of the world. There were other messiahs at the time of Jesus who sought political power, in part to drive out the Romans. The Devil offers Jesus political power.

Seen in this light, the three temptations of Jesus are different ways to be a Messiah other than to be a Messiah who is rejected, tortured, and crucified.

PUBLIC MINISTRY STORIES

What is the Transfiguration?

The Transfiguration is a very important story and scene in the gospels in which Jesus appears along with Moses and Elijah. Moses represents the Law, and Elijah represents the Prophets. Jesus is shown as the fulfillment or continuation of the Law and the Prophets. Jesus is also seen as the fulfillment of the Hebrew Scriptures/Old Testament. At the time of Jesus, the Hebrew Scriptures were only the Law and the Prophets. The third piece were the writings, the Kethuvim, which would be added later.

Why is it called the Transfiguration?

In the gospels, the appearance of Jesus is described as being transformed: "And he was transfigured before them, and his clothes became dazzling white, such as no one on earth could bleach them. And there appeared to them Elijah with Moses, who were talking with Jesus" (Mark 9:2–4, NRSV; see also Matthew 17:1–13 and Luke 9:28–36). The Transfiguration is in the three synoptic gospels, but not in John. *The Transfiguration* (painted 1516–1520) was the last painting by Renaissance master Raphael.

What are the miracles of Jesus?

All four gospels describe Jesus working miracles. The miracle stories fit into one of these categories, which are described below:

- The Healings of Jesus
- Driving out Demons
- Raising People from the Dead
- Jesus Feeding the Multitudes
- Miracles over Nature

Renaissance artist Rafael's circa 1520 masterpiece *The Transfiguration,* which involves Jesus praying on a mountain, where he begins to glow brightly. Moses and Elijah then appear, and Jesus speaks with them.

No set of categories is perfect for trying to organize the miracles of Jesus. In some of the healing miracles, Jesus drives out demons. Three stories do not easily fit any category: the story of Jesus turning water into wine in the Gospel of John, the story of Peter finding a coin in the mouth of a fish to pay the Temple tax (Matthew 17:24–27), and the story of Jesus cursing the fig tree, which then withers up (Matthew 21:18–22, Mark 11:12–14).

Some people count about three dozen miracles in the gospels. In this counting, if the same miracle story appears in several gospels, it is only counted once.

What is the meaning of the term "miracle"?

Actually, there is no agreed-upon definition of what a miracle is. Even in the gospels, these events are given different labels, such as "powers" (*dynamis,* meaning mighty deeds), "signs" (*sēmeion*), and "wonders" (*teras*).

One definition provided by *Webster's College Dictionary* is that a miracle is "an extraordinary occurrence that surpasses all known human powers or natural forces and is ascribed to a divine or supernatural cause, especially to God." Christians today have many different views on how to understand and explain the miracles of Jesus. For some Christians, the miracles are proof that Jesus was not an ordinary person but was in fact the Son of God on earth.

Also, Christians have different views on whether miracles happen today or not. Typically, such miracles are expected in response to prayer. Some Christians expect miracles, such as healings, to occur frequently. Other Christians think miracles are very rare or never happen at all.

In the Roman Catholic Church, one piece of evidence that a holy man or woman should be declared a saint is that miracles have happened to people who have prayed invoking the saint's help to intercede with God to grant help. (Many other Christians reject the idea of praying for help to saints who have died.) Such claims of miracles are investigated to show they have no natural explanation, such as a healing that could be explained by ordinary medical treatment.

What are the miracles in the Gospel of John?

There are seven miracles in John's gospels in Chapters 1–20. The gospel appears to end in Chapter 20 with the conclusion: "Now Jesus did many other signs in the presence of [his] disciples that are not written in this book. But these are written that you may [come to] believe that Jesus is the Messiah, the Son of God, and that through this belief you may have life in his name" (John 20:30, NABRE). Many scholars think that Chapter 21 was added later by a different author. Chapter 21 includes an eighth miracle: a catch of fish by the apostles that is so large they cannot pull the catch into the boat. The number seven in the Bible symbolizes fulfillment, and the seven miracles performed by Jesus are:

- Changing water into wine at the wedding of Cana
- Healing of the official's son
- Healing of the crippled man
- Feeding five thousand people
- Walking on the water
- Healing the man born blind
- Raising Lazarus from the dead

Three of the miracle stories—changing water into wine, the healing of the man born blind, and the raising of Lazarus from the dead—are filled with many symbolic details.

What is the significance of Jesus healing the woman with the issue of blood?

The Gospels of Matthew, Mark, and Luke tell the story of Jesus healing a woman who could not stop bleeding. Here is Mark's account:

Jesus healed a number of lepers. What is leprosy?

In the Bible, the term "leprosy" applies to a wide range of skin conditions. To modern people, the word "leprosy" refers to a bacterial infection called Hansen's disease. There is no way to know if the lepers that Jesus healed had Hansen's disease or some other skin condition.

Now there was a woman who had been suffering from hemorrhages for twelve years. She had endured much under many physicians, and had spent all that she had; and she was no better, but rather grew worse. She had heard about Jesus, and came up behind him in the crowd and touched his cloak, for she said, "If I but touch his clothes, I will be made well." Immediately her hemorrhage stopped; and she felt in her body that she was healed of her disease. Immediately aware that power had gone forth from him, Jesus turned about in the crowd and said, "Who touched my clothes?" And his disciples said to him, "You see the crowd pressing in on you;

A fresco in the Roman catacombs showing Jesus healing the bleeding woman, one of his many miracles.

how can you say, 'Who touched me?'" He looked all round to see who had done it. But the woman, knowing what had happened to her, came in fear and trembling, fell down before him, and told him the whole truth. He said to her, "Daughter, your faith has made you well; go in peace, and be healed of your disease."

—Mark 5:25–34, NRSV (see also Matthew 9:20–22 and Luke 8:42–48)

The story becomes more interesting once one realizes the religious rules of the time. According to Jewish law, a man would be ritually impure if he contacted a woman during her period. Many readers of this gospel story assume the woman's hemorrhages (also translated as "issue of blood") were related to her female bodily functions. Thus, given the culture and time, the woman was not supposed to touch Jesus, and he was not supposed to be touched by her. However, Jesus challenged the religious rule by ignoring it and healing the woman based on her faith.

Are there many stories of Jesus driving out demons?

There are about two dozen references to Jesus casting out demons in the Gospels of Matthew, Mark, and Luke, such as: "So he went into their synagogues, preaching and driving out demons throughout the whole of Galilee" (Mark 1:39, NABRE). Even the enemies of Jesus admitted that Jesus cast out demons: "He [Jesus] was driving out a demon [that was] mute, and when the demon had gone out, the mute person spoke and the crowds were amazed. Some of them said, 'By the power of Beelzebul, the prince of demons, he drives out demons'" (Luke 11:14–15, NABRE).

It is important to note that at the time of Jesus, many illnesses and psychological problems were ascribed to demons. In a world without medical science, demons offered an explanation of illness, especially mental illness. Today, we have a label for epilepsy that has a medical explanation. It can be diagnosed and treated. Imagine in the ancient world, a person having a seizure. The idea that a demon came into the person and brought on the seizure would make perfect sense to ancient people.

How are modern readers supposed to understand these stories of demons?

Among Christians today, there is disagreement over how to interpret these stories by Jesus. Some believe that Jesus was healing people with conditions that today would have an ordinary medical diagnosis. Thus, Jesus was not literally driving out demons. However, other Christians believe that since the gospel text says "demons," Jesus was in fact driving out literal demons.

Also, today some people use the expression "dealing with your demons" or "dealing with your inner demons." This language is a metaphor for people dealing with emotional or psychological problems or emotional scars. Most people using the expression do not literally believe that a person is dealing with demons: evil spiritual beings that are tormenting that person. It is important to recognize that the gospel writers were not using the language of demons in a metaphorical way.

Today, the majority of Christians do not believe illness is caused by demons. They do, however, regularly pray for healing of physical and psychological problems. However, a minority of Christians see demons as still active in this world and in their prayers use the language of "driving out demons" in dealing with physical and psychological problems.

What is the story about Jesus driving demons into pigs, who then drown themselves?

An important, but curious, story of demons is found in the Gospel of Mark.

> When he [Jesus] got out of the boat, at once a man from the tombs who had an unclean spirit met him. The man had been dwelling among the tombs, and no one could restrain him any longer, even with a chain. In fact, he had frequently been bound with shackles and chains, but the chains had been pulled apart by him and the shackles smashed, and no one was strong enough to subdue him. Night and day among the tombs and on the hillsides he was always crying out and bruising himself with stones. Catching sight of Jesus from a distance, he ran up and prostrated himself before him, crying out in a loud voice, "What have you to do with me, Jesus, Son of the Most High God? I adjure you by God, do not torment me!" (He had been saying to him, "Unclean spirit, come out of the man!") He asked him, "What is your name?" He replied, "Legion is my name. There are many of us." And he pleaded earnestly with him not to drive them away from that territory.
>
> Now a large herd of swine was feeding there on the hillside. And they pleaded with him, "Send us into the swine. Let us enter them." And he let them, and the unclean spirits came out and entered the swine. The herd of about two thousand rushed down a steep bank into the sea, where they were drowned.

—Mark 5:2–13, NABRE

A similar story involving two men possessed by demons can be found in Matthew 8:28–34.

Many Christians do not give this passage very much attention because it is such a strange story to modern ears. Some ask, "What did the pigs do to deserve such a fate?" Others wonder about the financial loss of the pig owners. (The famous American preacher Billy Sunday [1862–1935] joked about the effect of this event on the price of pork belly futures.) To ancient hearers of the story, it probably showed Jesus as a wonder-worker with such great power that he could even drive out thousands of demons.

What are the stories of Jesus raising the dead?

Rembrandt's *The Raising of Lazarus* (1630–1631) depicts one of Jesus' most extraordinary miracles: raising the dead.

In the gospels, three people are raised from the dead by Jesus: a widow's son; the daughter of Jairus; and a friend of Jesus, Lazarus. The widow's son story is in Luke 7:11–17. The daughter of Jairus story is found in the three synoptic gospels: Matthew 9:18, 23–26, Mark 5:21–24, 35–43, and Luke 8:40–42, 49–56. The story of Lazarus is only found in John 11:1–44.

The raising of Lazarus story is particularly important because it is not just about raising one person from the dead; it also develops the Christian belief in the resurrection of dead. In the Gospel of John, Lazarus is the brother of Mary and Martha. "Now Jesus loved Martha and her sister and Lazarus" (John 11:5, NABRE). Jesus had heard that Lazarus was ill but delayed two days before going to him. When Jesus arrived, Lazarus had already died.

> Martha said to Jesus, "Lord, if you had been here, my brother would not have died. But even now I know that God will give you whatever you ask of him." Jesus said to her, "Your brother will rise again." Martha said to him, "I know that he will rise again in the resurrection on the last day." Jesus said to her, "I am the resurrection and the life. Those who believe in me, even though they die, will live, and everyone who lives and believes in me will never die. Do you believe this?" She said to him, "Yes, Lord, I believe that you are the Messiah, the Son of God, the one coming into the world."
>
> —John 11:21–27, NRSV

The Gospel of John is filled with symbols, and most of the miracle stories have symbolic meanings. However, this story can be a little confusing since there are two different ideas about the resurrection. The first is that Jesus raises Lazarus from the dead:

Then Jesus, again greatly disturbed, came to the tomb. It was a cave, and a stone was lying against it. Jesus said, "Take away the stone." Martha, the sister of the dead man, said to him, "Lord, already there is a stench because he has been dead four days." Jesus said to her, "Did I not tell you that if you believed, you would see the glory of God?" So they took away the stone. And Jesus looked upward and said, "Father, I thank you for having heard me. I knew that you always hear me, but I have said this for the sake of the crowd standing here, so that they may believe that you sent me." When he had said this, he cried with a loud voice, "Lazarus, come out!" The dead man came out, his hands and feet bound with strips of cloth, and his face wrapped in a cloth. Jesus said to them, "Unbind him, and let him go."

—John 11:38–33, NRSV

Lazarus is brought back to life and would later die again.

The second idea of the resurrection, which is what the story of Lazarus symbolizes, is the Christian belief in the resurrection of dead. However, this resurrection is not back to this life, as happened to Lazarus, but rather to life in Heaven in the next life.

What is the story of Jesus feeding the multitudes?

The scene is also known as the Multiplication of the Loaves and Fishes. Actually, there are two separate events: the first when Jesus feeds five thousand people and the second when Jesus feeds four thousand. The feeding of the five thousand is found in all four gospels. Here is Matthew's version:

When Jesus heard of it, he withdrew in a boat to a deserted place by himself. The crowds heard of this and followed him on foot from their towns. When he disembarked and saw the vast crowd, his heart was moved with pity for them, and he cured their sick. When it was evening, the disciples approached him and said, "This is a deserted place and it is already late; dismiss the crowds so that they can go to the villages and buy food for themselves." [Jesus] said to them, "There is no need for them to go away; give them some food yourselves." But they said to him, "Five loaves and two fish are all we have here." Then he said, "Bring them here to me," and he ordered the crowds to sit down on the grass. Taking the five loaves and the two fish, and looking up to Heaven, he said the blessing, broke the loaves, and gave them to the disciples, who in turn gave them to the crowds. They all ate and were satisfied, and they picked up the fragments left over—twelve wicker baskets full. Those who ate were about five thousand men, not counting women and children.

—Matthew 14:13–21, NABRE
(see also Mark 6:31–44; Luke 9:12–17; John 6:1–14)

In the second story, Jesus feeds four thousand people. This story is found in Matthew and Mark but not Luke or John. Here is Mark's version:

In those days when there again was a great crowd without anything to eat, he summoned the disciples and said, "My heart is moved with pity for the crowd, because they have been with me now for three days and have nothing to eat. If I send them away hungry to their homes, they will collapse on the way, and some of them have come a great distance." His disciples answered him, "Where can anyone get enough bread to satisfy them here in this deserted place?" Still he asked them, "How many loaves do you have?" "Seven," they replied. He ordered the crowd to sit down on the ground. Then, taking the seven loaves he gave thanks, broke them, and gave them to his disciples to distribute, and they distributed them to the crowd. They also had a few fish. He said the blessing over them and ordered them distributed also. They ate and were satisfied. They picked up the fragments left over—seven baskets. There were about four thousand people.

An illustration by Gustave Doré of Jesus' miracle in feeding the multitudes by turning five loaves of bread and two fish into enough food for thousands.

—Mark 8:1–9, NABRE (see also Matthew 15:32–39)

In the Gospel of Mark, Jesus refers to both events:

"Do you have eyes and not see, ears and not hear? And do you not remember, when I broke the five loaves for the five thousand, how many wicker baskets full of fragments you picked up?" They answered him, "Twelve." "When I broke the seven loaves for the four thousand, how many full baskets of fragments did you pick up?" They answered [him], "Seven." He said to them, "Do you still not understand?"

—Mark 8:18–21, NABRE

What is the meaning of the baskets of food left over?

Some have thought it strange that in working these miracles, Jesus would overproduce the amount of food necessary. However, in the time the gospels were written, this was an important symbol because for most people, having enough food was a chronic problem. There was never enough food. Thus, a miracle that produced such abundant food that there was food left over would seem truly amazing and impressive.

Were these really miracles?

Christians have understood these two stories in different ways. Many think of these as true miracles in which Jesus took the few loaves of bread (or bread and fish) and as he gave them to the disciples to distribute, more food appeared that had not existed earlier. Some other Christians have suggested this was not an actual miracle but rather the people, encouraged by Jesus, shared the food they had brought themselves and when they shared it, they found there was plenty for all. What do you think?

What are the miracles over nature of Jesus?

The miracles over nature of Jesus include: Jesus calming a storm on the Sea of Galilee, Jesus walking on water, and the miraculous catch of fish. Here is Mark's version of the first story:

> On that day, when evening had come, he said to them, "Let us go across to the other side." And leaving the crowd behind, they took him with them in the boat, just as he was. Other boats were with him. A great windstorm arose, and the waves beat into the boat, so that the boat was already being swamped. But he was in the stern, asleep on the cushion; and they woke him up and said to him, "Teacher, do you not care that we are perishing?" He woke up and rebuked the wind, and said to the sea, "Peace! Be still!" Then the wind ceased, and there was a dead calm. He said to them, "Why are you afraid? Have you still no faith?" And they were filled with great awe and said to one another, "Who then is this, that even the wind and the sea obey him?"
>
> —Mark 4:35–41, NRSV (see also Matthew 8:23–27 and Luke 8:22–25)

The scene of Jesus walking on water also takes place on the Sea of Galilee. Here is Mark's version:

> Immediately he made his disciples get into the boat and go on ahead to the other side, to Bethsaida, while he dismissed the crowd. After saying farewell to them, he went up on the mountain to pray. When evening came, the boat was out on the sea, and he was alone on the land. When he saw that they were straining at the oars against an adverse wind, he came toward them early in the morning, walking on the sea. He intended to pass them by. But when they saw him walking on the sea, they thought it was a ghost and cried out; for they all saw him and were terrified. But immediately he spoke to them and said, "Take heart, it is I; do not be afraid." Then he got into the boat with them and the wind ceased. And they were utterly astounded, for they did not understand about the loaves, but their hearts were hardened.
>
> —Mark 6:45–52 NRSV (see also Matthew 14:22–33 and John 6:16–21)

There are two stories of the miraculous catch of fish. The first is in the Gospel of Luke:

> Getting into one of the boats, the one belonging to Simon, he asked him to put out a short distance from the shore. Then he sat down and taught the crowds from the boat. After he had finished speaking, he said to Simon, "Put out into deep water and lower your nets for a catch." Simon said in reply, "Master, we have worked hard all night and have caught nothing, but at your command I

will lower the nets." When they had done this, they caught a great number of fish and their nets were tearing. They signaled to their partners in the other boat to come to help them. They came and filled both boats so that they were in danger of sinking. When Simon Peter saw this, he fell at the knees of Jesus and said, "Depart from me, Lord, for I am a sinful man." For astonishment at the catch of fish they had made seized him and all those with him, and likewise James and John, the sons of Zebedee, who were partners of Simon. Jesus said to Simon, "Do not be afraid; from now on you will be catching men."

—Luke 5:3–11, NABRE

Painters have often depicted these scenes. A viewer of such art can easily recognize which story has been depicted. In the Luke story, Jesus is in the boat. In the John version of the story, Jesus stands on the shore:

Simon Peter said to them, "I am going fishing." They said to him, "We also will come with you." So they went out and got into the boat, but that night they caught nothing. When it was already dawn, Jesus was standing on the shore; but the disciples did not realize that it was Jesus. Jesus said to them, "Children,

Fish and fishing are recurring motifs in the gospels, which is not surprising given the importance of the sea as a resource, but it is also clearly symbolic of Jesus' ministry.

Is there some significance to the number of fish: 153?

No one knows the meaning of this number. Some have suggested a mathematical significance to the number, despite the fact that the gospel writers were not interested in numerology as compared to the writer of the Book of Revelation. Some have suggested that the number refers to the nations of the world to whom the apostles were supposed to take the gospel message. However, this is just a guess.

The number 153 might simply be used to make the point of how big the catch was. What deer hunter who has shot a twelve-point buck would brag that the deer had big antlers and not mention the twelve points?

have you caught anything to eat?" They answered him, "No." So he said to them, "Cast the net over the right side of the boat and you will find something." So they cast it, and were not able to pull it in because of the number of fish. So the disciple whom Jesus loved said to Peter, "It is the Lord." When Simon Peter heard that it was the Lord, he tucked in his garment, for he was lightly clad, and jumped into the sea. The other disciples came in the boat, for they were not far from shore, only about a hundred yards, dragging the net with the fish.

When they climbed out on shore, they saw a charcoal fire with fish on it and bread. Jesus said to them, "Bring some of the fish you just caught." So Simon Peter went over and dragged the net ashore full of one hundred fifty-three large fish. Even though there were so many, the net was not torn.

—John 21:3–14, NABRE

Did Jesus identify himself as the Messiah?

Jesus did not refer to himself as the Messiah. However, in one important story, he let Peter call him the Messiah:

Jesus went on with his disciples to the villages of Caesarea Philippi; and on the way he asked his disciples, "Who do people say that I am?" And they answered him, "John the Baptist; and others, Elijah; and still others, one of the prophets." He asked them, "But who do you say that I am?" Peter answered him, "You are the Messiah." And he sternly ordered them not to tell anyone about him.

Then he began to teach them that the Son of Man must undergo great suffering, and be rejected by the elders, the chief priests, and the scribes, and be killed, and after three days rise again. He said all this quite openly. And Peter took him aside and began to rebuke him. But turning and looking at his disciples, he rebuked Peter and said, "Get behind me, Satan! For you are setting your mind not on divine things but on human things."

—Mark 8:27–33, NRSV (see also 16:13–20 and Luke 9:18–21)

This passage describes what is often called the "Messianic Secret," that Jesus kept it a secret that he was the Messiah. Jesus defines what it means to be the Messiah as one who would suffer, be rejected, and be killed. Peter rebukes Jesus over his definition of the Messiah. It does not say what Peter's objection was, but very likely he imagined Jesus as a Messiah of power and glory with a large following, precisely the kind of messiahship that the Devil used to tempt Jesus.

Notice that the response of Jesus to Peter is one of the harshest things to come from the mouth of Jesus. Was the reaction of Jesus in part because what Peter was suggesting was actually a temptation to Jesus? Was Peter in a sense offering the same thing as the temptation of the Devil to give Jesus all the kingdoms of the world? Was the strong rebuke by Jesus because Jesus himself was still tempted to take a different path to being a Messiah rather than the path of suffering, rejection, and death?

What is the gospel story of the woman caught in adultery?

An important scene in the gospels is the story of the woman caught in adultery. Jesus was teaching in the Temple area.

> Then the scribes and the Pharisees brought a woman who had been caught in adultery and made her stand in the middle. They said to him, "Teacher, this woman was caught in the very act of committing adultery. Now in the law, Moses commanded us to stone such women. So what do you say?" They said this to test him, so that they could have some charge to bring against him. Jesus bent down and began to write on the ground with his finger. But when they continued asking him, he straightened up and said to them, "Let the one among you who is without sin be the first to throw a stone at her." Again he bent down and wrote on the ground. And in response, they went away one by one, beginning with the elders. So he was left alone with the woman before him. Then Jesus straightened up and said to her, "Woman, where are they? Has no one condemned you?" She replied, "No one, sir." Then Jesus said, "Neither do I condemn you. Go, [and] from now on do not sin any more."

> —John 7:53–8:11, NABRE

Several things about this passage are interesting. First, this story is only found in the Gospel of John. Second, it is interesting that if the woman was caught in the act of adultery, where is the man she was involved with who should also be punished? Is this a sign that the Pharisees were not that interested in enforcing the law but rather trying to trap Jesus?

It says Jesus wrote on the ground. For centuries people have argued over what he might have been writing, possibly words of accusation for her accusers. An interesting interpretation of the scene is found in the 1927 silent movie *The King of Kings*. Also, this passage is used in the argument over whether or not Jesus could write.

Lastly, and most importantly, the woman in the story is not named. Later Christian tradition would wrongly identify her as Mary Magdalene, which would lead to the mistaken tradition that Mary Magdalene was a prostitute or an immoral woman.

The story of Jesus forgiving the adulteress in the book of John is somewhat controversial because the tale is not found in early Greek versions of the book, implying it is not original to the gospel (art by Gustave Doré).

What is the controversy over this passage?

Although many Christians have found this passage to be both moving and inspiring, scholars have argued over this passage for many years. The main problem is that the passage is missing from the early Greek manuscript copies of the Gospel of John. Also, the language and theme of the story do not match the rest of the Gospel of John.

THE FINAL STORIES

What events make up the last days of Jesus?

In all the gospels, the triumphal entry of Jesus into Jerusalem marks the beginning of the last days of Jesus. In the Gospels of Matthew, Mark, and Luke, the story of Jesus cleansing the Temple follows; and then the Last Supper, the Crucifixion, and the Resurrection. In the Gospel of John, the Cleansing of the Temple takes place at the beginning of the public career of Jesus, several years before the Crucifixion.

Many Christians recall the events of the Triumphal Entry of Jesus, the Last Supper, the Crucifixion, and the Resurrection during a time in the year called Holy Week.

What is Holy Week?

Over the centuries, the tradition developed among Christians of celebrating Holy Week to remember the events of the last days of Jesus leading up to the Resurrection. Holy Week starts with Palm Sunday to celebrate the entry of Jesus into Jerusalem. Holy Thursday, also called Maundy Thursday, celebrates the Last Supper of Jesus. On Good Friday, many Christians remember the crucifixion of Jesus. Holy Saturday commemorates the day that the body of Jesus lay in the tomb. Holy Saturday, the last day of Holy Week, is followed by Easter Sunday, which celebrates the Resurrection of Jesus.

The dates on the regular calendar for Holy Week vary from year to year because Holy Week is the week before Easter, and the date for Easter changes each year. Easter is celebrated on the first Sunday after the first full moon after the Spring Equinox. Look at a calendar for next spring and see when the next Holy Week and Easter will take place.

Among Christians, there is a wide range of attitudes about how much to celebrate Holy Week. Some Christians only celebrate Easter. Others celebrate Easter and Palm

Sunday, especially those Christian traditions that deemphasize the importance of ritual. Many other Christians have special celebrations for Palm Sunday, Holy Thursday, Good Friday, Holy Saturday, and then Easter. Some traditions, such as the Roman Catholic Church and Anglican Church, have elaborate rituals to mark these events and days. Christians in these traditions often find these to be some of the most meaningful and deeply religious rituals of the entire year.

What is the Easter Triduum?

The Easter Triduum, which is also called the Paschal Triduum, is the three days that recall the Last Supper, the Crucifixion, the time of Jesus in the tomb, and then the Resurrection. It includes Holy Thursday, Good Friday, Holy Saturday, and Easter.

The word *triduum* is Latin for "three days." This is confusing for many people because the events cover four days: Thursday, Friday, Saturday, and Sunday. However, the Easter Triduum is understood as three twenty-four-hour days starting Thursday evening and ending Sunday morning.

Did the entry of Jesus into Jerusalem actually take place the week before the Resurrection?

Although Christians celebrate all these events in eight days from Palm Sunday to Easter Sunday, there is no way to know the time frame of the actual events. In the gospels, with some exceptions, there is often a lack of details about when events happened. How much time transpired between the entry of Jesus into Jerusalem and his crucifixion? Many scholars who have examined the issue say that we do not know the exact time frame.

However, the Gospel of John is more specific and puts the entry of Jesus into Jerusalem five days before the Passover, which would likely be Sunday depending on how you count five days, so why not assume that John's account is the most accurate? Two details in the Gospel of John do not mesh with the other gospels. First, as mentioned above, John describes the Cleansing of the Temple much earlier in the career of Jesus. Second, in the Gospels of Matthew, Mark, and Luke, the Passover is on Thursday evening. In the Gospel of John, the Passover is on Friday. That is why many who have examined the issue admit that we do not know the precise amount of time that passed during the last days of Jesus.

When was Jesus crucified?

The synoptic gospels describe Jesus as dying on a Friday. Matthew, Mark, and Luke describe how the burial of Jesus was done quickly before sundown because no work was allowed on the Jewish Sabbath. The Sabbath is Saturday; however, it begins at Friday sundown and ends at Saturday sundown. The synoptic gospels also depict the Last Supper of Jesus as taking place the day before, on Thursday. The Last Supper of Jesus was a Jewish Passover meal, although Jesus reworked it to initiate a new Christian ritual.

As mentioned above, in the Gospel of John, the Passover is Friday evening. Very likely, the author of the Gospel of John moved the Passover so that Jesus would die at the same time that lambs were being sacrificed for the Passover meal. The point was to connect the symbolism of Jesus dying as a final sacrifice.

Can you say more about the Triumphal Entry of Jesus into Jerusalem?

All four gospels describe the entry of Jesus into Jerusalem. Here is the account from the Gospel of Luke:

A stained glass window in a Brussels cathedral shows Jesus' triumphant entry into Jerusalem.

> As he drew near to Bethphage and Bethany at the place called the Mount of Olives, he sent two of his disciples. He said, "Go into the village opposite you, and as you enter it you will find a colt tethered on which no one has ever sat. Untie it and bring it here. And if anyone should ask you, 'Why are you untying it?' you will answer, 'The Master has need of it.'" So those who had been sent went off and found everything just as he had told them. And as they were untying the colt, its owners said to them, "Why are you untying this colt?" They answered, "The Master has need of it." So they brought it to Jesus, threw their cloaks over the colt, and helped Jesus to mount. As he rode along, the people were spreading their cloaks on the road; and now as he was approaching the slope of the Mount of Olives, the whole multitude of his disciples began to praise God aloud with joy for all the mighty deeds they had seen. They proclaimed:

> "Blessed is the king who comes
> in the name of the Lord.
> Peace in Heaven
> and glory in the highest."

> Some of the Pharisees in the crowd said to him, "Teacher, rebuke your disciples." He said in reply, "I tell you, if they keep silent, the stones will cry out!"

> —Luke 19:29–40, NABRE
> (see also Matthew 21:1–11, Mark 11:1–11, and John 12:12–15)

Why does Jesus enter riding on a donkey?

Many people are so familiar with this scene that the impact of Jesus riding on a donkey is lost. (In the Gospel of Mark, Jesus rides a colt.) At the time of Jesus, if a king or a general entered a city, he would ride a magnificent horse, stand in a chariot, or be carried in a sedan by slaves. There would be a parade of soldiers with him. Jesus, on the other hand, comes on a lowly donkey, a symbol of great humility.

What happened to the Messianic Secret?

In the synoptic gospels, Jesus tries to avoid being proclaimed as the Messiah. Yet as he enters Jerusalem, Jesus does let the people proclaim him as the Messiah. However, he does this in the context of what lies ahead: he is soon to be arrested and executed. He is a Messiah who suffers and dies.

What is the story of the Cleansing of the Temple?

All four gospels describe the scene called the Cleansing of the Temple, when Jesus drove out the money changers. This event did not take place in the actual Temple building but in the courtyards outside the Temple. Only the High Priest went into the Temple itself once a year. As described before, the money changers played an important role for pilgrims in converting Roman coins, which could not be used to buy animals for sacrifice. In the synoptic gospels, the Cleansing of the Temple takes place shortly before the Crucifixion. This gives the impression that this may have been the key event leading to the arrest of Jesus. Here is the version from Matthew:

> Then Jesus entered the temple and drove out all who were selling and buying in the temple, and he overturned the tables of the money changers and the seats of those who sold doves. He said to them, "It is written, 'My house shall be called a house of prayer'; but you are making it a den of robbers."
>
> —Matthew 21:12–13, NRSV (see also Mark 11:15–19)

The Luke version is shorter:

> Then he entered the temple and began to drive out those who were selling things there; and he said, "It is written, 'My house shall be a house of prayer'; but you have made it a den of robbers."
>
> —Luke 19:45–46, NRSV

In the Gospel of John, the event takes place in the beginning of the public life of Jesus, several years before his crucifixion. Here is John's account:

> In the temple he found people selling cattle, sheep, and doves, and the money changers seated at their tables. Making a whip of cords, he drove all of them out of the temple, both the sheep and the cattle. He also poured out the coins of the money changers and overturned their tables. He told those who were selling the doves, "Take these things out of here! Stop making my Father's house a marketplace!"
>
> —John 2:14–26, NRSV

Did Jesus use violence in cleansing the Temple?

Some people have argued that Jesus used violence in cleansing the Temple. However, others argue that the actions of Jesus were quite restrained. Nowhere does it describe Jesus striking a human being. The whip of cords was likely used only on the livestock.

A 1678 painting by Giovanni Antonio Fumiani depicts Jesus cleansing the Temple of money changers. It might be that Jesus's actions there were one reason he was turned in to the Romans.

Did Jesus destroy property?

Jesus did not seem to destroy property. Although he spilled the coins of the money changers, they would be able to pick them up. (In the movie version of *Jesus Christ Superstar,* Jesus destroys the tables of the buyers and sellers, which is far from what the gospels describe.)

What about the doves?

There is no mention of Jesus breaking the cages of doves or freeing the doves. In Mark and Matthew, Jesus turned over the seats of those who sold doves. In the Gospel of John, Jesus told those selling doves to take them out. It is important to note this detail because in many movies about Jesus, he is seen breaking the cages or releasing the doves. Granted, it is a great piece of cinematography to see the doves fleeing into the sky, but it does not accurately depict the restraint Jesus showed. This cinematic tradition probably began with Cecil B. DeMille's 1927 film *The King of Kings*. In the film, a dove reappears at the Last Supper and at the Resurrection.

Why did Jesus cleanse the Temple?

Did Jesus cleanse the Temple of the money changers because he thought they were cheating the people? Or did he do it because it distracted from the proper prayerful atmosphere of the Temple? Is it possible that something more was at stake? The money changers and sellers of animals supported the Temple system of animal sacrifice. The whole purpose of animal sacrifice was to obtain forgiveness of sins. If you committed a sin, the only way to get forgiveness and be made right in the eyes of God was by sacrificing an animal in a process controlled by the priests. Was Jesus rejecting the whole system? In his teachings, Jesus forgave people's sins with no conditions. He simply forgave them. No animals had to die.

No wonder the priests of the Temple would want to get rid of Jesus. The whole religious justification for their existence was based on controlling the forgiveness of sins through animal sacrifice. It was also their livelihood. Jesus offered forgiveness for free! Jesus preached a forgiving God.

FROM THE LAST SUPPER
TO THE DEATH OF JESUS

Why is the Last Supper called "the Last Supper"?

It is the last meal that Jesus ate. It is one of the more important events in the gospels.

What happened at the Last Supper?

The Last Supper is described in all four gospels. In the synoptic gospels, the key moment is when Jesus blesses the bread and wine.

> While they were eating, Jesus took a loaf of bread, and after blessing it he broke it, gave it to the disciples, and said, "Take, eat; this is my body." Then he took a cup, and after giving thanks he gave it to them, saying, "Drink from it, all of you; for this is my blood of the covenant, which is poured out for many for the forgiveness of sins. I tell you, I will never again drink of this fruit of the vine until that day when I drink it new with you in my Father's kingdom."
>
> —Matthew 26:26–29, NRSV (see Mark 14:22–26 and Luke 22:15–20)

This passage and its parallels in Mark and Luke are the basis of the Christian ritual of the Lord's Supper, which is also called Communion, Mass, or Eucharist. Christians repeat this ceremony as a memorial of what Jesus did. However, Christians disagree on how to interpret the words of Jesus: "This is my body" and "This is my blood." Are these sentences to be understood literally or symbolically?

Is the Last Supper in the Gospel of John?

Although John's gospel includes the Last Supper, John's account is very different from the synoptic accounts of Matthew, Mark, and Luke. The scene in John, which begins with Jesus washing the feet of his disciples, lasts from Chapter 13 through 17. This section in John includes a very long discourse by Jesus that is not found in the synoptic gospels. Also, there is no blessing of the bread and wine by Jesus with the words "This is my body" and "This is my blood." In John's gospel, the Last Supper is not a Passover meal. The Passover in John would take place on Friday night.

Instead, the Gospel of John includes an earlier passage that is called the Bread of Life discourse, which is found in Chapter 6, verses 35 and 48–51.

> Jesus said to them, "I am the bread of life; whoever comes to me will never hunger, and whoever believes in me will never thirst."
>
> …
>
> "I am the bread of life. Your ancestors ate the manna in the desert, but they died; this is the bread that comes down from Heaven so that one may eat it and not die. I am the living bread that came down from Heaven; whoever eats this bread will live forever; and the bread that I will give is my flesh for the life of the world." (NABRE)

What about Judas at the Last Supper?

In all four gospels, Jesus warns that one of his followers will betray him. Here is the version in Matthew:

> And while they were eating, he said, "Amen, I say to you, one of you will betray me." Deeply distressed at this, they began to say to him one after another, "Surely it is not I, Lord?" He said in reply, "He who has dipped his hand into the dish with me is the one who will betray me. The Son of Man indeed goes, as it is written of him, but woe to that man by whom the Son of Man is betrayed. It would be better for that man if he had never been born." Then Judas, his betrayer, said in reply, "Surely it is not I, Rabbi?" He answered, "You have said so."
>
> —Matthew 26:21–25, NABRE

Who painted the most famous depiction of the Last Supper?

One of the most famous paintings is *The Last Supper* by Leonardo da Vinci, painted in the 1490s.

Of course, Leonardo da Vinci's fresco *The Last Supper* is the most renowned portrayal of this most famous of meals.

What happened after the Last Supper?

After the meal, Jesus went with his apostles to the Garden of Gethsemane outside of Jerusalem to pray. The scene is known as the Agony in the Garden. Today, there are four sites in Jerusalem that claim to be the location of the garden where Jesus went to pray. There is no way to know if any of the claims is accurate.

What is the "Agony in the Garden" of Jesus?

In the garden, Jesus prays in agony and despair, apparently with the knowledge of what is to happen next: that he will be convicted, crucified, and die. Matthew describes Jesus: "He advanced a little and fell prostrate in prayer, saying, 'My Father, if it is possible, let this cup pass from me; yet, not as I will, but as you will'" (Matthew 26:9, NABRE; see Mark 14:32–42 and Luke 22:40–46). The Gospel of Luke adds the detail: "And to strengthen him an angel from Heaven appeared to him. He was in such agony and he prayed so fervently that his sweat became like drops of blood falling on the ground" (Luke 22:43–44, NABRE; this passage is missing from the oldest manuscript copies of the Gospel of Luke).

There are many paintings of the Agony in the Garden. Many people find the image comforting when they themselves are going through loss, agony, or distress.

Is the "Agony in the Garden" scene in the Gospel of John?

In the Gospel of John, after the Last Supper, Jesus does go to a garden. However, Jesus does not show any stress, agony, or sign of weakness. In fact, Jesus seems to be in control of the entire situation.

> So Judas got a band of soldiers and guards from the chief priests and the Pharisees and went there with lanterns, torches, and weapons. Jesus, knowing everything that was going to happen to him, went out and said to them, "Whom are you looking for?" They answered him, "Jesus the Nazorean." He said to them, "I AM." Judas his betrayer was also with them. When he said to them, "I AM," they turned away and fell to the ground.
>
> —John 18:3–6, NABRE

It is also important to note that Jesus identifies himself by saying "I AM." In the Gospel of John, Jesus several times identifies himself this way. "I AM" is a translation of the Hebrew name for God, Yahweh. To emphasize this point, many English translations of the Gospel of John capitalize all the letters in "I AM."

Where are the accounts of the crucifixion of Jesus?

The gospels describe Jesus being stripped and nailed to the cross. The gospel accounts are Matthew 27:27–56, Mark 15:16–41, Luke 23:26–49, and John 19:13–37. All the gospels state that Jesus was stripped of his garments and then crucified. However, they do not mention specifically that he was nailed to the cross. The only reference to nails is found in the Gospel of John after the Resurrection, in the story of Thomas—later known as Doubting Thomas—who says he would not believe that Jesus had risen: "Unless I see the mark of the nails in his hands, and put my finger in the mark of the nails and my hand in his side, I will not believe" (John 20:25, NRSV).

The Gospels of Matthew, Mark, and John tell that Jesus was given a crown of thorns to increase his suffering. The crown of thorns is not mentioned in the Gospel of Luke.

What is the story of the Good Thief crucified with Jesus?

All four gospels describe Jesus being crucified with two criminals, one on either side. In rural areas today, sometimes Christians have placed three crosses on hillsides to remind people driving by of the crucifixion of Jesus. Luke's account adds more detail:

> When they came to the place called the Skull, they crucified him [Jesus] and the criminals there, one on his right, the other on his left.
>
> …
>
> Now one of the criminals hanging there reviled Jesus, saying, "Are you not the Messiah? Save yourself and us." The other, however, rebuking him, said in reply, "Have you no fear of God, for you are subject to the same condemnation? And indeed, we have been condemned justly, for the sentence we received corresponds to our crimes, but this man has done nothing criminal." Then he said, "Jesus, remember me when you come into your kingdom." He replied to him, "Amen, I say to you, today you will be with me in Paradise."
>
> —Luke 23:33, 39–43, NABRE

This story of the "Good Thief" is only found in the Gospel of Luke, and the two thieves crucified with Jesus are not named. Later tradition gave the Good Thief the name "Dismas," and he became St. Dismas. (Tradition gave the Bad Thief, the one who taunted Jesus, the name "Gestas," if it ever comes up in a trivia contest.) What is interesting about the Good Thief story is that the Romans did not crucify thieves. They crucified revolutionaries and brigands. The gospels call the two men "criminals." Ironically, calling them "thieves" waters down the impact of the message in Luke in which Jesus tells a serious criminal that his sins are forgiven and he will go to Heaven.

According to the Bible, Jesus was crucified along with two criminals at Calvary (Golgotha) outside Jerusalem. The gospels do not record the last words of Christ in the same way, interestingly.

57

This story also reinforces a key theme in the Gospel of Luke: that Jesus came for the poor and lowly.

What are the last words spoken by Jesus?

In the Gospels of Matthew and Mark, Jesus, on the cross, cries out, "My God, my God, why have you forsaken me?" Then he cries out in a loud voice and dies. In the Gospel of Luke, Jesus says, "Father, into your hands I commend my spirit" before dying. In the Gospel of John, the last words of Jesus are "It is finished." Not surprisingly, in the Gospel of John, where any details that show weakness or need on the part of Jesus are removed, the cry of Jesus, "My God, my God, why have you forsaken me?" is left out.

However, as mentioned earlier, it is possible that in his cry of "My God, my God, why have you forsaken me?", Jesus is referring to Psalm 22. This is the first line of the psalm. At the time of Jesus, psalms were not numbered but rather identified by the first line. Very possibly, Jesus was referring to the entire psalm, which begins with words of despair but ends in words of hope in God.

I have heard of a musical composition called "The Seven Last Words of Jesus." What is that?

"The Seven Last Words of Jesus" are not words but rather the last sentences spoken by Jesus from all the gospels put together (all seven quotes from NABRE):

- "Father, forgive them, for they don't know what they're doing." (Luke 23:34)
- "I assure you, today you will be with me in paradise." (Luke 23:43)
- "Dear woman, here is your son." (John 19:26)
- "My God, my God, why have you abandoned me?" (Mark 15:34)
- "I am thirsty." (John 19:28)
- "It is finished!" (John 19:30)
- "Father, I entrust my spirit into your hands!" (Luke 23:46)

Over the centuries, many composers, including Joseph Haydn, have set these sentences to music.

What happened when Jesus died?

Mathew, Mark, and Luke state that darkness came over the land from noon to three when Jesus died. Luke explains the darkness as an eclipse. Matthew gives a dramatic description of the death of Jesus:

> Then Jesus cried again with a loud voice and breathed his last. At that moment the curtain of the temple was torn in two, from top to bottom. The earth shook, and the rocks were split. The tombs also were opened, and many bodies of the saints who had fallen asleep were raised. After his resurrection they came out of the tombs and entered the holy city and appeared to many.

—Matthew 27:50–53, NRSV

The Gospels of Mark and Luke also mention the veil of the Temple being torn. Christians have different views on whether to take these events literally or symbolically.

What is the symbolism of the veil of the Temple being torn?

Jews at the time of Jesus believed that God was especially present in the Temple in Jerusalem in a room called the Holy of Holies, which was behind a large, cloth veil. This detail about the veil being torn probably is meant to symbolize that no longer will God be found in the Temple.

What is the detail about Jesus being pierced by a lance?

The Gospel of John tells this story:

> Since it was the day of Preparation, the Jews did not want the bodies left on the cross during the sabbath, especially because that sabbath was a day of great solemnity. So they asked Pilate to have the legs of the crucified men broken and the bodies removed. Then the soldiers came and broke the legs of the first and of the other who had been crucified with him. But when they came to Jesus and saw that he was already dead, they did not break his legs. Instead, one of the soldiers pierced his side with a spear, and at once blood and water came out.
>
> —John 19:31–34, NRSV

This detail about Jesus being pierced by a lance is only found in the Gospel of John, although most paintings and statues of Jesus on the cross show this chest wound.

Some people note the detail of blood and water flowing from the wound and claim that this gives information about how Jesus died. They argue that the water shows that fluid would have accumulated in the lungs of Jesus, indicating that he died of asphyxiation. Other people argue that the blood and water are symbolic images. The Gospel of

---

What is the legend of the dogwood tree?

The dogwood is a small tree with beautiful, white flowers that have five petals, each of which has a red dot. According to the Gospel of John, Jesus had five wounds. People saw the dogwood blossom with its five red dots as symbolic of the wounds of Christ. Someone then made up the legend that Jesus was crucified using wood from a dogwood tree; the story goes that at the time of Jesus, the dogwood was a large tree, but after the Crucifixion, the dogwood never grew big again.

Another legend developed around a seashell called a sand dollar. This flat shell has five holes in it that people have connected to the five wounds of Christ. One hole, representing the chest wound of Jesus, is different from the other holes. Also, if you break open a sand dollar, five pieces that look like doves fall out. If you do not know what a sand dollar looks like, do an online image search.

A fresco at the Carmelites church in Dobling, Austria, shows a resurrected Christ with His side bearing the wound of the lance.

John is filled with symbolic references, and in this case, the water symbolizes baptism and the blood symbolizes the Eucharist.

THE RESURRECTION
AND ASCENSION OF JESUS

How important is the Resurrection story in the gospels?

For many Christians, the most important scene in the gospels is the story of the Resurrection because belief in the Resurrection is the basis of Christian faith. The story is told in all four gospels, although the actual Resurrection of Jesus is not described. The gospels describe the followers of Jesus finding the empty tomb and then seeing the risen Jesus. However, there are differences in the details in the four accounts, and there is no way to combine the various stories and make every detail fit together. Perhaps the eyewitnesses had different accounts of what happened or the gospel writers knew different versions of the story.

What happened between the crucifixion of Jesus and the Resurrection?

To understand the Resurrection stories, it is necessary to back up to the Crucifixion. After Jesus died on the cross, he was hurriedly buried by Joseph of Arimathea. The Gospel of Matthew describes:

When it was evening, there came a rich man from Arimathea, named Joseph, who was also a disciple of Jesus. He went to Pilate and asked for the body of Jesus; then Pilate ordered it to be given to him. So Joseph took the body and wrapped it in a clean linen cloth and laid it in his own new tomb, which he had hewn in the rock. He then rolled a great stone to the door of the tomb and went away.

—Matthew 27:57–60, NRSV

According to the gospels, Jesus died on a Friday. The Jewish Sabbath began at Friday sundown, and no work was allowed. In the Gospels of Mark and Luke, they rushed the burial and did not follow the normal customs of washing the body and anointing it with spices and ointments. The Sabbath continued until Saturday sundown. Thus, the women who wanted to prepare the body of Jesus had to wait until Sunday morning. Also, note that the Jewish week ended with the Sabbath: Saturday. Thus, Sunday was the first day of the week. Today, many people see Sunday as the last day of the week and Monday as the first day of the week.

Where in the gospels are the Resurrection stories found?

If you are interested, you can read the four accounts of the Resurrection appearances of Jesus in Matthew, Chapter 28; Mark, Chapter 16; Luke, Chapter 24; and John, Chapters 21–22. Here is Matthew's account:

After the Sabbath, as the first day of the week was dawning, Mary Magdalene and the other Mary came to see the tomb. And behold, there was a great earthquake; for an angel of the Lord descended from Heaven, approached, rolled back the stone, and sat upon it. His appearance was like lightning and his clothing was white as snow. The guards were shaken with fear of him and became like dead men. Then the angel said to the women in reply, "Do not be afraid! I know that you are seeking Jesus the crucified. He is not here, for he has been raised just as he said. Come and see the place where he lay. Then go quickly and tell his disciples, 'He has been raised from the dead, and he is going before you to Galilee; there you will see him.' Behold, I have told you."

Then they went away quickly from the tomb, fearful yet overjoyed, and ran to announce this to his disciples. And behold, Jesus met them on their way and greeted them. They approached, embraced his feet, and did him homage. Then Jesus said to them, "Do not be afraid. Go tell my brothers to go to Galilee, and there they will see me."

—Matthew 28:1–10, NABRE

In Mark and Luke, the women do not see the risen Jesus. In Matthew, the women encounter an angel. In Mark, they encounter a young man in a white robe. In Luke, the women see "two men in dazzling garments" who tell them that Jesus has risen from the dead.

In the Gospel of Luke, the women are Mary Magdalene; Joanna; Mary, the mother of James; and others. In the Gospel of Mark, the women are Mary Magdalene; Mary, the mother of James; and Salome. The Gospel of John describes only Mary Magdalene at the tomb. She goes and tells Peter and the Beloved Disciple, who then go to the tomb. At the tomb, Mary sees two angels in white. When she turns around, she sees Jesus, although she does not initially recognize him.

As stated earlier, there is no way to take all the different versions of these stories and harmonize them into one account in which all the various details fit neatly. The gospel writers had different accounts of what happened.

Are there other stories of the appearance of Jesus?

The Gospel of Luke tells the story of Jesus appearing to two of his followers walking the road to Emmaus, who do not recognize Jesus. The men describe the stories they have heard about the death of Jesus and his appearances. Jesus explains the prophecies that predict what happened. They stop for the evening, and when they sit down to eat, the two men finally recognize Jesus as he breaks the bread and blesses it (Luke 24:13–35; see also Mark 16:12). The location of a town named Emmaus has never been found. The painter Caravaggio created a dramatic portrayal of this scene in his 1601 painting *Supper at Emmaus*. (You can find it online.) Caravaggio also painted a 1606 version of this scene, but it is far less dramatic.

In his first letter to the Corinthians, Paul wrote:

> For I handed on to you as of first importance what I in turn had received: that Christ died for our sins in accordance with the scriptures, and that he was buried, and that he was raised on the third day in accordance with the scriptures, and that he appeared to Cephas, then to the twelve. Then he appeared to more than five hundred brothers and sisters at one time, most of whom are still alive, though some have died. Then he appeared to James, then to all the apostles.

> —1 Corinthians 15:3–7, NRSV

Paul wrote several decades before the gospels were written. The gospels make no mention of the risen Jesus appearing to the five hundred.

All of these stories in the gospels and the various references in the epistles support the key belief of most Christians that Jesus truly died on the cross, yet was alive, physically present, and talking to his followers two days later.

What is the Ascension?

The last story about Jesus is where he leaves the earth, called the Ascension. After the Ascension, Jesus can no longer be seen on earth. Belief in the Ascension of Jesus is based mostly on the story in the Gospel of Luke that is repeated in the book Acts of the Apostle. The writer of Luke also wrote Acts. Luke states: "As he blessed them he parted from them and was taken up to Heaven" (24:50–51, NABRE). The gospel does not say when this happened but makes it appear that this happened the same day as the Resurrection. In Acts, more detail is given to clarify the sequence of events: "He [Jesus] presented himself alive to them by many proofs after he had suffered, appearing to them during forty days and speaking about the kingdom of God" (Acts 1:3, NABRE). The Acts story relates:

> So when they had come together, they asked him, "Lord, is this the time when you will restore the kingdom to Israel?" He replied, "It is not for you to know the times or periods that the Father has set by his own authority. But you will receive power when the Holy Spirit has come upon you; and you will be my witnesses in Jerusalem, in all Judea and Samaria, and to the ends of the earth." When he had said this, as they were watching, he was lifted up, and a cloud took him out of their sight. While he was going and they were gazing up toward Heaven, suddenly two men in white robes stood by them. They said, "Men of Galilee, why do you stand looking up toward Heaven? This Jesus, who has been taken up from you into Heaven, will come in the same way as you saw him go into Heaven."

—Acts 1:6–11, NRSV

A mosaic showing the Ascension can be viewed in the Neamt Monastery in Vanatori, Romania. The Ascension is a theme commonly found in numerous works of Christian art.

The Ascension is mentioned briefly in the Gospel of Mark: "Then, after speaking to them, the Lord Jesus was taken up into Heaven and took a seat at God's right hand" (Mark 16:19, NABRE). However, most scholars recognize that this passage is a later addition to the gospel and not part of the original text. The Ascension is not mentioned in the Gospels of Matthew and John.

The forty-day period between the Resurrection and the Ascension parallels the forty days Jesus spent in the desert after his baptism. Many Christians, but not all, celebrate Ascension Thursday forty days after Easter.

THE TEACHINGS OF JESUS

OVERVIEW

What is the right attitude to take in exploring the teachings of Jesus?

This chapter is an exploration of the teachings of Jesus on what his followers were to believe and how they were to live and behave. From the time of Jesus down to the present, Christians have disagreed on how to understand and apply the teachings of Jesus. Today, there are many different views among Christians about how to live out this teaching. In exploring the teachings of Jesus, do not be surprised if you find new or different ideas, or even ideas with which you disagree. Keep an open mind and just remember that a diversity of opinion exists over how to understand the teachings of Jesus.

What are the different kinds of teachings of Jesus?

The gospels present the teachings of Jesus, which cover a wide range of topics. It is not easy to categorize the teachings of Jesus. However, four categories cover most of his teachings:

- Teachings about the Kingdom of God
- Teachings about faith
- Ethical teachings
- Important Parables of Jesus
- Jesus on Jesus

What things did Jesus not teach about?

There are many things that Jesus did not cover. Jesus never gives a complete description of what he is. Mainline Christians believe that Jesus was both man and God, yet Jesus never says that himself in the synoptic gospels nor does he describe what it is like to be such a being. (However, in the Gospel of John, Jesus does speak of himself and his relation to God the Father.) Jesus does not directly address many important ethical issues such as abortion, capital punishment, the role of government in providing for the needy, homosexuality, the morality of war, and many others. Although in the Gospel of Matthew, Jesus speaks of Peter being the foundation of the church of Jesus, Jesus says almost nothing about what that church should be in the future.

Down through the centuries, Christians have tried to fill out the teachings implied in the sayings of Jesus. Sometimes, these efforts seem consistent with the gospel messages, while other times, the efforts seem to be at great variance from the original message and intent of Jesus.

What does Jesus teach about the Kingdom of God?

A key theme of the teachings of Jesus in the Gospels of Matthew, Mark, and Luke is the Kingdom of God. Down through the centuries, readers of the gospels have struggled to figure out what Jesus meant by the "Kingdom of God." Common explanations of the Kingdom of God are that it refers to the Christian Church, or to a specific Christian denomination, or to Heaven when ones dies, or an inner spirituality. However, none of these explanations seem to exactly match what Jesus described. He seems to have in mind a present reality where his followers would see God as the Father and treat others according to a new set of values, such as those stated in the Beatitudes. The Kingdom

Jesus is always portrayed as a very patient and kind teacher who used parables to make his lessons easy to understand for all.

of God preached by Jesus was once described as the "Fatherhood of God and Brotherhood of man." This idea was proposed decades before the use of inclusive language.

The Gospel of Luke tells this story:

> Once Jesus was asked by the Pharisees when the kingdom of God was coming, and he answered, "The kingdom of God is not coming with things that can be observed; nor will they say, 'Look, here it is!' or 'There it is!' For, in fact, the kingdom of God is among you."
>
> —Luke 17:20–21, NRSV

The last line of this passage is sometimes wrongly translated as "the Kingdom of God is within you," which implies it as an interior state within people. However, Jesus seems to indicate that the Kingdom of God is among his followers.

What else did Jesus say about the Kingdom of God?

The Gospel of Mark describes the beginning of the public ministry of Jesus:

> After John had been arrested, Jesus came to Galilee proclaiming the gospel of God: "This is the time of fulfillment. The kingdom of God is at hand. Repent, and believe in the gospel."
>
> —Mark 1:14, NABRE

In Matthew and Luke, Jesus tells two important parables about the Kingdom (see more about Jesus' parables below).

> He [Jesus] put before them another parable: "The kingdom of Heaven is like a mustard seed that someone took and sowed in his field; it is the smallest of all the seeds, but when it has grown it is the greatest of shrubs and becomes a tree, so that the birds of the air come and make nests in its branches." He told them another parable: "The kingdom of Heaven is like yeast that a woman took and mixed in with three measures of flour until all of it was leavened."
>
> —Matthew 13:31–33, NRSV (see also Luke 13:18–21 and Mark 4:30–32)

However, note in this passage that there is no explanation of exactly what the Kingdom of Heaven is.

Does Jesus call it the Kingdom of God or the Kingdom of Heaven?

In Matthew, Jesus refers to his kingdom as the Kingdom of Heaven. Matthew wrote to a Christian community with a Jewish background. According to Jewish law, it was forbidden to say the name of God. Matthew avoids the word "God" by using "Heaven."

What does the word "gospel" mean?

The word "gospel" means simply "good news."

A kingdom is a political term. Did Jesus have something political in mind?

Although Jesus uses the political language of "kingdom," he does not talk in political terms. In fact, he never says anything about a king: the Kingdom of God of Jesus does not have a king. Although Christians would later speak of Jesus as the king, the label has no political meaning. The Kingdom of God that Jesus describes is not political, and it is not about power.

Down through the centuries at numerous times, political power has been linked to Jesus as if Jesus supported such political power. In England still today, a new king or queen is crowned in a Christian religious ceremony. But again, the Kingdom of God of Jesus rejects political power.

Are there other passages in the gospels that indicate what Jesus had in mind in preaching the Kingdom of God?

The key descriptions of the Kingdom of God are seen in the Beatitudes, which are found in Matthew and Luke and which are described below. The Beatitudes in both gospels are then followed by important passages that lay out key ethical teachings of Jesus.

What did Jesus say about religious faith in God the Father?

An essential point of the teachings of Jesus is to see God as a father. Jesus used the term "abba," which meant "daddy," as the term to address God. This is most famously seen in the prayer that becomes known as the Our Father. There are two versions found in Matthew and Luke. In Matthew, Jesus speaks:

> This is how you are to pray: Our Father in Heaven, hallowed be your name, your kingdom come, your will be done, on earth as in Heaven. Give us today our daily bread; and forgive us our debts, as we forgive our debtors; and do not subject us to the final test, but deliver us from the evil one.
>
> —Matthew 6:9–13, NABRE

The Gospel of Luke describes this scene:

> He was praying in a certain place, and when he had finished, one of his disciples said to him, "Lord, teach us to pray just as John taught his disciples." He said to them, "When you pray, say: Father, hallowed be your name, your kingdom come. Give us each day our daily bread and forgive us our sins for we ourselves forgive everyone in debt to us, and do not subject us to the final test."
>
> —Luke 11:2–4, NABRE

What does Jesus say about faith?

Jesus states in Mark:

> Have faith in God. Truly I tell you, if you say to this mountain, "Be taken up and thrown into the sea," and if you do not doubt in your heart, but believe that

what you say will come to pass, it will be done for you. So I tell you, whatever you ask for in prayer, believe that you have received it, and it will be yours.

—Mark 11:22–24, NRSV

Christians typically take this imagery of the power of faith as a metaphor since no one has yet been able to literally move a mountain by faith.

In many of his healings, Jesus refers to the faith of those being healed. In the Gospel of Mark, after Jesus heals the woman who had been afflicted with hemorrhages, he tells the woman: "Daughter, your faith has saved you. Go in peace and be cured of your affliction" (Mark 5:34, NABRE).

Mark relates this story:

Jesus said to him in reply, "What do you want me to do for you?" The blind man replied to him, "Master, I want to see." Jesus told him, "Go your way; your faith has saved you." Immediately he received his sight and followed him on the way.

—Mark 10:51–52, NABRE (see also the story in Luke 17:11–19)

Jesus often criticizes his followers for their lack of faith, for example:

And when he [Jesus] got into the boat, his disciples followed him. A windstorm arose on the sea, so great that the boat was being swamped by the waves; but he was asleep. And they went and woke him up, saying, "Lord, save us! We are perishing!" And he said to them, "Why are you afraid, you of little faith?" Then he got up and rebuked the winds and the sea; and there was a dead calm.

—Matthew 8:23–26, NRSV

Other versions of this story are found in Mark 4:36–41 and Luke 8:22–25. (For another story where Jesus criticizes the apostles for their lack of faith, see Matthew 16:5–12 and Mark 8:14–21.)

THE PARABLES OF JESUS

What is the style of the teachings of Jesus?

In the synoptic gospels of Matthew, Mark, and Luke, Jesus teaches in parables (short stories that illustrate a point) and short sayings. In addition, there are longer discourses, such as the Sermon on the Mount in Matthew and the Sermon on the Plain in Luke. The Gospel of Luke also contains several long and famous stories such as the Good Samaritan and the Man with Two Sons (also known as the Prodigal Son story). In the synoptic gospels, Jesus rarely says anything about himself.

The Gospel of John is very different. It includes long discourses of Jesus that often go on for several pages. Also, unique to John is that Jesus says much about himself and his relationship to God the Father.

What is the famous parable of the sower and the seed?

And he [Jesus] told them many things in parables, saying: "Listen! A sower went out to sow. And as he sowed, some seeds fell on the path, and the birds came and ate them up. Other seeds fell on rocky ground, where they did not have much soil, and they sprang up quickly, since they had no depth of soil. But when the sun rose, they were scorched; and since they had no root, they withered away. Other seeds fell among thorns, and the thorns grew up and choked them. Other seeds fell on good soil and brought forth grain, some a hundred-fold, some sixty, some thirty."

Jesus used images that everyone could understand in his parables, such as the story of the farmer sowing crop seeds; the seeds represent people hearing His word, but not all of the seeds will germinate and thrive just as only some people will take the message and allow it to grow in their hearts.

Jesus explains the parable:

Hear then the parable of the sower. When anyone hears the word of the kingdom and does not understand it, the evil one comes and snatches away what is sown in the heart; this is what was sown on the path. As for what was sown on rocky ground, this is the one who hears the word and immediately receives it with joy; yet such a person has no root, but endures only for a while, and when trouble or persecution arises on account of the word, that person immediately falls away. As for what was sown among thorns, this is the one who hears the word, but the cares of the world and the lure of wealth choke the word, and it yields nothing. But as for what was sown on good soil, this is the one who hears the word and understands it, who indeed bears fruit and yields, in one case a hundredfold, in another sixty, and in another thirty.

—Matthew 13:3–8, 19–23, NRSV (see also Mark 4:2–20 and Luke 8:4–15)

However, noteworthy in this parable is that the content of the "word of the kingdom" is never described. (Luke refers to the "word of God.") This parable describes what happens to the message of the Kingdom of God yet never defines what that message is.

What is the parable of the Good Samaritan, and what is the meaning of the story?

In the Gospel of Luke, Jesus tells an important parable.

Just then a lawyer stood up to test Jesus. "Teacher," he said, "what must I do to inherit eternal life?" He said to him, "What is written in the law? What do you read there?" He answered, "You shall love the Lord your God with all your heart, and with all your soul, and with all your strength, and with all your mind; and your neighbor as yourself." And he said to him, "You have given the right answer; do this, and you will live." But wanting to justify himself, he asked Jesus, "And who is my neighbor?" Jesus replied, "A man was going down from Jerusalem to Jericho, and fell into the hands of robbers, who stripped him, beat him, and went away, leaving him half dead. Now by chance a priest was going down that road; and when he saw him, he passed by on the other side. So likewise a Levite, when he came to the place and saw him, passed by on the other side. But a Samaritan while traveling came near him; and when he saw him, he was moved with pity. He went to him and bandaged his wounds, having poured oil and wine on them. Then he put him on his own animal, brought him to an inn, and took care of him. The next day he took out two denarii, gave them to the innkeeper, and said, 'Take care of him; and when I come back, I will repay you whatever more you spend.' Which of these three, do you think, was a neighbor to the man who fell into the hands of the robbers?" He said, "The one who showed him mercy." Jesus said to him, "Go and do likewise."

—Luke 10:25–37, NRSV

This is an important story about caring for those in need. The Samaritan cares for the injured man while the priest and the Levite keep walking. What is noteworthy is that the priest and Levite are very likely ignoring him for religious reasons. Both know they would be ritually defiled by having contact with a dead body and would be unable to fulfill their religious duties. They do not bother to find out that the man is still alive.

However, the story was even more startling to the listeners of the time because it was a Samaritan who did the right thing. The Samaritans were a religious and ethnic group within the Jewish world that held to an older version of the Bible and had their own temple. The Samaritans were a despised minority who were shunned for various reasons. Their religion was not seen as authentic. Jesus flips things on their heads by having the hated Samaritan be the true follower of God.

A stained glass window in Roxton Chapel in Bedfordshire, England, illustrates the tale of the Good Samaritan. It is important that superficially religious people in Jesus' parable ignore the man in need, while a member of a rejected minority does the right thing.

Due to this story, the word "Samaritan" has entered the English language as someone who helps strangers. Some people get bogged down in the application of this story over the wisdom of helping people along the roadside. However, helping people is not limited to such situations. Many people need help in many different ways.

What is the parable of the Sheep and Goats, and what is the meaning of the story?

In Matthew Chapter 25, Jesus gives this important parable about how we treat others:

> When the Son of Man comes in his glory, and all the angels with him, he will sit upon his glorious throne, and all the nations will be assembled before him. And he will separate them one from another, as a shepherd separates the sheep from the goats. He will place the sheep on his right and the goats on his left. Then the king will say to those on his right, "Come, you who are blessed by my Father. Inherit the kingdom prepared for you from the foundation of the world. For I was hungry and you gave me food, I was thirsty and you gave me drink, a stranger and you welcomed me, naked and you clothed me, ill and you cared for me, in prison and you visited me." Then the righteous will answer him and say, "Lord, when did we see you hungry and feed you, or thirsty and give you drink? When did we see you a stranger and welcome you, or naked and clothe you? When did we see you ill or in prison, and visit you?" And the king will say to them in reply, "Amen, I say to you, whatever you did for one of these least brothers of mine, you did for me."
>
> Then he will say to those on his left, "Depart from me, you accursed, into the eternal fire prepared for the devil and his angels. For I was hungry and you gave me no food, I was thirsty and you gave me no drink, stranger and you gave me no welcome, naked and you gave me no clothing, ill and in prison, and you did not care for me." Then they will answer and say, "Lord, when did we see you hungry or thirsty or a stranger or naked or ill or in prison, and not minister to your needs?" He will answer them, "Amen, I say to you, what you did not do for one of these least ones, you did not do for me." And these will go off to eternal punishment, but the righteous to eternal life.
>
> —Matthew 25:31–46, NABRE

This very powerful passage states that Christians will be judged based on how they treat the lowliest people in society. It can provide an important motivation for better treatment of those who are at the bottom. However, the message of this passage seems to be often ignored.

This passage is also important in the debate on what is necessary for salvation. Some Christians believe that salvation is based on faith and good works. This passage is often cited to argue for the importance of good works. Other Christians insist that salvation is based on faith alone and downplay the importance of this passage.

What is the parable of the Man with Two Sons, and what is the meaning of the story?

The story of the Man with Two Sons is one of the most famous parables in the gospels. It is also called the Prodigal Son story, and it is explained in detail below. The reader can decide which title is the best. Is the story about the younger son, the prodigal son, or about both of the sons? Jesus tells this story:

A man had two sons, and the younger son said to his father, "Father, give me the share of your estate that should come to me." So the father divided the property between them. [*Normally the son would get his share of the estate when his father died. Apparently, to this son, it does not matter whether his father is alive or dead.*] After a few days, the younger son collected all his belongings and set off to a distant country where he squandered his inheritance on a life of dissipation. [*Note that no details are given about how the younger son wasted his money.*]

When he had freely spent everything, a severe famine struck that country, and he found himself in dire need. So he hired himself out to one of the local citizens who sent him to his farm to tend the swine. And he longed to eat his fill of the pods on which the swine fed, but nobody gave him any. [*The pigs are eating better than he is! Also, for someone of the Jewish tradition, to be taking care of pigs would be a great dishonor.*] Coming to his senses he thought, "How many of my father's hired workers have more than enough food to eat, but here am I, dying from hunger. I shall get up and go to my father and I shall say to him, 'Father, I have sinned against Heaven and against you. I no longer deserve to be called your son; treat me as you would treat one of your hired workers.'" [*He prepares his speech so he can apologize to his father and be taken back as a servant. He does not expect to be restored as a son.*] So he got up and went back to his father.

While he was still a long way off, his father caught sight of him, and was

A painting by nineteenth-century artist Carl Johann Nepomuk Hemerlein on display at Schottenfelder Church in Vienna, Austria, illustrates the tale of the Prodigal Son, otherwise known as the Man with Two Sons.

73

filled with compassion. He ran to his son, embraced him and kissed him. [*The father sees his son a long way off because he is looking for him to come back. He wants his son back. Then the father runs out to him. The father does not stand waiting for the son to grovel and beg for forgiveness.*] His son said to him, "Father, I have sinned against Heaven and against you; I no longer deserve to be called your son." But his father ordered his servants, "Quickly bring the finest robe and put it on him; put a ring on his finger and sandals on his feet. [*The finest robe means that they are going to celebrate. This is the equivalent of a tuxedo today. Obviously, he would take a bath before putting it on. Also, the ring restored the son to his status as a son. The sandals meant that he would not be a servant.*] Take the fattened calf and slaughter it. Then let us celebrate with a feast, because this son of mine was dead, and has come to life again; he was lost, and has been found." Then the celebration began. [*A fattened calf would only be eaten at very special events.*]

[*For many people, the whole point of the story is over. The story is about forgiveness: the father forgives his son for the great wrong and insult that he has done and the son is welcomed back. The father symbolizes God, and the son symbolizes sinners. However, if that is the point to the story, then why does the story continue?*]

Now the older son had been out in the field and, on his way back, as he neared the house, he heard the sound of music and dancing. [*The older son does not do the normal thing of going in to find out what is going on and then join the party.*] He called one of the servants and asked what this might mean. The servant said to him, "Your brother has returned and your father has slaughtered the fattened calf because he has him back safe and sound." [*Notice that the servant does not say "Great news, your brother is back!" because the servant knows the elder brothers will not be happy that the younger brother is back nor happy that the father has forgiven the younger brother.*]

He became angry, and when he refused to enter the house, his father came out and pleaded with him. He said to his father in reply, "Look, all these years I served you and not once did I disobey your orders; yet you never gave me even a young goat to feast on with my friends. But when your son returns who swallowed up your property with prostitutes, for him you slaughter the fattened calf." [*How did the older brother know that the younger brother spent the money on prostitutes? Maybe that is what the older son would have done had he had the guts to run away. Also, note that the older son's definition of being a good, loving son is the definition of being a good servant.*] He said to him, "My son, you are here with me always; everything I have is yours. But now we must celebrate and rejoice, because your brother was dead and has come to life again; he was lost and has been found."

—Luke 15:11–32, NABRE

The point of the story seems not only to be about God's forgiveness of sinners but also about how religious people who have followed the rules resent God for forgiving those who did not always follow the rules. This story might refer to Jewish attitudes toward Christians. Many Jews who followed the law resented the Christian teaching that the followers of Jesus would be forgiven for their sins without having to follow all the Laws of Moses. At the time, some Jews spoke of everyone as a "Son of God," yet Jews were the elder sons (inclusive language and inclusive thinking did not exist then). This was at a time when the eldest son had greater honor and privileges than younger sons. Lastly, this parable could be for Christians who still followed the Jewish law yet resented Christians who did not follow the law.

THE ETHICAL TEACHINGS OF JESUS

Where in the gospels do you find the ethical teachings of Jesus?

The Gospel of Mark is the shortest gospel and contains little ethical teachings by Jesus. In John's gospel, Jesus speaks in long, theological discourses, yet these do not include much about how the followers of Jesus are to live. That leaves the Gospels of Matthew and Luke, where most of the ethical teachings of Jesus can be found. The main sources for the ethical teachings of Jesus are as follows:

- The Beatitudes in Matthew and Luke
- Matthew 5:17 through 7:12
- Luke 6:27–42

As the Beatitudes are so important, it is necessary to quote them in full. They are found in the Gospels of Matthew and Luke. As they are only found in these two gospels, they are considered key texts that came from the Q Source, a missing document that scholars speculated was a source of quotes used in the gospels of Matthew and Luke.

Why are the Beatitudes called the Beatitudes?

The word "beatitude" comes from the Latin word *beautus*, which means "blessed." The key lines of the Beatitudes begin with "Blessed are" or in older versions "Blessed be." The word "beatitude" is not derived from the "be-attitudes."

Where do the Beatitudes appear in the gospels?

Here is the version from the Gospel of Matthew, which is often called the Sermon on the Mount since Jesus gave this teaching on a mountain. In the Gospel of Matthew, this is meant to be a parallel image to Moses receiving the Law on Mount Sinai.

Blessed are the poor in spirit,
for theirs is the kingdom of Heaven.

Blessed are they who mourn,
for they will be comforted.

Blessed are the meek,
for they will inherit the land.

Blessed are they who hunger and thirst for righteousness,
for they will be satisfied.

Blessed are the merciful,
for they will be shown mercy.

Blessed are the clean of heart,
for they will see God.

Blessed are the peacemakers,
for they will be called children of God.

Blessed are they who are persecuted for the sake of righteousness,
for theirs is the kingdom of Heaven.

Blessed are you when they insult you and persecute you and utter every kind of evil against you [falsely] because of me.

Rejoice and be glad, for your reward will be great in Heaven. Thus they persecuted the prophets who were before you.

—Matthew 5:3–16, NABRE

Where is the other version?

Here is the version from the Gospel of Luke. It is sometimes called the Sermon on the Plain, where Jesus gave it.

And raising his eyes toward his disciples he said:

"Blessed are you who are poor,
for the kingdom of God is yours.

Blessed are you who are now hungry,
for you will be satisfied.

Blessed are you who are now weeping,
for you will laugh.

Blessed are you when people hate you,
and when they exclude and insult you,
and denounce your name as evil
on account of the Son of Man.

Rejoice and leap for joy on that day! Behold, your reward will be great in Heaven. For their ancestors treated the prophets in the same way.

But woe to you who are rich,
for you have received your consolation.

But woe to you who are filled now,
for you will be hungry.

The Church of the Beatitudes is near the Sea of Galilee and is said to be at or near where Jesus delivered his famous Sermon on the Mount.

> Woe to you who laugh now,
> for you will grieve and weep.
>
> Woe to you when all speak well of you,
> for their ancestors treated the false prophets in this way."
>
> —Luke 6:20–26, NABRE

In the Beatitudes, Jesus sets forth the values of those who belong to the Kingdom of God. Jesus turns upside down the values of the world. The rich are not blessed but rather the poor. The Kingdom of God is not about the powerful but rather the meek.

What are the key passages in Matthew and Luke?

The passages in Matthew and Luke after the Beatitudes contain many of the ethical teachings of Jesus. These are the ethical topics found in Matthew 5:17–7:12:

- Teaching on the Law of Moses
- Anger
- Adultery and removing one's eye
- Divorce
- Oaths
- Retaliation

77

- Love of enemies
- Almsgiving
- God and money
- Judging others
- The Golden Rule

The ethical topics in Luke 6:27–42 are love of enemies and judging others.

What was the Jewish Law?

According to Jewish tradition, God gave Moses the Law on Mount Sinai. The Law includes the Ten Commandments but also hundreds of other laws, totaling 613 laws. The laws are found in the first five books of the Bible, which are called the Torah: Genesis, Exodus, Leviticus, Numbers, and Deuteronomy. Religious Jews believe that they are bound by these laws. Modern Jews disagree on how strictly to follow these laws. Orthodox Jews are the most strict, Reform Jews are less strict and emphasize the moral laws, and Conservative Jews are in the middle. These laws are called the Jewish Law, or the Law of Moses, or the Torah.

At the time of Jesus, Jews who took their religion seriously followed the Law of Moses. One religious group, the Sadducees, focused on the written law. Another group, the Pharisees, followed both the written law and an oral tradition of interpretations of the law. About two hundred years after Jesus, this oral tradition would be written down as the Talmud. The Talmud is a collection of writings commenting on the Law.

What did Jesus say about the Law itself?

In Matthew, Jesus stated:

> Do not think that I have come to abolish the law or the prophets; I have come not to abolish but to fulfill. For truly I tell you, until Heaven and earth pass away, not one letter, not one stroke of a letter, will pass from the law until all is accomplished. Therefore, whoever breaks one of the least of these commandments, and teaches others to do the same, will be called least in the kingdom of Heaven; but whoever does them and teaches them will be called great in the kingdom of Heaven. For I tell you, unless your righteousness exceeds that of the scribes and Pharisees, you will never enter the kingdom of Heaven.
>
> —Matthew 5:17–20, NRSV

What did Jesus say about the Law of Moses?

Jesus came from a Jewish background, and not surprisingly, Jesus frequently mentioned the Law of Moses and gave his interpretation of it. In many cases, he went against the prevailing Jewish understanding of how to follow the law.

However, as noted above, Jesus often interpreted the laws differently than Jewish religious teachers. Another story in Luke shows the attitude of Jesus to the law:

> Just then a lawyer stood up to test Jesus. "Teacher," he said, "what must I do to inherit eternal life?" He said to him, "What is written in the law? What do you read there?" He answered, "You shall love the Lord your God with all your heart, and with all your soul, and with all your strength, and with all your mind; and your neighbor as yourself." And he said to him, "You have given the right answer; do this, and you will live."
>
> —Luke 10:25–28, NRSV

What did Jesus say about the religious people around him?

Jesus rejected the religious practices and attitudes of some people:

> Then Jesus said to the crowds and to his disciples, "The scribes and the Pharisees sit on Moses's seat; therefore, do whatever they teach you and follow it; but do not do as they do, for they do not practice what they teach. They tie up heavy burdens, hard to bear, and lay them on the shoulders of others; but they themselves are unwilling to lift a finger to move them. They do all their deeds to be seen by others; for they make their phylacteries broad and their fringes long. They love to have the place of honor at banquets and the best seats in the synagogues, and to be greeted with respect in the marketplaces, and to have people call them rabbi."
>
> —Matthew 24:1–7, NRSV

What did Jesus teach about anger?

In Matthew, Jesus speaks against anger:

> You have heard that it was said to your ancestors, "You shall not kill; and whoever kills will be liable to judgment." But I say to you, whoever is angry with his brother will be liable to judgment, and whoever says to his brother, 'Raqa,' will be answerable to the Sanhedrin, and whoever says, 'You fool,' will be liable to fiery Gehenna. Therefore, if you bring your gift to the altar, and there recall that your brother has anything against you, leave your gift there at the altar, go first and be reconciled with your brother, and then come and offer your gift. Settle with your opponent quickly while on the way to court with him. Otherwise your opponent will hand you over to the judge, and the judge will hand you over to the guard, and you will be thrown into prison. Amen, I say to you, you will not be released until you have paid the last penny.
>
> —Matthew 5:21–26, NABRE

Over the centuries, Christians have argued over how to apply this teaching. Was Jesus exaggerating in saying someone will be sent to Gehenna for calling someone "You fool"?

During Jesus' time, Gehenna was a trash heap that was always burning like hell; today, the hilly area in Jerusalem is peaceful, green, and dotted with old olive trees.

What is Gehenna?

Gehenna was the trash dump just outside the walls of Jerusalem that was constantly burning. Jesus uses it to symbolize the place of punishment in the afterlife.

Did Jesus teach that people should tear out their eyes if their eyes cause them to sin?

Jesus stated:

> You have heard that it was said, "You shall not commit adultery." But I say to you, everyone who looks at a woman with lust has already committed adultery with her in his heart. If your right eye causes you to sin, tear it out and throw it away. It is better for you to lose one of your members than to have your whole body thrown into Gehenna. And if your right hand causes you to sin, cut it off and throw it away. It is better for you to lose one of your members than to have your whole body go into Gehenna.
>
> —Matthew 5:27–30, NABRE (see also Mark 9:43–48)

Jesus seems to be making the point that wrongdoing is not just about what we do but also about what is in our minds and hearts. Lustful desire is wrong even if no actions take place. However, many who have thought about this passage would add that having a desire to do wrong and not doing it is less bad than having the desire and also doing it. What Jesus seems to call for is a change of heart that goes beyond merely following the moral rules, or for the audience of Jesus, following the Law of Moses.

> ## Did Jesus mean to literally tear out one's own eye?
>
> **N**o. Very likely, he was exaggerating to make his point. Jesus often used the literary device of hyperbole: exaggeration. Storytellers and teachers of the time of Jesus often used hyperbole, and the audience of Jesus would have recognized the words of Jesus as an exaggeration that was not to be taken literally.

What did Jesus say about divorce?

Four passages in the gospels give the teaching of Jesus on divorce. The gospel of Matthew includes two passages. Here is the longer version:

> Some Pharisees came to him, and to test him they asked, "Is it lawful for a man to divorce his wife for any cause?" He answered, "Have you not read that the one who made them at the beginning 'made them male and female,' and said, 'For this reason a man shall leave his father and mother and be joined to his wife, and the two shall become one flesh'? So they are no longer two, but one flesh. Therefore what God has joined together, let no one separate." They said to him, "Why then did Moses command us to give a certificate of dismissal and to divorce her?" He said to them, "It was because you were so hard-hearted that Moses allowed you to divorce your wives, but from the beginning it was not so. And I say to you, whoever divorces his wife, except for unchastity, and marries another commits adultery."
>
> —Matthew 19:3–9, NRSV

The short version in Matthew quotes Jesus: "It was also said, 'Whoever divorces his wife must give her a bill of divorce.' But I say to you, whoever divorces his wife (unless the marriage is unlawful) causes her to commit adultery, and whoever marries a divorced woman commits adultery" (Matthew 5:31–32, NABRE). Part of the background to keep in mind on this passage is that in the time of Jesus, a divorced woman might not have any means to support herself. In Luke, Jesus states, "Everyone who divorces his wife and marries another commits adultery, and the one who marries a woman divorced from her husband commits adultery" (Luke 16:18, NABRE).

The passage in Mark reads, "He [Jesus] said to them, 'Whoever divorces his wife and marries another commits adultery against her; and if she divorces her husband and marries another, she commits adultery.'" This passage is slightly different in talking about a woman initiating divorce, which may reflect a different audience for the Gospel of Mark, where that was legally possible.

What does the phrase in Matthew "unless the marriage is unlawful" mean?

The Gospel of Matthew grants an exception on divorce: "unless the marriage is unlawful." Perhaps this applies to non-Jewish converts to Christianity. Matthew's audience was primarily Christians with Jewish backgrounds. Jewish rules on what was a lawful marriage were different from Roman legal rules on marriage. Perhaps Christians who were married under the broader Roman rules were allowed to divorce and remarry if their marriages did not conform to the traditional Jewish rules. However, this is an educated guess.

Sometimes, this rule is called the "Mathean Exception." The Greek text uses the word *porneia* and is sometimes translated as "in cases of immorality." Although *porneia* is the root of the English word "pornography," it is unclear today how the word was understood by the original audience of Matthew's gospel. Under what circumstances did some Christian communities allow members to divorce and remarry? We do not know for certain.

Jesus makes it clear that divorce is not acceptable except if "the marriage is unlawful"; some churches will not allow divorced people to remarry, but most are more lenient in these modern times.

What is the modern Christian view on divorce and remarriage?

In modern times, many Christians have struggled over how to interpret these four passages. On the one hand, Christians want to encourage healthy marriages and discourage divorce. On the other hand, many Christians want to be sensitive to those who have needed to get divorced and encourage them to remain in the community if they have been remarried.

The question sometimes comes down to whether or not a divorced person is allowed to remarry in a particular Christian church. For some Christians, this is not an issue. Although they regret when divorces happen, there is no problem getting remarried in many Christian churches. However, for some Christians, such as Roman Catholics, it can get very complicated.

In all Roman Catholic teaching, a validly married person who gets divorced cannot later remarry in the Catholic Church. However, if a Catholic was married and gets divorced and then can show that the marriage was not valid sacramentally, the person can be granted an annulment and is then allowed to marry a second time in the Catholic Church. A full analysis and explanation of annulment is beyond the scope of this book.

One strategy that many denominations have taken on the problem of the frequency of divorce is to create training programs to help create more successful marriages.

What does Jesus say about swearing oaths?

Jesus spoke against swearing oaths in the Gospel of Matthew:

Again you have heard that it was said to your ancestors, "Do not take a false oath, but make good to the Lord all that you vow." But I say to you, do not swear at all; not by Heaven, for it is God's throne; nor by the earth, for it is his footstool; nor by Jerusalem, for it is the city of the great King. Do not swear by your head, for you cannot make a single hair white or black. Let your 'Yes' mean 'Yes,' and your 'No' mean 'No.' Anything more is from the evil one."

—Matthew 5:33–37, NABRE

Very possibly, Jesus was commenting on the question being debated at the time about whether it was lawful to swear by Heaven or by God's throne in Heaven. Jesus was also arguing for honesty of answers that did not need to be backed up with oaths. This teaching is reaffirmed in the Epistle of James (5:12).

Did Jesus mean to prohibit all oaths or only some of them? Some Christians, such as the Quakers, Amish, and Mennonites, understand this to prohibit all oaths, including legal oaths. Other Christians interpret this to prohibit swearing using God's name. It also seems likely that calling cuss words "swear words" is an attempt to find a biblical text against cussing.

What did Jesus say on retaliation?

Matthew contains this important passage of Jesus:

You have heard that it was said, "An eye for an eye and a tooth for a tooth." But I say to you, do not resist an evildoer. But if anyone strikes you on the right cheek, turn the other also; and if anyone wants to sue you and take your coat, give your cloak as well; and if anyone forces you to go one mile, go also the second mile. Give to everyone who begs from you, and do not refuse anyone who wants to borrow from you.

—Matthew 5:38–42, NRSV

Christians have argued over the meaning of this passage for centuries. Some see Jesus as describing an insult situation and thus see this passage as having a limited application. The detail about being struck on the right cheek implies that Jesus is describing a back hand slap by a right-handed person.

Others use this passage as indicative of a rejection by Jesus of all violence. It is important to note that Jesus never expands on this teaching by directly talking about issues such as the morality of war and the morality of capital punishment. Christian groups such as the Amish, Mennonites, and Quakers and Christian monks reject all violence as being against the teachings of Jesus and often cite this passage as proof of the attitude of Jesus.

Jesus clearly rejects all retaliation and the principle from the Law of Moses: "An eye for an eye." This rule is called the *Lex Talionis*. Many acts of violence are done in retaliation. "He did this to me that hurt me; therefore, I can hurt him back!" "That nation hurt us; therefore, we can hurt them back!" One of the problems with retaliation is that rarely does the other feel that things are equal and settled. The other side often feels a need to retaliate for the prior act of retaliation.

Another problem with violence is that it rarely fixes things. Unfortunately, many movie plots are based on the idea that once the good guys get enough weapons and do enough violence to the bad guys, then all will be well. Real life rarely works that way.

What was the teaching of Jesus on violence?

Christians have argued for centuries over whether or not Jesus rejected all violence. Many Christians believe that he did. As noted above, Quakers, Amish, Mennonites, and many other Christians insist that Christians should not use violence.

Many Christians believe strongly that Jesus was a pacifist and that they, too, should reject all violence. Included among these are the Amish (shown here), Mennonites, and Quakers.

Other Christians have argued that violence against other people is permitted under some circumstances, although Jesus never specifically stated such a principle. Such Christians cite the passage where Jesus cleansed the Temple and argue that Jesus used violence. However, as noted before, the acts of Jesus in that incident are very restrained. Nowhere does Jesus strike any person, although he does make a whip of words to drive out the livestock.

What about the Two Swords?

Other Christians argue that Jesus justified violence because of the presence of a sword or two swords among his followers at the arrest of Jesus. All four gospels mention the incident, although they disagree on who uses the sword. In Mark, it is a bystander. In Matthew, it is "one of those who accompanied Jesus." This may or may not have been one of his Twelve Apostles. In Luke, it is one of the disciples, which also may or may not mean one of the Twelve Apostles. In John, Simon Peter uses the sword.

The Gospel of Mark states: "One of the bystanders drew his sword, struck the high priest's servant, and cut off his ear" (Mark 14:47, NABRE). However, it is a bystander and not one of the apostles. Matthew's account states, "And behold, one of those who accompanied Jesus put his hand to his sword, drew it, and struck the high priest's servant, cutting off his ear. Then Jesus said to him, 'Put your sword back into its sheath, for all who take the sword will perish by the sword'" (26:51–52, NABRE).

The Gospel of John states: "Then Simon Peter, who had a sword, drew it, struck the high priest's slave, and cut off his right ear. The slave's name was Malchus. Jesus said to

Peter, 'Put your sword into its scabbard. Shall I not drink the cup that the Father gave me?'" (John 18:10–11, NABRE)

Here is the version from the Gospel of Luke:

He said to them, "But now, the one who has a purse must take it, and likewise a bag. And the one who has no sword must sell his cloak and buy one. For I tell you, this scripture must be fulfilled in me, 'And he was counted among the lawless'; and indeed what is written about me is being fulfilled." They said, "Lord, look, here are two swords." He replied, "It is enough."

...

When those who were around him saw what was coming, they asked, "Lord, should we strike with the sword?" Then one of them struck the slave of the high priest and cut off his right ear. But Jesus said, "No more of this!" And he touched his ear and healed him.

—Luke 22:36–38, 49–51, NRSV

Why in the Gospel of Luke does Jesus tell his followers to buy a sword? Jesus is trying to fulfill the prophecy of Isaiah: "They made his grave with the wicked and his tomb with the rich, although he had done no violence, and there was no deceit in his mouth" (Isaiah 53:9, NRSV). Jesus hints at the prophecy in all three synoptic gospels: "At that hour Jesus said to the crowds, 'Have you come out with swords and clubs to arrest me as though I were a bandit? Day after day I sat in the temple teaching, and you did not arrest me'" (Matthew 26:55, NRSV; see also Mark 14:48 and Luke 22:52).

So why did Jesus tell his followers to bring two swords?

In Luke, Jesus had his disciples bring two swords as a symbolic act to fulfill the prophecy. Jesus had no intention that they would be used because two swords would be totally inadequate. Ten other apostles had no swords. When the sword is actually used, the ear of a servant is struck. If this were an effective defense, the sword might be used against an actual soldier and the sword wielder might go for something other than an ear.

To summarize: the call of Jesus for his followers to bring a sword was a symbolic act to fulfill the prophecy of Isaiah. It was not to show the approval of Jesus to use violence. Jesus himself did not resist the violence toward himself. Furthermore, if Jesus taught "love your enemies," then how can any act of violence be justified?

What did Jesus say about loving one's enemies?

A very important teaching of Jesus is his call to love one's enemies: "But I say to you that listen, love your enemies, do good to those who hate you, bless those who curse you, pray for those who abuse you" (Luke 6:27–28, NRSV; see also Matthew 5:38–42). This radical teaching of Jesus rejects the typical attitude of many people, which is to love friends and hate enemies or to love one's own people and hate those who are different.

85

Many Christians seem to ignore this teaching of Jesus. Down through the centuries, many examples can even be found of Christians intensely hating other Christians.

What is almsgiving? What did Jesus say about almsgiving?

Almsgiving is giving money to help the poor or those in need. It is also called charity. Jesus stated:

Giving alms for the poor should be a humble deed and not one done in order to gain praise from others for one's generosity.

> [But] take care not to perform righteous deeds in order that people may see them; otherwise, you will have no recompense from your Heavenly Father. When you give alms, do not blow a trumpet before you, as the hypocrites do in the synagogues and in the streets to win the praise of others. Amen, I say to you, they have received their reward. But when you give alms, do not let your left hand know what your right is doing, so that your almsgiving may be secret. And your Father who sees in secret will repay you.
>
> —Matthew 6:1–4, NABRE

What did Jesus say about money?

Jesus often spoke about money. His most famous passage states: "No one can serve two masters. He will either hate one and love the other, or be devoted to one and despise the other. You cannot serve God and mammon" (Matthew 6:24, NABRE). The word "mammon" means money. In the Gospel of Luke, Jesus states, "Blessed are you who are poor, for the kingdom of God is yours…. But woe to you who are rich, for you have received your consolation" (Luke 21:20, 24, NABRE).

Over the centuries, Christians have argued over the teachings of Jesus on poverty: whether they are an essential part of Christianity or optional. Some Christians believe that having wealth is not a problem as long as a person is not too attached to it. This is a common attitude among wealthy Christians, although it is important to note that Jesus never made that distinction. Other Christians, such as St. Francis of Assisi, see poverty as an essential value of Christianity.

In an important story, Jesus calls a wealthy man to give up his wealth:

Now someone approached him [Jesus] and said, "Teacher, what good must I do to gain eternal life?" He answered him, "Why do you ask me about the good? There is only One who is good. If you wish to enter into life, keep the commandments." He asked him, "Which ones?" And Jesus replied, "'You shall not kill'; 'you shall not commit adultery'; 'you shall not steal'; 'you shall not bear false witness'; 'honor your father and your mother'; and 'you shall love your neighbor as yourself.'" The young man said to him, "All of these I have observed. What do I still lack?" Jesus said to him, "If you wish to be perfect, go, sell what you have and give to [the] poor, and you will have treasure in Heaven. Then come, follow me." When the young man heard this statement, he went away sad, for he had many possessions. Then Jesus said to his disciples, "Amen, I say to you, it will be hard for one who is rich to enter the kingdom of Heaven. Again I say to you, it is easier for a camel to pass through the eye of a needle than for one who is rich to enter the kingdom of God" (Matthew 19:16–24, NABRE; see also Mark 10:17–25 and Luke 18:18–25).

However, Christians have argued over the meaning of this story. Is Jesus stating a general principle, or is this a specific calling addressed to only one man? Some claim that the call of Jesus for this man to give up his possessions was only because the man was too attached to his wealth and possessions. Other Christians note that Jesus did not make such a distinction and that the words of Jesus about how hard it is for the rich to enter the Kingdom of Heaven indicate the wealth itself was a problem for Jesus.

What did Jesus say about judging others?

Jesus stated:

> Do not judge, so that you may not be judged. For with the judgment you make you will be judged, and the measure you give will be the measure you get. Why do you see the speck in your neighbor's eye, but do not notice the log in your own eye? Or how can you say to your neighbor, "Let me take the speck out of your eye," while the log is in your own eye? You hypocrite, first take the log out of your own eye, and then you will see clearly to take the speck out of your neighbor's eye.
>
> —Matthew 7:1–5, NRSV

> Do not judge, and you will not be judged; do not condemn, and you will not be condemned. Forgive, and you will be forgiven.
>
> —Luke 6:37, NRSV

There seem to be at least three problems with judging others. First, Jesus rejects it as the wrong attitude to take in dealing with others. Second, we often are wrong in our judgments. We get the facts wrong, or we misinterpret a person's actions, or we fail to understand the background behind other people's actions. Third, judging others is often hypocritical in that in pointing out other people's failings, we ignore our own failings.

What is the Golden Rule? What did Jesus say about it?

A key teaching of Jesus is stated in Matthew: "Do to others whatever you would have them do to you" (Matthew 7:12, NABRE). The version in Luke is: "Do to others as you would have them do to you." Sometimes this is called the Golden Rule and phrased as "Do unto others as you would have them do unto you." Sometimes the negative version of this is called the Silver Rule: "What you do not want done to yourself, do not do to others."

Jesus was not the first one to state the principle of the Golden Rule. It was stated some five hundred years earlier by both the Buddha in India and by Confucius in China. Was it a new idea for them, or was that concept even older? It is also stated in the book of Tobit, which is found in Catholic Bibles: "Do to no one what you yourself hate" (Tobit 4:15, NABRE).

The Golden Rule says that you should treat others with the same respect and kindness you would want from them.

In the Gospel of Matthew, Jesus expresses the same idea in the context of the Law of Moses:

> "You shall love the Lord your God with all your heart, and with all your soul, and with all your mind." This is the greatest and first commandment. And a second is like it: "You shall love your neighbor as yourself." On these two commandments hang all the law and the prophets.

> —Matthew 22:37–40, NRSV (see also Mark 12:28–31)

What else did Jesus teach about forgiveness?

Jesus frequently gave a very important and dramatic example of forgiveness by his contact with sinners. The opposite strategy of the Pharisees was to avoid all contact with sinners. The name "Pharisee" meant to be "set apart." Jesus spent time with sinners and even ate meals with them.

> And as he [Jesus] sat at dinner in the house, many tax collectors and sinners came and were sitting with him and his disciples. When the Pharisees saw this, they said to his disciples, "Why does your teacher eat with tax collectors and sinners?" But when he heard this, he said, "Those who are well have no need of a physician, but those who are sick."

> —Matthew 9:10–12, NRSV

This is often called "Table Fellowship." In the Mediterranean world at the time of Jesus, to eat dinner with someone would usually mean you then became part of their family. Eating dinner was not typically seen as casually eating with acquaintances. Jesus ate with sinners, which meant he became part of their families. This was shocking to religious people such as the Pharisees. This is strikingly illustrated in the story of Zacchaeus.

What is the story of Zacchaeus?

> He [Jesus] came to Jericho and intended to pass through the town. Now a man there named Zacchaeus, who was a chief tax collector and also a wealthy man, was seeking to see who Jesus was; but he could not see him because of the crowd, for he was short in stature. So he ran ahead and climbed a sycamore tree in order to see Jesus, who was about to pass that way. When he reached the place, Jesus looked up and said to him, "Zacchaeus, come down quickly, for today I must stay at your house." And he came down quickly and received him with joy. When they all saw this, they began to grumble, saying, "He has gone to stay at the house of a sinner." But Zacchaeus stood there and said to the Lord, "Behold, half of my possessions, Lord, I shall give to the poor, and if I have extorted anything from anyone I shall repay it four times over." And Jesus said to him, "Today salvation has come to this house because this man too is a descendant of Abraham. For the Son of Man has come to seek and to save what was lost."
>
> —Luke 19:1–10, NABRE

The people were upset that Jesus would eat dinner with Zacchaeus, whom they probably hated. Perhaps the people wanted Jesus to condemn Zacchaeus in the hopes that that would change him. Such criticism is rarely effective. Instead, Jesus offers friendship, and Zacchaeus changes and offers to give up most of his wealth.

Why were tax collectors considered sinners?

The tax collectors of the time of Jesus worked for the hated Roman occupiers. They were often seen as traitors to their own people. Furthermore, many strict Jews avoided contact with the Romans. Most importantly, tax collectors were hated because they extorted people to get more money, which they would keep for themselves. Many tax collectors acted like Mafia figures today. For all these reasons, tax collectors were seen as sinners.

Is forgiveness an important concept of Jesus?

Forgiveness is a key concept for Jesus. He stated: "But if you do not forgive others, neither will your Father forgive your trespasses" (Matthew 6:15, NRSV). The key line in the Our Father prayer states: "Forgive us our sins as we forgive those who sin against us." In another saying, Jesus answers Peter: "Then Peter approaching asked him, 'Lord, if my brother sins against me, how often must I forgive him? As many as seven times?' Jesus answered, 'I say to you, not seven times but seventy-seven times'" (Matthew 18:21–22, NABRE).

In his healings, Jesus is often forgiving sins with no conditions. Jesus went against the Jewish religion of his time, which required animal sacrifice for forgiveness. Interestingly, Jesus rarely talks about punishment for sins, except for religious people.

JESUS ON JESUS

What does Jesus say about himself?

In the synoptic gospels, Jesus says very little about himself. However, in the Gospel of John, Jesus frequently speaks about himself, such as in his "I am" statements.

What are the "I am" statements of Jesus?

There are several "I am" statements of Jesus in the Gospel of John.

1. "I am the bread of life. Whoever comes to me will never be hungry, and whoever believes in me will never be thirsty." (6:35, NRSV)

2. "I am the light of the world. Whoever follows me will never walk in darkness but will have the light of life." (8:12, NRSV)

3. "I am the gate. Whoever enters by me will be saved, and will come in and go out and find pasture." (10:9, NRSV)

4. "I am the good shepherd. The good shepherd lays down his life for the sheep." (10:11, NRSV)

5. "I am the resurrection and the life. Those who believe in me, even though they die, will live, and everyone who lives and believes in me will never die." (11:25–26, NRSV)

6. "I am the way, and the truth, and the life. No one comes to the Father except through me." (14:6, NRSV)

7. "I am the true vine, and my Father is the vine-grower.... I am the vine, you are the branches." (15:1, 5, NRSV)

How are these passages to be understood?

Many Christians would agree that statements 3, 4, and 7 are metaphorical statements since Jesus was not in fact a gate, a shepherd, or a vine. As for the other statements, many Christians would not see them as metaphorical. In particular, the first statement of Jesus that he is the "bread of life" will be understood very differently by Christians depending on their views about what happens in the Christian ritual of Communion or the Lord's Supper.

What other passages are important?

The opponents of Jesus asked:

What or who is Jesus Christ? The Good Shepherd. The Bread of Life. The Light of the World.

"Are you greater than our father Abraham, who died? The prophets also died. Who do you claim to be?" Jesus answered, "If I glorify myself, my glory is nothing. It is my Father who glorifies me, he of whom you say, 'He is our God,' though you do not know him. But I know him; if I would say that I do not know him, I would be a liar like you. But I do know him and I keep his word. Your ancestor Abraham rejoiced that he would see my day; he saw it and was glad." Then the Jews said to him, "You are not yet fifty years old, and have you seen Abraham?" Jesus said to them, "Very truly, I tell you, before Abraham was, I am."

—John 8:53–59, NRSV

In this important passage, Jesus identifies himself with the term "I AM." "I AM" in all caps is an English translation of the name of God, Yahweh, which was given to Moses in the Book of Exodus: "God replied to Moses: 'I am who I am.' Then he added: 'This is what you will tell the Israelites: I AM has sent me to you'" (Exodus 3:14, NABRE).

What was the reaction of the crowd to such a claim of Jesus?

Since what Jesus said was the equivalent to blasphemy, which is the sin of claiming to be God, the opponents of Jesus picked up stones to throw at Jesus. Stoning was the punishment for blasphemy.

What did Jesus say about his relationship to God the Father?

In the Gospel of John, Jesus states, "The Father and I are one" (10:30). Here is another key passage:

Jesus said to him, "I am the way, and the truth, and the life. No one comes to the Father except through me. If you know me, you will know my Father also. From now on you do know him and have seen him." Philip said to him, "Lord, show us the Father, and we will be satisfied." Jesus said to him, "Have I been with you all this time, Philip, and you still do not know me? Whoever has seen me has seen the Father."

—John 14:6–9, NRSV

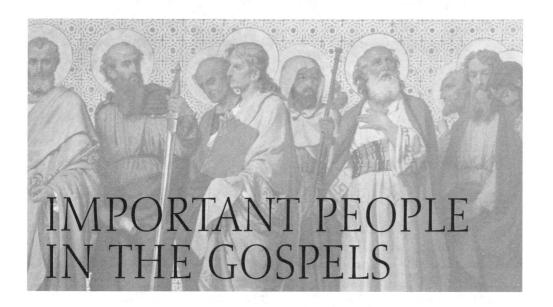

IMPORTANT PEOPLE IN THE GOSPELS

THE THREE KINGS

Who are the three Wise Men in Matthew's gospel?

In the Gospel of Matthew, the infant Jesus is visited by travelers from the East called Magi. The word "Magi" means astrologers. Astrologers looked at the position of the stars, the sun, and the moon and made predictions about the future. In Matthew's gospel, the Magi followed a star in the East. Later Christians became uncomfortable with the idea that the Magi were astrologers and renamed them as the three Wise Men or the Three Kings. The Gospel of Matthew does not say how many there were, although they brought three gifts of gold, frankincense, and myrrh. Later Christian tradition assumed the three gifts required three gift givers. Christian tradition would also give them the names of Casper, Melchior, and Balthasar. Also, a later tradition developed that Balthasar was of African descent. In many nativity sets, which are statues of the manger with Jesus, Mary, Joseph, the shepherds, and the animals, Balthasar is depicted with black skin.

A popular Christmas carol, "We Three Kings of Orient Are," describes the kings. Verses 2, 3, and 4 describe each of the three kings bringing his gift: gold, frankincense, and myrrh. In the song title, "of Orient" means "from the East." The title is a portion of the first line of the song: "We three kings of Orient are bearing gifts, we traverse [travel] afar."

Did the Three Kings come from the East?

The Gospel of Matthew states that the Magi came from the East. However, in the story in Matthew, they are following the star in the East: "We saw his star at its rising and come to do him homage." If they are coming from the East and traveling to the East, they are going the wrong way.

The problem is solved by understanding that this passage is filled with symbolism that need not be taken literally. The greater symbolism of the Magi is that they are foreigners coming to honor and worship Jesus while the local Jewish King Herod is bent on killing Jesus. For many early Christians, this symbolized the rejection of the Christian faith by many Jewish people.

THE FAMILY OF JESUS

What happened to Joseph, the father of Jesus?

The early chapters of the Gospels of Matthew and Luke describe Joseph, the father of Jesus and the husband or betrothed of Mary. Joseph does not appear in the later chapters, nor does he appear in the Gospels of Mark and John. Why? The traditional Christian answer is that Joseph died before Jesus began his public ministry or before Jesus was crucified. However, the gospels do not specifically answer the question of what happened to Joseph.

The death of Joseph became an important tradition for some Roman Catholics. Many older Roman Catholic churches have an altar to St. Joseph on the right side of the main altar. Often there is an image of Joseph dying with Mary and Jesus at his side. Typically, in these images, Jesus is pointing to Heaven. For some Catholics, Joseph became the "patron of a happy death." A happy death is dying of old age at peace and with your loved ones around you.

In Roman Catholic paintings and statues of Joseph, he is often seen holding a lily, which is a symbol of purity. According to Catholic teaching, Mary remained a virgin after the birth of Jesus. This would have required Joseph to remain chaste and not have sex. The lily is a symbol of his chastity. The lily symbol also shows up in many paintings of Mary.

I thought Jesus was an only child. Who are the brothers of Jesus?

In the Gospels there are several references to the "brothers of Jesus."

> "Is not this the carpenter, the son of Mary and brother of James and Joses and Judas and Simon, and are not his sisters here with us?" (Judas is not Judas Iscariot but the other Judas, often called Jude.)
>
> —Mark 6:3, NRSV

> "Is not this the carpenter's son? Is not his mother called Mary? And are not his brothers James and Joseph and Simon and Judas? And are not all his sisters with us?"
>
> —Matthew 13:55–56, NRSV

> Jesus did this, the first of his signs, in Cana of Galilee, and revealed his glory; and his disciples believed in him. After this he went down to Capernaum with his mother, his brothers, and his disciples; and they remained there for a few days.
>
> —John 2:11–12, NRSV

In his Epistle to the Galatians, Paul writes, "Then after three years I went up to Jerusalem to confer with Cephas [Peter] and remained with him for fifteen days. But I did not see any other of the apostles, only James the brother of the Lord" (1:18–19, NABRE).

Down through the centuries, Christians have argued over who these brothers and sisters might be. One answer is that they are other children of Joseph and Mary born after Jesus.

Another different answer is to claim that the brothers of Jesus might be half-brothers, and the sisters might be half-sisters. They are Joseph's sons and daughters from a previous marriage. Joseph was a widower before he married Mary. Although none of these details are stated in the gospels, some people hold this view.

Jesus' earthly father, Joseph, is considered by some Christians to be the "patron of a happy death" for living to an old age and then passing into Heaven surrounded by his family.

A final view is that the words "brothers" and "sisters" refer to cousins and other kinfolk. In this case, the brothers and sisters would be relatives who did not have Joseph as their father or Mary as their mother.

Why is "Who are the 'brothers of Jesus'?" even a question?

Christians have argued over who the brothers of Jesus were because of different understandings of the Christian belief that Mary was a virgin when she gave birth to Jesus. Most Christians agree that she was a virgin up until the birth of Jesus. Christians disagree about whether she remained a virgin or not. If she remained a virgin, as Roman Catholics and others contend, then the brothers and sisters of Jesus could not have been children of Mary and Joseph. They had to be either children of Joseph from a previous marriage, or they are some sort of cousins or relatives.

Many Protestants cite Matthew 1:25 about Joseph: "He [Joseph] had no relations with her [Mary] until she bore a son, and he named him Jesus." This passage implies—but does not state—that Mary and Joseph did have relations after the birth of Jesus. Many Protestants use this passage, along with the references to the brothers of Jesus in the gospels, to assert that Joseph and Mary had other children after the birth of Jesus, and thus, Mary did not remain a virgin. Interestingly, a number of early Protestant figures such as Martin Luther and Huldrych Zwingli believed that Mary remained a virgin.

The concept that Mary remained a virgin is called the "perpetual virginity of Mary." It is held by the Catholic Church, the Orthodox churches, the Anglican Church, and some Protestant churches. For those who believe that Mary remained a virgin, the brothers of Jesus are thought to be either sons from a first marriage of Joseph or kinsmen of Jesus.

Was James the brother of Jesus?

There are several references in the New Testament to a James who is the brother of Jesus. There are also numerous references in early Christian writings to this James. So, who was James? The first thing to note is that there are at least three New Testament followers of Jesus named James:

1. James, son of Zebedee and brother of John the Apostle. He is often called James the Great, or James the Greater, meaning that he is older than the other James.

2. James, the son of Alphaeus, called James the Less or James the Lesser, meaning that he is the younger James.

3. James the Just was an important early leader of the Christian community in Jerusalem. Some later Christians would call him the first bishop of Jerusalem. (There was no way to know if James saw himself as being a bishop or whether or not he even used the term for himself.)

In 2002 the discovery of the James ossuary was announced to the public. The first-century tomb includes the Hebrew inscription "James, son of Joseph, brother of Jesus." Owned by Israeli engineer Oden Golan, there is some question as to the tomb's authenticity.

It is this third James, the Just, who is often, but not always, identified as the brother of Jesus. This James is also often identified as the author of the Epistle of James, although there is no way to be certain.

This is a bit confusing. How do all these details fit together?

In trying to make sense of all the references to James in the New Testament, a question has to be asked about the assumptions that are being used. The question is whether or not we assume that all these little details in the various gospels and epistles should all fit together. A biblical literalist might make such an assumption. On the other hand, someone who does not take every detail literally would argue that given that these documents were written by different people in different places over a fifty-year-or-longer period, we would not expect that all the details fit together nicely and neatly. Also, there might even be contradictions in some of the details. What do you think?

Why is Mary important?

Mary, the mother of Jesus, plays an important role in the gospels. She appears in the infancy narratives in Matthew and Luke. She is present at the crucifixion of Jesus. She also appears in the Acts of the Apostles at Pentecost when the followers of Jesus receive the Holy Spirit. In the Gospel of John at the Wedding of Cana, it is Mary who points out to Jesus the problem that the wedding host has run out of wine.

Among Christians there is a great diversity of opinion on how to treat Mary. All Christians agree that as the mother of Jesus, she is a figure deserving of honor and respect. Protestants and similar denominations stop at that point. Other Christians, such as the Roman Catholic Church and the Eastern Orthodox tradition, assign Mary a much greater role. For some Christians, their devotion to Mary gets more attention than their devotion to Jesus.

Some Christians have statues, paintings, icons, and stained glass windows depicting Mary. Much Christian art has been dedicated to Mary. Cathedrals have been dedicated to her, such as Notre Dame in Paris. "Notre Dame" means "Our Lady."

What is the Magnificat of Mary?

The Magnificat is the prayer of Mary when she greets Elizabeth, who is six months pregnant with John.

My soul proclaims the greatness of the Lord;
my spirit rejoices in God my savior.

For he has looked upon his handmaid's lowliness;
behold, from now on will all ages call me blessed.

The Mighty One has done great things for me,
and holy is his name.

His mercy is from age to age
to those who fear him.

He has shown might with his arm,
dispersed the arrogant of mind and heart.

He has thrown down the rulers from their thrones
but lifted up the lowly.

The hungry he has filled with good things;
the rich he has sent away empty.

He has helped Israel his servant,
remembering his mercy,
according to his promise to our fathers,
to Abraham and to his descendants forever.

—Luke 1:46–55, NABRE

This prayer is called the Magnificat because of the opening line in Latin: *Magnificat anima mea Dominum*. *Dominum* is the Lord, *anima* is soul, *mea* is my, and *magnificat* means to magnify, glorify, or proclaim.

This prayer of Mary is based on numerous lines taken from the Old Testament/Hebrew Scriptures—in particular, lines from a number of the Psalms and 1 & 2 Samuel. If you look up this passage in a Bible that provides cross references, you can see how the Magnificat is based on numerous Old Testament phrases.

For Christian monks, this prayer is said every evening. Also, the theology of this passage, which speaks of throwing down rulers, lifting up the lowly, filling the hungry with good things, and sending the rich away empty, fits in with the overall theology of the Gospel of Luke that Jesus has come for the poor and lowly, not for the rich and powerful.

Are there other women named Mary in the gospels?

The gospels mention four other women named Mary:

- Mary of Bethany, the sister of Martha. In the Gospel of John, she and Martha are sisters of Lazarus
- Mary Magdalene
- Mary, the mother of James
- Mary Salome

JOHN THE BAPTIST

What is the story of the birth of John the Baptist?

The first chapter of the Gospel of Luke describes the events leading up to the birth of John. Zachariah is a priest in the Temple. He is elderly, as is his wife, and they have no children. The Angel Gabriel appears to Zachariah to tell him that his wife, though old and barren, will become pregnant and give birth to a son named John. This scene is reminiscent of the Old Testament/Hebrew Scriptures passage in the Book of 1 Samuel that describes the events leading up to the birth of Samuel to Hannah, whose husband was a Temple priest. Hannah had been barren until she prayed in the Temple. (See 1 Samuel 1:1–20.)

Who was John the Baptist?

John the Baptist is an important figure in the gospels as he points the way to Jesus. He appears in all four gospels, although he is not mentioned elsewhere in the New Testament. The Gospel of Matthew describes him: "John was clothed in a garment of camel's hair, and wore a leather belt around his waist. Grasshoppers and wild honey were his food" (Matthew 3:4 NABRE). The Gospel of Luke describes John:

> He went throughout [the] whole region of the Jordan, proclaiming a baptism of repentance for the forgiveness of sins, as it is written in the book of the words of the prophet Isaiah:

> "A voice of one crying out in the desert: 'Prepare the way of the Lord, make straight his paths. Every valley shall be filled and every mountain and hill shall be made low. The winding roads shall be made straight, and the rough ways made smooth, and all flesh shall see the salvation of God.'"

> —Luke 3:3–6, NABRE

A painting by Giuseppe Ghezzi at the Church of St. Sylvester in Rome, Italy, depicting St. John baptizing the faithful. The act of being baptized was a ritual form of repentance that was practiced by the Essenes on the west side of the Dead Sea, so some scholars think John may have been influenced by them.

The Gospels of Luke and Matthew give samples of the preaching of John the Baptist (Matthew 3:1–12, Luke 3:7–18; look them up on online if you are interested).

Some readers debate about the preaching of John. Are these words the actual preaching of John the Baptist, or do they reflect the views of the gospel writers? This is an unanswered question.

Do we know anything more about John the Baptist?

We actually know nothing about John the Baptist outside of the references to him in the gospels. Because he is performing baptisms and working from the desert, some people have wondered whether or not he might have come from the Jewish community called the Essenes or perhaps even lived at the site called Qumran. Like John, the Essenes lived ascetic lives of prayer and little food. Some Essenes lived in the desert and practiced water immersion. Although the connection of John the Baptist to the Essenes is an interesting possibility, there is no actual evidence to prove it.

What else does Luke say about John the Baptist?

As mentioned above, the Gospel of Luke opens up with the Angel Gabriel appearing to Zachariah telling him that his wife Elizabeth will bear a son even though she is barren. When Elizabeth is six months pregnant with John, Mary visits Elizabeth after Mary has received her own visit from Gabriel. This detail in Luke has led to the current Christian tradition of celebrating the birth of John the Baptist, six months before the birth of Jesus, on June 24. The scene of Gabriel visiting Mary is called the Annunciation. The scene of the meeting of Mary and Elizabeth is called the Visitation.

How did John get in trouble?

John criticized the Jewish king Herod Antipas for marrying Herodias, who had been the wife of Herod's brother. Very likely, Herodias had a role in having John arrested for his criticism of her.

How did John die?

The Gospel of Mark describes the death of John the Baptist:

> She [Herodias] had an opportunity one day when Herod, on his birthday, gave a banquet for his courtiers, his military officers, and the leading men of Galilee. Herodias's own daughter came in and performed a dance that delighted Herod and his guests. The king said to the girl, "Ask of me whatever you wish and I will grant it to you." He even swore [many things] to her, "I will grant you whatever you ask of me, even to half of my kingdom." She went out and said to her mother, "What shall I ask for?" She replied, "The head of John the Baptist." The girl hurried back to the king's presence and made her request, "I want you to give me at once on a platter the head of John the Baptist." The king was deeply distressed, but because of his oaths and the guests he did not wish to break his word to her. So he promptly dispatched an executioner with orders to bring back his head. He went off and beheaded him in the prison. He brought in the head on a platter and gave it to the girl. The girl in turn gave

it to her mother. When his disciples heard about it, they came and took his body and laid it in a tomb.

—Mark 6:21–29, NABRE (see also Matthew 14:1–12)

This well-crafted story has several interesting characters. The reader can understand these characters not by descriptions given by the author but rather by the details in the story. Herod comes off as a weak character, as he is manipulated into executing John the Baptist against his own wishes. (Apparently, Herodias was wearing the toga in that family.) Perhaps Herod was drunk in making his offer to the girl of anything she would want, including half the kingdom. What king would so flippantly make that offer? Was he drunk or stupid or both? And why swear an oath over the offer? Although he makes his oath in a culture in which people were bound by such verbal promises, he was the king! He could do whatever he wanted. Also, if he told his friends at the party that he changed his mind and would not execute John, they probably would have understood that he had had too much to drink and not held it against him. Herod appears weak and spineless.

The depiction of the daughter of Herodias is equally revealing. She also seems under the control of Herodias. What girl who was offered anything she wanted would not choose something else: perhaps jewels or new clothes? Would that not be the normal response? And when she asks Herodias, the daughter does not even argue with her mother. Instead, she willingly goes and asks for the head of John the Baptist. Apparently, she adds the detail to put the head on a platter. (Like mother, like daughter!)

Again, this is a great story because of how it is crafted and what it tells us about all the characters in the story through the details. The scene of the execution of John the Baptist is dramatically illustrated in the 1608 painting by Caravaggio: *The Beheading of St. John the Baptist*. (Do an online image search for the painting if you are interested.)

SALOME

What is the name of the daughter of Herodias?

The daughter of Herodias is not named in the gospels. The ancient Jewish writer Josephus gave her name as Salome, which is pronounced SAH-low-may.

Another Salome is also mentioned in the gospels. This Salome, the follower of Jesus, is present at the Crucifixion: "There were also women looking on afar off: among whom was Mary Magdalene, and Mary the mother of the younger James and of Joses, and Salome" (Mark 15:40, NABRE). She also goes to the tomb on Sunday morning: "And when the Sabbath was past, Mary Magdalene, and Mary the mother of James, and Salome, had bought sweet spices, that they might come and anoint him" (Mark 16:1, NABRE). In some traditions, this Salome is identified as the mother of the sons of Zebedee. She is sometimes called Mary Salome.

What is the importance of the story of the dance of Salome, the daughter of Herodias?

In Mark's gospel, it says that the dance of Salome "delighted Herod and his guests." The gospel does not say why. Many have assumed the dance was highly sensuous, which is why it pleased Herod and the guests. That could be the case, but it could also not be the case. There is no way to know.

However, the idea that Salome did a very erotic dance has caught the imagination of many. A seductive Salome has been the subject of numerous paintings. (For example, the 1870 painting *Salomé* by Henri Regnault.) The famous playwright Oscar Wilde (1854–1900) wrote his tragic play *Salome* based on the biblical story. Wilde developed the dance scene into the Dance of the Seven Veils. The German composer Richard Strauss would use Wilde's play to create his opera *Salome*. It included his own "Dance of the Seven Veils." The dance

The 1870 painting *Salomé* by Henri Regnault is a famous example of how the daughter of Herod is often depicted in a highly sensual manner.

of Salome even shows up in movies about Jesus, such as a seductive dance by Salome in the 1961 film *The King of Kings*. (The Dance of the Seven Veils from Strauss's opera can be seen on YouTube as well as Salome's dance scene from *The King of Kings*.)

THE FOLLOWERS OF JESUS

Who is the beloved disciple?

In the Gospel of John, there are six references to the "disciple whom Jesus loved." This figure is also known as the "beloved disciple." Who is this disciple?

Going back to the early Christian centuries, this figure has often been identified as John, one of the Twelve Apostles and the author of the Gospel of John. John 21:24 says, "It is this disciple who testifies to these things and has written them, and we know that his testimony is true." However, many scholars think that Chapter 21 was added on to the original Gospel of John. The important Christian writer Augustine of Hippo (354–430 C.E.) held that this beloved disciple was John the Apostle and the writer of the Gospel of John. This John in the Christian tradition is also called John the Evangelist. In traditional Christian art, he is young and beardless with long hair and typically holding a writing quill and a scroll or book.

However, many scholars do not think the Gospel of John was written by John the Apostle. This is based on the fact that the gospel was written at least sixty years after the crucifixion of Jesus, and the writing style, language, and theology are very different from what is expressed in the synoptic gospels.

Some writers have suggested that the beloved disciple might refer to Lazarus, or James, the brother of Jesus, or some unknown disciple. Another possibility is that the beloved disciple is a literary device in the Gospel of John. The Gospel of John is filled with symbolism such as light and dark, bread and wine. Thus, the beloved disciple represents the ideal Christian.

A final possibility is that the author of the Gospel of John was not John the Apostle; however, the author created the character "the beloved disciple" and placed him at key moments in the life of Jesus as a witness who would then write down his testimony. Whether the writer of the Gospel of John identified the beloved disciple as John the Apostle or not is unclear.

What are the names of the Twelve Apostles?

In the Gospel of Matthew and Mark, the Twelve Apostles are Simon (also called Peter), Andrew, James, John, Philip, Bartholomew, Thomas, Matthew, James, Thaddaeus, Simon, and Judas Iscariot (Matthew 10:2–4, Mark 3:13–19).

Simon and Andrew were brothers. James and John were also brothers, the sons of Zebedee. There are two Simons: Simon called Peter, and Simon the Canaanite. There are two Jameses: James the son of Zebedee and James the son of Alphaeus. Later Christian tradition would call the first James the Greater (meaning that he was older) and the second James the Lesser (meaning that he was younger). In Christian art, by the time of the Renaissance, the custom had developed of often painting James the Lesser without a beard, and also, John was painted without a beard.

In the Gospel of Luke, the name Thaddaeus is replaced by Judas, the son of James. Thus, in Luke's list, there are two apostles named Judas. Also, the Simon who is not called Peter is called Simon the Zealot. The Zealots were revolutionaries against the Romans. (The term "zealot" was not used during the time of Jesus, but it was used during the time of the writing of the gospels.) The author of the Gospel of Luke also wrote the New Testament book the Acts of the Apostles. The lists of the Twelve Apostles are the same in Luke and Acts (Luke 6:12–16, Acts 1:13).

In the Gospel of John, the name Bartholomew is replaced by the name Nathaniel. Also, Judas, the son of James, is called Jude. The Gospel of John mentions "the Twelve" but does not list them all. Three apostles are not named in John: Matthew, James the Lesser, and Simon the Zealot.

103

In the gospels, Judas Iscariot betrays Jesus and then commits suicide. In the first chapter of the Acts of the Apostles, the disciples vote to replace Judas with Matthias.

Do I understand this correctly? There is no one definitive list of the names of the Twelve Apostles?

That is correct.

What are the symbols associated with the Twelve Apostles?

Down through the centuries, the Twelve Apostles have often been depicted in Christian paintings and in stained glass windows. Different symbols have been assigned to each apostle. Here are the typical symbols used for each disciple. Keep in mind that there is some variation in the use of the symbols. Also, those Christian denominations that have windows and paintings of the apostles typically called the apostles "saints."

1. St. Peter (who is also called Simon or Simon Peter): The symbol for Peter is two keys based on this passage from Matthew's gospel: "And so I say to you, you are Peter, and upon this rock I will build my church, and the gates of the netherworld shall not prevail against it. I will give you the keys to the kingdom of Heaven. Whatever you bind on earth shall be bound in Heaven; and whatever you loose on earth shall be loosed in Heaven" (Matthew 16:18–19, NABRE). Also, Simon's name of Peter comes from this passage. The Aramaic word for rock is *cephas*, which in Greek becomes *petros*, which becomes Peter. Ancient carvings on rock are called "petroglyphs."

2. St. Andrew: Andrew's symbol is an X-shaped cross. According to tradition, he was crucified on an X-shaped cross rather than a T-shaped cross. This symbol of St.

Jesus was followed by twelve apostles, some of whom are prominent in the Bible and well known, while others seem to fade into the background. Indeed, their exact names are not even definitively given in the gospels.

Andrew would eventually become part of the British flag. One of the most famous golf courses in the world is named after him: St. Andrews Links in Scotland. Sometimes, an alternative symbol for St. Andrew is a fish.

3. St. James the Greater (who is called the son of Zebedee and the brother of John): St. James the Greater (the elder) is often seen with a shell. He is the patron saint of pilgrims, and the shell was used to drink water as one traveled. The city of Santiago de Compostela in Spain has a shrine to St. James. Many people walk the pilgrim's trail to the shrine. The trail has existed since the ninth century. The city's name "Santiago" comes from the Latin for St. James. In Spanish, the name James is Diego, thus the California city of San Diego is named after St. James.

4. St. John: His symbol is sometimes a chalice with a poisonous snake inside or an eagle. The eagle symbolizes the Gospel of John. Many images show John writing the Gospel of John or holding a book, which represents either the Bible or the Gospel of John. The poisonous snake in the chalice probably comes from a legend that he was offered a chalice of poisoned wine. When he blessed the wine, the poison turned into a snake and left the chalice, leaving John unharmed. According to Christian tradition, John the Apostle wrote the Gospel of John. However, many scholars think that the gospel was not written by an eyewitness but rather written by a later Christian writer and named after John the Apostle.

5. St. Philip: His symbol is a basket because he was present at the feeding of the five thousand by Jesus with loaves and fishes.

6. St. Bartholomew: The symbol for St. Bartholomew is typically a knife. According to Christian tradition, he was skinned alive, which is also called being flayed. In the famous painting of Michelangelo on the wall of the Sistine Chapel, called *The Last Judgment*, to the right of Jesus can be seen a man holding his skin. That is St. Bartholomew.

7. St. Thomas: Thomas the Apostle is best known for the story of him in the Gospel of John: "But Thomas (who was called the Twin), one of the twelve, was not with them when Jesus came. So the other disciples told him, 'We have seen the Lord.' But he said to them, 'Unless I see the mark of the nails in his hands, and put my finger in the mark of the nails and my hand in his side, I will not believe.' A week later his disciples were again in the house, and Thomas was with them. Although the doors were shut, Jesus came and stood among them and said, 'Peace be with you.' Then he said to Thomas, 'Put your finger here and see my hands. Reach out your hand and put it in my side. Do not doubt but believe.' Thomas answered him, 'My Lord and my God!' Jesus said to him, 'Have you believed because you have seen me? Blessed are those who have not seen and yet have come to believe'" (John 20:24–29, NRSV). Because of this story, he is called "Doubting Thomas." This later becomes an expression as when one is called a "doubting Thomas." The term "didymus" means twin. Around the year 1601, the painter Caravaggio painted a dramatic image of the scene called *The Incredulity of St. Thomas*. (The painting can

be viewed with an online image search for "Caravaggio St. Thomas.") The Gospel of John is filled with symbolism that is designed to help the reader understand the Christian message and believe in it. In this story, Thomas is the model for later Christians who believe without ever having seen Jesus for themselves. There are a number of very old traditions that Thomas brought Christianity to India around the year 50 C.E. However, there is no way to prove or disprove these traditions. The symbols for St. Thomas include a spear and a carpenter's square. According to the legend, he went to India and built the church with his own hands; thus, his symbol is a carpenter's square. He was killed by arrows and then a lance. Two apocryphal writings, writings that did not get accepted into the New Testament, are attributed to Thomas: the *Gospel of Thomas* and the *Acts of Thomas*. Christians disagree over the value of these writings.

8. St. James the Lesser (the son of Alphaeus): The symbol for this James is a saw or a fuller's bat. Different legends tell of James being killed for his faith with a saw or a fuller's bat. A fuller's bat was used to beat clothes during washing and bleaching.

9. St. Thaddaeus or St. Jude: The symbol for Thaddaeus is typically a large club, with which he was beaten to death. Thaddaeus is also spelled "Thaddeus." The symbol for St. Jude is a ship. Sometimes, the names are combined as St. Jude Thaddaeus, who is the patron saint of hopeless causes. Danny Thomas (1912–1991) prayed to St. Jude Thaddaeus asking for career guidance. Thomas became a popular actor and comedian. His TV show, *Make Room for Daddy*, was one of the longest-running sitcoms in television history. In gratitude for his success, Thomas helped create the famous St. Jude Children's Research Hospital in Memphis, Tennessee.

10. St. Simon (the Zealot): The symbol for Simon is often a scimitar, a curved sword, with which he was martyred. A fish is another symbol used for him.

11. St. Matthew: Several different symbols have been used for St. Matthew. Often he is shown with moneybags since he was a tax collector. According to Christian tradition, he was killed with an ax, so he is sometimes shown with an ax. Matthew is also shown with a book or writing a book, since the Gospel of Matthew is named after him. According to Christian tradition, Matthew the Apostle wrote the Gospel of Matthew. However, many scholars think that the gospel was not written by an eyewitness but rather written by a later Christian writer and named after Matthew the Apostle.

12. Judas Iscariot: Judas is described below. He was not recognized as a saint.

13. St. Matthias (the replacement for Judas Iscariot): The symbol for Matthias, the replacement for Judas, is a lance based on the tradition that he was killed by a lance. The selection of Matthias is described in Acts of the Apostles 1:15–26.

Why did Jesus choose twelve apostles?

In ancient Israel, there were twelve tribes that descended from the twelve sons of Jacob in the Book of Genesis. Jesus chose twelve apostles as a symbol of the Twelve Tribes.

The Twelve Tribes structure of ancient Israel is called an amphyctyony. An amphyctyony is a society divided into twelve groups, each of which is required to take care of the central shrine for one month of the year.

Lastly, there is the joke: "Why did Jesus pick twelve apostles?" "So they wouldn't fight over the donuts."

Why did Jesus only pick men as the Twelve Apostles?

The best answer for this question is that Jesus was a product of his time, when the roles of men and women in society were very unequal. In fact, the idea of men and women being equal is a very modern concept that only gets embraced by most people in America after the 1960s.

The gender of the apostles becomes an issue when deciding whether or not women can be Christian ministers today. A number of Christian groups allow female ministers, arguing that the choice of Jesus to limit the role of apostle to men was determined by the culture of his time. Other Christian denominations insist that only men can be ministers and cite the twelve male apostles as one of the main reasons. In this view, the apostles are the prototypes of the Christian minister and reflect an unchanging requirement that Christian ministry and leadership be restricted to men. Some people note that the apostles were also Jewish and illiterate, yet those characteristics are not required for the ministry.

Why is Peter important?

Peter appears in the gospels as the most important apostle. He is the first one to identify Jesus as the Messiah.

> He said to them, "But who do you say that I am?" Simon Peter answered, "You are the Messiah, the Son of the living God." And Jesus answered him, "Blessed are you, Simon son of Jonah! For flesh and blood has not revealed this to you, but my Father in Heaven. And I tell you, you are Peter, and on this rock I will build my church, and the gates of Hades will not prevail against it. I will give you the keys of the kingdom of Heaven, and whatever you bind on earth will be bound in Heaven, and whatever you loose on earth will be loosed in Heaven."

—Matthew 16:15–19, NRSV

A statue of St. Peter takes a prominent spot in Vatican City. Peter is seen as the most important of the apostles because he becomes the leader of the church after Jesus' death.

107

This passage has played an important role in later Christian tradition. For Roman Catholics, this passage is particularly significant. Most Christians believe that Jesus chose Peter to be the leader of the early Christian Church. Catholics believe that the authority given to Peter was passed down to his successors on to the present age. In the Catholic understanding, Peter went to Rome, where he became the first bishop of Rome. When he was killed, that authority given to Peter by Jesus was passed on to the next bishop of Rome. According to Catholic tradition, the first bishops of Rome were Peter, Linus, Cletus, and Clement. The authority given to Peter has been passed down over the centuries to the current pope. According to the Catholic Church, the authority of the current pope over the Catholic Church comes from the authority originally given to Peter some two thousand years ago.

Protestants who reject the idea of the pope do recognize the leadership role of Peter in the early church, but they do not believe that authority was passed on to anyone else. Some Protestants also point out that the position of the bishop of Rome took many decades after the death of Peter to develop.

Who was Mary Magdalene?

Mary Magdalene was an important follower of Jesus. She is mentioned some dozen times in the gospels, more than any one of the Twelve Apostles. Most importantly in the gospels, she is one of the first witnesses of the risen Jesus. This is an important detail because in the culture of the time of Jesus, women were not considered reliable witnesses, yet Mary is the witness of the risen Jesus.

Beyond these details, we know nothing about Mary Magdalene. However, down through the centuries, details have been added to her story, many of which are erroneous.

Is there a story about Jesus driving demons from Mary Magdalene?

The Gospel of Luke states, "Accompanying him [Jesus] were the Twelve and some women who had been cured of evil spirits and infirmities, Mary, called Magdalene, from whom seven demons had gone out" (Luke 8:1–2, NABRE; see also Mark 19:9). There is no way to know for certain what this passage means. It could mean that she was healed of some physical ailments or some psychological problems. Both phys-

A reenactment of Mary Magdalene recognizing the risen Jesus. Mary is an important figure in the New Testament, which is interesting given that women were not seen as reliable witnesses in Jesus' day.

> ## What details were added to the story of Mary Magdalene?
>
> Later Christian tradition has filled in many details about Mary Magdalene. Many of these details are distortions. The most prominent added detail is the idea that Mary Magdalene was a former prostitute. Many people believe this even though there is no evidence for it in the gospels. This inaccurate detail can be traced back as far as Pope Gregory I, who died in 604.
>
> Another inaccuracy is to identify Mary with other unnamed women in the gospels, such as the woman caught in adultery in the Gospel of John and the penitent woman who anoints the feet of Jesus. The anointing story is found in Matthew 26:6–13 and Mark 14:3–9. In John 12:1–8, the feet of Jesus are anointed by a Mary, but that is Mary of Bethany.

ical illness and psychological conditions were blamed on demons in the ancient world. (The 1927 silent movie *The King of Kings* depicts Jesus driving out the seven demons and gives an interesting interpretation as well as impressive special effects for 1927. However, the movie reinforces the false idea that she was a wayward woman.)

What is the "composite Magdalene"?

The "composite Magdalene" is a label given by scholars to the effort of taking the references to Mary Magdalene in the gospels and combining them with the stories of the penitent woman and the woman caught in adultery. The result is a more developed story of Mary Magdalene, who has a dramatic history of repentance and conversion.

A number of books, plays, musicals, and movies have created such a Mary Magdalene. One problem with doing an adaption of the gospels is that only the character of Jesus is fully developed. The other characters, even though important, appear in snippets. As a result, Mary Magdalene is often portrayed as a reformed prostitute. She is often depicted as the same age as Jesus. In several stories, Mary has a romantic interest in Jesus or a romantic relationship. This can be seen in Martin Scorsese's movie *The Last Temptation of Christ*, or Andrew Lloyd Webber's musical *Jesus Christ Superstar*, where Mary sings, "I don't know how to love him."

Due to the belief that St. Mary Magdalene had been a prostitute, she became the patroness of "wayward women," and Magdalene asylums became established to help save women from prostitution.

Is Mary Magdalene in Leonardo da Vinci's famous painting *The Last Supper*?

Because of the success of the book by Dan Brown, *The Da Vinci Code*, which became a popular movie, many people believe that Mary Magdalene was married to Jesus, they had children, and she was painted into Leonardo's famous *The Last Supper*. Brown's book is a work of fiction even though it makes many historical references, yet many or most of his historical references are very inaccurate. According to *The Da Vinci Code*, Leonardo painted Mary Magdalene sitting to Jesus' right.

The figure does appear to be a woman with long hair. If it is not Mary Magdalene, then who is it? It is the Apostle John. During the Renaissance, the tradition developed of portraying John as a young man, without a beard, with long hair, and with somewhat feminine features. This became the standard style for portraying John. Do an online search for paintings of St. John and see what you find. This tradition can also be seen in the stained glass windows in many older churches.

Also, if Mary Magdalene is in the painting, who is the missing apostle? There are twelve figures sitting with Jesus. Although Judas would leave the meal before the others, he can be seen in the painting as the third person on Jesus' right. (To the viewer, he is on the left of Jesus.) His elbow is on the table, and his hand clutches his bag of money. In the time of Leonardo, all twelve of the apostles were identified in the painting with St. John sitting on Jesus' right. Leonardo's notebook identified them.

Was Mary Magdalene the same age as Jesus?

Most readers of the gospels imagine Mary Magdalene to be of the same age as Jesus, yet there is no evidence in the gospels either way. Is it possible that Mary Magdalene was much older than Jesus? Could she have been the prototype of the elderly "church lady"?

PEOPLE INVOLVED IN THE CRUCIFIXION

Who was Barabbas?

All four gospels mention Barabbas in their accounts of the trial of Jesus by Pontius Pilate. As Mark states: "A man called Barabbas was then in prison along with the rebels who had committed murder in a rebellion" (Mark 15:7, NABRE). The Gospel of Matthew describes what happens next:

> Now on the occasion of the feast [of Passover] the governor was accustomed to release to the crowd one prisoner whom they wished. And at that time they had a notorious prisoner called Barabbas. So when they had assembled, Pilate said to them, "Which one do you want me to release to you, Barabbas, or Jesus called Messiah?" …The chief priests and the elders persuaded the crowds to ask for Barabbas but to destroy Jesus. The governor said to them in reply, "Which of the two do you want me to release to you?" They answered, "Barabbas!"
>
> —Matthew 27:15–27, NABRE
> (see also Mark 15:6, Luke 23:18–25, and John 18:39)

Although this custom of releasing a prisoner is mentioned in the gospels, no other references to it exist outside the gospels.

Very likely, the name of Barabbas was originally "Jesus Barabbas," which can be found in the older manuscripts. Later, the "Jesus" was dropped to avoid confusion with the other Jesus. In 1950, Pär Lagerkvist wrote his novel *Barabbas*, which follows the later story of Barabbas. This would become a movie.

Can you tell me more about Judas? Why did Judas Iscariot betray Jesus?

All four gospels depict Judas betraying Jesus. In fact, his betrayal has become so famous that other traitors are often called by the term "Judas." Because of his betrayal of Jesus, Judas does not get the designation of "saint."

However, the gospels do not give a clear explanation of why Judas betrayed Jesus. The gospel writers focus on the story of Jesus and his teachings. Every other character gets limited attention. For example, most of the apostles only get a mention of their names. As a result, writers creating plays, movies, and books telling the life of Jesus have often had to flesh out the other characters by adding details. Such writers need more developed characters for the other people in the gospels to make them more interesting and to give them motivations for their actions.

The gospels give very little background on Judas. The one exception is the story in John's gospel where Mary of Bethany anoints the feet of Jesus with oil. "But Judas Iscariot, one of his disciples (the one who was about to betray him), said, 'Why was this perfume not sold for three hundred denarii and the money given to the poor?' (He said this not because he cared about the poor, but because he was a thief; he kept the common purse and used to steal what was put into it.)" (John 12:4–6, NRSV).

Modern readers sometimes find it frustrating that the gospels do not give a clear motivation of why Judas betrayed Jesus. However, modern people are influenced by mysteries, crime novels, and movies that often go into great detail exploring the motivation of those who do wrong. The gospel writers had no such interest and focused only on Jesus.

As a result in plays, movies, and books on the life of Jesus, a motivation is often given to Judas. In the rock opera *Jesus Christ Superstar*, the story revolves around the character of Judas. In the 1927 movie *The King of Kings*, the motivation of Judas is that Judas had been in love with Mary Magdalene, who then rejects him because of her faith in Jesus. Other stories give Judas the motivation that he is trying to force Jesus to go in front of the religious leaders, where Jesus will have to prove his power and authority. Another motivation given to Judas is that he is angry at Jesus because the Kingdom of God that Jesus promises is for

The Kiss of Judas by Giotto di Bodone illustrates the apostle's betrayal of Jesus in the Garden of Gethsemane.

111

the poor and the meek, not the wealthy and powerful as Judas had imagined it. A final idea might be that he was motivated simply by the money he could gain by betraying Jesus. However, as said before, the gospels do not clearly explain the motivation of Judas.

How did Judas die?

The death of Judas is described in the Gospel of Matthew:

> When Judas, his betrayer, saw that Jesus was condemned, he repented and brought back the thirty pieces of silver to the chief priests and the elders. He said, "I have sinned by betraying innocent blood." But they said, "What is that to us? See to it yourself." Throwing down the pieces of silver in the temple, he departed; and he went and hanged himself. But the chief priests, taking the pieces of silver, said, "It is not lawful to put them into the treasury, since they are blood money." After conferring together, they used them to buy the potter's field as a place to bury foreigners.
>
> —Matthew 27:3–7, NRSV

In later centuries, the term "potter's field" would be used for cemeteries to bury poor and homeless people. In the potter's field on Hart Island in New York City, over a million people have been buried, making it the biggest tax-funded cemetery in the world.

Who was Pontius Pilate?

Pontius Pilate was the Roman official who decided to execute Jesus. His title could have been either "procurator" or "prefect." There is much we do not know about him since he is mostly known from the references in the New Testament. There are only a few brief references to him outside the Bible, such as by the Roman writers Tacitus and Philo of Alexandria and the Jewish writer Josephus. Pilate's name was also found carved on a stone.

All four gospels describe a trial of Jesus before Pilate. Some historians have wondered how the followers of Jesus could have known what transpired since such trials were not open to the public. Here is Matthew's version of part of the trial:

> While he [Pilate] was still seated on the bench, his wife sent him a message, "Have nothing to do with that righteous man. I suffered much in a dream today because of him."
>
> ...
>
> Pilate said to them, "Then what shall I do with Jesus called Messiah?" They all said, "Let him be crucified!" But he said, "Why? What evil has he done?" They only shouted the louder, "Let him be crucified!" When Pilate saw that he was not succeeding at all, but that a riot was breaking out instead, he took water and washed his hands in the sight of the crowd, saying, "I am innocent of this man's blood. Look to it yourselves." And the whole people said in reply, "His blood be upon us and upon our children."

112

—Matthew 27:19, 22–25, NABRE

Pontius Pilate (shown here condemning Jesus in a church fresco in Dubrovnik, Croatia) was a Roman official who was charged with governing Judea. He had a bad reputation for being cruel, even among the Romans, and was eventually removed from office.

Possibly, the gospel writers wanted to downplay his role to make the gospel message more palatable in the Roman world in which Christianity was growing. From what we know about Pilate, he was a very harsh ruler, and he would have had no reluctance to execute a potential revolutionary or insurrectionist as he very likely saw Jesus. He also operated under Roman law, which thought in terms of the concept of guilty until proven innocent. He was eventually removed from his position because of his brutality.

His name is mentioned in the Nicene Creed: "For our sake he [Jesus] was crucified under Pontius Pilate, he suffered, died, and was buried." Adding Pilate's name probably had to do with affirming the historical context for the death of Jesus.

Who were Annas and Caiaphas?

Caiaphas was the Jewish High Priest who, according to the gospels, was responsible for the arrest and trial of Jesus. Annas, the father-in-law of Caiaphas, had previously been the high priest. He still had influence over religious affairs in Jerusalem. In the Gospel of John, Annas is involved in questioning Jesus after his arrest. Caiaphas is mentioned nine times in the New Testament, while Annas is mentioned four times.

OTHER SIGNIFICANT PEOPLE
IN THE GOSPELS

Who were Joachim and Anna?

Joachim and Anna (or Anne) were the parents of Mary, the mother of Jesus. Their names are not mentioned in the gospels. Their names and their stories come from the Gospel of James, which is, of course, not in the Bible. Written around 150 C.E., the Gospel of James—also called the Infancy Gospel of James—is one of several dozen writings called the New Testament Apocrypha, which are writings that did not make it into the Bible. However, do not get confused. There is an Epistle of James in the New Testament.

Many Christians accept these stories, and many Christians do not. The Gospel of James adds details such as how Joseph was selected as the spouse of Mary thanks to the intervention of an angel, the idea that Joseph was a widower with children before marrying Mary, and that Mary remained a virgin the rest of her life. For those Christians who accept these stories, such as Roman Catholics and some Orthodox, the parents of Mary are called St. Joachim and St. Ann (or St. Anna, or St. Anne).

If you do an online image search for "painting St. Anne with Mary," you will see a number of paintings. A common image is of St. Anne teaching the young Mary how to read. However, when Mary lived, it was extremely rare for a woman to read and write. If you want to read the Gospel of James, it is available online.

Who was Simon of Cyrene?

Simon of Cyrene appears in the synoptic gospels in Matthew 27:32, Mark 15:21, and Luke 23:36. The Roman soldiers taking Jesus to be crucified forced Simon to help Jesus carry his cross. Cyrene today is the nation of Libya. Simon does not appear in the Gospel of John. In John's gospel, Jesus shows no weakness or any need of help, so he carries his own cross.

Some Christians remember the Crucifixion by praying the Fourteen Stations of the Cross. The Fifth Station is the scene of Simon helping Jesus to carry his cross.

Who was Joseph of Arimathea?

In the synoptic gospels, Joseph of Arimathea is a member of the Jewish High Council, the Sanhedrin. According to the Gospel of Matthew, he is also the one responsible for getting the body of Jesus and burying it in his own tomb.

In the Middle Ages, a number of legends developed around King Arthur and his knights and their search for the Holy Grail, which was the cup of Jesus. In the stories, the knights hunt for the Grail in Britain and France. These legends seem to have developed after the Muslims retook the Holy Land, which had been conquered by Europeans in the Crusades. As a result, Europeans could not make pilgrimages to the Holy Land. Thus, the legends of King Arthur told of knights searching for the Grail in Europe.

A piece of legend was created to explain how the Holy Grail got to Europe: Joseph of Arimathea brought the cup that Jesus used at the Last Supper as well as the spear that pierced Jesus on the cross. In another version of the legend, Joseph of Arimathea used the cup to catch some of the blood from Jesus on the cross, which he also brought to Europe. There is a church in Bruges, Belgium, that claims to have the blood of Jesus. It is not the actual blood of Jesus.

BASIC BELIEFS OF MAINLINE CHRISTIANS

Who are mainline Christians?

Mainline Christians are those Christians who accept the ideas of the Nicene Creed. The Nicene Creed was a statement of Christian belief written in the year 325. The text of the Nicene Creed is given below along with a detailed analysis.

Christian churches that accept the Nicene Creed include the Roman Catholic Church; Christian Orthodox Churches; and the Protestant Church, such as the Episcopalians, Anglicans, Lutherans, Reformed Churches, and many Evangelical Churches. (This is not a complete list.)

There are also Christians, such as some Baptists, who accept the ideas of the Creed but do not have a written creed.

What are some Christian groups that reject these beliefs and the statements of the Nicene Creed?

Mormons, Christian Scientists, and Jehovah's Witnesses are the more prominent examples.

THE SEVEN BASIC CHRISTIAN BELIEFS

What are the basic beliefs of mainline Christians?

There are seven basic beliefs:

1. Monotheism
2. Messiah
3. Resurrection
4. Incarnation

117

5. Trinity
6. The role of the Bible
7. Continuous community

What is "monotheism"?

"Mono" means "one." The prefix "mono" is added to "theism," which means a belief in God. "Monotheism" is the belief in one God and only one God. Three major world religions are labeled as monotheism: Christianity, Islam, and Judaism. (Polytheism is the belief in many gods and is found in the Ancient Greek and Ancient Roman religions.)

Christians are monotheists who believe in one God, although, as will be shown below in the discussion of the Trinity, the Christian understanding of the monotheist belief in one God is a bit complicated.

What does the word "divine" mean?

The word "divine" is an important word to understand, although it has several meanings. The first meaning is when the word is used for something that is very good. Someone might say "You look divine!" or "This dish tastes divine." There is even a candy called "divinity fudge."

The second meaning of the word "divine" is to be like God or to be Godlike. However, one has to be careful about the meaning of "like." To be like something is not to actually be it.

The final meaning of the word "divine" is to be God. Monotheists believe that God is divine.

What is the meaning of the word "deity"? How is the word pronounced?

The word "deity" can be pronounced with either a long "e" sound or a long "a" sound: "DEE-it-tee" or "DAY-it-tee." The word "deity" can be used in several ways to mean God, or a god or goddess. The word comes from the Latin word for God, *deus*.

What is the Christian belief in Jesus as the Messiah?

The second key Christian belief is that Jesus is the Messiah: the Chosen one of God. Christians believe that Jesus was uniquely chosen by God to bring salvation to believers.

Christians call Jesus both the Messiah and the Christ. Is there a difference in the two terms?

No. Basically, the two words mean the same thing. "Messiah" is based on a Hebrew word, and "Christ" is based on the Greek version of the Hebrew word.

What is the history of the term "Messiah"?

The word has a long and complicated history in the Old Testament/Hebrew Scriptures in which the term referred to kings, priests, and prophets. At the time of Jesus, many

> ## What is the origin of the word "Messiah"?
>
> The English word "Messiah" comes from the Hebrew word מָשִׁיחַ, which is often spelled as *mashiach*. The word "Messiah" means the "anointed one." In the Old Testament/Hebrew scriptures, kings, priests, and prophets were designated by being anointed with perfumed olive oil poured on their heads. As the Christian gospels were written in Greek, Christians adopted the Greek version of the word: Christ. In Greek, it is pronounced *Christos* and written as Χριστoσ.

people hoped and expected a Messiah to save the people. For many Jews, the big political problem was that their land was occupied and controlled by the foreign Romans. Many Jews resented the Romans with their foreign Roman religion, which included many gods. Even the Roman leader Caesar was believed to be a god. Many Jews desperately wanted God to send a Messiah to rescue their land from the Romans.

Yet, there was no agreement among the people about what kind of Messiah to expect. Some people wanted a great political king or a military leader to lead a revolt against the Romans who occupied Judea. Others expected a prophet in the model of Elijah. Probably the reason why Jesus was reluctant to use the term "Messiah" for himself was that there were so many different expectations around the title.

Before, during, and after the life of Jesus, a number of Messiahs appeared who attempted to lead revolts against the Romans and free the land of Israel. Most Messiahs and their followers were brutally killed by the Romans, and their attempts at revolution were crushed.

Did Jesus call himself the Messiah?

Jesus avoided using the term "Messiah" for himself and instead preferred to refer to himself with the expression the "son of man." When Jesus did accept the label of Messiah, as stated by Peter, Jesus redefined the term as one who would suffer and die. There are three versions of this important story found in the gospels: Matthew 16:13–20; Mark 8:27–38; and Luke 9:18–27.

What is the Messianic Secret?

In the three Bible passages mentioned above, Peter, one of the followers of Jesus, identifies Jesus as the Messiah. However, Jesus, after redefining what Messiah means, tells his followers to keep it secret. Jesus' reluctance to be identified as the Messiah is often called the "Messianic Secret." Very likely, Jesus was concerned that his message and ministry would be confused with the messages of other Messiahs of the time, who had political and revolutionary goals.

As discussed earlier, the key to understanding the story of Jesus and the temptations offered by the Devil is that the temptations were different ways to be a Messiah. In the end, Jesus rejected the three visions offered by the Devil and instead chose the path of suffering and death, which would lead to his crucifixion.

What did later Christians do with the term "Messiah"?

Later Christians removed all the political and revolutionary connotations and redefined the word "Messiah" to refer to Jesus who suffered and died to redeem humans from their sins. Christians adopted the Greek version of the word, Christ, and began referring to Jesus as Jesus Christ. "Christ" is not the last name for Jesus; rather, it is a title that can be better understood when stated as "Jesus the Christ."

Also, Christians begin using the word to label themselves as Christians ("Christ"ians).

What else does one need to know about the word "Messiah"?

As stated before, Christians use the Greek version of the word, which was pronounced as *Christos* and written as "Χριστος." The Greek letters of this word have become important Christian symbols. The first letter looks like an "X." It is called "chi." The second letter looks like a "P." It is called "rho." Christians combined these two letters in the symbol called the "chi-rho." In those churches that use art, this symbol is very common. Have you seen it before?

Also, the "X" for the first letter of "Christ" in Greek is why you can abbreviate "Christmas" as "Xmas." So "Xmas" is still "keeping Christ in Christmas."

How important is the Christian belief in the Resurrection?

The belief in the Resurrection of Jesus is one of the most important Christian beliefs and is key to understanding Christian teachings. When Christians speak of the Resurrection of Jesus, they usually have in mind three interrelated aspects:

1. Jesus died and rose from the dead.
2. The death and Resurrection of Jesus brings salvation.
3. Christians expect to be resurrected themselves.

What is the Christian understanding of the Resurrection?

Most Christians believe that Jesus died on the cross and was alive three days later. They believe that Jesus really died. They

The chi-rho was an early symbol of Christianity. It is a combination of the first two letters in the Greek "Christos."

reject the idea that Jesus went into a coma and came out of it in the tomb. To repeat: most Christians believe that Jesus died on the cross but was seen alive three days later.

Different Christians have different ways to explain the nature of the resurrected Jesus. Some Christians say that the actual body of Jesus was raised up and brought back to life. Others describe the body of Jesus as somehow transformed. It was the same body, yet somehow different.

Most Christians reject the idea that the followers of Jesus saw a ghost or a spirit. Instead, most Christians believe the resurrected Jesus had a physical body.

Lastly, for most Christians, the Resurrection is not understood as merely symbolic, that "Jesus lives on our hearts." No, most Christians believe that Jesus rose from the dead with some sort of physical body.

What is the second aspect?

The core teaching of Christianity is that the death and Resurrection of Jesus bring salvation. The theology runs like this: humans commit sin and separate themselves from God. However, humans cannot overcome the gap between themselves and God because the sin is so great. Only Jesus, by his death and Resurrection, can bridge the gap. Jesus pays the price for sin. He became a sacrifice offered to God for human sin. Jesus redeems human beings and brings salvation. Thus, humans are saved from sin and the penalty of sin, which is to die and not go to Heaven. Christians call Jesus their "Savior" and "Redeemer." (These terms are explained in detail below.)

What is the third aspect?

Christians expect to be resurrected after death—but not back to this life. Christians expect to be resurrected into Heaven to live forever with God. As Jesus stated in the Gospel of John: "I am the resurrection and the life. Those who believe in me, even though they die, will live, and everyone who lives and believes in me will never die" (John 11:25–26, NRSV).

How important is the Christian belief in the Resurrection?

The Resurrection is at the core of Christian belief. St. Paul stated:

> If there is no resurrection of the dead, then Christ has not been raised; and if Christ has not been raised, then our proclamation has been in vain and your faith has been in vain. We are even found to be misrepresenting God, because we testified of God that he raised Christ—whom he did not raise if it is true that the dead are not raised. For if the dead are not raised, then Christ has not been raised. If Christ has not been raised, your faith is futile and you are still in your sins.

> —1 Corinthians 15:13–17, NRSV

What is the meaning of the word "incarnation"?

Incarnation is a key concept for Christians. The word "incarnation" is based on the Latin word *carnis*, which means "flesh," "meat," or "body." The English word "carnivore" is

A circa 1250 plaque depicts saints rising from the dead. The concept of resurrection for the faithful followers of Jesus is central to the Christian faith.

also based on *carnis*. Incarnation is the belief that in Jesus, God has taken on human flesh. (There is a Hindu term "reincarnation," but that is a very different idea.)

According to mainline Christians, Jesus is both God and man at the same time. They state that Jesus was truly man and truly God at the same time. In other words, he was both human and divine. The word "divine" means to be God. The formula states that Jesus is one person with two natures: a divine nature and a human nature.

This may not be an easy concept to understand. If you say Jesus was just a good man, you are disagreeing with mainline Christian belief. If you say Jesus was God but not man, you are disagreeing with mainline Christian belief. To say Jesus was an angel is to disagree with mainline Christians.

Again, the mainline Christian belief asserts that Jesus is both human and divine. To deny that Jesus is God is a heresy called Arianism. To deny that Jesus is human is a heresy called monophysitism. ("Monophysitism" means "one nature.")

What other concepts are part of the belief in the incarnation?

For Christians, another key concept that supports the idea of the incarnation is the belief that Jesus was born of the Virgin Mary. Most Christians believe that when Jesus was born, his mother Mary was still a virgin. Jesus was not conceived through the normal biological process. Instead, according to Christian belief, by a miracle, God's power came over Mary, and she became pregnant.

The first chapter of the Gospel of Luke describes a scene called the "Annunciation" in which the angel Gabriel announces to Mary that she will give birth to Jesus. Down through the centuries, many painters have created images of Gabriel appearing to Mary. Often in these paintings, the Holy Spirit as a dove is seen. A white lily, often held by Gabriel, can also be seen as a symbol of the purity or virginity of Mary.

Mary carried in her womb Jesus, who was both human and divine. Christians believe that Mary gave birth to Jesus, who was both human and divine. Since Jesus was born human and divine, some Christians call Mary the "Mother of God." Orthodox Christians refer to Mary as "Theotokos," the "bearer of God" or the "carrier of God." The point of the term "Theotokos" is to assert that Mary carried in her womb Jesus, who was both God and human.

Some Christians avoid the term "Mother of God" for Mary because they think it confuses people and puts too much emphasis on Mary. However, most Christians agree with the concept that Mary gave birth to Jesus, who was God and human.

Jesus is sometimes spoken of as the "Word." Sometimes, he is called the "Word made flesh" or even the "Incarnate Word." Now you know what these titles mean.

The belief in the Trinity does not seem like it is an easy concept to understand. Is it?

The Trinity is a key concept for mainline Christians, yet many Christians are confused about what it means. Many ministers never take the time to try to explain the concept to their congregations. The Trinity is perhaps the hardest Christian belief to understand. What makes it difficult is that there is nothing with which one can compare the Trinity to try to understand it. The idea of the Trinity is a paradox in that it requires one to hold two different ideas in the mind at the same time. On the one hand, the Trinity is the belief in one God. On the other hand, this God is made of three divine persons. What follows is an attempt to explain the Trinity in straightforward language. However, some Christians may find this explanation unsatisfactory.

What is the Christian belief in the Trinity?

Notice that the beginning of the word "trinity" is "tri," which means "three," as in "tricycle" and "triceratops." Christians are monotheists who believe in one God; however, this one God is made of three persons: Father, Son, and Holy Spirit. The three persons are the Trinity. Yet these three persons are not human persons; they are divine persons. The formula that expresses the essence of the idea of the Trinity is "One God, yet three divine persons."

A painting at the Church of the Annunciation in Seville, Spain, shows the Father, Son, and Holy Spirit, which commonly is depicted in the form of a dove.

What does it mean to be a person? To be a person is to have a separate awareness. You are a human who has a separate

123

awareness. You know you are you and not someone else. In a similar way, there are three separate "awarenesses" in the Trinity. The Father knows he is the Father and not the Son or the Holy Spirit. The Son knows he is the Son and not the Father or the Holy Spirit. The Holy Spirit knows it is the Holy Spirit and not the Father or the Son. (Traditional gender pronouns are being used here to keep this as simple as possible. Yet the three persons are still one God.)

How can one get a clearer understanding of the Christian belief in the Trinity?

It is important to look at two heresies regarding the Trinity. Understanding these heresies helps to get a clearer idea of what the orthodox teaching of mainline Christians is on the Trinity. According to mainline Christians, these heresies are wrong ways to think about the Trinity. The first heresy is tritheism, which is the idea that the Father, Son, and Holy Spirit are three separate gods.

The second heresy is called modalism. Modalism is the idea that there is one divine person who plays three different roles, one at a time. A mode is a role. For example, a student may have three different roles: being a student, being on a sports team, and holding a job. The student has three different roles and is in three different modes: student mode, athlete mode, and employee mode, yet he or she is still one person.

According to the heresy of modalism, there is one divine person who plays the first role as God the Father, then plays a second role as Jesus, then plays a third role as the Holy Spirit. Each role is played one at a time. The simplest argument against modalism is to examine the passages in the gospels where Jesus prays to the Father. Jesus and the Father would have to be separate beings, unless somehow Jesus was praying to himself.

Just to clarify: tritheism and modalism are heresies and considered wrong ideas by mainline Christians, yet understanding these heresies helps to get a clearer picture of what Christians think about the idea of the Trinity.

I have heard the term "Holy Spirit," but I have also heard the term "Holy Ghost." What is the Holy Ghost?

"Holy Ghost" is simply the older version of the term "Holy Spirit." Some years ago, there was concern that the word "ghost" brought to mind images of Halloween costumes of children in white sheets pretending to be the ghosts of dead people. Most churches embraced the new term "Holy Spirit."

Is the word "Trinity" mentioned in the Bible?

No, the term is not mentioned in the Bible. It was created by an early Christian writer Tertullian (c. 155–c. 240 C.E.) in his attempt to explain the relationship of the Father, Jesus the Son, and the Holy Spirit.

What is the Christian Bible?

The Christian Bible is made of two parts: the Old Testament and the New Testament. Put simply, the Old Testament is before Jesus and the New Testament is Jesus and after. A typical printed Bible is about fifteen hundred pages long. The Old Testament starts with the story of Creation and then moves through the history of ancient Israel up to the centuries before Jesus. The New Testament covers the life of Jesus and the activities of the first several generations of his followers.

What is the Christian view of the role of the Bible?

All Christians believe that the Bible is the guide for what to believe and how to live. They agree on the importance of the Bible, yet they often disagree about what the Bible means and how to understand it. For example, Christians who believe in the Bible disagree on many issues, such as same-sex marriage, abortion, capital punishment, women ministers, and many other issues. Over the centuries, many churches have been split over different views about what is in the Bible. Christians have even killed other Christians over what the Bible means, yet, all Christians agree that the Bible is the guide for what to believe and how to live.

What is the Christian belief of a continuous community?

Christians believe that the Christian community starts with the first generation of the followers of Jesus. Christianity is not reinvented each generation; it is part of a long tradition going back to the first apostles.

Christianity is a community activity. As Jesus stated: "For where two or three are gathered in my name, I am there among them" (Matthew 18:20, NRSV). Although the hermit alone praying by himself is a part of Christian tradition, it is a very small part, and in fact, most monks who pray by themselves are part of larger groups.

Christian communities have rituals. Two rituals are found in all Christian churches: baptism and Communion. Communion is also called Mass, the Lord's Supper, and Eucharist.

THE NICENE CREED

What is the Nicene Creed?

In the year 325, several dozen Christian bishops from lands around the Mediterranean Sea met in the city of Nicaea to create a statement of basic Christian beliefs. Today, Nicaea is in Turkey, which is a predominantly Muslim country. For the first centuries of the Christian era, before the rise of Islam, this area was Christian.

The bishops met at the urging of Emperor Constantine, who was troubled by the fighting among various Christian groups over different ideas about who and what Jesus

This cathedral in Iznik, Turkey, which is now in ruins, is where the Council of Nicea met and wrote the Nicene Creed, an effort to define the nature of Jesus.

was. Constantine had a political motivation. He was hoping Christianity could be the glue to keep his empire of very diverse populations together. The bishops came to an agreement on a number of points defining the nature of Jesus. They wrote up their points in a document that today is called the Nicene Creed. The seven Christian beliefs listed above are explanations of the ideas within the Nicene Creed.

What is the text of the Nicene Creed?

Here is one of the modern versions of the Nicene Creed:

We believe in one God,
the Father, the Almighty,
maker of Heaven and earth,
of all that is seen and unseen.

We believe in one Lord, Jesus Christ,
the only Son of God,
eternally begotten of the Father,
God from God, Light from Light,
true God from true God,
begotten, not made, one in Being with the Father.
Through him all things were made.

For us men and for our salvation
he came down from Heaven:
by the power of the Holy Spirit
he was born of the Virgin Mary, and became man.
For our sake he was crucified under Pontius Pilate,
he suffered, died, and was buried.
On the third day he rose again
in fulfillment of the Scriptures;
he ascended into Heaven
and is seated at the right hand of the Father.
He will come again in glory to judge the living and the dead,
and his kingdom will have no end.

We believe in the Holy Spirit, the Lord, the giver of life,
who proceeds from the Father and the Son.
With the Father and the Son he is worshipped and glorified.
He has spoken through the Prophets.
We believe in one holy catholic and apostolic Church.
We acknowledge one baptism for the forgiveness of sins.
We look for the resurrection of the dead
and the life of the world to come.
Amen.

What is the importance of the Nicene Creed?

Many Christians consider the Nicene Creed to be an essential statement of their faith. In a number of denominations, the Nicene Creed is recited each Sunday during the church service. Other Christians only recite the Creed on special occasions.

The Nicene Creed also provides an important measurement for trying to sort out different Christian groups. A rough division of different Christian denominations can be made along these lines: 1. Those denominations that agree with the Nicene Creed and use the text; 2. Those denominations that agree with the beliefs stated in the Nicene Creed but do not use the actual text; and 3. Those denominations that reject the ideas in the Nicene Creed.

An icon showing Emperor Constantine and several bishops holding part of the Nicene Creed. Constantine wanted a definitive statement from the Church about its beliefs in Jesus and hoped Christianity could help unite a diverse Roman Empire.

What was the effect of the Nicene Creed?

The goal of the Nicene Creed was to clearly state the basic beliefs of Christians. These would be the orthodox beliefs (the correct beliefs). The Creed was also used to identify false or heretical beliefs. In particular, the Creed rejected the heresies of monophysitism, Arianism, and Gnosticism.

What is Gnosticism? Why is it important to know about Gnosticism?

Gnosticism was one of the religious ideas current at the time the Nicene Creed was written. The Creed directly rejects several beliefs of Gnosticism. Many people who know the Nicene Creed read or recite the condemnations of Gnosticism, yet do not recognize that several statements are directed particularly at Gnosticism.

Gnostics believed that there were two separate realms: a spiritual realm and a physical realm. They saw the spiritual realm as good and the physical realm as bad. The physical realm is a place of dirt, disease, sin, and death. Gnostics believed that God created the spiritual realm but not the physical realm. They held that a perfect and good God could not create the flawed physical world. Gnostics believed that another being called a Demiurge created the physical world. However, a good God could not create the less-perfect Demiurge. According to Gnostic thought, the Demiurge "fell away from" or "emanated" from God.

Gnostics rejected the idea of the incarnation. A good God could not become a human being with a physical body. According to Gnostics, the physical body of Jesus was only an illusion.

After reading the Nicene Creed above, I still have trouble understanding all the statements in it. Can the text of the Creed be clarified?

Here is the Creed with detailed comments.

> We believe in one God,
> the Father, the Almighty,
> maker of Heaven and earth,
> of all that is seen and unseen.

These first four lines assert the belief in monotheism and reject Gnosticism. "Seen and unseen" is sometimes translated as "visible" and "invisible." These words refer to the physical realm and the spiritual realm. Gnostics rejected the idea that God created the physical realm. This first sentence also describes the first person of the Trinity: God the Father.

> We believe in one Lord, Jesus Christ,
> the only Son of God,
> eternally begotten of the Father,
> God from God, Light from Light,
> true God from true God,
> begotten, not made, one in Being with the Father.

These six lines describe the second person of the Trinity: Jesus, the Son. These lines also reject Arianism. Jesus is not created. He is the Son of God.

Through him all things were made.
For us men and for our salvation
he came down from Heaven:
by the power of the Holy Spirit
he was born of the Virgin Mary, and became man.

These lines describe the incarnation and also reject monophysitism. Also, the virgin birth of Jesus is stated. "For us men" is understood to refer to all humans.

For our sake he was crucified under Pontius Pilate,
he suffered, died, and was buried.
On the third day he rose again
in fulfillment of the Scriptures;
he ascended into Heaven
and is seated at the right hand of the Father.

These lines describe the death and Resurrection of Jesus. The reference to Pontius Pilate establishes the time when Jesus died.

He will come again in glory to judge the living and the dead,
and his kingdom will have no end.

This sentence wraps up the beliefs about Jesus with the belief in the Second Coming of Jesus.

We believe in the Holy Spirit, the Lord, the giver of life,
who proceeds from the Father and the Son.
With the Father and the Son he is worshipped and glorified.
He has spoken through the Prophets.

These lines describe the third person of the Trinity: the Holy Spirit.

We believe in one holy catholic and apostolic Church.

These lines describe the four identifying marks of the Christian Church. The church is supposed to be united, holy, catholic—which means universal—and based on the teachings of the first followers of Jesus, the apostles.

We acknowledge one baptism for the forgiveness of sins.
We look for the resurrection of the dead
and the life of the world to come. Amen.

These last sentences emphasize the importance of baptism and the belief that believers will live again after death.

Can you say more about the four marks of the Christian church?

The Nicene Creed calls for belief in "one holy catholic and apostolic Church." As stated above, the Christian church is supposed to be united, holy, catholic, and based on the teachings of the apostles of Jesus.

These marks are ideals of the Christian church that Christians have frequently failed to meet down through the centuries. The Nicene Creed calls for one united church, yet Christians are anything but united. In fact, Christians have split into many thousands of different groups and new groups start up all the time. There are a few examples of different groups, joining together, such as the United Methodists and the United Churches of Christ. However, these are the exceptions rather than the rule.

The Christian church is supposed to be holy. Sadly, there are many, many examples of church members and church leaders failing to lead holy lives. In fact, there are many scandalous stories about church leaders.

The word "catholic" is not capitalized. The word means "universal," the original intent of the term in the creed. Most Christians understand that the Nicene Creed does not mean Catholic as in the "Roman Catholic Church." Centuries later, the word became the name of largest Christian denomination.

THE GOSPEL OF JOHN ON THE TRINITY

What does the Gospel of John say about the Trinity?

Although the word "Trinity" did not exist when the Gospel of John was written, the gospel mentions all three persons of the Trinity: the Father, the Son (Jesus), and the Holy Spirit. The term "Holy Spirit" is not in John, but rather, the terms used are "the Advocate" or "the Comforter."

Many Christians describe Jesus as "the Word," "the Word of God," or "the Word of God made flesh" based on the Gospel of John. What do these terms mean?

The writer of John wanted a label for the Son, before the Son became Jesus. He chose the Greek word *Logos*. He used a term that had been used in both Greek philosophy and Jewish thought. (For example, Stoic philosophers saw the Logos as the reason of the universe.) The writer of the Gospel of John wrote, "In the beginning was the Logos, and the Logos was with God, and the Logos was God. He was with God in the beginning. Through him all things were made; without him nothing was made that has been made. The Logos became flesh and made his dwelling among us" (John 1:1–3, 14, NABRE).

Again, the writer of John wanted a label for the Son, before the Son became Jesus. He wanted to say that the Son was there at the beginning, that the Son was with God, that the Son was God, and that the Son became human as Jesus and lived among us humans. The Gospel of John was written in Greek. In English translations, if the term "Logos" had been left as "Logos," then readers would have understood it as a label for the Son who became Jesus. However, Logos was translated as the word "Word," which has caused some confusion. "In the beginning was the Word, and the Word was with God, and the Word was God. He was with God in the beginning. Through him all things were made; without him nothing was made that has been made.… The Logos became flesh and made his dwelling among us" (John 1:1–3, 14, NABRE).

When people hear the English translation as "In the beginning was the Word, and the Word was with God, and the Word was God," some people assume that "Word" refers to the normal meaning that a word is a sound that is written out with letters. Some people want to ask, "Well, what is the word that I'm supposed to hear?" Other people think that the term means the message of God. However, in the beginning of the Gospel of John, the Word is the Son of God before the Son of God becomes Jesus.

If you have an interest, you might read the first chapter of the Gospel of John, verses 1–14. This important text is often called the Prologue of John. Notice also that it starts with "In the beginning," the same words as the start of the book of Genesis.

From these lines in John comes another title for Jesus. Jesus is called the Incarnate Word or the Word Incarnate. This term means that Jesus is the Logos, the Son of God, who became human and took on a human body.

SAVIOR AND REDEEMER

What does the title "Savior" mean?

Christians believe that Jesus died for their sins and saved them both from the effects of their sin but also from the punishment for their sins. Many Christians believe that the

The titles "Savior" and "Redeemer" when applied to Jesus means that He paid the price for human sins so that those who believe in Him can enter Heaven.

punishment they deserved for their sins was eternal damnation in Hell. However, Jesus died for their sins and paid the price for their sins. So, Jesus saved them from the punishment for sin. Hence, many Christians call Jesus their Savior. He saved them from their sins and brought them salvation. Christians believe that because Jesus saved them from eternal punishment, they will go to Heaven.

For many Christians, however, this salvation is only available if one accepts and believes what Jesus did by dying and rising. Many Christians call this acceptance of Jesus as "being saved." Some Christians describe it as "accepting Jesus as your Lord and Savior." Some Christians ask people, "Are you saved?" Many Christians remember the date when they were saved by accepting Jesus. However, there also many Christians who do not insist on using the language of Jesus as one's personal Savior.

What does the title "Redeemer" mean?

The title "Redeemer" was easier to understand in the ancient world, where people often had to be redeemed with money to get back their freedom. Enemy prisoners were sometimes ransomed for money—especially important prisoners. People could be held captive or enslaved because of debt and had to be ransomed. In these cases, someone who paid for their freedom would redeem them and become their redeemer. Today, the term "redeem" is used for using coupons. It also applies in a pawn shop, where one pays back money to redeem the item that was pawned.

Since for Christians, Jesus paid the price of dying on the cross for human sin, he redeemed sinners from the punishment for their sins. Hence, Christians call Jesus their Redeemer and state that Jesus brought redemption. The act of Jesus bringing salvation is often called the Redemption.

In the Old Testament/Hebrew Scriptures, Job states, "As for me I know my redeemer lives," although he was not referring to Jesus (Job 19:25). Charles Wesley (1707–1788) wrote the classic hymn "I Know My Redeemer Lives" about Jesus.

> I know that my Redeemer lives,
> And ever prays for me;
> A token of his love he gives,
> A pledge of liberty.
> I find him lifting up my head,
> He brings salvation near,
> His presence makes me free indeed,
> And he will soon appear.

THE BIBLE

STRUCTURE OF THE OLD AND NEW TESTAMENTS

What do the terms "Old Testament" and "New Testament" mean?

For most people, the word "Bible" brings to mind a Christian Bible made of two parts: the Old Testament and the New Testament. The Old Testament starts with the story of the Creation, moves through the history of ancient Israel, and ends in the centuries before Jesus. The New Testament describes the life and teachings of Jesus and the teachings of the first several generations of the followers of Jesus. Simply put, the Old Testament is before Jesus, and the New Testament is Jesus and after.

The titles "New Testament" and "Old Testament" are Christian labels. The world "testament" means a contract or agreement. Another word for testament is "covenant." The meaning of these terms is that there was an old agreement between God and the ancient people of Israel. This old agreement was augmented or superseded by a new agreement between God and the Christian church through Jesus. (Christians have different views and use different words to explain why the New Testament is "new" and the Old Testament is "old." Here, the words "augmented" and "superseded" are used as possible words. Some Christians would have other explanations.)

The Old Testament is about three quarters of the Christian Bible. The Old Testament is broken into a number of sections that are called "books." The first five books of the Old Testament are Genesis, Exodus, Leviticus, Numbers, and Deuteronomy. Christians disagree on the number of books in the Old Testament. In a Protestant Bible, there are thirty-nine books; in a Catholic Bible, there are forty-six books. The New Testament is broken down into twenty-seven books.

What are the names of the books in the Old Testament?

Old Testament Books

Protestant Bible	Catholic Bible
Genesis	Genesis
Exodus	Exodus
Leviticus	Leviticus
Numbers	Numbers
Deuteronomy	Deuteronomy
Joshua	Joshua
Judges	Judges
Ruth	Ruth
1 Samuel	1 Samuel
2 Samuel	2 Samuel
1 Kings	1 Kings
2 Kings	2 Kings
1 Chronicles	1 Chronicles
2 Chronicles	2 Chronicles
Ezra	Ezra
Nehemiah	Nehemiah
	Tobit
	Judith
Esther	Esther
	1 Maccabees
	2 Maccabees
Job	Job
Psalms	Psalms
Proverbs	Proverbs
Ecclesiastes	Ecclesiastes
Song of Songs	Song of Songs
	Wisdom
	Sirach
Isaiah	Isaiah
Jeremiah	Jeremiah
Lamentations	Lamentations
	Baruch
Ezekiel	Ezekiel
Daniel	Daniel
Hosea	Hosea
Joel	Joel
Amos	Amos
Obadiah	Obadiah
Jonah	Jonah
Micah	Micah
Nahum	Nahum
Habakkuk	Habakkuk
Zephaniah	Zephaniah

Protestant Bible	Catholic Bible
Haggai	Haggai
Zechariah	Zechariah
Malachi	Malachi

How does the Christian Old Testament compare to the Jewish Bible?

The Christian Old Testament is the same set of writings as the Jewish Bible. (The Jewish Bible contains basically the same readings as the Protestant Old Testament.) Jews typically do not refer to the Jewish Bible as the Old Testament since "Old Testament" is a Christian label with a Christian meaning. The Jewish Bible is divided into three sections: the Torah, the books of Law; the Neviim, the books of the prophets; and the Kethuvim, the writings. The first letters of the names of these three parts, T, N, and K are used to create the word "Tanak" (also Tanakh), which is another name for the Jewish Bible.

What are the names of the books in the Jewish Bible?

The books are organized as follows:

Torah: The Five Books of Moses (the books of Law)

Genesis
Exodus
Leviticus
Numbers
Deuteronomy

Neviim: The Eight Books of the Prophets

Joshua
Judges
Samuel
Kings
Isaiah
Jeremiah
Ezekiel
The Twelve (minor prophets)

Kethuvim: The Eleven Books of the Writings

Psalms
Proverbs
Job
Song of Songs
Ruth
Lamentations
Ecclesiastes
Esther
Daniel
Ezra/Nehemiah
Chronicles

If one compares the list of books of the Protestant Old Testament and the Jewish Bible, one will notice many similarities and also some differences. While the books of Samuel, Kings, and Chronicles are single books in the Jewish Bible, they are each split into two parts in the Old Testament. Chronicles is the last book on the Jewish Bible list. Also, the twelve Minor Prophets are combined in the Jewish Bible but kept separate in the Old Testament.

Are there other names for the Jewish Bible?

The Jewish Bible is also called the Jewish Scriptures, the Hebrew Scriptures, the Hebrew Bible, and the Tanakh. As mentioned above, Jews typically do not call their Bible the Old Testament. When the term "Hebrew Scriptures" is used for the Old Testament, the term "Christian Scriptures" is

The Tenakh scrolls (also called the Tanach, Tanakh, Mikra, or simply the Hebrew Bible) contain the text used as the source for the Christian Old Testament.

often used for the New Testament. However, Jews do not recognize the Christian Scriptures as sacred texts. Some non-Jews use the terms "Hebrew Scriptures" and "Christian Scriptures" to be more sensitive.

Why is the Protestant Old Testament different from the Catholic Old Testament?

The Old Testament, from the early centuries of Christianity through the Middle Ages, had forty-six books in it. In the 1500s, when Martin Luther broke away from the Catholic Church, he decided to create a translation of the Bible in German, which was the language of the people around him. In deciding on the Old Testament, he only chose those thirty-nine books that were originally written in Hebrew. He excluded seven books that were first written in Greek. The Catholic Church retained the complete set of forty-six books, including those originally written in Greek.

What are the seven books that are in a Catholic Old Testament but not the Protestant Old Testament?

Tobit, Judith, 1 Maccabees, 2 Maccabees, Wisdom, Sirach (also called Ecclesiasticus), and Baruch.

What are the Major and Minor Prophets?

In the Old Testament, four books are called the Major Prophets because the books are long: Isaiah, Jeremiah, Ezekiel, and Daniel. There are also twelve short books of prophecy that are called the Minor Prophets: Hosea, Joel, Amos, Obadiah, Jonah, Micah, Nahum, Habakkuk, Zephaniah, Haggai, Zechariah, and Malachi. The books of Jeremiah, Ezekiel, and the Minor Prophets are all named after the prophet who gave that particular message. The Book of Daniel tells various stories about Daniel. The composition of the Book of Isaiah is described below.

Of the Minor Prophets, the Book of Amos is particularly important because of its calls for justice. Amos states: "Let justice surge like waters, and righteousness like an unfailing stream" (Amos 5:24, NABRE).

What are the twenty-seven books of the New Testament?

The New Testament begins with the four Gospels: Matthew, Mark, Luke, and John. It is followed by a book called Acts of the Apostles, which is a sequel to the Gospel of Luke. Twenty-one letters follow, which were actual letters written by early Christian leaders and sent to Christians in various parts of the Roman Empire. The early Christian teacher Paul (St. Paul) wrote a number of them addressed to Christian communities, such as in the cities of Rome and Corinth. These letters are called "Paul's Letter to the Romans" and "Paul's First Letter to the Corinthians." In the past, these letters were often called "epistles," which is simply an older word for "letters." The last book of the New Testament is the Book of Revelation. Here is the list:

The Major Prophets of the Old Testament—Daniel, Ezekiel, Isaiah, and Jeremiah—are depicted in this fresco found in the Church of the Gesù in Rome, Italy. The word "major" is not used because they are more important, but, rather, because the books named after these prophets are longer than those of the twelve Minor Prophets.

4 Gospels: Matthew, Mark, Luke, and John
1 Acts of the Apostles
21 Letters or Epistles
1 Revelation
27 Total Books

What are the names of the books in the New Testament?

Matthew
Mark
Luke
John

137

Acts (of the Apostles)
Romans
1 Corinthians
2 Corinthians
Galatians
Ephesians
Philippians
Colossians
1 Thessalonians
2 Thessalonians
1 Timothy
2 Timothy
Titus
Philemon
Hebrews
James
1 Peter
2 Peter
1 John
2 John
3 John
Jude
Revelation

What are the apocryphal books?

Apocryphal books are books that did not make it into the Bible. Sometimes, these are called the "Apocrypha," which comes from the Greek word for "hidden." Some examples are the Book of Enoch and the Gospel of Thomas.

Among Christians, there are three different categories of apocryphal books. The first group is books that most Christians agree do not belong in the Old Testament, such as the Book of Enoch and the Book of Jubilees.

The second group called "Apocrypha" are the seven books mentioned above that are not in the Protestant Old Testament but are in the Catholic Old Testament (Tobit; Judith; 1 Maccabees; 2 Maccabees; Wisdom; Sirach, also called Ecclesiasticus; and Baruch). Protestants believe that these seven books do not belong in the Old Testament and often call them apocryphal books. However, Catholics include these books and believe that they are part of the Bible.

The third group is New Testament Apocrypha. Since Christians agree on the list of the twenty-seven books in the New Testament, there is little dispute on which writings belong to this group. There are about two dozen early Christian writings that did not make it into the New Testament, such as the Gospel of Thomas and the Acts of Thomas. However, Christians disagree on whether or not these writings add any insight into the life of Jesus.

DIFFERENT VIEWS ON HOW TO READ THE BIBLE

How old is the earth?

Some Christians believe that the world was created in six days about six thousand years ago. Science says the earth is 4.6 billion years old. Who is right: science or the Bible? The key is how to read the Bible. Christians disagree on many, many things, including how to read the Bible. There are two approaches to reading the Bible: the literalist and the nonliteralist approach.

What is the literalist view on reading the Bible?

Literalists believe that the Bible should be taken literally because it is the Word of God. Typically, literalists also believe that the Bible is "God words." This is the idea that God told the biblical writers what to write down, word for word. Therefore, if God told them what to write, there cannot be any mistakes in the Bible. Thus, if the Bible says the earth is six thousand years old, it is six thousand years old! (A literalist might argue that God would know how old the earth is because he was there at creation.) Typically, literalists do not believe in evolution since it is not mentioned in the Bible. Furthermore, evolution could not have happened in the short time of creation described in the Bible. In the Bible, there is the story of Jonah, who was thrown overboard from a ship. Jonah was swallowed by a big fish and lived in the belly of the fish for three days before being spat out. Literalists believe this actually happened. This approach to reading the Bible is the literalist view.

What do you call the nonliteralist view?

The nonliteralist view for reading the Bible can be called the contextualist view. The word "contextualist" is a new term to make this simpler. The older term for this approach to reading the Bible is the historical-critical method. A person who reads the Bible in its context is called a contextualist.

The contextualist view holds that the Bible was written by humans. To understand

A literal interpretation of the Bible would have some figure out that Earth is a mere six thousand years old, while science has shown that it is about 4.6 *billion* years old. However, one can still interpret the Bible in a way that it does not disagree with science.

any human writing, speech, or communication, one has to understand the "context" or setting. If someone says to me, "You are such a stupid idiot!", I have to know the context to know how to interpret the remark. Is someone who does not like me calling me a stupid idiot? Is it a friend just teasing me? Is someone who really loves me just mad at me? If I am a boss, do I need to fire the employee who called me a stupid idiot? Am I an actor in a play? How you would understand "You are such a stupid idiot!" totally depends on the context.

The view of contextualists is that if humans wrote the Bible, there could be historical mistakes. If four different humans wrote the story of Jesus, there will be differences in how they tell the story. Ancient people did not have science to explain the world around them, so they often told myths. Typically, contextualists think that the stories in the first part of the Book of Genesis are religious myths and not a scientific or historical description of how the universe came into being.

Contextualists believe the story of Jonah was meant to teach a lesson. It turns out that the Book of Jonah is a very profound teaching story about religious hatred. Contextualists do not believe that Jonah actually lived in the belly of a fish for three days since that would be physically impossible to do. Contextualists believe you have to try to think like ancient people, who had no science and very little written history and no archeology, to know about what happened before them. There are two kinds of contextualists.

What are the two kinds of contextualists?

1. Those contextualists who believe the Bible was written solely by humans. In this view, the Bible is an interesting ancient religious text but nothing more than that.

2. Those contextualists who believe the Bible was written by humans but inspired by God. The Bible is God's message written by humans in their own words using ancient styles of literature. The Bible is "God's Word"—meaning God's message but not "God's words."

So how many views are there on how to read the Bible?

There are three basic views on how to read the Bible:

- Literalist view
- Contextualist view—solely a human product
- Contextualist view—a human product inspired by God

Which view makes more sense to you?

Who are fundamentalists?

Fundamentalists are Christians who insist on taking the Bible literally. Many literalists believe the earth is six thousand years old and that there was no evolution. Some Christian fundamentalists are active in opposing theories about evolution and opposing the teaching of evolution in schools. Most fundamentalists are afraid that a nonliteral reading of Genesis will undermine the Bible and Christian faith and morals. One of the reasons for the growth of the Christian homeschool movement is to set up schools that do not teach evolution.

A famous song, written in the 1920s, questions a literal interpretation of the Bible. It is called "It Ain't Necessarily So!" from the opera *Porgy and Bess*, written by George Gershwin. Check it out on YouTube.

What is form criticism?

Form criticism is the attempt in reading the Bible to recognize that the Bible is made of many different kinds of literature. It includes histories, prayers, proverbs, letters, sagas, parables, and many other different kinds of writings. According to form criticism, it is important to understand what kind of literature is a particular part of the Bible in order to know how to understand that part of the Bible. For example, the three gospels of Matthew, Mark, and Luke are examples of one literary form. The Gospel of John is actually a different literary form. The epistles are yet another form. Lastly, the Book of Revelation falls in its own category or form of literature.

Form criticism identifies different types of literature, which are also literary genres. By way of comparison, a newspaper is made of different literary genres. The front page is different from the sports page which is different from the opinion page which is different from the comics. An alert reader instantly recognizes the difference and reads each genre differently.

Television is filled with many different forms, and most people seem to be able to sort them out. Commercials are different from the actual show, serious news is different from a comedy newscast such as on *Saturday Night Live*, and a comedy sitcom is different from a serious drama. In the same way, the Bible is made of different literary forms that an alert reader should recognize.

READING THE BIBLE

Which Bible translation should I read?

Many good Bible translations are available. The New Revised Standard Version (NRSV) is highly respected. Some people prefer the older King James Version (KJV) of the Bible. The New International Version (NIV) is also available. The New American Bible Revised Edition (NABRE) is an excellent and very readable Catholic translation. Printed versions of the NABRE include helpful headings in the text such as "Sermon on the Mount" and "The Feeding of the Four Thousand."

Are the translations of the Bible all that different?

Although many people think there are vast differences in the different translations, typically the wording is somewhat similar, and passages from the different versions say about the same thing. (As noted above, Catholic Bibles include seven extra Old Testament books. Protestant Bibles do not include these books.) If you are curious, take a Bible passage that you like and look at the different translations.

What is a Bible concordance?

A Bible concordance is an index of every significant word used in the Bible. If you wanted to know every place the word "hand" or "angel" is used in the Bible, a concordance will tell you. If you want to find a Bible passage and you can only remember part of the passage, a concordance will help you find it in the Bible.

In the days of computers, it is easy to imagine creating a concordance by doing computer searches of digitized Bibles. However, the first concordances were written before computers. Someone had to by hand go through a Bible and make a list of where every word was used.

When selecting a Bible to read, there are several versions from which to choose. Protestant Bibles have various edits in language, some of which use more modern colloquialisms to make them easier for laypeople to understand. The Catholic Bible has the significant difference in that it includes an extra seven books in its Old Testament.

The most famous written concordance is *Strong's Exhaustive Concordance of the Bible*. Because there are different translations of the Bible, online concordances ask you to specify which Bible you are searching. Some online concordances are easier to use than others. Some sites have ads and promote specific religious messages. However, a concordance is not always needed today to find the location of a Bible passage. Usually, an online search of the key words in the passage will identify the passage.

CHRISTIAN USE OF
THE OLD TESTAMENT

Why do Christians include the Old Testament in the Bible if Christianity is based on the New Testament?

Although Christianity is based on the life and teachings of Jesus that are found in the New Testament, most Christians see the Old Testament as an important part of their tradition. Readings from the Old Testament are used in church services, many Christians read the Old Testament, and many Christians see the life and teachings of Jesus as a continuation of what was in the Old Testament. Many Christians also see the Old Testament stories as part of the history of their own religious tradition. Many stories in the Old Testament are important for Christians.

Also, Jesus saw himself as following the Old Testament/Hebrew Scriptures. In his teachings, Jesus frequently commented upon and interpreted the Law of Moses. In the famous scene of the Transfiguration, Jesus is presented as the continuation of the Law and the Prophets.

Why are the first chapters of Genesis important for Christians?

The first eleven chapters of Genesis describe the Creation, the stories of Adam and Eve, and the Noah stories. For literalist Christians, these stories become an important issue in faith requiring the belief that things happened exactly as described in Genesis. Contextualists see the stories for their description of the relationship between God and humans.

The story of the first man and woman—called Adam and Eve—who disobey God and eat from the tree from which they were forbidden is a key story. For some Christians, this is the first sin of humans. Some Christians call this "Original Sin." Other Christians see this as a story that illustrates the tendency of humans to disobey God and become alienated from God. Many Christians believe that the first sin of Adam and Eve makes necessary the eventual redemption of humans by the death and Resurrection of Jesus.

The stories of Adam and Eve, found in Chapters 2 and 3 of Genesis and including the story of their temptation by the snake, are well known. Two things must be pointed out. The story never says that the snake was the Satan—the Devil—and the fruit is never specified as an apple.

Why is the story of Abraham important for Christians?

Christians see Abraham as a key figure in their faith tradition. For many Christians, he is a model of faith and trust in God. Christians share this belief with Jews and Muslims. All three religions are called "Abrahamic Faiths" for tracing their spiritual lineage back to Abraham. The stories of Abraham and his wife, Sarah, can be found in Genesis Chapters 11–25. At first, they are named Abram and Sarai.

Abraham had two sons. The first by the maidservant Hagar was called Ishmael. The second son, Isaac, was born of Sarah. He is the ancestor of the people of Israel. Isaac had two sons: Esau and Jacob. Jacob would have twelve sons, who would become the ancestors of the Twelve Tribes of Israel.

Is Abraham part of the Islamic tradition?

Yes, he is a key model of faith for Muslims. He is also the ancestor of the Arabic peoples through Ishmael. However, in the Islamic version of the story, Hagar is not a maidservant but, rather, a second wife. In Islam, the name Abraham is "Ibrāhīm," and the name Ishmael is "Ismaī'īl."

What is the importance of Moses?

Three important things happened during the Moses period. Moses learned the name of God, he led the Hebrews out of Egypt in the Exodus, and he went up Mount Sinai, where

143

Abraham is a key figure in the Bible, as well as being the patriarch of the Jewish and Islamic faiths (*Abraham and the Angels* by Aert de Gelder).

he received the Ten Commandments and hundreds of other laws. For many Christians, these stories and events are important parts of their faith tradition. Many Christians find the dramatic story of Moses leading the people out of Egypt to be an exciting and dramatic story.

According to Jewish tradition, Moses received 613 laws, which included the Ten Commandments. The Book of Exodus described the story of Moses going up Mount Sinai to receive the Commandments from God. Most Christians follow the Ten Commandments and ignore the other 603 laws. In Judaism, there are different divisions based on how strictly the 613 laws are followed. Orthodox Jews strictly follow all the laws while Reform Jews are less strict, just focusing on the moral laws. Conservative Jews are in between.

What is the importance of King David?

David was the second king of Israel after Saul, the first king. David lived in about the year 1000 B.C.E. His life and career are extensively covered in the Bible, although almost no evidence of him exists outside the Bible. David conquered a Jebusite city and made it his capital of Jerusalem. David brought the Arc of the Covenant to Jerusalem. The Arc was a box believed to go back to the time of Moses that contained the Tablets of the Law that Moses had received from God. The name Jerusalem means "city of peace"; however, it has been fought over many times.

What happened after King David?

David's son Solomon became the third king. He built the first Temple in Jerusalem. At Solomon's death, in 921 B.C.E., the people revolted and split the Kingdom of Israel into two kingdoms. The northern kingdom retained the name Israel. The southern kingdom took the name of its largest tribe, Judah. For two hundred years, two kingdoms with two different kings existed.

In about 722 B.C.E. the northern kingdom of Israel was conquered by the Assyrians, and most of the people were deported to Assyria in Mesopotamia (modern-day Iraq). Only the kingdom of Judah survived. Since only people in Judah survived, it is at this point that we call these people "Jews." During the threat of the Assyrian conquest, the prophets Amos, Hosea, and Isaiah were actively warning the people.

A statue in Jerusalem of King David, the second king of Israel. He established the city of Jerusalem as the capital and was responsible for bringing the Ark of the Covenant there.

What happened next?

In 587 B.C.E., the Babylonians conquered the southern kingdom of Judah. The Temple of Solomon was destroyed, and the Arc of the Covenant disappeared. Many Jews were taken away to Babylon in a period known as the Babylonian Captivity. During their exile, the Jews started worshipping in local buildings called synagogues. They also started writing the Hebrew Bible.

In 537 B.C.E., some Jews returned to rebuild Jerusalem, and under the leadership of Ezra they rebuilt the Temple. This is called the Second Temple.

In 332 B.C.E., the Greeks conquered the region, called Palestine at this point. The Jews came under Greek control. The Greeks oppressed the Jewish religion, took over the Temple, and dedicated it to Zeus. The Jews eventually revolted in what is known as the Maccabean Revolt. In about 167 B.C.E., they retook the Temple from the Greeks. A legend tells that when they went to relight the Temple lampstand, called the menorah, which had seven lamps on it, they only had enough oil for one day; however, by a miracle, the lamp stayed lit for eight days. This legend is behind the Jewish tradition of Hanukkah.

For a brief period, the Jews had independence as the Hasmonean Kingdom until the Romans entered in 63 B.C.E. Of course, the Romans were present at the time of Jesus.

The story of the Greek and Roman conquests is told in the books of 1 & 2 Maccabees, which are neither part of the Hebrew Bible nor the Protestant Bible. However, both Jews and Protestants recognize the importance of these books for the history of these tumultuous years.

Under the Romans, a Jewish king, Herod the Great, ruled. He undertook many building projects, including a massive restoration of the Temple complex. Some of the walls he built can still be seen today. Herod died around 4 B.C.E., right around the birth of Jesus. Jesus was probably born between 6 and 4 B.C.E. and crucified between 27 and 30 C.E. Some thirty years after Jesus, the Jews revolted against the Romans. Although initially successful in driving out the Romans, the Romans returned with a large army that eventually destroyed the city of Jerusalem and leveled the Temple (the Second Temple). The place where the Temple stood can be seen in Jerusalem today.

ISAIAH AND JONAH

Why is the prophet Isaiah important for Christians?

The prophet Isaiah lived in the 700s B.C.E. at the time of the Assyrian conquest of the northern kingdom of Israel. His teachings were written down. Later, teachings of prophets from the 500s B.C.E. were added to his writings to create the Book of Isaiah. Chapters 1–39 of the Book of Isaiah are the teachings of the original Isaiah. Chapters 40–55 were written in the 500s B.C.E. during the period known as the Babylonian Captivity. Chapters 56–66 were written even later.

Many Christians find prophecies in the Book of Isaiah that point to Jesus, such as: "Therefore the Lord himself will give you a sign; the young woman, pregnant and about to bear a son, shall name him Emmanuel" (Isaiah 7:14, NABRE). In the Gospel of Matthew, this passage is quoted as: "Behold, the virgin shall be with child and bear a son, and they shall name him Emmanuel, which means 'God is with us'" (Matthew 1:23, NABRE; note that the word for young woman in Hebrew in Isaiah is less specific than the Greek word used for virgin by Matthew).

Another popular text from Isaiah is: "For a child is born to us, a son is given to us; upon his shoulder dominion rests. They name him Wonder-Counselor, God-Hero, Father-Forever, Prince of Peace" (Isaiah 9:5, NABRE). This text is used in the famous 1741 choral piece *Messiah* by George Frideric Handel. (It can be found on YouTube under "For unto us a child is born," and it runs about four minutes.)

Many Christians see the following passage as a prophecy of Jesus:

For he grew up before him like a young plant, and like a root out of dry ground; he had no form or majesty that we should look at him, nothing in his appearance that we should desire him. He was despised and rejected by others; a man of suffering and acquainted with infirmity; and as one from whom others hide their faces he was despised, and we held him of no account.

Surely he has borne our infirmities and carried our diseases; yet we accounted him stricken, struck down by God, and afflicted. But he was wounded for our transgressions, crushed for our iniquities; upon him was the punishment that made us whole, and by his bruises we are healed.

—Isaiah 53:2–5, NRSV

Why is Jonah important?

The Book of Jonah tells the short story of Jonah. It is a popular story that gets a lot of attention. However, most readers miss the whole point of the story. For biblical literalists, the story of Jonah is often seen as an important test of faith, as they believe that Jonah actually lived in the belly of a fish for three days. Contextualists argue that this is a teaching story with a moral point and deny that anyone could live in the belly of a fish for three days.

So what is the story of Jonah?

In the story, Jonah hates the Assyrians. He wants God to punish and destroy them, but God does not want to destroy the Assyrians. Instead, God wants Jonah to preach to them, so they can be forgiven. After trying to run away from his assignment—sailing in the opposite direction, being swallowed by a fish (or whale), and then being spat out exactly where he started—Jonah winds up going to the Assyrian city of Nineveh and preaching. The people repent! Jonah is the most successful prophet in the Bible! Yet, Jonah is furious because he wanted God to destroy his enemies.

Then Jonah goes up on a hillside to watch what will happen to the city. A plant grows up and gives him shade, but then it dies, and Jonah is again mad. God asks Jonah why he is so concerned about his little plant. Should not God be more concerned about all the people in the city of Nineveh?

The profound message of the Jonah story is that God does not hate whom we hate. (This is a Bible lesson apparently missed by such groups as the Westboro Baptists.) Over the centuries, many Christians and other religious people have hated other people for many reasons. Such people often assume their hate is consistent with God's hatred for the same people. To Jonah's surprise and to the surprise of the listener of the story, God does not hate the people that religious people hate.

More important than his being swallowed by a giant fish is Jonah's successful ministry in the Assyrian city of Nineveh. The fact that God does not destroy the Assyrians whom Jonah hated is a lesson in tolerance for others (illustration by Gustave Doré).

THE PSALMS

What are the Psalms?

The Old Testament/Hebrew Scriptures contains the Book of Psalms. It is found right in the middle of a Christian Bible. The Psalms are prayers. The 150 Psalms were originally meant to be sung along with instruments. Some of the psalms include references to musical instruments, such as Psalm 150.

> Hallelujah!
> Praise God in his holy sanctuary;
> give praise in the mighty dome of Heaven.
> Give praise for his mighty deeds,
> praise him for his great majesty.
> Give praise with blasts upon the horn,
> praise him with harp and lyre.
> Give praise with tambourines and dance,
> praise him with strings and pipes.
> Give praise with crashing cymbals,
> praise him with sounding cymbals.
> Let everything that has breath
> give praise to the LORD!
> Hallelujah! (NABRE)

There are several kinds of psalms. Some are songs or poems of praise, such as Psalm 104. Many are prayers in times of need, such as Psalm 86. Some are prayers recognizing one's sinfulness, such as Psalm 51. Some were used when making a pilgrimage up to Jerusalem, such as Psalm 122.

Which is the best-known psalm?

Psalm 23 is the best-known psalm. Many people who know nothing else about the Bible can recognize the opening lines of this psalm.

> A Psalm of David.
> The Lord is my shepherd, I shall not want.
> He makes me lie down in green pastures;
> he leads me beside still waters;
> he restores my soul.
> He leads me in right paths
> for his name's sake.
>
> Even though I walk through the darkest valley,
> I fear no evil;
> for you are with me;
> your rod and your staff—
> they comfort me.

You prepare a table before me
in the presence of my enemies;
you anoint my head with oil;
my cup overflows.
Surely goodness and mercy shall follow me
all the days of my life,
and I shall dwell in the house of the Lord
my whole life long. (NRSV)

Is there a psalm that describes the Crucifixion?

Many people have found parallels between Psalm 22 and the Crucifixion of Jesus. Some Christians cite Psalm 22 as a prediction of the Crucifixion. In the Gospels of Matthew and Mark, Jesus quotes the first line of the psalm as he dies on the cross. The gospels also quote some of the lines of Psalm 22. Here are some of the more important lines of the psalm:

My God, my God, why have you abandoned me?
Why so far from my call for help,
from my cries of anguish?
…

But I am a worm, not a man,
scorned by men, despised by the people.
All who see me mock me;
they curl their lips and jeer;
they shake their heads at me:
"He relied on the LORD—let him deliver him;
if he loves him, let him rescue him."
…

Like water my life drains away;
all my bones are disjointed.
My heart has become like wax,
it melts away within me.
As dry as a potsherd is my throat;
my tongue cleaves to my palate;
you lay me in the dust of death.
Dogs surround me;
a pack of evildoers closes in on me.
They have pierced my hands and my feet
I can count all my bones.
They stare at me and gloat;
they divide my garments among them;
for my clothing they cast lots.

—Psalms 22:2, 7–9, 15–19, NABRE   149

How do Christians use the Psalms?

Christians use the Psalms in many ways. Many Christians use them in their private Bible reading and prayer. Most of the prayers said by monks in monasteries are the Psalms. A book of daily prayers built around the Psalms is called the Divine Office. In the services of many denominations, the Psalms are often read aloud. Many Christian services are built around an Old Testament reading, a psalm, a reading from an epistle, and finally, a gospel reading. The psalm is often called a Responsorial Psalm with one person reading most of the psalm aloud, while the congregation repeats one line of the psalm at regular intervals.

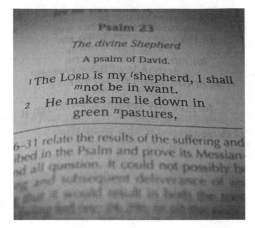

Many Christians draw inspiration from the beautiful, moving text of the Psalms, all of which have, at one time or another, been set to music.

THE GOSPELS

What are the synoptic gospels?

The Christian New Testament contains the four gospels: Matthew, Mark, Luke, and John. If you read all four of these carefully, you would probably notice that Matthew, Mark, and Luke are somewhat similar, while John is very different in style and in content. Because they are similar, Matthew, Mark, and Luke are called the synoptic gospels. The word "synoptic" is made from "syn," which means "same," and "optic," which means "eye" or "view," so synoptic means "same view." Matthew, Mark, and Luke—the synoptic gospels—describe Jesus in a similar way.

Why are the synoptic gospels so similar?

A biblical literalist would say that God told the gospel writers of Matthew, Mark, and Luke what to write, so of course they would be similar. On the other hand, a contextualist would say that humans wrote the gospels, so a different explanation is required. Over the last several hundred years, biblical scholars have tried to develop explanations of how the different pieces of these gospels fit together based on the text in the gospels themselves. The only statement in the gospels themselves about the writing process is found in the Gospel of Luke.

> Since many have undertaken to set down an orderly account of the events that have been fulfilled among us, just as they were handed on to us by those who from the beginning were eyewitnesses and servants of the word, I too decided,

after investigating everything carefully from the very first, to write an orderly account for you, most excellent Theophilus, so that you may know the truth concerning the things about which you have been instructed.

—Luke 1:1–4, NRSV

Many scholars agree that the similarity of the three synoptic gospels has a simple explanation: somebody copied something from somebody. Such copying was common in ancient writing and was not considered plagiarism.

Scholars have studied this in great detail and have come up with a widely accepted theory of who copied from whom. The Gospel of Mark was written first. It is the earliest gospel. Then the authors of Matthew and Luke used Mark in writing their gospels. This would explain all the places in the gospels where Mark, Matthew, and Luke are the same—sometimes word for word. The author of Matthew and Luke copied from Mark. However, there is material that is in Matthew and Luke but not in Mark. From where did this material come?

What are some passages in Matthew and Luke that are not in Mark?

The Lord's Prayer given by Jesus—also called the Our Father—is one example. Here is the text from Luke:

Father, hallowed be your name,
your kingdom come.
Give us each day our daily bread
and forgive us our sins
for we ourselves forgive everyone in debt to us,
and do not subject us to the final test.

—Luke 11:2–4, NABRE (the prayer in Matthew is in 6:9–15)

The Beatitudes found in Matthew and Luke are another example.

So where did this material come from that is in Matthew and Luke but not Mark?

Scholars have concluded that there must have been another source that Matthew and Luke had but that Mark did not. This source may have been written, or it may have been an oral source of remembered sayings of Jesus. Scholars nicknamed this source "Q." The name comes from the German word *quelle*, which means "source."

Matthew and Luke used as their sources the Gospel of Mark and "Q." Sometimes, this approach is called the "two-source" theory for the synoptic gospels. In addition, Matthew and Luke had sources unique to each of them, which would explain the stories that are in Matthew or Luke and not in any other gospels.

So is that the Synoptic Problem and its answer?

Yes. The three synoptic gospels of Mathew, Mark, and Luke share many passages that are similar or word for word the same. The Gospel of Mark, which was written first, was

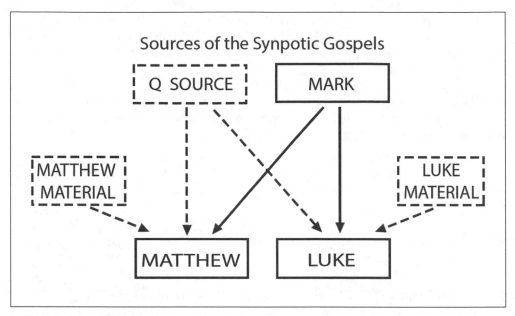

In the above diagram, solid-line boxes represent known documents, and dotted-line boxes are hypothetical source material; solid-line arrows are likely source relationships, and dotted-line arrows mean there is no scholarly consensus about their relationship.

used by Matthew and Luke. However, Matthew and Luke also had another source of sayings of Jesus called the "Q Source." In addition, the writer of Matthew had material used only in the Gospel of Matthew, and the writer of Luke had material used only in the Gospel of Luke. The following diagram illustrates the interconnections of the synoptic gospels.

What is unique about the Gospel of Matthew?

Matthew's gospel is addressed to a Christian audience that has a strong Jewish background. In Matthew's gospel, Jesus is presented as a new Moses. In the early chapters of Exodus, the baby Moses survives the plan of the Pharaoh of Egypt to kill all the baby Hebrew boys. In the Gospel of Matthew, Jesus survives the plan of King Herod to kill all the baby boys. Jesus and his parents, Mary and Joseph, flee to Egypt. Just as Moses led the people out of the Egypt, a few years later, the Holy Family comes out of Egypt and settles in Nazareth.

Later in the gospel, Jesus gives his core teachings, the Beatitudes, on a mountain. This famous "Sermon on the Mount," in which Jesus gives his new law, parallels Moses on Mount Sinai receiving the old law.

What is unique about the Gospel of Mark?

Mark is the shortest gospel. It was written first, even though it is listed second in the New Testament. It does not include stories about the birth of Jesus.

What is the problem with the ending of the Gospel of Mark?

There are discrepancies among the various ancient manuscripts as to how the Gospel of Mark should end. In other words, the oldest Greek copies of Mark have different endings. The main discrepancy is what should follow after Mark 16:1–8. The longer ending, which is not found in the oldest manuscripts, is verses 9–20. This longer ending describes Jesus appearing to Mary Magdalene, Jesus appearing to two disciples, Jesus commissioning the eleven apostles, and the Ascension. The shorter ending would come right after 16:1–8 and states: "And they reported all the instructions briefly to Peter's companions. Afterward, Jesus himself, through them, sent forth from east to west the sacred and imperishable proclamation of eternal salvation. Amen."

In the Book of Matthew, parallels are clearly seen between the life of Moses (shown in this stained glass window) and that of Jesus. In other words, it presents Jesus as the new Moses.

What is unique about the Gospel of Luke?

The Gospel of Luke, like Matthew, has stories about the birth of Jesus. These are called "infancy narratives." Luke also includes stories about the birth of John the Baptist. The Gospel of Luke also has some of the best-known parables taught by Jesus, such as "The Good Samaritan" and "The Prodigal Son."

In the Gospel of Luke, there are also numerous references to Jewish rituals. The first character to appear in the gospel is Zachariah, who is a priest in the Temple where the angel Gabriel appears to him telling him that he will have a son who will be named John. The son becomes John the Baptist.

On the eighth day after his birth, Jesus is circumcised and receives his name according to Jewish custom. Also, as was Jewish custom, Mary goes to the Temple for the ritual of purification after giving birth. In the offerings made in the Temple at the Presentation of Jesus, Joseph offers two doves, which was the offering for poor people.

When Jesus is twelve years old, he is left behind in Jerusalem during a pilgrimage by his family to Jerusalem. When Joseph and Mary discover that he is missing from their entourage, they return and search for Jesus. They find him, symbolically on the third day, in the Temple talking to the priests and teachers, who are amazed at his wisdom and knowledge. Presumably, Jesus and the elders were talking about religious faith and the Jewish law. This incident takes place when Jesus is twelve. The gospels do not describe a bar mitzvah for Jesus. However, this story is the symbolic equivalent. In a bar mitzvah, a boy reads from the Scriptures in a synagogue to fulfill the Law of Moses.

What is different in Luke about the message of Jesus?

In Luke's gospel, the message is that Jesus has come for the poor and lowly. In the prayer of pregnant Mary, called the "Magnificat," she exclaims about God: "He has shown might with his arm, dispersed the arrogant of mind and heart. He has thrown down the rulers from their thrones but lifted up the lowly. The hungry he has filled with good things; the rich he has sent away empty" (Luke 1:51–53, NABRE).

In Luke, the family of Jesus is portrayed as being poor. Jesus is born in a stable or a manger because there is no room at the inn. However, one must set aside modern ideas about staying at hotels where a family would have their own room. At the time of Jesus, rooms at an inn would be large, often crowded, with the rooms shared by a number of people who slept on the floor. The baby Jesus is visited by shepherds who were the witnesses of the newborn child. Shepherds were often at the very bottom of the social order and were often considered as unreliable witnesses.

In the Beatitudes in Luke, Jesus states:
Blessed are you who are poor,
for the kingdom of God is yours.
Blessed are you who are now hungry,
for you will be satisfied.
…

But woe to you who are rich,
for you have received your consolation.
But woe to you who are filled now,
for you will be hungry.

—Luke 6:20–21, 24–25, NABRE

What is unique about the Gospel of John?

John's gospel is very different in style and content. It is the most theologically rich gospel.

What makes the Gospel of John so different from the synoptic gospels?

The biggest difference is the way Jesus speaks in the Gospel of John. In the synoptic gospels, Jesus speaks in short lessons or short stories, and he rarely speaks about himself. In John's gospel, Jesus gives long speeches that sometimes go on for pages. These speeches are very theological and sometimes difficult to follow. Often in John, Jesus speaks about himself with statements such as "The Father and I are one" and "No one comes to the Father, except through me." Also, there are only seven miracles in the gospel, and they often contain symbolic meaning.

What are the seven miracles in the Gospel of John?

The seven miracles are:

- Changing water into wine at the wedding of Cana
- Healing of the official's son
- Healing of the crippled man
- Feeding five thousand people
- Walking on the water
- Healing the man born blind
- Raising Lazarus from the dead

Chapter 21 includes an eighth miracle: a catch of fish by the apostles that is so large, they cannot pull the catch into the boat. Many scholars think that Chapter 21 was added later by a different author.

Why is it that Jesus speaks so differently in John's gospel than in the synoptics?

The traditional answer is that Jesus spoke one way in public and another way in private. In the synoptic gospels, one finds the public teaching of Jesus. In John, one finds also the private teaching of Jesus. Some people claim that John was the closest disciple to Jesus, so he heard these private conversations of Jesus. (However, some of the teachings of Jesus unique to John were in public, such as in the scene of the raising of Lazarus.)

A fresco in the Spoleto Cathedral in Italy shows the miracle of the 153 fish that is included in John 21. Many scholars are inclined to believe this tale was added later by a different author.

Some contextualists propose a different answer, but a difficult one. The synoptic gospels reflect how Jesus spoke—short sayings and stories. The speeches of Jesus in the Gospel of John are not how Jesus actually spoke; rather, these speeches were created by the writer of the Gospel of John to explain the message of Jesus. The speeches of Jesus in the Gospel of John reflect the early Christian understanding of Jesus and not his actual words.

As noted, this second answer is a challenging one. Keep in mind that ancient writings did not follow modern rules about quoting and citing sources. The writer of John was trying to express what he saw as the truth about Jesus, not the actual words spoken by Jesus.

Did John the Apostle write the Gospel of John, the three Epistles of John, and the Book of Revelation?

The traditional answer is that he did. That is one of the reasons John the Apostle was depicted as a young man in many paintings. He had a long life to live in order to survive until he wrote the Book of Revelation.

Now, most biblical scholars think that John the Apostle did not write the Gospel of John, although the gospel was named for him. It was probably written by a community of his followers. The three Epistles of John, also called the Johannine epistles, were probably written by the same person but not the Apostle John nor the writer of the Gospel of John. The Book of Revelation was written by another man named John from the island of Patmos. However, this John did not write any of the earlier works.

Most biblical scholars think that the aforementioned writers—Apostle John; the writer of the Gospel of John; the writer of the Epistles of John; and John of Patmos, who wrote the Book of Revelation—were all different people. This conclusion is based on differences in writing styles and different theologies in the various writings.

What is left out of the Gospel of John?

The Gospel of John drops any details that show Jesus as weak or in need. There is no baptism of Jesus in John, although John the Baptist appears. Although Jesus is arrested in the garden in John, Jesus shows no distress or agony about what is to happen. In fact, he seems to be in control of the situation:

> Then Jesus, knowing all that was to happen to him, came forward and asked them, "For whom are you looking?" They answered, "Jesus of Nazareth." Jesus replied, "I am he." Judas, who betrayed him, was standing with them. When Jesus said to them, "I am he," they stepped back and fell to the ground.
>
> —John 18:4–6, NRSV

In the crucifixion story in the Gospel of John, there is no Simon of Cyrene to help Jesus carry the cross. Jesus needs no help. At his moment of death, Jesus does not cry out "My God, my God, why have you forsaken me?" Instead, Jesus says, "It is finished." (John 19:30)

I have heard that there are animal symbols for the various gospels. What are these symbols?

The New Testament Book of Revelation mentions four animals that stand before the throne of God in Heaven: a lion, an ox (or a calf), a man, and an eagle.

> In front of the throne was something that resembled a sea of glass like crystal. In the center and around the throne, there were four living creatures covered with eyes in front and in back.
>
> The first creature resembled a lion, the second was like a calf, the third had a face like that of a human being, and the fourth looked like an eagle in flight.
>
> The four living creatures, each of them with six wings, were covered with eyes inside and out. Day and night they do not stop exclaiming: "Holy, holy, holy is the Lord God almighty, who was, and who is, and who is to come."
>
> —Revelation 4:6–8, NABRE

The detail that the animals are covered with eyes means that the creatures are all-knowing. Later, Christians matched these four figures up with the gospels:

Christ is surrounded by the four gospel writers in the form of a winged lion, eagle, ox, and man in this architectural carving at the Church of St. Trophime in Arles, France.

- Mark, the lion
- Luke, the ox
- Matthew, a man or angel
- John, the eagle

In Christian churches that make use of art and images, one can often find similar images for the gospel writers. Sometimes, these images will be on the podium where the gospels are read.

Here is a simple way to remember the images. Mark is the lion. The Gospel of Mark starts in the desert with John the Baptist. Lions would be in the desert. Luke is the ox. The Gospel of Luke, in the first chapters, has several references to Jewish ceremonies at the Temple, where they sacrificed oxen. Matthew is the man. Matthew's gospel emphasizes the humanity of Jesus. John is the eagle. The theology of the Gospel of John soars like an eagle.

THE REST OF THE NEW TESTAMENT

What is the Book of Acts about?

Acts of the Apostles is a sequel to the Gospel of Luke and was written by the same author. Acts begins with the Ascension of Jesus. Then Pentecost follows, which is when the apostles receive the Holy Spirt.

> When the day of Pentecost had come, they were all together in one place. And suddenly from Heaven there came a sound like the rush of a violent wind, and it filled the entire house where they were sitting. Divided tongues, as of fire, appeared among them, and a tongue rested on each of them. All of them were filled with the Holy Spirit and began to speak in other languages, as the Spirit gave them ability.
>
> —Acts 2:1–4, NRSV

Many Christians see this moment as the beginning of the Christian church. The stories of Peter and Paul follow in the next chapters of Acts. Acts of the Apostles ends with Paul in Rome in chains for his faith.

What are the letters? What is an epistle?

The New Testament includes twenty letters written to different early Christian communities. "Epistle" is an older word for a letter. Paul is the author who wrote the most letters. (The epistles are described in detail in *The Handy Bible Answer Book* by Jennifer R. Prince.)

What is the Book of Revelation?

The Book of Revelation is an example of apocalyptic writing. Apocalyptic writing typically takes place in a time of crisis and is filled with weird imagery, signs, and symbols that are meant to interpret events at the time the writing was completed or in the very near future. Typically, apocalyptic writings are not predictions of the far distant future. Apocalyptic writings are usually designed to warn people that God's judgment is soon to fall on people for their wrongdoings or lack of faith.

What is the meaning of the Book of Revelation?

Christians have been arguing and disagreeing over the meaning of the Book of Revelation since it was written. In the distant past, many predictions about the future have been made based on Revelation. All of these predictions have turned out not to be true. Today, many people are making predictions about the Book of Revelation. There are so many different predictions, they cannot all be right.

Is the Book of Revelation worth reading?

Everyone should read the Book of Revelation. A careful reader will note that the meaning of the book is not obvious at all. Many people find the book both confusing and frustrating to read. It is difficult to figure out how the different scenes in the book fit together.

Reading the book and seeing that it is not an easy book to interpret should make one skeptical of people who claim to have the complete interpretation of Revelation. It should also make one skeptical of those who think the book makes predictions about the future. Read the book and make your own assessment of it.

What is the Book of Revelation about?

There is much disagreement about what the meaning of the Book of Revelation is. The most common notion is that it is a prediction of the end of the world. Many people think it describes when Jesus will return in glory. Down through the centuries, many people have believed that they lived in the End Times predicted by the Book of Revelation and were convinced that the events of their times matched the symbols in Revelation. They expected Jesus to come into their lives very soon. However, none of these predictions were accurate. Most Christians believe that the Second Coming of Jesus has not yet happened.

However, there is an entirely different way to look at the book. This view says that Revelation was written around the year 100 C.E. to Christians being persecuted in Asia Minor. (Asia Minor is modern-day Turkey.) At the time the Book of Revelation was written, there was intense persecution of Christians in this region. The Book of Revelation was written to encourage Christians, who were being harassed, imprisoned, and even killed. In other words, the book is not about the future or the present. The Book of Revelation is about the past.

A third view is that the persecution of Christians in Asia Minor at that time was actually not that severe. It was not a time of crisis for Christians, but somehow, the writer of the Book of Revelation saw it as such. He criticized Christians for not being as fanatical as himself.

Is the Book of Revelation about the Apocalypse?

The Book of Revelation was originally written in Greek. The Greek word for "revelation" is αττοκάλμψη (apokálypsis). Thus, the Apocalypse is the title for the book. Over the centuries, the word "apocalypse" has come to mean a battle between good and evil at the end of time.

Do you have any suggestions for reading the Book of Revelation?

The Appendix of this book includes a chapter-by-chapter overview of Revelation. This guide helps the reader understand the confusing imagery of Revelation.

A common interpretation about the Book of Revelation is that it forecasts the end of the world—the Apocalypse—as a result of the ultimate battle between good and evil.

SALVATION HISTORY

What is salvation history?

Salvation history is an attempt to describe the overall arc of the Bible. It asks the question: What is the story of the Bible from Genesis to Revelation? Salvation history occurs in four phases: creation, the fall, covenant, and redemption. The first two phases are based on stories in Genesis. It must be noted that one does not have to take the stories in Genesis literally to believe in God as the creator of the universe and of humans and to believe that humans by their sins have alienated themselves from God.

What is creation?

Salvation history begins with creation as described in Genesis:

> In the beginning when God created the Heavens and the earth, the earth was a formless void and darkness covered the face of the deep, while a wind from God swept over the face of the waters. Then God said, "Let there be light"; and there was light.
>
> —Genesis 1:1–3, NRSV

God creates the universe, which is good. Humans—both men and women—are created in the image of God.

What is the fall?

The first man and woman disobey God. They were forbidden to eat from the tree of the knowledge of good and evil, yet they ate from it anyway. They fall from God's grace.

They heard the sound of the Lord God walking in the garden at the time of the evening breeze, and the man and his wife hid themselves from the presence of the Lord God among the trees of the garden. But the Lord God called to the man, and said to him, "Where are you?" He said, "I heard the sound of you in the garden, and I was afraid, because I was naked; and I hid myself."

—Genesis 3:8–10, NRSV

Humans alienate themselves from God. Alienation is the nature of the human relationship to God. This story implies that before the man and woman disobeyed, they would not have hid when God walked in the garden.

What is the covenant?

God does abandon humans. He reaches out through agreements called "covenants." God made his first covenant with Noah. The second covenant is with Abraham. God promises Abraham that he will have land and descendants in response to his faith.

The descendants of Abraham grow in number, but they become enslaved in Egypt. God promises to Moses:

Therefore, say to the Israelites: I am the LORD. I will free you from the burdens of the Egyptians and will deliver you from their slavery. I will redeem you by my outstretched arm and with mighty acts of judgment. I will take you as my own people, and I will be your God....

—Exodus 6:6–7, NABRE

God next makes a covenant with Moses that is based on the Commandments. God gives the Commandments, and the Hebrews will be his people.

It was not because you were more numerous than any other people that the Lord set his heart on you and chose you—for you were the fewest of all peoples. It was because the Lord loved you and kept the oath that he swore to your ancestors, that the Lord has brought you out with a mighty hand, and redeemed you from the house of slavery, from the hand of Pharaoh king of Egypt. Know therefore that the Lord your God is God, the faithful God who maintains covenant loyalty with those who love him and keep his commandments, to a thousand generations....

—Deuteronomy 7:7–9, NRSV

Do the people live up to their part of the covenant?

No. Although the people of Israel are called to follow the commands of the Lord (the Ten Commandments and the other laws in the Torah), they continuously disobey God. The Old Testament/Hebrew Scriptures is not a success story! It is a story of continual failure on the part of the people but continual love and forgiveness by God.

Over a two-hundred-year period, starting in c. 922 B.C.E. with the division of the Kingdom of Israel into the northern Kingdom of Israel and the southern Kingdom of Judah, there were two kings. Most of the Kings received negative ratings. For example:

> In the thirty-eighth year of Azariah, king of Judah, Zechariah, son of Jeroboam, became king over Israel in Samaria for six months. He did what was evil in the LORD's sight, as his ancestors had done, and did not desist from the sins that Jeroboam, son of Nebat, had caused Israel to commit.
>
> —1 Kings 15:8–9, NABRE

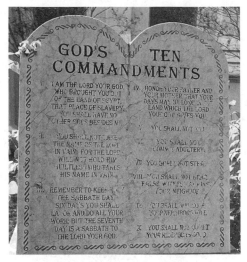

One example of a covenant is the Commandments given to Moses, which the Hebrews were supposed to follow as God's chosen people.

Does God abandon the people?

God does not abandon his people but rather sends prophets to warn them of their failure to follow God's commands. The more famous prophets are Isaiah, Jeremiah, and Ezekiel. Here are the words of Jeremiah:

> The days are surely coming, says the Lord, when I will make a new covenant with the house of Israel and the house of Judah. It will not be like the covenant that I made with their ancestors when I took them by the hand to bring them out of the land of Egypt—a covenant that they broke, though I was their husband, says the Lord. But this is the covenant that I will make with the house of Israel after those days, says the Lord: I will put my law within them, and I will write it on their hearts; and I will be their God, and they shall be my people. No longer shall they teach one another, or say to each other, "Know the Lord," for they shall all know me, from the least of them to the greatest, says the Lord; for I will forgive their iniquity, and remember their sin no more.
>
> —Jeremiah 31:31–34, NRSV

However, despite the warnings of the prophets, the people fail to follow God's commands. The people are punished by being invaded by first the Assyrians and then the Babylonians.

What are the references to harlotry by the prophets?

Often, the failure of Israel is compared to adultery and/or harlotry. In the Book of Hosea, Hosea is told by God to marry a harlot, Gomer. However, she returns to her harlotry. She is a symbol of Israel being unfaithful.

The imagery of an unfaithful spouse who commits adultery becomes a metaphor for unfaithful Israel. This metaphor has several layers of meaning. The people were unfaithful because they worshipped other gods, such as the Canaanite god Baal and his female consort Asherah. These were fertility gods. When they had sex, the world became fertile. Male followers honored these gods by going to temple harlots to have sex. It was seen as a religious act. Thus, the comparison of unfaithful Israel to a religious harlot had a double meaning.

What is redemption?

In the final phase of salvation history, God the Father sends his Son Jesus to die for human sin and redeem mankind. As Paul stated:

> For since death came through a human being, the resurrection of the dead came also through a human being. For just as in Adam all die, so too in Christ shall all be brought to life....
>
> —1 Corinthians 15:20–22, NABRE

Because the death and Resurrection of Jesus become the way to salvation, the actions of Jesus are often called the "New Covenant."

The term "Old Testament" means "Old Covenant," which is superseded by the New Covenant, or the "New Testament."

What about the Second Coming?

Some Christians add a fifth phase: the Second Coming of Jesus at the end of time. The Bible ends with the Book of Revelation promising that Jesus will come again and triumph over all evil.

The Book of Revelation ends with words "Come, Lord Jesus."

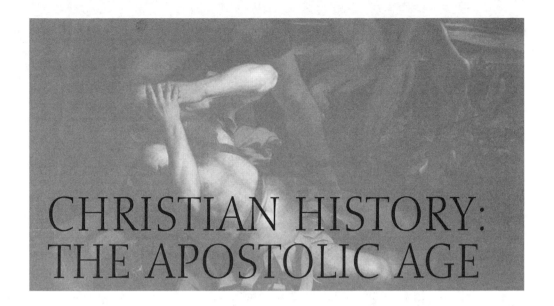

CHRISTIAN HISTORY: THE APOSTOLIC AGE

Any suggestions on exploring Christian history?

There is value in holding a generally respectful attitude to others with different positions. Keeping an open mind is a good thing to do. However, this does not mean that every belief or action has to be respected. In the following overview of Christian history, a number of examples will be given of people who believed they were acting in the name of Jesus yet did horrific things that were at variance with the message of Jesus in the gospels. Perhaps the most dramatic illustration is the First Crusade from 1095 to 1099. Christian armies brutally killed countless Muslims, Jews, and other Christians in the name of Jesus. It is acceptable to pass moral and theological judgments on some of the stories that follow. The big question is whether or not the actions and beliefs that are described are consistent with the life and teachings of Jesus. Perhaps the old bumper sticker said it best: "What Would Jesus Do?"

What are the lessons that can be learned from Christian history?

A first lesson that can be learned is that Christianity was diverse from the beginning. There was never just one way to be a Christian.

A second lesson is that almost all questions that Christians struggle with today have already been argued over. This is one of the values of studying Christian history: to see how Christians from the past dealt with these issues. The one exception would be the questions brought up by modern technology such as "Should we have video screens in church?" or "Is it moral to turn off medical equipment for a terminal patient so the person can die and stop suffering?" All the other questions of Christianity have been debated for centuries.

A third lesson is that Christian history provides a rich treasure trove to mine. There are many interesting, and sometimes heroic, women and men who struggled to live out the Christian faith in their own times. Many Christians today see these people as sources of inspiration or examples to emulate. Also, many Christian writers have left behind an immense body of writings. Many of these writings are still insightful and inspiring to modern-day Christians.

What are the periods of Christian history?

There are many ways to divide the past two thousand years of Christian history. Here is one way that will be followed in this book:

- The Apostolic Age: Jesus to the year 100
- Early Christianity: 100–800
- Christianity in the Middle Ages and the Renaissance: 800–1500
- The Protestant Reformation and the Catholic Counter-Reformation: the 1500s
- Christianity in Europe from the 1600s to the present
- Christianity in America: 1492 to the present

JESUS TO THE YEAR 100

What is the Apostolic Age?

The Apostolic Age is the period after Jesus when his followers—the Twelve Apostles, Paul, and others—began to spread Christianity throughout much of the Roman Empire and beyond. In the next centuries, Christianity would spread easily throughout the Roman Empire because of what is known as the Pax Romana, the Roman Peace. The Roman Empire had a great road system protected by Roman soldiers, so bandits were typically not a problem. Also, the Roman Navy kept the oceans free of pirates. Two languages were spoken throughout much of the Roman Empire: Greek and Latin. This made communication possible throughout an empire of many diverse peoples and languages.

However, one thing must be remembered about the Pax Romana. It was created by brutally conquering countless kingdoms, tribes, and peoples. In conquering Gaul, the area that would later become France and Belgium, the armies of Julius Caesar killed perhaps a million people.

What was the Council of Jerusalem?

The Council of Jerusalem, which met around the year 50, was the first Christian church council where leaders came together to resolve issues. Present were Simon Peter, Barnabas, Paul, and James. The central issue was whether non-Jewish converts to Christianity had to follow the Jewish Law. It was decided that they did not, so converts to Christianity did not need to be circumcised. This decision removed a significant barrier to converting Gentiles to Christianity. However, Jewish rules about not eating meat unless it was properly butchered—so that all blood was removed—were still to be followed. The council also agreed that fornication—sex outside of marriage—and idolatry were also forbidden. The Council of Jerusalem is described in Acts of the Apostles in Chapter 15. It is also described in Chapter 2 of Paul's Letter to the Galatians. (Over the years, some scholars have argued over the differences between these two versions of the Council and whether there might be inaccuracies in the description found in Acts.)

Why is Paul important?

Paul of Tarsus played a key role in the development and shaping of Christianity. He lived from about 5 B.C.E. to 67 C.E. He was the most important early missionary for Christianity, helping it to spread around the Mediterranean. He also wrote letters to Christian communities in cities such as Rome and the Greek city of Corinth. A number of these letters became part of the New Testament and are known as the Letters or Epistles of Paul. ("Epistle" is simply an older word for "letter.") It is important to note that Paul wrote his letters years before the gospels were written.

Paul played a key role in shaping Christian thought and belief. The Gospels of Matthew, Mark, and Luke describe the life and teaching of Jesus, but there is not much of an explanation of what it all means. It was Paul who worked out the meaning of Christianity in terms of Jesus dying for human sin to bring salvation to believers.

What is the story of Paul's life?

About half of Acts of the Apostles deals with the story of Paul. Originally named Saul, he was a fanatical Jew who wanted to stop the early Christian movement by persecuting the first Christians. He appeared at the stoning of Stephen, the first Christian martyr. In a dramatic event, Saul was struck from his horse and heard a voice calling to him. His conversion soon followed, and he took the name of Paul. This happened around the years 33–36 C.E. Paul then began preaching his Christian message and writing letters to various Christian communities. However, he was arrested for his faith. The latter part of Acts of the Apostles describes several trials and ends with Paul in prison in Rome. Although not described in the Book of Acts, Paul was executed in Rome for being a Christian.

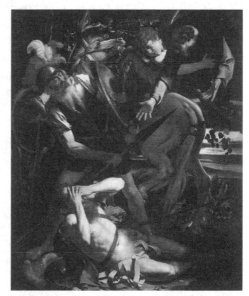

The Conversion of St. Paul by Caravaggio illustrates the dramatic story of how Saul was converted to Christianity after being struck by a bright light and hearing the voice of Jesus.

What is the story of Paul's conversion?

There are several versions of Paul's conversion. Here is the account in Acts of the Apostles:

Now as he was going along and approaching Damascus, suddenly a light from Heaven flashed around him. He fell to the ground and heard a voice saying to him, "Saul, Saul, why do you persecute me?" He asked, "Who are you, Lord?" The reply came, "I am Jesus, whom you are persecuting."

—Acts 9:3–6, NRSV (see also Acts 22:6–21 and 26:9–18)

Paul writes in his Letter to the Galatians:

You have heard, no doubt, of my earlier life in Judaism. I was violently persecuting the church of God and was trying to destroy it. I advanced in Judaism beyond many among my people of the same age, for I was far more zealous for the traditions of my ancestors. But when God, who had set me apart before I was born and called me through his grace, was pleased to reveal his Son to me, so that I might proclaim him among the Gentiles....

—Galatians 1:13–16, NRSV

One of the most famous paintings of St. Paul is Caravaggio's *Conversion of Saint Paul on the Road to Damascus*, found in the church of Santa Maria del Popolo in Rome (the church name translates as "Holy Mary of the People").

Which epistles did Paul write?

There are thirteen epistles that claim Paul as the author. However, many scholars do not think they were all actually written by Paul. This assessment is based on analyzing differences in writing styles and theological content in the various letters. Most scholars list seven as genuine letters written by Paul: First Thessalonians (c. 50 C.E.), Galatians (c. 53), First Corinthians (c. 53–54), Philippians (c. 55), Philemon (c. 55), Second Corinthians (c. 55–56), and Romans (c. 57). As for the letters Colossians and Second Thessalonians, scholars are divided on whether or not these were written by Paul. Four letters are regarded by most scholars as not written by Paul: Ephesians, First Timothy, Second Timothy, and Titus.

What does the word "Gentile" mean? Why is Paul called the "Apostle to the Gentiles"?

The word "Gentile" is a Jewish term to identify those who are not Jewish. Paul called himself the Apostle to the Gentiles (Romans 1:15, 11:13, Galatians 2:8). Jesus, his Twelve Apostles, and most of his early followers were all Jewish. As the Jewish Saul, Paul had persecuted Christians. However, after his conversion, Paul began working to convert Gentiles to Christianity. He played a key role in dropping the requirements that Christians had to follow the Jewish Law and in particular the requirement to be circumcised. As mentioned earlier, circumcision had been a barrier to attracting Gentile converts. Then, in his letters, Paul worked out the theology that rejected the older Jewish theology that salvation came from following the Law. Instead, Paul proposed salvation by faith in what Jesus did.

What is the theology of Paul?

Paul is particularly important for working out the theology of the meaning of the death and Resurrection of Jesus. After exploring the Gospels of Matthew, Mark, and Luke, a reader might still wonder, "What is the point of the death and resurrection of Jesus?" Paul worked out the meaning. He stated: "For if we believe that Jesus died and rose, so too will God, through Jesus, bring with him those who have fallen asleep" (1 Thessalonians 4:14, NABRE).

Paul's theology began with the idea that all humans have sinned and deserved to be punished for their sins. Paul rejected the idea that following the Jewish Law brought salvation. According to Paul, the Law only served to show humans how they have failed to follow God's law. The punishment for human sin would be eternal damnation after death.

The key for Paul to salvation was having faith in what Jesus did by dying and rising. According to Paul, Christians are justified by their faith in Jesus. To be justified means to be made right in the eyes of God.

> Therefore, since we are justified by faith, we have peace with God through our Lord Jesus Christ, through whom we have obtained access to this grace in which we stand; and we boast in our hope of sharing the glory of God.
>
> —Romans 5:1–2, NRSV

For Paul, Abraham was a model of faith.

Humans are redeemed and saved from eternal punishment by having faith in the death and Resurrection of Jesus. This means that those who have such faith in Jesus will be resurrected in Heaven after they die. According to Paul, Jesus died as the final sacrifice for human sin.

> For since death came through a human being, the resurrection of the dead came also through a human being. For just as in Adam all die, so too in Christ shall all be brought to life....
>
> —1 Corinthians 15:20–22, NABRE

For Paul, baptism was key:

> Do you not know that all of us who have been baptized into Christ Jesus were baptized into his death? Therefore we have been buried with him by baptism into death, so that, just as Christ was raised from the dead by the glory of the Father, so we too might walk in newness of life.
>
> —Romans 6:3–4, NRSV

According to Paul, in baptism, believers share in the death and Resurrection of Christ.

Did Paul believe in the Second Coming of Jesus?

Yes, Paul believed that Jesus would return soon:

For since we believe that Jesus died and rose again, even so, through Jesus, God will bring with him those who have died. For this we declare to you by the word of the Lord, that we who are alive, who are left until the coming of the Lord, will by no means precede those who have died. For the Lord himself, with a cry of command, with the archangel's call and with the sound of God's trumpet, will descend from Heaven, and the dead in Christ will rise first. Then we who are alive, who are left, will be caught up in the clouds together with them to meet the Lord in the air; and so we will be with the Lord forever.

—1 Thessalonians, 4:14–17, NRSV

What did Paul say about the body of Christ?

Paul saw the Christian church as the body of Christ.

As a body is one though it has many parts, and all the parts of the body, though many, are one body, so also Christ. For in one Spirit we were all baptized into one body, whether Jews or Greeks, slaves or free persons, and we were all given to drink of one Spirit.

…

Now you are Christ's body, and individually parts of it. Some people God has designated in the church to be, first, apostles; second, prophets; third, teachers; then, mighty deeds; then, gifts of healing, assistance, administration, and varieties of tongues.

—1 Corinthians 12:12–13, 27–28, NABRE

This concept is sometimes called the "mystical body."

Paul described the importance of the Lord's Supper:

The cup of blessing that we bless, is it not a participation in the blood of Christ? The bread that we break, is it not a participation in the body of Christ? Because the loaf of bread is one, we, though many, are one body, for we all partake of the one loaf.

—1 Corinthians 10:16–17, NABRE

What did Paul say about love?

One of the most famous passages of St. Paul is from his first letter to the Corinthians:

If I speak in the tongues of mortals and of angels, but do not have love, I am a noisy gong or a clanging cymbal. And if I have prophetic powers, and understand all mysteries and all knowledge, and if I have all faith, so as to remove mountains, but do not have love, I am nothing. If I give away all my possessions, and if I hand over my body so that I may boast, but do not have love, I gain nothing. Love is patient; love is kind; love is not envious or boastful or arrogant or rude. It does not insist on its own way; it is not irritable or resentful; it does not rejoice in wrongdoing, but rejoices in the truth. It bears all things, believes all things, hopes all things, endures all things. Love never ends.

—1 Corinthians 13:1–8, NRSV

This passage is often read at weddings. Paul also wrote: "And now faith, hope, and love abide, these three; and the greatest of these is love" (1 Corinthians 13:13, NRSV).

WRITING OF THE GOSPELS AND THE NEW TESTAMENT

When were the gospels written?

Most scholars think that the gospels were written in the period from about 70 C.E. to around 100 C.E., although there is no way to know for sure. One key in dating the gospels is that there is a reference in the Gospel of Mark to the destruction of the Temple by the Romans. This took place in 70 C.E., so Mark had to be written after 70 C.E. The gospel states, "As he [Jesus] came out of the temple, one of his disciples said to him, 'Look, Teacher, what large stones and what large buildings!' Then Jesus asked him, 'Do you see these great buildings? Not one stone will be left here upon another; all will be thrown down'" (Mark 13:1–2, NRSV). Not all agree with this conclusion. Some believe that this was an actual prediction by Jesus.

Is there really a forty-year gap between the death of Jesus and the writing of the first gospel?

Yes, Jesus was crucified around the year 30 and the first gospel was written after the year 70; that means there is a forty-year gap between the life of Jesus and the writing of the gospels. The teachings of Jesus were passed down orally before being written down. That means that there was time for changes, additions, and deletions. This gap has led to the ongoing debate by some over how accurately the gospels depict Jesus and how accurately they pass on the actual sayings of Jesus. However, this was an oral culture with the tradition of remembering stories and sayings fairly accurately.

A painting by Rembrandt shows the evangelist Matthew writing down the story of Jesus as told to him by an angel. There is about a forty-year gap between the death of Jesus and the best estimates of when the gospels were penned.

171

Why did they write the gospels?

Very likely, there are at least four reasons for writing the gospels. The first was that the Second Coming of Jesus, the Parousia, did not happen. The second was the death of the eyewitnesses. The third reason was that as Christianity spread throughout the Roman Empire, written accounts of the life of Jesus would be helpful for evangelization, which is the preaching of the gospels. Fourth, the gospels were helpful in fighting heresy. We know from Acts of the Apostles and the epistles of Paul that already in the first generation of Christianity, there were fights over what the correct beliefs and practices were.

Why didn't Christians write the gospels sooner?

We do not know. One possibility is that they expected Jesus to return soon and did not see a need for written accounts of Jesus. Also, many of the eyewitnesses were still around.

The gospels come first in the New Testament. Are they the oldest writings in the New Testament?

No, some of the epistles are the earliest writings. Paul wrote his letters in the middle of the first century. Interestingly, the Letter to the Philippians contains a prayer or hymn describing Jesus Christ:

> Who, though he was in the form of God,
> did not regard equality with God something to be grasped.
> Rather, he emptied himself,
> taking the form of a slave,
> coming in human likeness;
> and found human in appearance,
> he humbled himself,
> becoming obedient to death, even death on a cross.
> Because of this, God greatly exalted him
> and bestowed on him the name
> that is above every name,
> that at the name of Jesus
> every knee should bend,
> of those in Heaven and on earth and under the earth,
> and every tongue confess that
> us Christ is Lord,
> to the glory of God the Father.

> —Philippians 2:6–11, NABRE

Very possibly, this hymn was not Paul's creation, but rather, he was quoting an existing hymn. If that is the case, then this prayer might be one of the oldest examples of Christian literature.

The letters of Paul were written first. The other epistles were written over the next several decades. The gospels were written in the period from about 70 to about 100. The book Acts of the Apostles was written as a sequel to the Gospel of Luke by the same author. In fact, the book of Acts begins, "In my first account, Theophilus, I dealt with all that Jesus did and taught until the day he was taken up to Heaven having first instructed the apostles he had chosen through the Holy Spirit" (Acts 1:1–2, NABRE). The Book of Revelation was written around the year 100.

Why is the introduction to the Gospel of Luke important?

The first verses of the Gospel of Luke are one of the few times in the Bible where the writer explains what he is doing:

> Since many have undertaken to set down an orderly account of the events that have been fulfilled among us, just as they were handed on to us by those who from the beginning were eyewitnesses and servants of the word, I too decided, after investigating everything carefully from the very first, to write an orderly account for you, most excellent Theophilus, so that you may know the truth concerning the things about which you have been instructed.

—Luke 1:1–4, NRSV

No other gospel writer gives a similar introduction. Several things are interesting about this passage. By saying he is basing his gospel on what has been handed down by the eyewitnesses, the writer of Luke is admitting that he is not an eyewitness. Also, he is recognizing that others have undertaken similar narratives. Lastly, Theophilus might be some important person to whom the writing is dedicated. In the ancient world, one way to get attention to a written work was to dedicate it to someone famous or claim that someone famous wrote it. However, the name Theophilus in Greek means "one who loves God." This might be a literary device that dedicates the gospel to anyone who loves God. In the same way, a modern sportscaster might say, "Welcome, baseball fans." There is no one named "Baseball Fan."

Was Luke a physician?

The claim that Luke, the author of the gospel, was a physician is based on Paul's

St. Luke is important not only as the author of one of the four gospels but also for writing Acts, which means more material in the New Testament is the result of his pen than any other author.

letter to the Colossians: "Luke the beloved physician sends greetings" (Colossians 4:14, NABRE). This Luke, a traveling companion of Paul, is also mentioned in 2 Timothy 4:11 and Philemon 24. However, the bigger question is whether Luke, the companion of Paul, is the writer of the Gospel of Luke.

Is Luke, who is the companion of Paul, the author of the Gospel of Luke and Acts of the Apostles?

The Gospel of Luke and Acts of the Apostles were written by the same author. If Luke was a companion of Paul, it would explain why Luke could describe the journeys and preaching of Paul in such detail in Acts. However, several things are striking about the portrayal of Paul in Acts. For example, Paul's conversion is described differently than Paul's own version of it. Also, in the Gospel of Luke and in the Book of Acts, none of Paul's theology comes through, even in speeches by Paul in the Book of Acts. If Luke had known and traveled with Paul, one would expect to see more of Paul's theology in Luke's writings. Many scholars have thus concluded that Luke, the traveling companion of Paul, was not the author of the Gospel of Luke and Acts of the Apostles.

Are there any other important early Christian writings?

The *Didache* is an important Greek writing from the first century that gives us a window into Christian thought and practice. The word *didache* means "the teaching." The *Didache* is also called *The Teaching of the Twelve Apostles*. It is the oldest known Christian catechism. A catechism is a writing or book for teaching the Christian faith. The *Didache* begins: "There are two Ways, one of Life and one of Death; but there is a great difference between the two Ways."

The *Didache* covers Christian morals, the rituals of baptism and Eucharist, and Church leadership. For example, it states: "Be not prone to anger, for anger leads to murder; nor given to party spirit, nor contentious, nor quick-tempered (or, passionate); for from all these things murders are generated" (Chapter 3:2). For baptism, two options are given: immersion and pouring water on the head. The roles of prophets, bishops, and deacons are described: "Elect therefore for yourselves Bishops and Deacons worthy of the Lord, men meek, and not lovers of money, and truthful, and approved; ..." (Chapter 15:1). Regarding prophets, the *Didache* states: "But whosoever says in the spirit: 'Give me money or any other thing,' you shall not listen to him; but if he bid you to give for others that lack, let no one judge him" (Chapter 11:12).

If you are interested, you can find the entire *Didache* online. It takes about fifteen minutes to read. What is particularly interesting is that the *Didache* shows how much of what would become standard Christian practice and moral teaching was already established by the time of its writing.

CHURCH STRUCTURE

Did the early church have any kind of structure with designated leaders?

A church structure appeared very early in the Christian church. Three roles developed: bishop, presbyter, and deacon. All three terms can be found in the New Testament in the Book of Acts and in various epistles. The role of the prophet mentioned in the epistles and the *Didache* disappeared in most communities.

What is a bishop?

The word "bishop" comes from the Greek word Εττίοκοττος *(epískopos)*, which means "overseer" or "supervisor." In the Epistle of Titus, the qualifications for a bishop are described:

> For a bishop, as God's steward, must be blameless; he must not be arrogant or quick-tempered or addicted to wine or violent or greedy for gain; but he must be hospitable, a lover of goodness, prudent, upright, devout, and self-controlled. He must have a firm grasp of the word that is trustworthy in accordance with the teaching, so that he may be able both to preach with sound doctrine and to refute those who contradict it.
>
> —Titus 1:7–9, NRSV

1 Timothy 3:1–7 also describes the qualifications of a bishop:

> This saying is trustworthy: whoever aspires to the office of bishop desires a noble task. Therefore, a bishop must be irreproachable, married only once, temperate, self-controlled, decent, hospitable, able to teach, not a drunkard, not aggressive, but gentle, not contentious, not a lover of money. He must manage his own household well, keeping his children under control with perfect dignity; for if a man does not know how to manage his own household, how can he take care of the church of God? He should not be a recent convert, so that he may not become conceited and thus incur the devil's punishment. He must also have a good reputation among outsiders, so that he may not fall into disgrace, the devil's trap. (NABRE)

The English word "bishop" comes from the distortion of the sound of the original Greek word *epískopos*. However, the Greek word can be seen in the English adjective "episcopal." For example, a bishop's house could be called the "episcopal residence." The Greek word can also be found in the denomination called the Episcopalians.

What is a presbyter?

The word "presbyter" means "elder." It comes from the Greek word ττρεσβύτερος *(presbyteros)*. The term is used several times in the New Testament, for example:

They appointed presbyters for them in each church and, with prayer and fasting, commended them to the Lord in whom they had put their faith.

—Acts 13:23, NABRE (see also Acts 11:30, 15:22, 20:17, and 1 Peter 5:1)

For this reason I left you in Crete so that you might set right what remains to be done and appoint presbyters in every town, as I directed you, on condition that a man be blameless, married only once, with believing children who are not accused of licentiousness or rebellious.

—Titus 1:5–6, NABRE

Presbyters were leaders in the church. The role developed over time, and the word would eventually become the word "priest." However, many denominations do not call their ministers "priests." Instead, many churches have elders who run their congregations. Obviously, the word "presbyter" shows up in the name of the denomination the "Presbyterians."

Initially, a bishop served the entire Christian community and led all the services because Christian communities were small. In time, as the communities grew, a bishop would be the local head in a city assisted by presbyters who did the services for the different congregations.

What is a deacon?

The role of a deacon appeared in the earliest days of Christianity when men were specially chosen for duties of service to the Christian community. The English word "deacon" comes from the Greek word διάκονος *(diákonos)*. The Book of Acts describes the origin of the role of the deacon:

And the twelve called together the whole community of the disciples and said, "It is not right that we should neglect the word of God in order to wait at tables. Therefore, friends, select from among yourselves seven men of good standing, full of the Spirit and of wisdom, whom we may appoint to this task, while we, for our part, will devote ourselves to prayer and to serving the word."

—Acts 6:2–4, NRSV

The requirements to be a deacon are described in the epistle 1 Timothy:

Deacons likewise must be serious, not double-tongued, not indulging in much wine, not greedy for money; they must hold fast to the mystery of the faith with a clear conscience. And let them first be tested; then, if they prove themselves blameless, let them serve as deacons. Women likewise must be serious, not slanderers, but temperate, faithful in all things. Let deacons be married only once, and let them manage their children and their households well; for those who serve well as deacons gain a good standing for themselves and great boldness in the faith that is in Christ Jesus.

—1 Timothy 3:8–13, NRSV

St. Stephen was one of the first deacons in the Church, and he was also the first martyr, being stoned for his faith. Above is the site, preserved at the Greek Orthodox Church of St. Stephen in the Kidron Valley near Jerusalem, where the stoning is said to have happened.

There is some uncertainty over the reference to women in the above passage. Does this mean that women served as deacons, or does it refer to the wives of male deacons?

In the next centuries, the role of these three positions—bishop, presbyter, and deacon—would evolve and change. Today among the countless Christian groups are many different ideas and disagreements between Christians about these roles.

Who was St. Stephen?

The story of Stephen is described in Acts of the Apostles in Chapters 6 and 7. Stephen was one of the first deacons chosen to help the apostles in their work. At the time, there was tension between Jewish officials and the growing Christian movement. Stephen was taken before the Jewish High Council, the Sanhedrin, where he gave a long discourse on the history of Israel starting with Abraham, then describing Moses, and ending with the Temple of Solomon. He then gave a stinging criticism of the Sanhedrin. Next, Stephen described a vision where he saw Jesus standing at the right hand of God the Father. Infuriated, the members of the High Council took Stephen outside the city and stoned him to death. Stoning was the penalty of the time for anyone uttering blasphemy, which is the crime of speaking something that is offensive to God. Present at the stoning was Saul.

How was Christianity spread?

Christianity began spreading throughout the Roman Empire. As stated earlier, the excellent road system of the Romans, safety when sailing the seas, and common languages made possible the spread of Christianity in the Empire. A further impetus was the disasters of the Jewish rebellion in Jerusalem and its being crushed by the Romans. The numerous journeys of Paul were also particularly important. (Go online and pull up a map of Paul's journeys to get a feel for his extensive travels. However, keep in mind that we cannot precisely pin down where he went in each different journey.) Christianity also spread beyond the Roman Empire, including along the Silk Road trade routes into India and eventually into China.

Stephen is the first Christian martyr or saint. He is often called Stephen the Protomartyr. The prefix "proto" means "the first." Some Christians give him the title "saint," while many do not.

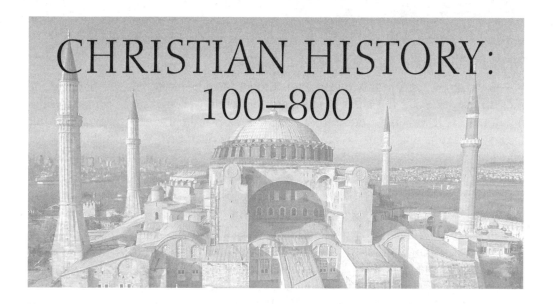

CHRISTIAN HISTORY: 100–800

Do we know much about early Christianity?

There is much we do not know about the early period of Christianity and much we do know. For example, we know of a number of important early Christian writers. Many of their writings have survived and can be found and read online. Here are eight of the more important early Christian writers:

- Ignatius (c. 35–c. 107) was bishop of Antioch, Syria. His six letters survived.

- Polycarp (69–155) was bishop of Smyrna in Asia Minor (modern-day Turkey). He wrote *Polycarp's Letter to the Philippians*.

- Justin Martyr (100–165). Most of his writings have been lost. However, his *First Apology*, *Second Apology*, and *Dialogue with Trypho* survived.

- Irenaeus (d. c. 202) was bishop of Lugdunum, part of the Roman Empire (now Lyon, France). His most important work was *Against Heresies*.

- Origen (c. 184–c. 253). A brilliant writer and biblical scholar, Origen wrote extensively on many topics related to Christianity. However, because some of his views were controversial, his writers were not copied by later generations, and most of his writings have been lost.

- Lactantius (c. 250–c. 325). His most important writing is the *Divine Institutes*.

- Tertullian (c. 155–c 240) lived in Carthage in North Africa. Tertullian is called "the father of Latin Christianity." He created the term "Trinity." He believed that persecutions of Christians showed their courage; in the end, rather than discouraging people from becoming Christian, the act led to more Christians. As Tertullian said, "The blood of martyrs is seed."

- Eusebius (c. 260–c. 339) lived in Caesarea (modern-day Israel). He wrote *History of the Church*, the first history of Christianity.

What don't we know about early Christianity?

We do not know what ordinary Christians thought and believed. It turns out that for most of history, we do not know the thoughts of ordinary people since ordinary people did not write. It was only around the 1700s that many ordinary people started writing letters and expressing their thoughts, so for the American Civil War (1861–1865), we know much about the thoughts of common soldiers because so many of their letters have survived, but in the early centuries of Christianity, ordinary people did not write, so we know very little about them.

How uniform was early Christianity?

The early Christian church was incredibly diverse with little uniformity. Christianity spread rapidly and countless Christian communities sprang up, yet there was limited communication between various groups and often little or no coordination. As a result, many different kinds of Christians existed with often very diverse views. As the later centuries passed, church organizations evolved and gained more control so that much of this diversity disappeared; however, it was there in the early centuries.

What are the different forms of Christianity?

As Christianity spread throughout the Roman Empire, various styles developed. Early on, a Latin style and a Greek style developed. The Latin form of this early period is often known as Western Christianity because it developed in Western Europe. The Greek form is known as Eastern Christianity or Orthodox Christianity. Eventually, the two forms would split in 1054 to become the Roman Catholic Church and the Orthodox Christian Church. Today, one part of Orthodox Christianity is called the Greek Orthodox Church.

There was also a third form of Jewish Christians who believed in Jesus yet retained many Jewish beliefs and customs. The Ebionites were one such group, and the Nazarenes were another. There is much that is not known about the Jewish Christian movement. This third branch of Christianity was often attacked by leaders of other Christian Churches and it disappeared for various reasons, including the later rise of Islam.

ROMAN PERSECUTIONS

Were Christians persecuted by the Romans?

Christianity spread rapidly throughout the Roman Empire. The general attitude of the Romans was to be tolerant of different religions as long as people made some attempt to honor the Roman gods and remain loyal to Rome. Jews were tolerated in the Roman Empire even though they would not honor the Roman gods. However, as time passed and Christians became more numerous, there were periodic attempts to suppress Christians that are called "persecutions."

This 1876 painting by Henryk Siemiradski shows one of the more monstrous forms of Christian persecution by the Roman emperor Nero, who liked to tie up Christians to posts and light them up as "Christian candlesticks."

The word "persecute" means to harass or mistreat people because of their religion or beliefs. Sometimes persecution can lead to violence, imprisonment, and even killing people for their religions. The word "persecute" is different from the word "prosecute," which is to take legal action against someone, so for example, a prosecuting attorney takes legal action to bring a criminal to trial to be punished. Sadly, religious persecution continues today. Often, it goes hand in hand with ethnic persecution.

Why were Christians hated by the Romans?

As is typical in periods of hatred toward other groups, the hatred is often based on misinformation. Christians would not eat meat that was sacrificed to the Roman gods. They would also not make offerings to statues of Roman gods and to statues of the Roman emperors as gods. To the Romans, these seemed to be actions of political disloyalty. Christians often avoided the theater, religious festivals, and various games—all of which included religious aspects. Many Christians were pacifists and refused to join the Army. As a result, many Christians were seen as unpatriotic and disloyal to the Roman Empire.

Christians were seen as "haters of humanity" and antisocial for not participating in social activities. They were also accused of being atheists because they only worshiped one God, and because in their services they talked about loving one another and eating the bread, which is the body of Christ, they were falsely accused of being sexually immoral and cannibals.

In the first three centuries of Christianity, there were frequent but sporadic persecutions of Christians. The severity of the persecutions depended on whether local leaders wanted to go after Christians or not. The biggest persecution was under the Roman

181

Emperor Diocletian. It started in 303 and lasted for ten years. A number of Christians died for their faith as martyrs and became saints: for example, Ignatius of Antioch, Polycarp, Perpetua, and Felicity.

Because of persecution and anti-Christian attitudes, a number of early Christian writers, such as Justin and Tertullian, became apologists, writing to defend the Christian faith against its many critics.

Who are the better-known emperors who persecuted Christians?

Four emperors are important. Nero (37–68) was the first one to persecute Christians. Marcus Aurelius (121–180) also persecuted Christians. However, he is also known for writing his important book of Stoic philosophy, called the *Meditations*.

Decius (201–251) passed an edict in 250 demanding that everyone perform a sacrifice to the Roman gods and for the emperor's well-being. Many Christians refused to do this. It is not known how many Christians were put to death for refusing to offer the sacrifice; however, several prominent Christian leaders, such as Pope Fabian, were killed. The severest persecution under Diocletian (244–312) was known as the Great Persecution. This was the last persecution because the next emperor, Constantine, legalized Christianity.

Who were the Christian martyrs?

A martyr is someone who is killed for his or her religious faith. Often, a martyr is killed after refusing to renounce his or her faith. The word "martyr" comes from the Greek word for "witness." Countless Christians were martyred in the first centuries. However, keep in mind that there are also martyrs in other religious faiths.

Although the names of most early Christian martyrs have been lost, the names of many are remembered and honored by later generations such as Polycarp of Smyrna, Justin Martyr, Perpetua and Felicity, St. Sebastian, and St. Valentine.

If St. Valentine was a Christian martyr, what does he have to do with sending cards and flowers on St. Valentine's Day?

Nothing. There was a Christian martyr named Valentine of Terni who died in the third century and was later honored as a saint and given the feast day of February 14. Nothing is known about him. Making

Some of the bones of the third-century saint Valentine are kept at the church of Santa Maria in Cosmedin, Rome. While many believe St. Valentine's Day is named after this Christian saint, there were actually a number of saints by this name; also, the holiday is more closely based on Roman customs, including the mythology of Cupid.

it even more confusing is that almost a dozen men named Valentine were also honored as saints. The tradition of sending love letters, cards, and gifts on St. Valentine's Day developed in the last several centuries and has nothing to do with the original saint. In fact, St. Valentine's Day is more influenced by Roman mythology, in which the god Cupid shoots arrows that cause people to fall in love.

Were Christians fed to the lions at the Coliseum in Rome?

Although a few Christians may have been executed as criminals at the Coliseum, most executed Christians were killed at the Circus Maximus, a horse racetrack nearby. (The word "coliseum" can also be spelled as "colosseum.") A few of the Christian martyrs may have been fed to lions, but most were not. Also, it is now recognized that early Christians exaggerated the number of martyrs who died at the hand of the Romans. There were far fewer Christians martyred by the Romans than most people imagine.

EMPEROR CONSTANTINE

Who was Constantine, and why was he important?

Constantine, who lived from about 272 to 337, had little education but was a valiant soldier. His father was emperor of part of the Roman Empire. When his father died, the army proclaimed Constantine the new emperor. Constantine had a number of rivals for the position. He defeated all of them, although he killed several relatives in the process.

A key event for Constantine was a battle at the Milvian Bridge in what today is Italy. According to the legend, he had a vision of a cross in the sky with the words "In This Sign Conquer." He became a Christian, his army won, and Constantine became emperor.

Constantine is important for his Edict of Toleration in 313 C.E., which legalized Christianity in the Roman Empire. The Edict was a very important turning point for Christians in the Roman Empire. Christianity moved from being illegal and persecuted to becoming legal. In the decades after Constantine, Christianity became the official religion, and Christians would begin persecuting non-Christians.

Constantine moved his capital from Rome to Byzantium. Today, the area is the country of Turkey. He renamed his capital city after himself: Constantinople, which means "Constantine's City." (In 1453 the Ottoman Turks conquered the city and started using the Greek name for the city, Istanbul, which means "the city.")

What else did Constantine do to shape Christianity?

In 325, Constantine called leading bishops to the Council of Nicaea (today the location, the city of Nicaea, is in modern Turkey) to settle the growing dispute over the nature of Jesus. Constantine had hoped that Christianity would be the glue to hold together his empire with all of its diverse peoples. However, the disputes over Jesus were creating great divisions. Constantine wanted the bishops to settle the dispute. The bishops cre-

The painting *The Emblem of Christ Appearing to Constantine* (1622) is artist Peter Paul Rubens' interpretation of Emperor Constantine's conversion to Christianity when his vision of a cross converted him, allowing him to then defeat his opponents. Historians have long said that Constantine adopted Christianity as a way to unite his subjects and keep power.

ated the Nicene Creed, a statement of the core beliefs of Christianity. However, the fighting over the nature of Jesus would go on for several centuries.

Historians debate over whether Constantine was a good Christian or not. He rarely attended services, and he surrounded himself with non-Christian philosophers. In his letters to bishops, he cared little for theology, though he suppressed religious dissent for political reasons. He probably supported Christianity because he thought it would purify Roman morals and unify the empire. During his reign, the Christian church in some areas became wealthy.

Lastly, Constantine was baptized on his deathbed. However, this was not unusual. At this time in Christian history, there was no ritual of confession. When you were baptized, all your sins were taken away. However, if you committed later sins, they could not be forgiven. As a result, many people delayed baptism for as long as possible. Later, the ritual of confession would develop to solve the problem of later sins committed by baptized people.

What is the Nicene Creed?

The Nicene Creed is a very important statement of Christian faith. It was created at the Council of Nicaea in the year 325 C.E. Many Christians recite the Creed today as a summary of their Christian beliefs. (The Nicene Creed was explored in great detail in "Beliefs about Jesus.")

Were there other church councils after the Council of Nicaea in 325?

The Council of Nicea is counted as the first ecumenical council. Catholics count twenty-one of these. The earlier Council of Jerusalem is not included in this list. Here are the first seven. The major task of these councils was to define the nature of Jesus and reject various heresies. The councils are named for the city where they were held.

Church Councils

Year	Council
325	Nicaea
381	Constantinople I
431	Ephesus (in modern-day Turkey): This council rejected the heresy of Nestorianism that held that Mary was not the Mother of God. The council insisted that Mary was the Mother of God and used the title for Mary of Theotokos: the bearer of God.
451	Chalcedon (in modern-day Turkey near Istanbul)
553	Constantinople II
680–681	Constantinople III
787	Nicaea II: This council answered the bitter fight over the use of religious images by Christians. The council rejected the Iconoclasts, who wanted to destroy religious images.

I have heard of another creed: the Apostle's Creed. What is that?

The Apostle's Creed is an early Christian statement of faith. Here is the Creed:

I believe in God, the Father Almighty, Creator of Heaven and earth; and in Jesus Christ, His only Son, our Lord: who was conceived by the Holy Spirit, born of the Virgin Mary; suffered under Pontius Pilate, was crucified, died and was buried.

He descended into Hell; the third day He rose again from the dead; He ascended into Heaven, is seated at the right hand of God the Father Almighty; from thence He shall come to judge the living and the dead.

I believe in the Holy Spirit, the holy catholic Church, the communion of Saints, the forgiveness of sins, the resurrection of the body, and life everlasting. Amen.

The Apostle's Creed took its present form later than the Nicene Creed, probably in the 700s C.E.

Why does the Apostle's Creed say about Jesus that "He descended into Hell"?

In Christian thought, salvation comes from the death and Resurrection of Jesus. After the death and Resurrection, Christian believers will go to Heaven when they die. What happens to those holy people, such as Abraham and Moses, who died before Jesus? The Apostle's Creed expresses the idea that between his death on the cross and Resurrection, Jesus went into Hell to rescue all the holy people who had already died. The scene is sometimes called "The Harrowing of Hell." The word "harrow" is not a reference to a farm implement; rather, it means to ravish or despoil.

Who were the emperors who played important roles in Christianity becoming the dominant religion in the Roman Empire?

Constantine, Theodosius I, and Justinian I. Put simply, Constantine legalized Christianity, Theodosius (347–395) made it the official religion of the Roman Empire, and Justinian persecuted those who were not Christian. This last part is ironic and tragic since Christians themselves were persecuted before the time of Constantine.

EMPEROR JUSTINIAN AND THE HAGIA SOPHIA

Who was Emperor Justinian?

Justinian I (c. 482–565) was the Eastern Roman emperor who ruled from the city of Constantinople, where he built the magnificent basilica, the Hagia Sophia (a basilica is a large church or cathedral). Justinian created a uniform code of laws, called the *Corpus Juris Civilis* (the Body of Civil Laws). Theodora, the wife of Justinian, was very influential. Justinian supported the Church, giving it much legal support, and he also fought against heretics. He also had great control over the Church because he wanted religious conformity to help create unity in his empire. The branch of Christianity under his control would eventually be called Orthodox Christianity. Justinian pushed for religious conformity, persecuted those practicing the older Roman pagan religion and Greek philosophy, and restricted the rights of Jews. (Do an online image search for "Justinian and Theodora" to see mosaic images of the emperor and his wife.)

What are mosaics?

Mosaics are artwork done with brightly colored pieces of glass cemented onto a wall. Sometimes clear glass is used with a very thin layer of gold leaf behind it. (Search online for "mosaics." Then search for "Ravenna mosaics.")

The architecturally gorgeous Hagia Sophia basilica in Instanbul, Turkey, was constructed by order of Justinian I from 532 to 537.

What are Ravenna mosaics?

Ravenna is a city in northern Italy just south of Venice. In the 400s, it served as the capital city of the Roman Empire. Eight Christian buildings, churches, and mausoleums were built in the 400s and 500s with magnificent mosaics.

What is the Hagia Sophia?

The Hagia Sophia was built as a magnificent Orthodox Christian church with a massive dome. The words "Hagia Sophia" mean "holy wisdom." Built by Emperor Justinian I, it was completed in the year 537 C.E. For a thousand years, it was the largest church in the world. It stands today in the city of Istanbul in modern Turkey, although at the time it was built, the city was called Constantinople. In the year 1453, the region was conquered by the Muslim Ottoman Turks, and the Hagia Sophia was converted into a mosque. Four towers, called minarets, were added. Five times a day, a man called a muezzin would go to the top of each tower to call Muslims to prayer. In 1935, the Hagia Sophia became a museum and is visited by many tourists each year. (Do an online image search to see pictures of the Hagia Sophia.)

AUGUSTINE

Who was Augustine? Why was Augustine so important?

Augustine, who lived from 354 to 430 in North Africa, was one of the first Christian writers to think out all the dimensions of Christianity. A very prolific writer, he covered so much that later generations would look back to him and cite his writings to support their views. He became one of the most important authorities on Christian teachings—second, for many, only to the Bible.

Augustine had great influence on the Roman Catholic Church but also on Protestant thinkers such as Martin Luther and John Calvin, who read Augustine.

How do you pronounce the name of Augustine?

Roman Catholics call him a saint and tend to put the accent on the first syllable of his name and pronounce the last syllable as "teen," which is how most people pronounce the city named after him: St. Augustine, Florida. Protestants tend to put the accent on the second syllable and pronounce the last syllable as "tin." Many Protestants also drop the saint title.

If Augustine was from Africa, would he have had black skin?

Augustine was from the town of Hippo in North Africa, an area that had been settled by peoples from the Mediterranean. He would have had light skin, typical of people around the Mediterranean today.

What is the *Confessions* of Augustine?

This is Augustine's most famous writing. The first nine chapters are the most readable part, where Augustine describes his early life and his conversion to Christianity. Many readers find the second half a difficult read because it is a theological exploration that says little about Augustine's life.

Two stories from the *Confessions* are particularly well known. The first is when Augustine as a young man goes with some of his friends and steals pears from a tree. Here is Augustine's account:

> There was a pear tree close to our own vineyard, heavily laden with fruit, which was not tempting either for its color or for its flavor. Late one night—having prolonged our games in the streets until then, as our bad habit was—a group of young scoundrels, and I among them, went to shake and rob this tree. We carried off a huge load of pears, not to eat ourselves, but to dump out to the hogs, after barely tasting some of them ourselves. Doing this pleased us all the more because it was forbidden. Such was my heart, O God, such was my heart—which thou didst pity even in that bottomless pit. Behold, now let my heart confess to thee what it was seeking there, when I was being gratuitously wanton, having no inducement to evil but the evil itself. It was foul, and I loved it.

—Augustine, *Confessions,* Book II, 9

Augustine looked back on this incident and saw it as an example of doing wrong just for the thrill of doing wrong. For Augustine, it illustrated the inmate human desires that lead us to do bad or immoral things.

The second memorable story is the moment of conversion for Augustine. He hears a voice say, "Take up and read," and Augustine opens the Bible at random:

I was saying these things and weeping in the most bitter contrition of my heart, when suddenly I heard the voice of a boy or a girl I know not which—coming from the neighboring house, chanting over and over again, "Pick it up, read it; pick it up, read it." Immediately I ceased weeping and began most earnestly to think whether it was usual for children in some kind of game to sing such a song, but I could not remember ever having heard the like. So, damming the torrent of my tears, I got to my feet, for I could not but think that this was a divine command to open the Bible and read the first passage I should light upon....

So I quickly returned to the bench where Alypius was sitting, for there I had put down the apostle's book when I had left there. I snatched it up, opened it, and in silence read the paragraph on which my eyes first fell: "Not in rioting and drunkenness, not in chambering and wantonness, not in strife and envying, but put on the Lord Jesus Christ, and make no provision for the flesh to fulfill the lusts thereof." I wanted to read no further, nor did I need to. For instantly, as the sentence ended, there was infused in my heart something like the light of full certainty and all the gloom of doubt vanished away.

—Augustine, *Confessions,* Book VIII, 29

The Conversion of St. Augustine by Fra Angelico, c. 1430–1435. It portrays Augustine's feelings of guilt, his repentance, and his conversion to Christianity.

189

The Bible passage that Augustine read was from St. Paul's letter to the Romans, 13:13. The words "chambering and wantonness" are often translated as "orgies and drunkenness." Augustine read this passage—which called for putting away one's immoral ways and accepting Jesus—as applying directly to him.

Why did Augustine give his book the title the *Confessions*?

Augustine gave his book the Latin title *Confessiones*. However, translating the title into English as the *Confessions* is a bit misleading. Although the book does include Augustine confessing some of his wrongdoings, a better translation of the Latin title *Confessiones* would be *The Testimony* or perhaps *My Testimony*. Augustine gives his testimony of how he came to the Christian faith.

What are other important writings by Augustine?

The important writings of Augustine include *On Christian Doctrine*, *The Enchiridion* (The Manual), *On the Trinity,* and *The City of God*. Augustine wrote extensively on many things. His collected works are the size of a set of encyclopedias.

One thing to keep in mind when reading Augustine is the style of his writing. Often, rather than giving definitive answers, Augustine is thinking out questions and exploring different possible answers. Much of his writing is speculation rather than final answers to questions about faith.

THE BATTLE AGAINST HERESY

Why study heresies since they are considered by many Christians to be wrong views?

It is important to know about several heresies to better understand the period of Early Christianity. The Council of Nicaea was called to define Christian teachings about Jesus. The resulting creed defined Christian belief but also rejected many heresies. "Heresy" was defined early as wrong belief. Early Christianity was shaped by the fights against heresy. Four heresies were particularly important: Gnosticism, Marcionism, Monophysitism, and Arianism. Furthermore, understanding these various heresies often helps one understand the orthodox Christian beliefs.

What is the heresy of Gnosticism?

The word "Gnosticism" comes from the Greek word for knowledge: *gnosis*. The "g" is silent. So, Gnosticism sounds like "NAHS-ti-cis-em," like "knowledge" sounds like "NAH-ledge." A believer in Gnosticism is called a Gnostic.

At the time of the Nicene Creed in 325, there were several different types of Gnosticism: a generic Gnosticism, a Jewish version of Gnosticism, and a Christian version of

Gnosticism. Christian Gnosticism held the belief that Jesus came to bring secret knowledge for salvation. (Most Christians believe that Christian Gnosticism is heresy because there is nothing secret about the message of Jesus and salvation comes from the death and Resurrection of Jesus, not a secret message that he left with his followers.)

Gnostics also had different ideas about God and the creation of the earth. Gnostics were troubled by the idea that an all-perfect God could create the world around us that is so flawed and so filled with sickness and death and change. They concluded that God did not create the physical world around us. Instead, Gnostics believed in a figure called the Demiurge, a lesser and imperfect being who created the flawed physical world around us. They believed that God created the spiritual realm, which was perfect, and the Demiurge created the physical world.

Can you tell me more about Gnosticism?

Gnostics believed that the physical realm was evil and only the spiritual realm was good. The physical world is made of disease, decay, suffering, pain, and death. The physical world is also constantly changing. The spiritual realm is good because it is unchanging and not filled with disease, decay, suffering, pain, and death.

Gnostics believed that trapped within each person's physical body is a divine spark, a part of the spiritual realm. The goal therefore was to free this divine spark from the physical body.

A few Gnostics took this to its logical conclusion that the best way to free one's inner divine spark from the body was to kill oneself. However, Gnostics also believed that doing violence to oneself was wrong; therefore, the only option was starvation. Some Gnostics did starve themselves to death to free their divine inner spark from their corrupt physical bodies. However, starvation is not an easy way to die, and this never became very popular.

Other Gnostics chose to live an ascetic life with few possessions and few attachments. However, some Gnostics took the opposite approach: since only the spiritual was good, it did not matter what one did with the physical body. Thus, some Gnostics pursued physical pleasures, believing the physical world to be irrelevant to the spiritual realm.

Many Gnostics had different views about Jesus. Since the material, physical world is bad, Jesus—a spiritual being—could never have had a real body. Thus, Gnostics denied the Incarnation. Gnostics denied the idea that Jesus was God in human flesh.

One group of Gnostics said that although Jesus appeared to have a human body, this was only an illusion. This branch of Gnosticism is called "Docetism." The term "docetism" comes from the Greek work for "to seem." Also, since Jesus did not have a human body, he could not die on the cross and rise from the dead. These Gnostics believed that the death of Jesus on the cross was an illusion that was proved by the fact that later Jesus appeared alive. He did not die and rise; it was only an illusion.

What is the heresy of Marcionism?

Marcionism is a heresy named for Marcion, who was a wealthy ship owner in Rome who died in the year 160. He founded religious communities throughout the Roman Empire. He said that Christianity was entirely a gospel of love, so the old laws of the Old Testament no longer applied. Marcion rejected the Old Testament and its image of God. (For example, many people find the actions of God in the Book of Joshua to be very harsh.) Marcion saw the Old Testament image of God to be at odds with the teachings of Jesus.

Gnosticism has a long history in Christianity, and it is still around today. Certain aspects of Christian Science teachings are similar to what the Gnostics taught.

What are the heresies of Arianism and Monophysitism?

According to the Nicene Creed, in Jesus, God has become human. This is the Christian belief in the Incarnation. Jesus is both God and man, or to put it another way: Jesus is both divine and human; or yet another way: Jesus has both a divine nature and a human nature. Two heresies deny one or the other nature: Arianism and Monophysitism.

Arianism was started by Arius (c. 256–336), who lived in Alexandria, Egypt. Arius denied the divinity of Jesus. He said that Jesus was not God. Jesus was created by God, but he was not God.

Monophysitism denied the humanity of Jesus. Jesus had only one nature: he was only divine. The word for nature in Greek is *physis*. So, Jesus had only one (mono) nature. The Nicene Creed rejected both of these heresies.

Who were the Iconoclasts?

In the Byzantine Christian world, around Constantinople in the 700s, there was a big fight over the use of religious images. Some Christians, taking the second Commandment seriously—"Thou shall have no graven images before me"—rejected any use of statues, paintings, and mosaics depicting God, angels, and holy people. Some went so far as to smash images and paintings. Since the paintings were often called icons, these image breakers were called "iconoclasts." Their movement was called "iconoclasm." Those who defended the use of images were called "iconodules." The Council of Nicaea II rejected iconoclasm and defended the veneration of religious images.

Iconoclasm would flare up again in the Byzantine world in the 800s. It would reappear in the Protestant Reformation of the 1500s as some groups destroyed images and churches. Today, Christians are divided on the issue. Some churches have statues, paintings, and stained glass windows depicting religious figures. Other Christian churches have no such decoration or only a simple, wooden cross.

What are religious icons?

In the Greek Christian world, the practice developed of praying to images of Jesus, Mary, and saints. These are painted in a special style. Do an online image search for "religious icons" to see the stylized way that icon images are painted. Images of Mary holding the baby Jesus and of Jesus are particularly popular. The veneration of icons is still an important part of the Christian Orthodox tradition. The paintings are understood as a window into the sacred world. However, it is understood that one is not worshipping the wood or the paint.

MONASTICISM

What is monasticism?

Monasticism is the life of monks living in monasteries devoting their lives to prayer.

Did Christians invent monasticism?

Christians did not invent monasticism. Buddhist monks had been living the monastic life for five hundred years before Jesus. The monastic tradition in Hinduism is even older.

Why was monasticism important?

Although monks and monasteries are few and far between today, for most of Christian history, monasteries were extremely important. In the Middle Ages, there were thousands of monasteries all across Europe from small ones of a dozen or so men to enormous monasteries with hundreds of men. Monasteries served both religious and societal functions in their time. For example, in many families, the eldest son would alone inherit the family farm because if the land were divided among all the sons, the pieces each would be too small to farm. After the eldest son got the family land, what would happen to the younger sons? One answer was to send them to monasteries.

What is the monastic life?

To understand the monastic life, one must start by realizing that this tradition came from a view of God as harsh and demanding. The culture that supported the monastic life saw the Christian life as very difficult. If one wanted to follow Christ completely, then one had to withdraw from ordinary life and devote oneself to prayer.

Also, keep in mind that effective birth control is a modern reality, so becoming celibate and giving up sex freed one from all the demands of having and raising children.

This freed one up to follow God completely. It is sometimes difficult for modern people to appreciate the reasons for celibacy.

Monks were not married. "Mono" in Greek means "one" and from this comes the word "monk." Although monks were alone in terms of not being married, they usually lived in communities with other monks.

A monk lives in a "monastery." A monk lives a "monastic" life. The head of a monastery is called the "abbot." This comes from the word for father, "abba." Sometimes, a monastery is called an "abbey."

Women who wanted to follow the monastic life lived in monasteries for women called "convents." They were called "nuns." The head of a convent was called "Mother Superior." She might also be called an "abbess." For both men in monasteries and women in convents, they live a life closed off from the outside world in what is called a "cloister."

In London many centuries ago, there was an abbey. The road in front of it was called Abbey Road. The recording studio for the Beatles was on Abbey Road, so the Beatles named one of their famous albums *Abbey Road*.

What did the monks do?

The most important duty of the monks and sisters in convents was to pray. The sequence of prayers was called the Divine Office. Eight times during the day and night, monks and nuns went to the chapel to pray with their community. Two passages from Psalm 119 were cited for determining the number of times to pray during a twenty-four-hour period: "At midnight I rise to praise you because of your righteous judgments" (v. 62); and "Seven times a day I praise you because your judgments are righteous" (v. 164, NABRE).

The traditional times of prayer were as follows (the words "Prime," "Terce," "Sext," and "None" are based on the Latin words for first, third, sixth, and ninth):

- Prayer at midnight, called Matins, Vigils, Nocturns, or the Night Office. (The French word *matin* means "morning.")
- Lauds or Dawn Prayer at Dawn, or 3 A.M. ("Lauds" is based on the Latin word for praise.)

How did one become a monk?

To become a monk, a man took three vows. (A vow is a promise.) The three vows were celibacy (no marriage, no sex), poverty (to not own anything), and obedience (to obey the abbot). In a monastery, most men were not priests and called each other "brother." A few became priests, and they would be called "father."

Nuns took the same vows, although the first vow was called "chastity." The nuns called each other "sister," although the leader of the convent was often called "mother."

- Prime or Early Morning Prayer at the First Hour, typically at 6 A.M.
- Terce or Mid-Morning Prayer at the Third Hour, typically at 9 A.M.
- Sext or Midday Prayer at the Sixth Hour, typically at 12 noon.
- None or Mid-Afternoon Prayer at the Ninth Hour, typically at 3 P.M.
- Vespers or Evening Prayer, typically at 6 P.M.
- Compline or Night Prayer, typically at 9 P.M.

The core prayers of the Divine Office were the Psalms. At each prayer time, one or more of the Psalms was chanted. Often, they were chanted in choir style with one side of the chapel or church saying one line of the psalm and the next line chanted by the other side of the chapel. It went back and forth from one side to the next until the psalm was completed.

The Canticle of Zachariah, also called the Benedictus, from the Gospel of Luke was usually chanted during morning prayers, and the Canticle of Mary, called the Magnificat, also from the Gospel of Luke, was chanted at Vespers. Typically, the Psalms would be chanted as music. The most common style of monastic music was called the Gregorian Chant.

BENEDICT

Why is Benedict important?

Benedict, often called St. Benedict, was born in 480 and died in either 543 or 547 C.E. He set up a number of monasteries in Italy. Most importantly, he wrote a guidebook on being a monk called the *Rule of St. Benedict*. His rule book became so influential that he is often called the Founder of Western Monasticism. One group of monks, called the Order of St. Benedict, is still around today.

However, Benedict did not invent Christian monasticism. Early Christian men and women living the monastic life existed in the second century. Famous monks such as St. Antony and the Desert Fathers in Egypt lived in the third and fourth centuries. By the time of Benedict, there were many Christian monasteries and a long history of Christian monasticism.

A 1926 portrait of St. Benedict by artist Herman Nieg. Benedict literally wrote the book on how to be a Christian monk.

195

The *Rule of St. Benedict* is important because it became so influential. In writing his rule, Benedict tried to find a middle way of moderation. He wanted to avoid practices that were overzealous or fanatical, such as demands for extreme fasting. The problem with such practices is that they are very hard to maintain over the long term. On the other hand, Benedict wanted to avoid a monastic life that was too easy and that would encourage laziness and invite distractions from a life of prayer.

The motto of St. Benedict was "Ora and Labora," which means "pray and work." Monks were required to spend most of their time in prayer either in community or by themselves, yet monks were also required to work to support themselves. Initially, Benedict imagined monks supporting themselves through manual labor and farm work. He wanted to get away from monasteries that were supported solely by donations.

He expected his monks to live a simple life without possessions for fear that possessions would distract them from the spiritual life and also because more possessions would require more money to buy them.

What does the *Rule of St. Benedict* look like?

The text of the *Rule* can be found online if one wants to explore it. It is made up of seventy-three short chapters.

> The meals of the brethren should not be without reading. Nor should the reader be anyone who happens to take up the book; but there should be a reader for the whole week, entering that office on Sunday. Let this incoming reader, after Mass and Communion, ask all to pray for him that God may keep him from the spirit of pride. And let him intone the following verse, which shall be said three times by all in the oratory: "O Lord, open my lips, and my mouth shall declare Your praise." Then, having received a blessing, let him enter on the reading.

> And let absolute silence be kept at table, so that no whispering may be heard nor any voice except the reader's.

THE DOCTORS OF THE CHURCH

Who are the Doctors of the Christian Church?

The Doctors of the Christian Church were important Christian writers and theologians from the period of Early Christianity. There were originally four Latin Doctors of the Western Church and four Greek Doctors of the Eastern Church.

Starting in the 1500s, the Catholic Church recognized other theologians as Doctors of the Church. The current list has thirty-six names, including four women: Teresa of Ávila, Catherine of Siena, Thérèse of Lisieux, and Hildegard of Bingen.

Who were the original four Doctors of the Western Church?

Gregory the Great, Ambrose, Augustine, and Jerome. All four are considered saints by many Christians.

Who was Gregory the Great?

Gregory lived from c. 540 to 604 and became the bishop of Rome in 590. He did much to shape the influence and authority of the bishop of Rome over Western Christianity, which included his efforts to send out missionaries in Europe. He is called Pope Gregory I, although the word "pope" was not used during his time as the bishop of Rome. His numerous writings have survived, including his sermons and letters. A style of music used by monks for chanting the Psalms from the Bible developed at this time and is named after him: the Gregorian Chant.

Who was Ambrose?

Ambrose lived from c. 340 to 397. He became an influential bishop in the city of Milan (in Italy today). During his career, he had numerous struggles with Arian Christians who rejected parts of the Nicene Creed. Ambrose wrote extensively, including letters and homilies on the Old Testament. Augustine lived in Milan and was influenced by Ambrose.

Who was Jerome?

Jerome (347–420) was important for his extensive writings, including a Latin version of the Bible. In writing the Latin Old Testament, he used the original Hebrew version and Greek translation called the Septuagint. His Latin Bible is called the Vulgate, which means it was written in common Latin. His Latin translation of the Bible was the official Bible of the Catholic Church up until the modern age. Even English translations were based on his Latin version.

Jerome lived in several places, including Rome. During his last years, he lived in Jerusalem and then in a cave in Bethlehem that he believed was the cave where Jesus was born. He also wrote extensive commentaries on the Scriptures.

Who were the original four Doctors of the Eastern Church?

The four Doctors of the Eastern Church were John Chrysostom, Basil the Great, Gregory of Nazianzus, and Athanasius of Alexandria.

John Chrysostom (c. 349–407), who served as archbishop of Constantinople, was a prolific writer who created the *Divine Liturgy of Saint John Chrysostom*: a set of prayers used in services. He also left behind numerous homilies. Basil the Great (c. 329–370), a theologian and bishop of Caesarea Mazaca in Asia Minor (modern-day Turkey), was known for his care for the poor. He wrote guidelines for monasteries and is known as the Father of Eastern Monasticism.

Gregory of Nazianzus (c. 329–390) was the archbishop of Constantinople. He is known as an important theologian, especially for his writings on the Trinity. Athanasius

197

of Alexandria (c. 296–373) was the bishop of Alexandria in Egypt. Also called Athanasius the Great, he is known for his tireless fight against the heresy of Arianism.

FALL OF THE ROMAN EMPIRE AND THE DARK AGES

What happened to the Roman Empire?

Although people often speak of the Fall of the Roman Empire, it was not one event but rather a series of transformations caused by numerous factors over several centuries. In the 300s, Constantine moved his capital to Constantinople in the eastern half of the empire. This would become the Christian Byzantine Empire, which would last for over a thousand years.

In the western half of the Empire, the control exercised by Rome diminished in the face of economic decline and invading tribes. Rome could no longer produce the large armies that had created the empire, which were now needed to keep local peoples under control and keep out invaders. As a result, tribal people, often called barbarians, began carving up the pieces of the Western Roman Empire and settling down. This period is known as the Dark Ages.

What were the Dark Ages?

The Dark Ages were the period between the collapse of the Roman Empire and the Middle Ages in Western Europe. There was a decline of the sophisticated Roman culture. Also, writing and literature declined dramatically so that the Dark Ages are "dark" in the sense that there was little knowledge passed on in writing that survives today. Coincidentally, this period was marked by climate change, with Europe getting colder for several centuries, leading to agricultural, economic, and social decline.

Many tribal cultures such as the Goths, Franks, Germanic, and Norse tribes were active in this period. These peoples had sophisticated cultures with great craftsmanship in metals, clothes, and wood. They also had extensive oral traditions of myths and stories. However, these cultures did not have writing. The bulk of their myths

The Roman Empire declined in the fourth century C.E., eventually splitting into the Eastern and Western Roman Empires in 395. The East fared better, becoming the Byzantine Empire, while the West disintegrated into barbarism and smaller, warring kingdoms.

and stories have been lost. Also, they did not build in stone as did the Romans and Greeks. The ruins of countless Greek and Roman temples still exist. The wooden halls built by tribal people are long gone. As a result, much of this tribal culture has been lost.

Who are some important Christian missionaries of this period?

St. Augustine of Canterbury (d. 604) brought Christianity to England. He is a different person from Augustine of Hippo (354–430).

St. Boniface (c. 675–754) brought Christianity to the Germanic tribes. One legend tells how he chopped down the sacred tree of Thor (called Donner in German) in a village. When he was not struck dead by lightning, the villagers believed his god was more powerful than Thor, so they converted.

St. Cyril (826–869) and St. Methodius (815–885) were two brothers who are known as the "apostles to the Slavs" for their missionary work with the Slavic people in Eastern Europe. They created a special alphabet for translating the Bible. Called the Cyrillic alphabet, it is named after Cyril. Today, the script is used for languages such as Russian.

Who was St. Patrick?

St. Patrick is known as the "Apostle of Ireland" for helping to bring Christianity to Ireland. He lived in the late 400s. He grew up in Britain but was captured by Irish pirates at about the age of sixteen. He worked as a slave for the next six years until he escaped to his family in Britain. He became a priest and returned to Ireland as a missionary. He eventually became a bishop. He is remembered for bringing Christianity to Ireland.

Did St. Patrick drive the snakes from Ireland?

St. Patrick is given credit for the lack of snakes in Ireland. However, this legend has no basis in history. There is no fossil evidence that snakes existed in Ireland since the time of the glaciers.

Why is the shamrock the symbol of St. Patrick?

There is a legend that Patrick used the shamrock to teach people about the Trinity. Just as the shamrock has three leaves, the Trinity has three persons in one God. However, since the legend first appears in writing in the 1700s, there is serious doubt whether or not St. Patrick actually used the shamrock as a teaching device.

The feast of St. Patrick is March 17. Many people use shamrocks as decorations to remember St. Patrick, especially in areas that have populations with an Irish heritage. Ironically, many bars decorate with shamrocks as people celebrate St. Patrick's Day by drinking, with little interest in the religious beliefs supposedly behind the symbol.

Who was Clovis? Why is he important?

Clovis I (c. 466–511) became the first king of the Franks by uniting all the Frankish tribes into one kingdom that included the area of modern-day France, Belgium, and Germany. He also converted to Christianity under the influence of his wife, Clotilde. Widespread conversion to Christianity of most of the Frankish people followed.

CHRISTIANITY AND ISLAM

What else happened during this period?

In the year 570, Muhammad was born in the city of Mecca in what today is Saudi Arabia. According to Muslim tradition, at the age of forty, he began receiving revelations from the Angel Gabriel. In the next years, a new religion, Islam, was built on these revelations. Eventually, the revelations were written down as the holy book of Islam, the Qur'an. Muhammad was honored as the final prophet of Allah's message. "Allah" is the Arabic word for God.

Muhammad died in 632. In the next centuries, his followers spread Islam over the Mideast, North Africa, and what today is Spain. There were numerous conflicts as the Islamic world and the Christian world clashed.

What is the Battle of Tours, and why is it important?

The Battle of Tours, also called the Battle of Poitiers or the Battle of the Palace of the Martyrs by Arab sources, took place in what today is France in the year 732. Charles Martel led Frankish and Burgundian forces and defeated Islamic forces coming from what today is Spain, who were led by Abdul Rahman Al Ghafiqi.

In the early 700s, Muslim armies conquered much of what is now Spain. The next goal was the land of Gaul, which today is France. Had the Muslims won the Battle of Tours, the later history of Europe would have been very different, as much of Europe would have been Muslim. Instead, Charles Martel won and helped establish a Christian empire. Christianity became the dominant religion in Europe except in the lands that would eventually become Spain. Eventually, the Muslims were driven out of Spain in the 1500s under King Ferdinand and Queen Isabella.

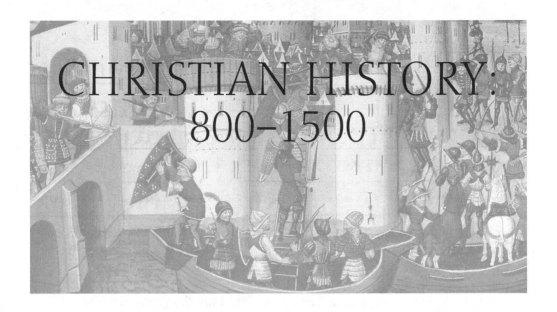

CHRISTIAN HISTORY: 800–1500

THE MIDDLE AGES: 800–1300

When were the Middle Ages? What is the Medieval Period?

The Middle Ages and the Medieval Period are the same thing. Historians give different centuries for this era. This book will use the years 800 to 1300 as the Medieval Period.

To better understand the Middle Ages, one must note that most people, but not all, thought the world was flat. They also thought that the sun, moon, and stars were small objects a few miles up in the air. Most people had no idea that earth was a planet in a vast, vast universe, so most people believed Heaven was "up there, beyond the stars" and that Hell was down below the earth. By the Middle Ages, the concepts of Heaven and Hell were well developed.

Why start the Middle Ages at 800?

The year 800 marks a convenient point for starting the Middle Ages. In that year, the king of the Franks, Charlemagne, was crowned the Holy Roman Emperor by Pope Leo III. The pope wanted to re-create an empire on the model of the old Roman Emperor, only this time, it would be a Christian empire. Charlemagne did create a large kingdom that would include what today are France, Germany, and part of Italy. However, the Holy Roman Empire never lived up to its name. It was very small compared to the original Roman Empire. It was not that Roman, and although Charlemagne and the succeeding rulers were Christians, their conduct was often anything but holy.

However, the title and role of the Holy Roman Emperor lasted in Europe down to the First World War. Over the centuries, the Holy Roman Emperors, who were French, Spanish, and German, had great influence over what happened in Europe.

How is the medieval view of the afterlife different from modern views of the afterlife?

It is hard for many modern Christians to understand the medieval religious world. For many Christians today, salvation is not that hard to achieve. According to some Christians, all one has to do is to sincerely accept Jesus as "my Lord and Savior," and one is saved. Although this acceptance of Jesus needs to be followed up by living out a moral, faith-filled life, achieving salvation is fairly easy. This view is very different from the medieval view that getting to Heaven was very difficult and arduous. In the medieval world, people held to a view of God as harsh, demanding, and punishing, so getting to Heaven was not easy, and people went to great lengths to achieve salvation. For example, many people made pilgrimages by walking all the way from Europe to Jerusalem in the hope of achieving salvation.

Why is the medieval view of salvation so different from the views of modern Christians?

After the Middle Ages, in the 1500s in Europe, the Protestant movement would arise, starting with Martin Luther. This movement would break away from the Roman Catholic Church and offer a different vision of salvation based solely on having faith in the death and Resurrection of Jesus. In time, the Catholic Church also softened its view about salvation, and many of the harshest medieval ideas about salvation and the practices to achieve salvation disappeared.

Most Christians today, regardless of their denomination, live a Christian faith influenced, in one way or another, by the Protestant shift in emphasis about salvation.

What was the medieval view of the afterlife?

In the Middle Ages, the dominant religion in Western Europe was the Roman Catholic Church. The only other religions to be found were Judaism and outlier Christian groups such as the Albigensians. Jews were a minority of the population and typically lived in

---

What is the famous book about the afterlife written by Dante in the Middle Ages?

The Italian writer Dante Alighieri (1265–1321) wrote *The Divine Comedy*, describing the medieval view of the afterlife. The word "comedy" does not mean it is a humorous story but rather that it has a happy ending. *The Divine Comedy* is a poem made up of one hundred parts called "cantos," dividing into three sections: The Inferno Hell, Purgatorio Purgatory, and Paradiso Paradise or Heaven.

In the poem, Dante is led through Hell and Purgatory by the Roman writer Virgil. Beatrice, Dante's image of the ideal woman, leads him through Paradise.

the cities. The vast majority of Europeans had been baptized as infants in the Roman Catholic Church and held the Catholic view of the afterlife.

In the Catholic view, there were three options when a person died: Heaven, Hell, or Purgatory. In the Middle Ages, the common belief was that it was very hard to get into Heaven. One had to be very holy and religious. Being a monk, nun, or priest improved one's chances of getting to Heaven. On the other hand, it was not difficult to wind up in Hell. If you had not been baptized, you could not get into Heaven and would go to Hell. Even innocent unbaptized infants could not get into Heaven. If you were baptized but later committed a serious sin, you would go to Hell, unless you had seen a priest and gone to confession. In that case, your sin was forgiven, and you would not go to Hell.

Don't these views seem very harsh?

Yes, the medieval view of God tended to be that God was harsh, demanding, and ready to punish. This fit well with the medieval world, where life was harsh, demanding, and full of suffering. Illness and death were common. Wars were frequent. Laws could be harsh. Punishments were brutal and included torture and executions using techniques such as burning at the stake and ripping people to pieces, so for many people, their image of God often matched their life experience.

What is the concept of Purgatory?

Purgatory was the place for baptized people who had died with unforgiven sin, but the sin was not serious enough to send them to Hell. Purgatory was a place to go to pay the penalty for unforgiven sins. It was a place of suffering, like Hell, but not permanent.

A lot of energy was spent in the Middle Ages worrying about Purgatory. People would pray and make offerings for deceased relatives whom they believed were in Purgatory. Sometimes, wealthy people would leave endowments so that monks would pray for them after they died to shorten their time in Purgatory.

I know someone who is Protestant and never heard much about Purgatory. Why is that?

The Protestant movement began in the 1500s with Martin Luther. Luther rejected the belief in Purgatory because he could not find the concept in the Bible.

If the concept of Purgatory is not in the Bible, why did the Catholic Church believe in it?

The concept of Purgatory gained acceptance under Pope Gregory the Great, who died in 604. Purgatory solved a problem that had puzzled people. Some people were very holy, and they went to Heaven. Other people were very bad, and they went to Hell. But what happened to all those people who were not perfect but not bad enough to go to Hell? The concept of Purgatory was adopted to address this problem.

203

Purgatory, according to the Catholic view of the afterlife, was a place between Heaven and Hell, where some sinners who were not damned outright could be purified before entering Heaven (altar art at the City Church in Bad Wimpfen, Germany).

Furthermore, the Catholic position was that although the word "Purgatory" was not in the Bible, the concept could be found in the Bible, specifically in 2 Maccabees 12:46: "Thus he [Judas Maccabee] made atonement for the dead that they might be absolved from their sin." The books of 1 & 2 Maccabees are found in Catholic Bibles. However, in the 1500s, Martin Luther would remove those books from the Protestant Bible, which is why Protestants do not believe that the idea of Purgatory is in the Bible.

What was the Catholic idea of Limbo?

The idea of Limbo was never an official Catholic teaching; however, it was believed by many Catholics and until recent times often taught by Catholic priests and sisters. The idea of Limbo was based on the belief that only baptized people could go to Heaven. That meant that unbaptized babies, even though innocent, could not go to Heaven and would have to go to Hell. This seemed a bit harsh. In time, the idea developed of a special place for infants called Limbo. Some described Limbo as just outside of Heaven.

What is the current view of the Catholic Church about what happens to unbaptized infants who die?

In 2004 Pope John Paul II asked the International Theological Commission to look at the issues. The resulting report, *The Hope of Salvation for Infants Who Die without Being Baptized*, was released in 2007. It stated that, without minimizing the importance of baptism, there is hope of salvation for infants who die without receiving the sacrament of baptism.

Does the Catholic Church still believe in Purgatory?

Yes. Purgatory is defined in articles 1031 and 1032 in the *Catholic Catechism,* which is a book describing Catholic teachings:

> 1031 The Church gives the name *Purgatory* to this final purification of the elect, which is entirely different from the punishment of the damned.

Also, the Catholic Church accepts the practice of praying for the dead:

> 1032 This teaching is also based on the practice of prayer for the dead, already mentioned in Sacred Scripture: "Therefore [Judas Maccabeus] made atonement for the dead, that they might be delivered from their sin." From the beginning the Church has honored the memory of the dead and offered prayers in suffrage for them, above all the Eucharistic sacrifice, so that, thus purified, they may attain the beatific vision of God.

The phrase "attain the beatific vision" means to go to Heaven. Note that 2 Maccabees 12:46 is being quoted.

What are Indulgences?

In the Middle Ages, the practice of Indulgences developed. Indulgences were obtained by living people to shorten the time of specific persons in Purgatory. Thus, a living person might obtain an Indulgence for a deceased relative.

What was the thinking behind Indulgences?

Here is a simplistic explanation. Indulgences are based on the belief that the saints, those who go to Heaven, get there because of the merit of their holiness and good works. However, saints often have extra merit that could be assigned to other people to shorten their time in Purgatory. A document, called an Indulgence, transferred this merit. People were expected to make a donation for the Indulgence. In time, Indulgences were

---

What was the celibacy rule for priests?

Up until around the year 1000, the policy had developed that bishops and monks could not be married and had to live celibate lives. Priests, such as parish priests, were allowed to marry. In the Middle Ages, this policy changed under the influence of popes who had lived in monasteries, and as a result, all priests were required to live celibate lives. However, for several centuries, many priests ignored the rule. Today in the Orthodox Christian churches, the older policy is still followed that allows priests to marry, but monks and bishops remain celibate.

being sold to raise money. (The sale of Indulgences would become a lightning-rod issue in the 1500s, launching the career of Martin Luther.)

What was the Great Schism?

For some centuries, tension had been growing between Western Christianity under the leadership of the pope in Rome and Eastern Orthodox Christianity. A key issue was that the Eastern Christians did not believe that the pope was the head of the universal church. Also, there was a controversy over a word added to the Latin version of the Nicene Creed. There was also much misunderstanding between the two sides.

In 1054, things came to a head when Pope Leo IX excommunicated Patriarch Michael Cerularius (the head bishop) of Constantinople. Cerularius responded by excommunicating the pope. This break between the Western and Eastern Christian churches is called The Great Schism or the East–West Schism. (The word "schism" refers to break or division, especially within churches.) These two branches of Christianity have remained divided up to the present. However, starting in the mid-twentieth century, many efforts have been made to promote respect and understanding between them.

What was the Filioque Controversy?

The Latin Church added the word "filioque" to the Nicene Creed. The word means "and the Son" and was used in the sentence: "We believe in the Holy Spirit, the Lord, the giver of life, who proceeds from the Father and the Son." The Eastern Orthodox Church insisted that the Creed only described the Holy Spirit as proceeding from the Father. This disagreement is known as the "Filioque Controversy."

What was the place of Jews in the Middle Ages?

Jews played an important role in medieval Europe. Jews increased in numbers, although they were a minority of the overall population. Judaism was tolerated by the dominant Christian culture because of the Jewish background of Jesus. However, there were many laws and restrictions against Jews. For instance, Jews were often forbidden from owning property or belonging to the guilds, the equivalent of labor unions.

In some places, Jews were required to wear clothes that identified them as Jews. Sometimes, they were required to wear yellow stars. In some cities, Jews were required to live in specific areas called "ghettos." Also, under penalty of death, Jews were forbidden to convert Christians to Judaism.

In many places, there was significant anti-Semitism, which occasionally flared up into violence. During the Crusades, the peasant armies massacred Jews in several cities.

Is there a connection between Jews and banking that developed in this period?

In several passages in the Bible, the lending of money at usury is forbidden. Usury is to charge interest, so technically, Christians were forbidden to charge interest on loans. However, Jews understood this rule to mean that Jews could not lend money to other Jews at

Jews in the Middle Ages were forced to wear distinctive clothing to identify them, including some kind of yellow badge (it could be a star, circle, or square) or a distinctive hat, as shown in this thirteenth-century manuscript illustration.

interest. However, they could lend to non-Jews, so by this quirk in interpreting this rule of the Bible, some Jews found themselves as moneylenders in the medieval world. The problem was that in the growing economies of the Middle Ages, no one was willing to lend money unless there was some interest to cover the risk for lending the money.

Keep in mind that in the Middle Ages, no consumer protection laws existed. Many people today are not great at figuring percentages; most people in the Middle Ages could not do math. Not surprisingly, there was often mistrust and anger toward Jewish moneylenders, in some cases legitimate and in other cases not legitimate.

Today, modern Christians get around the biblical prohibition on lending money at usury by saying that usury means exorbitant interest rates. Although this is a helpful way around the issue, it ignores the original Bible intent that all charging of interest was forbidden.

THEOLOGIANS AND SAINTS

Who was Anselm of Canterbury?

Anselm, also called St. Anselm (c. 1033–1086), was an important theologian and archbishop in Canterbury in England. (The term "bishop" goes back to the New Testament. Over the centuries, bishops in large cities were called "archbishops.")

207

Anselm is often called "the Father of Scholasticism." Scholasticism was a philosophical and theological tradition that used reason to explore and explain Christian faith. Anselm wrote three important works: *Monologion* (the Monologue), *Proslogion* (the Discourse), and *Cur Deus Homo* (Why God was a Man). He tackled two important questions: Can reason be used to prove the existence of God? Why was the Incarnation necessary? In other words, why did God have to become human in Jesus?

Anselm proposed an argument to prove the existence of God. It would later be called the "ontological argument." God is that than which nothing greater can be conceived. According to the *Oxford Dictionary of the Christian Church* (Oxford University Press, 1983): "If we were to suppose that God did not exist we should be involved in a contradiction since we could at once conceive of an entity greater than a non-existing God—an existing God."

According to Anselm, God is the greatest thing we can imagine. Then he assumes it is better to exist than to not exist. Thus, if one says that God, the greatest thing one can imagine, does not exist, someone could respond that that is not the greatest thing a person could imagine. The greatest thing one could imagine is a God who does exist.

Some people get Anselm's argument; some people do not. His idea is that for God to be the greatest thing, God would have to exist. Some criticize Anselm's argument as being just a play with words.

Anselm also proposed the "satisfaction theory of atonement." Why did God have to become man in Jesus? Why did Jesus, the Son of God, have to die to bring salvation?

According to Anselm, Jesus died not to pay a debt to the Devil to ransom us but because humans had offended God's majesty. The justice of God demanded payment of a penalty. Anselm's theory is based on the medieval notion that sin is based on the rank of the offended person. So, punching a peasant was a minor offense compared to punching a Lord of the Manor. Since God is infinite, any sin against God is also infinite. Therefore, infinite satisfaction was required, but it must be offered by a human since humans are responsible for their sins. Thus, Jesus had to die, but he had to be an infinite being that was both divine and human.

Who was Peter Abelard?

Peter Abelard (1079–1142) was a brilliant theologian and writer. For many, he is best known for his relationship with Héloïse. In the famous Père Lachaise Cemetery in Paris, France, there is a tomb to Abelard and Héloïse. (Some claim that the tomb in Père Lachaise does not contain the bones of both Abelard and Héloïse.) It is one of the most visited tombs in the cemetery, although it competes with the tomb of Jim Morrison, singer of the rock group The Doors. Abelard wrote a number of works of theology, including *Sic et Non* (*Yes and No*), in which Abelard addresses 158 questions of theology and gives arguments for and against them.

Who was Peter Lombard?

Peter Lombard (c. 1096–1160) wrote *Four Books of the Sentences*, which became the textbook of theology in Europe. He was known as the "Master of the Sentences."

Who was Albert the Great?

Albert the Great (Albertus Magnus in Latin, c. 1200–1280) wrote extensively on theology, philosophy, astrology, ecumenism, music, and science. His science writings included works on mineralogy, alchemy, and zoology. He was a Dominican monk. The Dominicans were a new Roman Catholic order created in the Middle Ages dedicated to teaching Christian faith and fighting heresy.

Who was Thomas Aquinas?

Thomas Aquinas (1224–1274) was one of most influential Christian theologians of the Middle Ages. The most important writing of Thomas Aquinas was his *Summa Theologiae*, a comprehensive overview of all the Christian theological topics of the time. Aquinas is particularly important for integrating the thought of the Greek

One of the most important theologians of the Middle Ages was Thomas Aquinas, who is noted for writing the *Summa Theologiae*.

philosopher Aristotle with Christian thought. In the 1500s, during the Protestant Reformation in Europe, many Protestant writers rejected the teachings of Aquinas.

Who was St. Francis?

One of the most important figures of the Middle Ages was St. Francis (1182–1226). He is probably the most popular Catholic saint. He created a new religious order called the Franciscans, which emphasized voluntary poverty. He also oversaw the creation of an order for women, the Poor Clares. Many people today visit the city of Assisi in Italy to see the sites where he grew up and lived. It is also believed by many that Francis had the stigmata: the wounds of Christ on his hands, feet, and chest. Francis is also the patron saint of animals. The life story of Francis is told in the 1972 Franco Zeffirelli film *Brother Sun, Sister Moon*.

The prayer of St. Francis is attributed to him, although he did not write it. The earliest known version of the prayer is from 1912. It has been set to numerous musical compositions.

Who was St. Dominic?

Dominic de Guzmán (1170–1221) lived in Spain. He created a new religious order called the Order of Preachers, also known as the Dominicans. Dominic wanted to address the problem of religious ignorance by creating an order of well-educated monks to teach and preach to the people. His order played a key role in fighting heresy.

THE CRUSADES

What were the Crusades?

The Crusades were a series of military campaigns in the Middle Ages undertaken by European Christians to conquer the Holy Land: Jerusalem and the surrounding territory. At that time, the area was held by various Muslim rulers. The First Crusade began in 1095. The last Crusade ended in 1272.

The First Crusade conquered Jerusalem but with great bloodshed. Jerusalem was then retaken by the Muslims, and subsequent Crusades failed to reconquer it. By 1291 all the territory that had been conquered during the Crusades was in Muslim hands.

Can you give me an overview of the Crusades?

The Crusades were a series of very complicated events over two hundred years. What follows below is a very simple overview.

How many Crusades were there?

Some lists count nine Crusades. Other lists count eight by combining the last two Crusades as one. Here are the general dates:

The Crusades

Crusade	Years
First Crusade	1096–1099
Second Crusade	1147–1149
Third Crusade	1189–1192
Fourth Crusade	1202–1204
Fifth Crusade	1217–1221
Sixth Crusade	1228–1229
Seventh Crusade	1248–1254 (sometimes combined with the Sixth Crusade because both were led by Frederick II)
Eighth Crusade	1270
Ninth Crusade	1271–1272 (usually combined with the Eighth Crusade)

What was the cause of the Crusades?

The ruler of the Christian city of Constantinople, Emperor Alexius, wanted help fighting the Muslim Seljuk Turks, who were taking over parts of his territory. Also, the Seljuk Turks conquered Jerusalem and closed it to pilgrims coming from Europe. Despite the long distance, many Europeans traveled in those days to the Holy Land—Jerusalem and its environs—to visit the sites where Jesus lived and was crucified and buried.

Emperor Alexius wrote to the Pope in Rome asking for help. What Alexius had in mind was a small army of trained knights to help him. Instead, the pope launched a massive military campaign far beyond what Alexius had in mind. The pope set in motion a series of events that in the end would lead to the destruction of Christian Constantinople.

What happened in the First Crusade?

The First Crusade lasted from 1095 to 1099. In response to the letter of Emperor Alexius, Pope Urban II, in an open-air sermon in Clermont, France, called for a crusade on November 27, 1095. He wanted an army to rescue the Holy Land. He gave exaggerated accounts of Muslim atrocities against Christians. He offered the pardon of sins for those on the Crusade and freedom from their debts. Part of the motivation for Pope Urban was his hope that a crusade would unite the Christian kingdoms in Europe and stop the fighting between them.

What was the Peasants' Crusade?

Before the Crusader armies could be organized, a preacher named Peter the Hermit led a band of some five thousand peasants to go to Jerusalem to rescue the Holy Lands. However, the bands first attacked Jewish communities along the Rhine River (what today is Germany) and massacred many thousands of Jews.

They continued their journey by foot toward Constantinople killing and pillaging as they went. When they arrived at Constantinople, the emperor feared the unruly mob and ferried them across the Bosporus Strait. They were in the land that today is called Turkey. There, the peasant Crusaders attacked Christian cities such as Nicaea, where the Nicene Creed had been written in 325 C.E. The Peasants' Crusade was eventually destroyed by Muslim armies.

Taking of Jerusalem by the Crusaders, 15th July 1099 (1847) by Émile Signol shows the triumphant conclusion of the First Crusade.

What happened with the main body of Crusaders?

The main Crusade was made up of five armies from Europe. The most important leaders of the Crusade were Princes Hugh, Godfrey, Baldwin, Robert, Stephen, Raymond, Bohemond, and Tancred. There were many conflicts and disagreements between these leaders.

On their way to Jerusalem, they conquered the city of Antioch and slaughtered all the inhabitants. Their journey through the southern part of Anatolia—what is called Turkey today— was a nightmare of starvation, a lack of water, disease, and death.

What happened when they reached Jerusalem?

The Crusader armies finally arrived in Jerusalem. However, by now, Fatimid Muslims had conquered Jerusalem and were friendly to Christians and willing to let them visit the holy places. Nonetheless, the Crusaders wanted to conquer the city.

After a long siege, the Crusaders broke through the walls on July 15, 1099. They proceeded to slaughter a vast number of Muslims and Jews as they conquered the city and took over all the holy sites. They then established the Crusader States.

What were the Crusader States?

The Crusader States were established in what today is Syria, Lebanon, Jordan, Israel, and the Palestinian Territory. Two special orders of knights were created to defend the land and protect pilgrims coming from Europe to visit Jerusalem: the Knights Hospitaller and the Knights Templar.

What happened next?

In the wake of the Crusaders' conquest of so much territory, including Jerusalem, the Muslims started organizing to fight back. The Muslims' first step in 1144 was to reconquer the city of Edessa (today in modern Turkey), which had been conquered by the Crusaders on their way to Jerusalem.

What happened in the Second Crusade?

The Second Crusade lasted from 1147 to 1149. In response to the fall of Edessa, Pope Eugene III called for the Second Crusade. The fiery Bernard of Clairvaux was commissioned by the pope to preach the Crusade and build up support. The Crusader army was led by kings Conrad III and Louis VII. There was dissension and distrust among the various Christian armies. They decided to attack the city of Damascus, even though the city was an ally of Jerusalem, which was held by the Crusaders. Although they laid siege to Damascus, the Crusaders eventually gave up and went home. The whole Crusade was a debacle.

What happened after the Second Crusade?

The Muslim ruler Saladin came to power. In 1187 he conquered Jerusalem. He then destroyed much of the Crusader States.

What happened in the Third Crusade of 1187–1192?

This Crusade was led by German Emperor Frederick I Barbarossa, King Philip of France, and King Richard I of England, the Lionheart. Frederick drowned en route. Richard and Philip conquered the city of Acre, which is today in northern Israel. Richard made a deal with Saladin. Richard was allowed to rebuild the Crusader States, but Jerusalem remained under Saladin's control. The story of Robin Hood in England takes place while Richard is on this Crusade.

What happened in the Fourth Crusade of 1202–1204?

This Crusade was led by Count Baldwin. To get the city of Venice to pay for the ships he needed, he agreed to attack the Christian city of Zara, a trade rival of Venice. The Crusaders then attacked the Christian city of Constantinople. They looted and sacked the city in 1204.

What is the legacy of the Fourth Crusade?

The sacking of Constantinople greatly weakened it so that it would eventually be taken over by the Muslim Ottoman Turks in 1453. Ironically, defending Christian Constantinople and its surrounding territory had been the original catalyst for starting the Crusades.

The sacking of Constantinople led to great resentment on the part of Eastern Orthodox Christians toward Roman Catholic Christians. In some places, the resentment

A fifteenth-century work showing the 1204 siege of Constantinople during the Fourth Crusade. The Byzantine Empire captured the city and established the Latin Empire, which fell in 1261 to the Nicaeans.

still lingers. For many people today, the Fourth Crusade is one of several important illustrations of the fundamental immorality and un-Christian nature of the Crusades.

What was the Children's Crusade of 1212?

The story of the Children's Crusade is a mix of legend and fact, with no one sure what exactly happened. The legend is that a large band of children, perhaps thirty thousand, set out to free the Holy Land. It was led by Nicholas of Cologne, who was a shepherd, and Stephen of Cloyes, a twelve-year-old shepherd boy, who somehow came to the idealistic belief that the Muslim armies would surrender Jerusalem to a band of peaceful children. When the children arrived at the Mediterranean Sea, they were offered passage on ships. However, they were sold into slavery instead.

The historical evidence points to two groups of peasants of all ages. Both set out, but both groups fell apart before leaving Europe.

What was the Fifth Crusade of 1217–1221?

This Crusade was called by Pope Innocent III and led by King John of Jerusalem. His army sailed to Egypt to move toward Jerusalem from the west. The Crusaders conquered the Egyptian city of Damietta. At this point, the sultan, fearing the Crusaders, offered them the city of Jerusalem. However, the pope's representative, Cardinal Pelagius, overruled John and insisted that they attack Jerusalem.

The Crusader armies had to wait for more troops to arrive. In the meantime, the army was destroyed by floods on the Nile and the Egyptian army. The Crusade was a failure.

What was the Sixth Crusade of 1228–1229?

This Crusade was led by the German emperor Frederick II. Frederick did not want to go on a Crusade but was forced by Pope Innocent III. Once he got to the Holy Land, Frederick made a deal with the Muslims, called the Treaty of Jerusalem, and got control of Jerusalem. However, neither the Christians nor the Muslims liked the deal. Frederick eventually left and returned to Europe to protect his kingdom back home. In 1244, the Muslims retook Jerusalem.

What was the Seventh Crusade of 1248–1254?

This Crusade was led by King Louis IX, who would later become St. Louis. (The well-known city in Missouri is named after him.) Louis IX conquered the Egyptian city of Damietta. However, he was then captured. He paid a large ransom for his freedom and then returned with his forces to France.

What was the Eighth Crusade of 1270?

This Crusade was also led by King Louis IX. The plan was to take North Africa and then conquer Jerusalem. It failed, and King Louis died of the plague in North Africa.

What was the Ninth Crusade of 1271–1272?

The Crusade was led by Prince Edward of England and achieved nothing. Some historians list it as a second phase of the Eighth Crusade. In the next years, Muslim armies conquered all Crusader strongholds in what had been the Crusader States. The last to fall was the city of Acre in 1291.

What is the legacy of the Crusades today?

When people today make the claim that most wars have been fought over religion, the Crusades become their primary example. The truth is that most wars are fought over political and economic issues.

The Return of the Crusader (1835) is a sorrowful depiction by artist Karl Friedrich Lessing of the last crusader to return from the Holy Land in defeat.

However, the Crusades illustrate a problem that has occurred a number of times over the centuries when religion is used to promote very unreligious policies. A recent example is the 1995 genocide by Christian Serbians of Muslims from Bosnia and Herzegovina.

The Crusades also played an important role in creating friction between some Muslims and some Christians, which is still around today. However, the big source of resentment by some Muslims of the Mideast toward Western countries has to do with the economic, political, and military domination of many countries of the Mideast by both the British and then the Americans in the twentieth century. For example, in the Mideast, Britain and the United States have been involved in the overthrow of governments in Iran, Iraq, Syria, and Egypt. Most Americans do not know this history, but people in the regions do.

Also in the debate about the value of religion, the Crusades are often brought up. Some argue that religion has done more harm than good, and they bring up things such as the Crusades and the priest abuse scandal. On the other hand, people point out the value of religion in helping people reshape and reform their lives, promoting moral values, and providing charity work for the needy.

What is the influence of the Crusades on the medieval cathedrals?

One of the most dramatic examples of the influence of Christianity on medieval Europe was the building of magnificent Gothic cathedrals. While on the Crusades, Europeans were impressed with Muslim architecture, and they learned new building techniques that inspired them to create a new style of massive architecture: the Gothic style.

215

What were the church councils during this period?

Seven more councils took place from the ninth to thirteenth centuries:

Year	Council
869	Constantinople IV
1123	Lateran I
1139	Lateran II
1179	Lateran III
1215	Lateran IV
1245	Lyons I
1274	Lyons II

At the time, the pope lived in the Lateran Palace in Rome, so four church councils met there. A cathedral known as the Basilica of John in Lateran was built. It was the pope's church for many centuries. Only much later did the pope move to another area of Rome called the Vatican. Lyons is a city in southern France.

What happened with the position of the pope during the Crusade era?

The pope's influence and power over Western Europe continued to increase during the Middle Ages. Also, a number of popes were chosen who had been monks and brought monastic ideas with them, such as the idea of celibacy for priests. Three important popes

What was the Inquisition?

The word "Inquisition" often brings to mind images of torture and execution to force religious conformity. However, the actual history is far more complicated. First, one must distinguish between the medieval General Inquisition, which took place in Europe under the control of the pope, and the later Spanish Inquisition, which began in 1478. It is the Spanish Inquisition, set up by King Ferdinand and Queen Isabella with both political and religious aims, that was particularly inhumane.

The purpose of the General Inquisition was to take control of heresy trials away from political rulers so it could not be used for political purposes. Also, the investigations and trials were conducted by the Dominican and Franciscan orders, known for their theological training and for lacking worldly interests in money and power. The practices of the Inquisition often matched what happened in criminal proceedings of the time: the accused had few rights, and torture was used to force confessions. However, the General Inquisition did have standard procedures that lessened the abuses. Lastly, people accused of heresy were given the chance to recant their views and receive a penance, such as going on a pilgrimage or wearing a cross on one's clothing. Those who refused to repent could receive harsh punishments such as banishment, life in prison, or death.

of this period were Urban II (c. 1042–1099), Innocent III (1160–1216), and Boniface VIII (c. 1234–1303). Pope Urban called for the Crusades.

CHRISTIANITY IN THE RENAISSANCE: 1300–1500

What were the conflicts around the pope at this time?

There were two conflicts during this period involving the pope: the Avignon Papacy (1309–1376) and the Papal Schism (1378–1417). The authority of the pope comes from his role as the bishop of Rome. In the 1300s, there was a long fight over control of the papacy. The popes at the time were very much involved in politics, and many political figures wanted to control who was pope. In 1309, a bitter fight over who should be pope led to the election of Pope Clement V. The atmosphere in Rome was so hostile that he moved the entire court of the pope to the city of Avignon in southern France. A total of seven subsequent French popes ruled from Avignon. The French kings were able to exert influence on these popes. Finally, the seventh pope, Gregory XI, moved the papacy back to Rome.

When Gregory died, another fight broke out, and before long, there were three men claiming to be pope, including one in Rome and one in Avignon. Keep in mind that these fights had little to do with theology and much to do with political and church authority. Finally, at the Church Council of Constance in Germany, a single pope was agreed upon: Pope Martin V. These squabbles over who was pope did much to discredit the pope and his role in the minds of some Christians.

What were the church councils of this period?

Three councils took place in this period:

Year	Location
1311–1313	Vienne (in France)
1414–1418	Constance (in Germany)
1431–1439	Basel, Ferrara, and Florence (the council met in three different sessions: the first in Switzerland and the second two in Italy)

What was the Black Death?

The Black Death was the bubonic plague, which comes from the bacterium *Yersinia pestis*. Humans got the disease when they were bitten by fleas carrying the bacterium. The plague came in several waves. The worst outbreak peaked in the years 1347–1351, resulting in anywhere from seventy-five to two hundred million people dying in Europe and Asia. This plague started in Central Asia and then traveled along the Silk Road. It was probably carried by fleas on rats that traveled on ships. The devastation of so many deaths had a tremendous social and political impact.

Is not the Renaissance best known for the artists of the period?

Yes, the Renaissance was the age of famous artists such as Michelangelo, Raphael, and Leonardo da Vinci. However, the label "the Renaissance" was given to this period many centuries later.

What are *The Canterbury Tales*?

The Canterbury Tales were written by Geoffrey Chaucer between the years 1387 to 1400. The book is a collection of stories told by pilgrims on their way to the shrine of Thomas Becket in Canterbury, England.

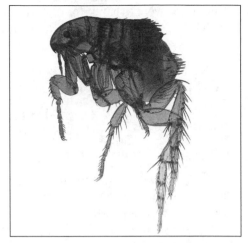

There is often a misperception that bubonic plague was spread by rats in Europe, but actually it was fleas like this one that carry the bacteria for the disease.

The Canterbury Tales gives a window into the late medieval feudal world. A number of the characters are religious figures, such as the Parson, the Monk, the Friar, the Pardoner, the Summoner, Nuns, Priests, and the Prioress (a woman in charge of a convent). The characters are all introduced in the Prologue.

Chaucer did not write about ideal models of these various religious roles. Rather, he describes monks and friars who are ignoring the precepts of their religious orders. Chaucer does this because they make more interesting characters. A monk or friar who followed the rules and spent all his time praying would actually be quite boring.

Some of the more popular tales are "The Miller's Tale," "The Reeve's Tale," "The Wife of Bath's Tale," and "The Pardoner's Tale." Although Chaucer wrote *The Canterbury Tales* in English, he used a much older form of English that modern readers find difficult to read. Chaucer also wrote in verse style, so rather than read the original, most readers today prefer a prose version in modern English. (Verse is short lines, such as in a poem. Prose is in the form of paragraphs.)

IMPORTANT FIGURES OF THE RENAISSANCE

Who was William of Ockham?

William of Ockham (c. 1287–1347) was a theologian and philosopher. He proposed the theory of nominalism, which when applied to Christianity meant that the Christian church was the individual members rather than the Church institution. He thought the church should focus on religious studies and not be involved politically. Ockham believed the final religious authority was the Bible and that popes and church councils could err. He had great influence on the Reformation two hundred years later.

Who was Catherine of Siena?

Catherine of Siena (c. 1347–1380; Siena is a city in Italy) exerted great influence on the Catholic Church in her time through her letters and personal contact. She played a key role in encouraging Pope Gregory XI to move the papacy back to Rome from Avignon. She was also a theologian, philosopher, and mystic, and she wrote *The Dialogue*. She was later declared a Doctor of the Church.

Who was John Wycliffe? Why was he important?

John Wycliffe (c. 1320–1384; pronounced WICK-liff) taught theology at Oxford University in England. In his studies, he focused on the Bible, which was unusual for the time. He came to the conclusion that the Bible was the final authority in religious matters. Based on his studies of the Bible, Wycliffe began rejecting many Catholic beliefs and practices. He rejected the authority of the pope and idea of the monastic life, seeing no basis for either in the Scriptures. He also rejected the theology of transubstantiation, which was the standard explanation of how the bread and wine became of the Body and Blood of Jesus at Mass. Wycliffe believed in predestination of those who are chosen by God for salvation.

Wycliffe came to believe that sinners were not church members. This was a reaction against medieval culture, where almost everyone was baptized and therefore a member of the church whether they lived a moral life or not. Wycliffe rejected the wealth and worldliness of the clergy, and he believed the Church needed to get rid of its property.

Wycliffe believed that the Bible should be available to everyone, so he began creating an English translation, although most people could not read and write. He probably translated much of the New Testament and his followers translated the Old Testament, which they completed in 1384. The translations were based on the Latin Bible, called the Vulgate. Since the printing press had not yet been invented, these translations were written out as manuscripts.

Seen as a forerunner of the Protestant Reformation, John Wycliffe disagreed with many Catholic tenets and went so far as to translate the Bible into English because he felt everyone should be able to read it.

Wycliffe started an order of priests for parishes called Lollards. In his time, Wycliffe's teachings were condemned, and many of his followers died at the stake. Wycliffe is an important forerunner of the Protestant Reformation, which Martin Luther led in the 1500s.

Who was John Huss?

John Huss (1366–1415) lived in Prague in Bohemia, which today is the Czech Republic. He was influenced by the writings of Wycliffe, although he was prohibited from teaching and preaching on the ideas of Wycliffe. Huss ignored the prohibition. He insisted that the Bible was the final authority in deciding religious matters and the pope could err. Huss opposed wealthy clergy and insisted that during Mass, the Communion cup should be given to the laity—the people in the pews. He also rejected the gulf between clergy and laity, opposed the selling of Indulgences, and rejected having images in churches and even confessions to a priest. He also attacked church corruption. Eventually, Huss was excommunicated, arrested, and imprisoned. When he refused to take back or recant his beliefs, he was burned at the stake.

In 1999, Pope John Paul II apologized for the treatment and execution of John Huss.

Who was Joan of Arc?

Joan of Arc (Jeanne d'Arc in French; c. 1412–1431) was a young peasant girl who claimed she received visions from the Archangel Michael and several saints telling her to support the French king Charles VII and to help free France from English domination. Although she was poor and illiterate, she asked for armor and a horse to lead the forces. She was sent to the French city of Orléans, then under siege by the English. She rallied the French, and the siege was lifted. Several more French victories followed, which led to Charles VII being crowned as king in the French city of Reims. This set the stage for the ultimate French victory.

However, Joan was captured by Burgundians, who handed her over to the English. She was tried by the pro-English bishop of Beauvais. She was accused of both heresy and cross-dressing. She had worn men's clothing as a disguise so as not to be captured, and then in prison, she wanted to wear pants because she felt it gave her some protection from being raped by the guards. Found guilty in a trial that was rigged against her, she was burned at the stake on May 30, 1431. She was about nineteen years old.

In 1456 Pope Callixtus authorized a church court to examine the trial. Joan was found innocent of all the false charges that had been made against her and was declared a martyr. She became a Catholic saint in 1920. In the middle of the twentieth century, "Joan" became a popular name for Catholic girls.

Several movies have been made about her:

- *The Passion of Joan of Arc* (1928), a silent film.

- *Joan of Arc* (1948), starring Ingrid Bergman.

• *The Messenger: The Story of Joan of Arc* (1999).

> ### What happened to Wycliffe's Bible?
>
> The translation of Wycliffe and his followers was based on the standard Latin Bible of the time called the Latin Vulgate. Some parts of these translations later wound up in the Catholic version of the English Bible and also the Protestant King James version of the Bible.

Who was Thomas à Kempis?

Thomas à Kempis (c. 1380-1471) wrote *The Imitation of Christ,* which became one of the most popular Christian writings on religious devotion. Although he was German, he lived in the Netherlands. He joined a religious group of monks called the Brethren of the Common Life, who were part of the religious movement called Modern Devotion. He became a priest and was a prolific writer and copyist of manuscripts.

The Imitation of Christ, which emphasizes a withdrawal from the world to focus on the inner life of faith, is divided into four books: *Helpful Counsels of the Spiritual Life, Directives for the Interior Life, On Interior Consolation,* and *On the Blessed Sacrament.*

Some notable quotes from these books include:

• "At the Day of Judgement we shall not be asked what we have read, but what we have done; not how well we have spoken but how well we have lived." (Book I, Chapter 3)

• "For man proposes, but God disposes." (Book I, Chapter 19)

• "If, however, you seek Jesus in all things, you will surely find Him." (Book II, Chapter 7)

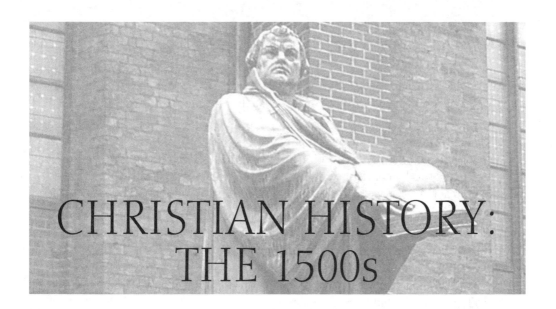

CHRISTIAN HISTORY: THE 1500s

What is the meaning of the terms "Protestant Reformation" and "Catholic Counter-Reformation"?

In the 1500s, Martin Luther started a movement that emerged in Europe in which numerous groups broke away from the Roman Catholic Church. This movement is called the Protestant Reformation. The Roman Catholic response is called the Catholic Counter-Reformation or simply the Counter-Reformation.

The term "Protestant Reformation" contains two words. The word "reformation" comes from an attempt to reform the Catholic Church of the time. There were many people calling for reform of the abuses of the medieval Church. The word "protestant" does not come from an act of protest of Luther nailing a document to the door of his local church. He did such an action in 1517, but as will be seen, it was not an act of protest. The word "protestant" comes from the action of German princes who took advantage of the religious turmoil of the time to break free from the political and legal control of the pope over Europe and to free themselves from taxes to Rome.

The Catholic Counter-Reformation included trying to stem the spread of Protestantism as well as addressing some of the problems within the Catholic Church. The Counter-Reformation also included the building of magnificent churches and sponsoring dramatic art in order to draw people into Catholic churches.

What were some of the problems within the Catholic Church in the 1500s that led to the Reformation?

There were a number of problems within the Catholic Church that many people recognized. One problem was the buying of church positions. Church positions, such as becoming a bishop of a city, were often sold to the highest bidder. This resulted in unqualified people often holding these positions. However, keep in mind that buying of positions was also common in the political world and in the military.

Another abuse was that since many of these positions had incomes, a man might buy several positions. He might be the bishop of several sees or dioceses. Often, there was no attempt to responsibly fulfill the duties of such multiple positions.

Yet another problem was that many of the ordinary clergy were uneducated. Some could barely read Latin. In many local parishes, there was a lack of theology, and often, the beliefs were closer to superstition than the true Christian religion. Furthermore, although the rule was that parish priests should be celibate, many still had wives or housekeepers who acted as wives.

Also, the Catholic Church had great political influence and, in some places, much wealth. All the kingdoms in Europe paid taxes to the pope in Rome. The Catholic Church in many places was the biggest landholder. Many people felt that many church officials were not living out the gospels and that the teachings of the Bible were being ignored. Lastly, some people felt that the rituals and ceremonies were a distraction rather than an aid to true religious faith.

KEY FIGURES

Who was William Tyndale?

William Tyndale (c. 1494–1536), a scholar who lived in England, played a leading early role in the Reformation. He is best known for his translation of the Bible into English. Rather than basing his translation on the Latin Bible, Tyndale used the original Hebrew and Greek texts for his translation. He also used the term "Jehovah" for God's name.

In 1528, Tyndale wrote *The Obedience of a Christian Man*, which influenced Henry VIII to break from the Roman Catholic Church. However, he would later oppose Henry's annulment of his first marriage.

In the 1400s, Johannes Gutenberg had invented the printing press with moveable type. This created a revolution in communication because now, many copies of writings could be printed cheaply. Tyndale's Bible was printed on such presses, and many people had access to copies. However, Tyndale's translation bothered Roman Catholic officials, and he was arrested in Brussels and accused of heresy. He was executed by strangulation, after which they burned his body at the stake.

In 1611, when the English King James Bible was created, it borrowed heavily from the translation of William Tyndale. In his translation, Tyndale influenced the English language by creating such words as "passover" and "scapegoat" and phrases such as "let there be light," "my brother's keeper," and "the powers that be."

Why is Martin Luther so important?

The Protestant Reformation began with Martin Luther. Unlike the earlier voices calling for reform such as John Huss, the followers of John Wycliffe, and William Tyndale, Luther was not executed. He survived.

What is the story of Martin Luther?

Martin Luther (1483–1546) was born in Germany and grew up a Roman Catholic. As a young man, he started to attend law school; however, one day while riding a horse to school, he was struck by lightning. Luther cried out, "St. Ann, I will become a monk." Luther thought the lightning strike was a sign from God. It reminded him of the story of St. Paul being knocked from a horse on the road to Damascus.

Luther entered a monastery and became very devout in his religious duties. Motivated by an overwhelming sense of his own sinfulness, he would pray and fast extensively. He was obsessive about his sins and would go into confession and confess long lists of fairly harmless things. One day his confessor told him, "Get out of here and don't come back until you commit some real sins!"

His religious superiors were concerned about Luther's overemphasis on his sins, so they suggested he put his energies into

Martin Luther (depicted in this statue by St. Mary's Church in Berlin, Germany) was the man responsible for the start of the Protestant Reformation. Disagreeing with many of the Catholic Church's practices, he was excommunicated by Pope Leo X.

learning the Bible to become a teacher of theology. Thus, Luther undertook the study of the Scriptures. While reading St. Paul's Letter to the Romans, Luther came across the concept of "justification by faith." This was a breath of fresh air to Luther when he realized that all his efforts to remove his sinfulness were futile. All he needed to do was to have faith in what Jesus had done by dying and rising for human sins. Luther realized that he was not justified by his own efforts but rather by his faith in Jesus.

The story could have ended there, with this German monk finding the answer to his spiritual crisis. However, Luther was greatly disturbed by the practice of selling Indulgences.

At the time of Luther, what was the view about what happened after death?

Christians at the time of Luther believed in three options when a person died: Heaven, Hell, and Purgatory. Christians had a view of God as very harsh and judging. In this view, only a few very holy people would go right to Heaven when they died. It was hard to go directly to Heaven. On the other hand, many people would wind up in Hell. Anyone who committed a serious sin—there were many things that were considered serious sins in those times—and who had not gone to confession for forgiveness would be

225

punished in Hell with eternal damnation. Everyone else would go to Purgatory, which was a place for sinners to be punished and pay the price for their sins until they were purified and could go to Heaven. (Note that the word Purgatory is similar to the word "purge," which means "to clean out.")

For many centuries, there had been a strong emphasis on Purgatory. It was an important part of medieval religion with people offering prayers and Masses for dead people who were believed to be in Purgatory, with the hope that such prayers and Masses could get them into Heaven.

The idea of an Indulgence developed. (What follows is the theory of Indulgences in a simplistic form.) When a holy person dies and goes to Heaven, that person often has extra merit that he or she did not need to get to Heaven. The Church was able to assign that merit to sinners still suffering in Purgatory to reduce their time in Purgatory. A document was written to recognize this transference of merit called an "Indulgence." Initially a donation was expected; however, in time, Indulgences were sold, often to raise money for church projects.

What did Luther think about Indulgences?

With his new understanding of justification by faith, Martin Luther thought that the sale of Indulgences was terribly wrong. If the only requirement for salvation was faith in what Jesus did, then having an Indulgence would be of no help. Also, if people believed that Indulgences would get them to Heaven, it might keep them from doing the one thing that actually could get them to Heaven, which was to have faith in what Jesus did. Luther thought the sale of Indulgences was a deception and tragedy.

Luther decided that he wanted to engage someone in a debate on Indulgences. He wrote up a document called the *95 Theses*, which listed points to be debated on Indulgences. His document was only about Indulgences and was not a manifesto lamenting everything else wrong with the Catholic Church. According to legend, on October 31, 1517, he nailed his *95 Theses* to the door of the Catholic Church in Wittenberg, Germany. He nailed it there because that was the bulletin board to post such announcements. He did not do it as an act of protest.

What happened next with Martin Luther?

Luther never got the debate he wanted over Indulgences. Instead, copies were made of the *95 Theses* and spread around. He found himself in the middle of a storm of controversy. In the next several years, he continued to write and criticize Catholic teachings and practices. He was summoned to several hearings by Church officials to explain his teachings and retracted them. (To retract means to admit he was wrong.) Luther refused, and in 1520, he was excommunicated (kicked out) by the Catholic Church. However, due to the protection of the German prince Frederick, Luther was not arrested and was not executed. After a period of hiding, Luther came out in the open and wrote extensively, helping to usher in the Protestant Reformation.

What was the effect of Luther's *sola scriptura* principle?

Luther thought he had solved the problem of resolving disagreements in Christianity by asserting that the final guide was the Bible. However, as would become very clear within a few short years, other Christians reading the exact same Bible would draw many different conclusions about faith and morals. All agreed on the principle of *sola scriptura,* but they came to very different conclusions about what the Bible meant.

What three principles guided Martin Luther's thought?

Three principles—stated in Latin— guided Luther: *sola scriptura, sola fide,* and *sola gratia.*

Sola scriptura means that Scripture alone is the final authority for answering questions of faith and morals. *Sola fide* means that salvation is based on faith alone. *Sola gratia* means that salvation is freely given by God and is not earned by anyone.

What other ideas did Luther embrace?

Using his principle of *sola scriptura,* Luther looked for the concept of Purgatory and found it was not in the Bible, so he rejected it. He also looked in the gospels for the seven sacraments of the Catholic Church, but he only found two sacraments: baptism and the Lord's Supper. Luther would hold on to ceremonies such as confirmation, marriage, and ordination, but they would not be called sacraments.

Luther had lived as a celibate—unmarried—monk. Luther could not find any Bible support for the concept that church ministers should be celibate. Luther insisted that ministers should normally be married, and he himself got married to a former Catholic nun. Luther also saw no biblical support for the concept of women living in convents and for men living in monasteries.

Luther also believed that religious services should be in the language of the people. Catholic services at the time were all in Latin. He also thought that the Bible should be available to all people. He created the first German translation of the Bible. Also, the practice at Mass was for the laity—the people in the pew—to only receive the bread and not drink from the cup of wine. Luther insisted that the laity should also drink from the cup.

Today, what denominations in the United States are descended from Luther's teachings?

The two main Lutheran denominations in America are the Lutheran Church–Missouri Synod and the Evangelical Lutheran Church in America (ELCA). (There are other Lutheran denominations in America such as the Wisconsin Synod.) The Missouri Synod is the more traditional branch. The word "synod" means the governing council of the

227

Church. The teaching of the Missouri Synod insists on a literal interpretation of the Bible. Only men are allowed to be priests. The church opposes abortion and same-sex marriage. One of the outreach ministries of the Missouri Synod is *The Lutheran Hour* radio show, which has been broadcasting since 1930.

The ELCA, the larger denomination, allows for women priests, does not insist on taking the Bible literally, has many members who take a pro-choice position, and allows same-sex marriage.

Who was John Calvin?

John Calvin (1509–1567) was the next figure in the Protestant Reformation. He was born in France but lived most of his life in Geneva, Switzerland. Calvin wanted to reform Christianity based on the Bible. In 1536 he published his theological teachings as *Institutes of the Christian Religion.*

Like Luther, Calvin explored St. Paul's Letter to the Romans, in which Calvin found the concept of predestination. Calvin would come to understand predestination as the idea that God has already predestined or predetermined who is going to Heaven and who is going to Hell. Furthermore, humans cannot by their actions or decisions change their destiny.

Calvin was trying to assert the sovereignty of God: God is in control of everything. Therefore, if humans had the choice on whether they got to Heaven or not, then God would not be control. From Calvin's time to the present, Christians have argued and disagreed over the concept of predestination. Calvin also insisted that Christians should live a strict moral life.

Although Martin Luther did not do much to change the actual church buildings, Calvin called for drastic changes. Calvin removed all statues, images in stained glass windows, and all decoration from his churches. He also did away with special clothes—called vestments—for the ministers, insisting instead that they wear simple, black academic robes. Calvin also got rid of elaborate music and complex choral pieces. Calvin wanted simple and austere church buildings with simple services so the congregation could focus on God and not be distracted.

John Calvin believed that God had already predetermined who would go to Heaven and, therefore, people could not change their destiny by their actions.

What happened with Calvin's teaching of predestination?

After Calvin died, a follower, named Jacobus Arminius (1560–1609), began developing his own theology in which he watered down the concept of predestination. Arminius wondered what the point of Christianity was if it is already determined whether you are going to Heaven or Hell and there is nothing you can do about it. What is the motivation for becoming a Christian? His views became known as Arminianism.

In 1618, a group of Calvinist leaders met in a Dutch town named Dort for a meeting called the Synod of Dort. At the meeting, they rejected the ideas of Arminius and insisted on five principles, reasserting the concept of predestination in very strong terms. The five principles are remembered with the acronym TULIP.

*T*otal depravity
*U*nconditional predestination
*L*imited atonement
*I*rresistibility of grace
*P*erseverance of the saints

What is the meaning of the five principles of TULIP?

Although you may not accept the concept of predestination, try to follow the inner logic of these principles. "Total depravity" is the idea that there is no natural goodness in humans. Therefore, all humans deserve condemnation to eternal damnation. "Unconditional predestination" means that God has already determined who is going to Heaven and who is going to Hell and there is nothing you can do to change that destiny.

"Limited atonement" is the idea that Jesus only died to redeem the saints, those who are going to Heaven. Jesus did not die for those who were condemned to Hell. This idea is different from the belief of typical Christians that Jesus died for everyone, although some may reject Jesus or live immorally and wind up in Hell. The "atonement" refers to the death and Resurrection of Jesus to redeem humans from sin and its punishments. According to Calvinist thought, the atonement is limited to the saints.

"Irresistibility of grace" is the belief that salvation is offered by God to those whom he chooses, and those chosen cannot refuse God's offer. This offer of salvation is called "grace."

If it is already determined whether you are going to Heaven or Hell, why not live an immoral life? If one cannot earn salvation by moral living or lose it by living sinfully, why not live immorally and have pleasure? "Perseverance of the saints" answers this objection. The saints—those who are predestined for Heaven—will live moral lives. They do not earn salvation by living morally; rather, moral living is a sign that they are predestined for Heaven.

Today, what denominations follow the teachings of John Calvin?

The most important denomination that follows Calvin is the Presbyterian Church. The name comes from the word "presbyter," which is based on the Greek word for "elder."

Other denominations include the Dutch Reformed Church and the German Reformed Church. In the 1960s, these two denominations merged with other groups to form the United Church of Christ.

Who was Henry VIII of England?

Henry VIII (1491–1547), the king of England, was a devout Catholic and a supporter of the pope. Henry even wrote an essay condemning Martin Luther and his teachings, for which the pope called Henry the "Defender of the Faith." However, Henry did not have a son. Henry desperately wanted a son to take the throne when he died. He feared a civil war if there was no clear successor to the throne.

Henry's wife was Catherine of Aragon from Spain. Catherine bore a daughter, Mary, but no son. Henry decided he would need another wife who could provide him a son. (At the time, they did not understand the process of conception—that it is the sperm of the male that determines the gender of a child.)

Henry asked the pope for an annulment to end his marriage so he could leave Catherine and marry Anne Boleyn. Normally, the pope would have agreed to such an annulment; however, the pope was under pressure from the Spanish to not annul the marriage. The Spanish wanted to keep the Spanish Catherine on the throne of England. The pope refused Henry's request.

Henry's response was to break away from the Catholic Church and create the Church of England, also known as the Anglican Church. He became head of this church. Henry soon found other benefits of breaking away from the pope. At the time, all European countries paid taxes to the pope in Rome. Henry could now keep that tax money in England. Also, any legal cases involving clerics or church property could be appealed to courts in Rome, which were favorable to the Catholic Church. Now, all such cases had to stay in England and be resolved in English courts.

Although Martin Luther rejected the idea of monks in monasteries as not biblical, Henry saw a practical advantage to getting rid of monasteries in England. Many of the monasteries were very large properties. Henry suppressed the monasteries, closed them down, and gave the land to lords who supported him. The

King Henry VIII of England was a faithful Catholic until the pope denied him his wish to divorce his first wife; he left the Church and created the Anglican Church, which, of course, permitted his divorce.

lords then created large estates. On some of these estates today, the old ruins of the medieval monasteries can still be seen. Some estates retained the names of the monasteries that were closed. Note the name of the popular PBS TV series *Downton Abbey*. An abbey is a monastery.

However, beyond these changes, the Church of England retained many of the elements of the Roman Catholic Church in terms of belief and liturgical practices. Many Christians in England were happy with things this way, while many others wanted more changes.

Who were the six wives of Henry VIII?

Henry VIII divorced Catherine and married Anne Boleyn. However, Anne did not produce a son. She was accused of being unfaithful to Henry and was beheaded. Four more wives followed. The six wives were:

- Catherine of Aragon—She gave birth to Mary. Henry had their marriage annulled.
- Anne Boleyn—She gave birth to Elizabeth. Anne was beheaded.
- Jane Seymour—She gave birth to Edward. She died twelve days later.
- Anne of Cleves—Henry had their marriage annulled.
- Catherine Howard—She was beheaded.
- Catherine Parr—She became a widow when Henry died.

   Their fates can be remembered as "divorced, beheaded, died, divorced, beheaded, lived."

Did Henry's son become king? What about his daughters?

Yes, his son, Edward, became King Edward VI. He became king in 1547 at age nine. He died at age fifteen.

Henry's daughter, Mary, took the throne in 1553 when Edward died. She tried to undo the religious changes of Henry VIII and take England back to the Catholic Church. During her reign, she burned over 280 religious dissenters at the stake. Her opponents called her "Bloody Mary."

In 1558 Elizabeth became queen. She took up the effort of Henry to create a Protestant England. She also executed many religious dissenters.

THE ANGLICAN CHURCH
AND THE PURITAN MOVEMENT

What is the *Book of Common Prayer*?

The *Book of Common Prayer* is an important book for Anglicans. It contains prayers for use by individuals in private prayer but also prayers to be used in all Anglican rituals and   231 ceremonies. Originally published in 1549, it was revised several times before taking its final form.

What are the *Thirty-nine Articles*?

The *Thirty-nine Articles* are a list of the essential principles of the Anglican Church. They were finalized in 1571. (King Henry had died in 1547.) The articles state basic beliefs about issues of faith, the Bible, and ministers. (The *Thirty-nine Articles* can be found online and can be read quickly if you are interested.)

What is the Puritan movement?

Within the Anglican Church, a movement developed of people who called themselves "Puritans." Puritans wanted to "purify" the church of Roman Catholic elements. They wanted to make the Church of England more Protestant and less "popish" or "Romish." Over the next centuries, the Puritans grew in strength and influence. However, they were a diverse group with many different views on how far the purification of the Church of England should go. Some Puritans even broke away from the Church of England.

Seeking greater religious freedom, some Puritans came to the New World to establish the colony of Plymouth and the Massachusetts Bay Colony (which would later become Boston). However, keep in mind that these Puritans wanted religious freedom for themselves. They were not interested in the religious freedom of others.

What are the two styles of the Anglican Church?

Two styles of liturgy and church design developed in the Anglican Church: high church and low church. High church congregations tend to have more elaborate buildings with more religious art and decoration. Their religious ceremonies tend to be more elaborate. The low church style has a much simpler liturgy and uses church buildings of simpler design. Low church congregations are closer to many Protestant groups.

The terms "high church" and "low church" are helpful when discussing various Christian denominations. Denominations with elaborate buildings and elaborate ceremonies are "high church." Denominations with simple buildings and simple ceremonies are "low church."

What happened to the Church of England (the Anglican Church) during the Revolutionary War?

The Anglican Church came to the American colonies. In several colonies, such as Virginia, it was the official religion. After the Revolutionary War, the Anglicans in America broke their ties with England and created the Episcopal Church. Their members are called Episcopalians. The word "episcopal" comes from the Greek word for bishop. They consecrated their own bishops in America rather than follow the previous practice of getting bishops from England.

THE ANABAPTISTS

After Martin Luther, John Calvin, and Henry VIII broke away from the Catholic Church, what other groups also broke away?

The next part of the Protestant Reformation is the story of a number of different groups that are called the "Anabaptists."

Did the Baptists come from the Anabaptists?

No, the Baptists are a different group that will be talked about in the next chapter.

Well, then, who are the Anabaptists?

The Anabaptists get their name from a word that meant to "re-baptize." The Anabaptists believed that only adult baptism mattered. They noted that infant baptism was not in the Bible. Therefore, if one was baptized as an infant, it did not count, and one had to be re-baptized. In Europe at the time, most people had been baptized as infants, yet many of these people did not live Christian lives. The Anabaptists realized that baptism did not make one a Christian. One could only be baptized as an adult when one could make a commitment to live a true Christian life.

Is the early Anabaptist history easy to understand?

The early history of the Anabaptist movement is complicated because there were a whole series of groups with different views and ideas. Most were very devout and moral Christians but not all them. One group took over the town of Münster in Germany in 1533 to create the Kingdom of God on earth. The leader of the group claimed he could have more than one wife. In the end, the local prince and the bishop brought an army and crushed what is called the Münster Rebellion. However, this extreme group was an exception.

Why are the Anabaptists called the Radicals of the Reformation?

The word "radical" means to go to the root of something. The Anabaptists did not think anyone had gone far enough in trying to reform Christianity. They believed that true Christians had to go further in getting to the root of the message of Jesus.

For Anabaptists, two key teachings of Jesus were important. Jesus said, "If some-

One of the central tenets of the Anabaptists is that one should choose to be baptized as an adult. Faith is a choice, and therefore, an infant's inability to choose to be baptized makes the ritual less meaningful.

233

one strikes you on one cheek, turn the other cheek" (Luke 6:29, NABRE). Anabaptists took this seriously. They would not use violence, even in self-defense. The Anabaptists were nonviolent pacifists. They would not fight in war nor would they be on a police force. They would not even defend themselves.

The Anabaptists focused on another teaching of Jesus to not swear oaths. The Anabaptists would not swear oaths. In our culture today, we occasionally swear oaths such as when testifying as a witness in court. However, in the 1500s there were all kinds of loyalty oaths that one had to swear. The Anabaptists would not swear such oaths. This created great resentment against them. Nonviolence and no oaths were key concepts for the Anabaptists.

What was the Anabaptist attitude toward heretics?

At the time, every other group of Christians used violence against those who held the wrong views. Arrest, prison, torture, and execution were commonly used against heretics. The Anabaptists said that such violence was not Christian. According to the Anabaptists, if someone had the wrong ideas, then all the Christian community could do was to ban that person from the church. If the heretic did not reform, then the community would do the next thing, which was to shun the person. Even family members were not supposed to talk to shunned people. Although this may seem harsh today, it was far more humane than what the other Christians would do, so Anabaptists practiced "banning and shunning."

Today, many Anabaptists still shun family members who do not accept the religious teachings of their communities. Frequently, the family will not talk to the person with the hope that one day the person will return to the community. By today's standards, most other Christians see this as harsh. Most other Christians will still maintain family relationships with those who do not belong to the same church.

What did the Anabaptists think about religious freedom?

Anabaptists believed that faith was a free choice. The early Anabaptists lived at a time when kingdoms had official religions. These official religions were often enforced by law. The Anabaptists thought it was wrong to force people to belong to a church. Anabaptists played an important early role in the development of the idea of religious freedom.

Anabaptists also believed that churches should be separate from government. They thought that government was about power, force, and violence. Therefore, government was not Christian. Anabaptists believed you should obey the laws, except when the laws went against the teachings of Christ.

What happened to the Anabaptist groups in Europe?

The Anabaptists in Europe found much persecution and rejection in Europe. Hundreds of Anabaptists were executed in the 1500s. Many Anabaptists remember the names and stories of these numerous Anabaptist martyrs. As the British colonies opened up in the

> ### How can I learn more about early Anabaptist beliefs?
>
> You could read the 1527 *Schleitheim Confession*, which can be found online. The *Confession* gives an overview of the essential Anabaptist beliefs. (It runs about thirty-seven hundred words in length.)

New World, many Anabaptists fled to America. The colony of Pennsylvania was particularly open to the Anabaptists. (Many of the other colonies did not want Anabaptists.)

I have never heard of a church called the Anabaptist Church, so who are the Anabaptists today?

The two most important Anabaptist groups are the Amish and the Mennonites. They were both started in Europe, but when they experienced religious persecution, they came to the colonies in the New World. The Mennonites were started in Europe by Menno Simons (1492–1559).

Who are the Amish?

Under the leadership of Jakob Ammann (1644–c. 1730), this group broke off from the main body of Mennonites in Europe. His followers then came to the American colonies.

Among many of the Amish today, there is rejection of modern technology. Their reason is rather simple. Their goal is to control the influence of technology and not have it control them. (Think for a moment about how technology controls your life.) Some Amish have a phone but not in the house. That way, they decide when they are going to use the phone and not the other way around. The Amish worry that non-Amish culture with all of its technology will distract people from their Christian faith.

The Amish in America continue to grow, in part because they have large families. There are large Amish communities in Pennsylvania, Kentucky, Indiana, Illinois, and Missouri.

Why do many Amish and Mennonite men wear black clothes? Why do the women wear traditional, simple dresses?

The goal with Amish and Mennonite clothes is to not wear anything that is decorative. For many Amish and Mennonites, their clothes often do not even have buttons, which are seen as decorations. Those Amish who use buggies typically do not want decorations even on their buggies. Initially, many fought state laws requiring them to put a bright orange triangle on the back of their buggies to avoid accidents. A black buggy on a highway is hard to see at night by a car moving 60 miles an hour. Most Amish buggies now have the safety triangles.

A group of Mennonites bow their heads in prayer. Compared to their Anabaptist cousins, the Mennonites are more accepting of modern technology, especially for farm use, but they embrace a lifestyle free of luxuries.

Is there only one kind of Amish and one kind of Mennonite?

There are a number of different Amish and Mennonite groups. These groups often have different rules about how to dress and what technology can be used. Also, despite their attempts to resist modern technology, it has made many inroads into Amish life, and things are changing for some Amish.

I have heard that many Amish do not participate in the American Social Security program. Is that true?

The goal of Social Security is to provide retirement income for elderly people. The Amish think that families and the local community should take care of the elderly and do not see such programs as necessary.

Are there any other important Anabaptist groups?

A third group, the Hutterites, is not as well known. They were founded by Jacob Hutter, who was executed in 1536 in Europe. This group thought private property was the enemy of love, so they held property in common. The Hutterites were expelled from Europe in 1622 and then settled in South Dakota, Montana, and Manitoba in Canada. They use modern things but work collectively.

What song did "Weird Al" Yankovich compose about the Amish?

The comic singer "Weird Al" Yankovich wrote a song and made a video entitled "Amish Paradise." It is based on Coolio's song and video called "Gangsta's Paradise." Many people have found this a charming parody of Amish life.

THE CATHOLIC
COUNTER-REFORMATION

What is the Counter-Reformation?

During the Reformation, various Protestant groups under the leadership of Martin Luther, John Calvin, Henry VIII, and various Anabaptist leaders broke away from the Roman Catholic Church to form their own churches. The Catholic Church response to the Reformation is called the Counter-Reformation. The Catholic Church wanted to defend its own beliefs and practices, address some of the problems within the church, and make the Catholic Church more attractive to ordinary people. To accomplish these goals, the Catholic Church called a series of meetings called the Council of Trent, created a new order of priests—the Jesuits—and promoted the building of new churches filled with dramatic artwork to attract people to the Catholic faith.

What was the Council of Trent?

The Council of Trent was three sets of meetings of Roman Catholic bishops in the Italian city of Trento. The first was in 1545, and the last one ended in 1563.

What does the word "Tridentine" mean?

"Tridentine" is an adjective based on the word "Trent," so the reforms coming from the Council of Trent can be called the Tridentine Reforms. The Catholic Mass that came out of the council is called the Tridentine Mass.

What was the origin of the Council of Trent?

For many years prior to the Reformation, a number of Catholics had been calling for a church council or meeting of the bishops to address the numerous problems within the Catholic Church. The popes in Rome resisted their calls because they did not want a council. They feared "Conciliarism," which was the idea that church councils should be the final decision-makers for the Church. Eventually, Pope Paul III, in response to the growing Protestant movement, gave in and agreed to allow the council. However, he and his successors did their best to control what happened at the council. (There were five popes from the beginning to the end of the Council of Trent.)

The council was called to respond to the Protestant Reformation and address problems within the Catholic Church. After several false starts, the council met for three periods: 1545–1547, 1551–1552, and 1562–1563. A total of 217 bishops attended the last session.

What was the purpose of the Council?

In the early calls for the Council, a number of voices proposed a meeting to reconcile the various divisions of the Christian Church. Their goal was to bring together the major

237

Protestant groups and the Catholic Church to try to put the pieces back together. However, once Trent got started, Catholic hardliners took over, and all hopes for reconciliation were dashed. Thus, the divisions between Catholics and Protestants grew deeper.

What did the Council of Trent do?

The Council produced a series of decrees on Catholic teachings. One set of decrees dealt with issues of doctrine about what to believe; another set dealt with issues of discipline that were rules about how the church should be run. For the most part, the doctrinal decrees were a rejection of the key points of Protestant theology and a clarification of Catholic teachings.

What are the important doctrinal decrees of the Council of Trent?

Here are eight of the most important doctrinal decrees:

1. Scripture and tradition are the two primary sources of divine revelation. Tradition is found in the writings of the Church fathers and the decrees of popes and councils. *This decree rejected Martin Luther's teaching that scripture alone is the only source of revelation for Christians.*

2. Man is justified with God's grace with man's free cooperation by good works of faith, hope, and charity. *Martin Luther insisted on faith alone as the requirement for salvation. At Trent, the bishops insisted that faith needed to be accompanied by good works such as charity to help those in need.*

3. Grace is an indispensable principle of supernatural life, which man can use or abuse. *This decree rejected the Calvinist principle of "Irresistibility of Grace."*

4. Grace is given to all, not merely to the elect, and is lost by mortal sin, although faith is driven out only by infidelity. *This was a rejection of John Calvin's teaching of predestination and a rejection of the corollary that Jesus only died for the elect.*

5. The sacraments are means of justification instituted by Christ, are seven in number, and produce their effect independent of the minister. *This decree rejected Martin Luther's teaching that Jesus only instituted two sacraments.*

6. Eucharist is the true sacrament in which Christ's body and blood are really and substantially contained with His divinity. Christ is present whole and entire under both species and each part of those species.

7. The substance of bread and wine is entirely changed into the substance of Christ's body and blood with the appearance of bread and wine remaining: this is aptly called transubstantiation. *These decrees affirm the Roman Catholic teaching that the bread and wine in Mass truly become the body and blood of Jesus. The term "transubstantiation" is the theological explanation made of the prefix "trans," which means "to cross over," and the root "substance," which means "essence." In Mass, the essence of the bread becomes the essence of the body of Christ. The essence of the wine becomes the essence of the blood of Christ. However, the ac-*

cidentals of the bread, such as the look, feel, and taste, remain the same. Doctrine number 6 also rejects the Protestant idea that laypeople should receive the cup during Mass. Since Christ is present in both the bread and wine, taking the bread alone is sufficient.

8. The sacrament of penance was instituted by Christ for remission of sins by absolution from a validly ordained priest having jurisdiction. *Protestants rejected the sacrament of penance. In this decree, the Catholic Church affirmed the belief in the sacrament of penance as something instituted by Jesus. Also, this decree affirms that penance done by a valid priest does take away one's sins.*

What are the important disciplinary decrees of the Council of Trent?

Here are nine key disciplinary decrees of the Council of Trent:

1. Choice of bishops and cardinals pertains to pope. *In this decree, the Catholic Churches asserted that the pope had the right to select bishops and cardinals. A number of kings had wanted to pick bishops and cardinals who would support their own interests.*

2. Bishops, cardinals, patriarchs, and archbishops are obliged to reside in their dioceses.

3. Bishops are to visit parishes to inquire into discipline and morals. *These two decrees required church officials to live in the territories assigned to them and to check up on the priests under them to make sure the priests were doing good work and following church rules.*

4. Benefices should not be multiplied. *A benefice was a church job with an income. Some clergy were holding several benefices to get all the income yet were ignoring most of their job responsibilities.*

5. No one shall be pastor without inquiry into his qualifications by the bishop.

6. Seminaries should be erected in each diocese, or where necessary, region. *These two decrees required that priests be qualified and properly trained at seminaries, which are special schools to train priests. The requirement that each diocese have a seminary was one of the more important decisions of the Council of Trent. It raised the educational standards for priests.*

7. Clerics of religious orders are to reside in their houses and follow vows and rules. *Monks were required to stay in their monasteries and follow the rules.*

8. Secret marriages were prohibited. Catholics must be married before a priest and two witnesses. *Secret marriages were a problem. A man could secretly marry a woman and later abandon her, claiming that they were never married.*

9. The Index of Prohibited Books was to be revised, with rules for enforcement. *The Index was a list of books that Catholics were not supposed to read. All of the Protestant writings would be added to it. Keep in mind that the Gutenberg press had been invented only a hundred years earlier. This had greatly increased the number of publications available for reading.*

239

THE JESUITS

Who were the Jesuits?

Another key point in the Counter-Reformation was the founding of the Jesuits, the Society of Jesus. The organization was started by Ignatius of Loyola (1491–1556). Ignatius grew up in Spain and became a soldier. However, his leg was injured by a cannonball. While recovering, he went to a place called Manresa, where he wrote his small book called the *Spiritual Exercises*.

He decided to commit his life to the church and went to study in Paris. He set up his own order of priests called the Society of Jesus. In 1540 Pope Paul III approved the order. Ignatius wanted to reform the church through education, the sacraments, preaching of the gospels, and missionary work. The slogan of Ignatius and the Jesuits is *Ad Majorem Dei Gloriam!* This is Latin for "To the Greater Glory of God."

What impact did the Jesuits have in North America?

Jesuits from Spain and France played an important early role as missionaries. The Jesuit Père Jacques Marquette (1637–1675) made several important trips to explore the Mississippi River. *Père* is the French word for "Father." The Jesuits would eventually establish some thirty colleges and universities in the United States.

What about Counter-Reformation art and architecture?

In order to pull people into the churches, the Catholic Church began building them in a dramatic style called the Baroque. The Church also supported Baroque artists, such as Caravaggio, to create dramatic religious images to stir the emotions.

Spanish priest and theologian Ignatius of Loyola founded the Jesuit order in 1541. The Jesuits were loyal to the pope and served as missionaries.

CHRISTIAN HISTORY IN EUROPE: 1600s TO THE PRESENT

What is the King James Bible?

The King James Bible was an English translation of the Bible completed in 1611. It was created during the reign of King James I of England and Ireland (1566–1625). The translation was not based on the Latin Catholic version but rather on the original Greek, Hebrew, and Aramaic texts. However, most of the King James Bible is based on the translations done by William Tyndale. The King James Bible became the standard Bible for most English-speaking Protestant congregations in Europe and America. Some churches still insist on using it today. The original King James Bible used an older form of English with words such as "thy" for "your," "thou" for "you," and "shalt" for "shall."

THE BAPTISTS

You have described the origin of the Anabaptists, but what about the Baptists?

The Baptist movement began with an English exile living in Amsterdam named John Smyth (pronounced Smith). Many English went to Amsterdam for religious freedom. In 1609, he began the practice of believer's baptism. He believed that people should only be baptized when they were old enough to make a commitment of faith and could live out that faith. This is the start of the Baptist movement. It was very diverse from the beginning. The Baptist tradition, in its several varieties, is the second largest religious group in the United States.

Baptists have strong beliefs about the ritual of baptism. They usually insist on baptism by full immersion for young people or adults. They do not baptize babies. Many Baptist churches have baptismal tanks within the church. Baptists reject the idea that baptism is a sacrament conferring grace. Rather, they recognize it as a ritual that admits one who has already been saved. It is a sign that one has already accepted Jesus and been saved. One has to have a conversion experience before being baptized.

The Baptist tradition is based on self-sufficient congregations, organized in loose associations. Each congregation is independent. Thus, different Baptist congregations have different beliefs. One of the reasons for the diversity of the Baptist tradition is that each congregation is on its own to hire and fire its ministers and to decide on its doctrine. For Baptists, the Bible is the sole source of faith, and they typically reject creeds such as the Nicene Creed as being man-made. However, many Baptists agree with many of the concepts within the Nicene Creed.

Within the Baptist tradition, there is disagreement over many issues. Some Baptists believe in predestination, while others, such as "Free Will" Baptists, reject predestination. They disagree on missionary work. The two concepts are linked. If people are predestined, there is no need for missionary work. Baptists disagree on whether the Bible should be taken literally or not, although many Baptist groups insist on a literal interpretation of the Bible.

What are the different Baptist groups today?

Counted together, the Baptists are the second largest religious group in America after Roman Catholics. The largest group of Baptists are those congregations affiliated with the Southern Baptist Convention. Also significant are the American Baptist Churches. For African Americans, the largest denomination is the National Baptist Convention. In addition, there are numerous Independent Baptist congregations.

THE QUAKERS

Who are the Quakers?

The Quaker movement was started in England by George Fox (1624–1691). Fox lived about a hundred years after Martin Luther. He thought that no one had gone far enough in getting back to basics. Fox asked, "Where ultimately does one find God?" Is it in buildings? Is it in rituals? Is it in church structures? Is it in the Bible? According to Fox, the answer is "no." The place where one ultimately finds God is in one's own heart. God is found within a person.

This was the life experience of George Fox. He was apprenticed as a shoemaker. As a young man in 1643, he left his family to seek religious truth. He had a profound religious experience that changed him and changed his thinking. Fox created the Doctrine of the Inner Light, which held that people find the Light of God within themselves. Fox thought that individuals can find truth on their own. He saw no need for ministers, liturgy, sacraments, music, a sanctuary, or consecrated buildings. The followers of Fox became known as the Quakers.

Fox abolished all liturgy and special buildings: there are no sacred buildings or sacred spaces. When Quakers get together for prayer, it is in a meetinghouse. Quaker services are very simple, with no formal structure. Quakers pray quietly until someone feels inspired by the Holy Spirit to speak or pray aloud. There are no ministers at Quaker services. Quakers emphasize the Holy Spirit and the experience of the Holy Spirit. The Quakers followed the Anabaptists in rejecting violence and rejecting the swearing of oaths. However, they did not take on the rejection of modern society.

During his life, George Fox made journeys to Ireland, the West Indies, and North America. Like the Anabaptists and other groups, the Quakers in Europe were frequently imprisoned and harassed. Thus, many Quakers headed for the American colonies. They received some friction in the

The Quakers (Religious Society of Friends) were founded by George Fox, the son of a weaver, who believed that one should live a simple life and that God is found in one's heart, not in rituals or expensive cathedrals.

colonies, but for the most part, they found more freedom than in Europe. The colony of Pennsylvania was set up by a Quaker, William Penn, on the principle of religious freedom.

How did they get the name Quakers? Is that their official name?

The full name for the Quakers is the Religious Society of Friends, which means "Friends of the Truth." "Quakers" is a nickname they picked up, perhaps because of the intense religious experience of early followers.

Quakers have often been vocal on issues of social justice. Many Quakers have spoken out against war and violence. Many Quakers played important roles in the anti-slavery movement and in reforming prisons and institutions for the mentally ill. Many were active in the fight of civil rights in America in the 1960s.

And, of course, there is the logo for Quaker Oatmeal showing a Quaker in traditional dress from several centuries ago.

JOHN WESLEY AND METHODISM

What is the origin of the Methodist Church?

The Methodist Church began as a movement within the Anglican Church led by John Wesley (1703–1791), the son of an Anglican minister. In 1784 he left the Anglican Church and formed the Methodist Church.

243

What is the story of the Methodist Church?

John Wesley was ordained as an Anglican priest. In 1738 he had a conversion experience that he called a "heart-warming experience." It changed his life. He had been religious all his life, but now, he found a new emotional depth to his faith. He began to preach salvation by faith to anyone who would listen.

Many Anglican churches did not let him preach, so Wesley preached in fields, stadiums, and factories. He appealed to the masses, and many listened. A few threw tomatoes and stones, but in general, his movement grew. He was successful in part because many of the clergy of the Church of England were not good ministers and preachers. Also, the Church of England, while well-established among the upper classes, did little for the growing working class, which was rapidly increasing in the 1700s due to the Industrial Revolution. Populations were growing, and many people were moving from the country to the cities.

The tireless John Wesley would eventually travel 250,000 miles in his life and preach forty-two thousand sermons. He even made it to the American colony of Georgia. In England, he organized lay pastors to help. He then trained some men to be ordained as ministers to be sent to the American Colonies, but the Anglican bishops would not ordain them. Wesley ordained them himself, and with that, his movement broke away from the Church of England.

The key to the Methodist tradition is the importance of an emotional conversion experience. Also, Methodism has a certain tolerance for differences of doctrine. Methodists realized that it was better to not fight about the details, especially if the Bible did not give a definite answer.

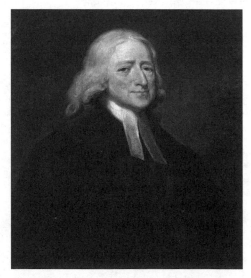

English cleric John Wesley founded the Methodist Church in 1784.

Methodism came to the American Colonies, and by the time of the American Civil War, it was the largest religion in America. It would eventually be passed over by the Baptists and Catholics. The rapid growth of Methodism in America was in part due to a system of traveling bishops, who set up parishes that could function by themselves. Today, a number of Methodist churches exist in the United States, with the largest being the United Methodist Church.

What is a good source to learn more about John Wesley?

The sermons of John Wesley can be found online if you want to explore them. Just do an online search for "Sermons of John Wesley."

THE 1800s

What is Liberal Protestantism?

This movement of the late 1800s into the 1900s tried to rethink Christianity and in the process rejected many traditional Christian doctrines. "Liberal Protestantism," the label for this movement, has nothing to do with the modern political definition of the word "liberal."

Two key figures in the Liberal Protestant movement were Albrecht Ritschl (1822–1889) and Adolph von Harnack (1851–1930). Ritschl saw that the traditional Christian teachings of the virgin birth, the miracles of Jesus, and the Resurrection of Jesus were unnecessary for understanding the historical Jesus who walked the earth. He saw the New Testament picture of Jesus as that of a perfect being taking up the ethical calling to live out God's love within the Christian community.

Harnack taught at several universities in Germany. A prolific writer, his two most important works are *What Is Christianity?* and *History of Dogma*. He thought that the original message of Jesus had been distorted by the Greek philosophy that had been used by Christian institutions to create Christian doctrine. Harnack wanted to remove the layers of doctrine to get back to the primitive gospel message of Jesus. Harnack found three essential themes in the gospel:

1. The coming of the Kingdom of God,
2. God the Father and the value of the human soul, and
3. A higher righteousness based on the commandments of love.

He wanted to separate the kernel of the original teaching of Jesus from the husk of later Christian doctrine. In the process, Harnack rejected the traditional understandings of the Incarnation and Trinity.

What is the crisis over the Bible?

In the 1800s, a crisis developed in Christianity that continues for some Christians today. It is the question over how to read the Bible. In earlier times, it had not been a big issue.

Most people took it for granted that the stories in the Bible were true the way they were written. Few people doubted stories such as Adam and Eve, Noah and the flood, and Jonah in the whale (or fish).

In the 1800s, a number of difficult questions were raised about the Bible that came from science, history, and literature. Although the studies of science and history were still developing, they raised serious and critical questions about how we understand the Bible.

The first set of questions came from geology, which in the 1700s and 1800s began to say that the earth was very old. Some geologists began talking about the earth as many millions or hundreds of millions of years old. (Eventually, in the twentieth century, the earth would be dated at 4.6 billion years old.) This went against the biblical notion that the earth was about six thousand years old.

At the same time, important advances were made in the study of ancient languages and writings. Archeologists were digging up clay tablets with ancient texts in Mesopotamia (the land of Iraq today). Scholars realized that the Bible was not such a unique document. There were other ancient documents that had some similarities to some parts of the Bible.

One discovery in particular was important. In England, a researcher translated the ancient story *The Epic of Gilgamesh*. The *Epic* includes a story of a flood and a boat of animals surviving the flood. This showed that the flood story was not unique to the Bible. Other scholars noticed that some of the biblical laws seemed to be based on the Code of Hammurabi. Therefore, the biblical writings were not unique. Furthermore, the Bible seemed to be the product of ancient human efforts.

Then came Charles Darwin (1809–1882), who published his book, *The Origin of Species,* in 1859. Darwin did not invent the idea of evolution, but he systemized it and added the driving mechanism: natural selection. Natural selection works like this. There are accidental genetic variations within a group of animals. Sometimes, these variations give some individuals a better chance at survival. Since these animals survive, the chances are better that their genetic difference will get passed on to the next generation and give them an advantage to survival.

Here is an example: coal smoke and dust became a problem in certain areas of England. There were some moths that were light-colored and stood out against the bark of a tree that had been darkened by coal dust. Predators could see them and eat them. A moth that had an accidental genetic variation and was slightly darker would have a better chance of blending in and not getting eaten. This darker moth survived and could reproduce. The offspring of this moth would more likely be darker and more likely to survive. In time, the darker moths would reproduce, and the lighter moths would get eaten up. The population of the moths would be darker. The color of the moths would evolve.

In working out his ideas on evolution, Darwin described the very long process of living creatures evolving from less-developed creatures. Darwin went on to say that humans had evolved from less-developed creatures over a long period of time. He concluded that humans were somehow related to apes.

However, evolutionary ideas seemed to be a threat to what the Bible said. If humans were related to apes, this seemed to deny the uniqueness of humans as God's creation. Also, there is no mention of evolution in the Bible. In the creation story in the book of Genesis, it says that humans were created on day six. According to the theory, evolution requires an immense amount of time. If the earth is only six thousand years old, there would not be enough time for evolution.

What were the responses to the crisis over the Bible?

Three responses developed to the questions raised about the Bible:

1. *Ignore the problem.* For many people, the answer was simple: focus on other parts of religion and ignore the threat to a literal reading of the Bible. Some people focused on spirituality, or the spiritual experience, or prayer, or ritual and did not let the problem bother them.

2. *Accept that science is right but still believe in the meaning of the Bible.* This is the second contextualist view described earlier: the Bible is a human writing inspired by God. In this view, the Bible is the religious experience of the ancient Jews and Christians

An 1855 photo of Charles Darwin around the time he was working on *The Origin of Species*. The theory of evolution threw into question how the Bible portrays the creation of the world by God.

247

It is important to note that the questions raised by geology, ancient literature, and evolution only challenge a literal reading of a small portion of the Bible, yet people who reject the conclusions of these disciplines often seem to think that the whole Bible is threatened. These people feel that if you question any part of the Bible, you undermine the whole thing.

Many other Christians have found that the contextualist approach frees one up to read and explore the Bible and understand it from the perspective of the original writers. This helps the reader to grasp the underlying story of religious faith.

written in a prescientific time. Thus, a Christian can accept science on the age of the earth and evolution, yet accept the value of the religious teaching and meanings of the Bible.

3. *Reject science and insist on the literal interpretation of the Bible*. This is the literalist position. It would be called the fundamentalist position and would lead to an influential and powerful movement in American Christianity.

THE WORLD COUNCIL OF CHURCHES AND VATICAN I AND II

What is the World Council of Churches?

In 1948 the World Council of Churches (WCC) was created in response to the ecumenical movement of the nineteenth and twentieth centuries. Many of the mainline Christian denominations belong to it. The ecumenical movement sought to get different Christian groups together to talk to one another to find common ground and understanding and to overcome centuries of animosity and misunderstanding between different Christian denominations. The WCC promotes justice and peace.

What happened at Vatican I?

Many centuries had passed since the previous Catholic church council—the Council of Trent from 1545 to 1563. Popes had avoided calling councils, preferring to decide church policy and practice on their own. However, Pope Pius IX, in the face of numerous political setbacks, decided to call a council at the Vatican.

The Council lasted from December 1869 to October 1870. The only significant teaching to come out of the Council was the teaching that the pope cannot err when teaching on matters of faith and morals. This is the teaching of "papal infallibility."

What happened at Vatican II?

In 1958 Pope John XXIII (1881–1963, born Angelo Giuseppe Roncalli) became pope, although not much was expected of the elderly man. To everyone's surprise, he called for a council to open the window of the church to the Holy Spirit. Starting in 1962 and lasting until 1965, the Council of Vatican II was a series of meetings of hundreds of bishops, archbishops, and cardinals from around the world. Pope John died in the middle of the Council, and Pope Paul VI was elected. Important Catholic theologians and thinkers such as Ives Congar, Karl Rahner, and Hans Kühn attended the Council.

The end result of the Council was sixteen documents that covered issues such as the Catholic Church in the modern world, the relation of the church to other Christians, the relation of the church to non-Christians, the priesthood, the role of sisters, and the Catholic teaching on Scripture. Particularly important was the *Declaration on Religious Freedom*, which held that people should be free in their choice of religion. This document represented a significant change in church policy from previous centuries. (A list of the documents of Vatican II can be found in the Appendix.)

What happened after the Council?

The Council closed in 1965, after which a number of changes happened to Catholic parishes, especially regarding church services. The altar was turned around, so the priest now faced the congregation. Services were in the language of the people, and new styles of more popular music emerged.

Among many Catholics, a great interest in studying the Bible developed. Bible study was encouraged in seminaries and in parishes. In some congregations, there was a toning down of devotion to Mary and a reemphasis on Jesus. There was also a toning down of focus on the Church structure and more of an emphasis on the People of God. Most importantly, the image of God changed from a judgmental God, all too ready to punish people for their sins, to the image of a loving and forgiving God.

For many Catholics, a great spirit of excitement and openness existed during and after the Council. There was much experimentation in liturgy, especially with music. Looking back, some of the music was not great music, but it reflected the period and times. Also, a willingness to talk to and respect people in other religions emerged. Previously, Catholics viewed other Christians and people of other religions with suspicion. In addition, a spirit of openness to the modern world emerged. John Paul II would become pope thirteen years after the Council. It is impossible to imagine such a public and visible role for the pope without Vatican II.

However, there were unforeseen changes. At the time of Vatican II, the number of priests and nuns was at its historic highest. Very soon after Vatican II, the numbers began to drop. The "vocation crisis" began, which still affects the Catholic Church today. The numbers of sisters and nuns has dropped dramatically. Some blame the Council for the drop of vocations, but a better explanation is that in the 1960s, the career options for men, and especially for women, greatly expanded. The choice of being a priest or sister could not compete with all the other choices.

Before the Council, there was a sense of absolute certainty about the Catholic faith and Catholic belief—that Catholics alone had the ultimate truth. This gave some Catholics a sense of security. After Vatican II, there was a new degree of honesty and openness. Maybe Catholics did not have all the answers. Perhaps other religious groups might have some of the truth. Some Catholics today regret that loss of certainty.

In recent years, some conservative Catholics have taken to bashing Vatican II as if it were the worst thing that ever happened to the Catholic Church. They blame it for the priest shortage, priest sexual abuse scandals, and anything else they do not like. (Many Catholics would argue that the priest sexual abuse scandals happened because the Church failed to live out the principles of Vatican II.) However, much of such criticism is based on misinformation and a failure to read the original documents. As noted before, the end result of Vatican II was sixteen documents. Explore them if you are interested. (They can be found on the Vatican website: http://www.vatican.va/archive/hist_councils/ii_vatican_council/index.htm.) Two short and easy-to-read documents are *Dignitatis Humanae: The Declaration on Religious Freedom* and *Nostra Aetate: The Declaration on the Relation of the Church to Non-Christian Religions.*

IMPORTANT FIGURES

Who were Vincent de Paul and Louise de Marillac?

Vincent de Paul (1581–1660) was a French Catholic priest who founded an order of priests dedicated to missionary work and an order of sisters dedicated to charity work. Vincent grew up in the peasant class in France. He was ordained in 1600 but was captured and enslaved by pirates. When he escaped, he decided to devote his life to charity. In 1624, he started a group of priests that would later be called the Congregation of the Missions with a focus on missionary work to spread the Catholic faith. His group would later get the nickname the "Vincentians." With Louise de Marillac (1591–1660), Vincent formed a group of religious sisters called the Daughters of Charity in 1633. Up to this point, religious women stayed in cloistered convents away from the outside world. The Daughters of Charity, and other orders of sisters created in this period, were different. They went out in the world to help the poor, to tend to the sick, and to educate. In the twentieth century, the Daughters of Charity were the largest congregation of religious women in America. In 1833, the Society of St. Vincent de Paul was formed in Paris as a group for laypeople to do charity work. Today in America, many Catholic parishes have a Society of St. Vincent de Paul to help needy people. Both Vincent de Paul and Louise de Marillac were later recognized as saints by the Catholic Church.

Up until 1964, the Daughters of Charity were recognized by their head coverings, called "cornettes." These large cornettes were designed to look like the caps worn by

French peasant women of the time. The goal was to blend in with the peasants and not stand out.

Who was Galileo, and why did he get in trouble with the Catholic Church?

Galileo Galilei (1564–1642) played a key role in the development of modern science. He wrote on astronomy, mathematics, and physics. He was also an engineer. Using the telescope that he built, he made a number of discoveries about our solar system. Galileo believed the writings of Copernicus that the sun was the center of the solar system and not the earth. This idea is called "heliocentrism." Because his views were controversial, he defended them in his 1632 writing *Dialogue Concerning the Two Chief World Systems*. However, Galileo's *Dialogue* made fun of those who held the older view that the earth was the center of the solar system. Unfortunately, Pope Urban VIII took offense. This alienated the pope, who had, up to that time, been a supporter of Galileo.

Galileo was eventually tried for heresy, convicted, and sentenced to house arrest, which meant he could not leave his estate. He never went to prison. Some church officials felt that the heliocentric view went against the Bible and the ideas of the philosophy of Aristotle. The whole episode was a complicated and messy affair involving

Galileo Facing the Roman Inquisition (1857) by Cristiano Banti illustrates the scientist's famous confrontation with the Church.

religion, politics, misunderstandings, and egos, all made worse by Galileo needlessly antagonizing several of his opponents.

The Galileo affair is often cited as evidence of a fundamental conflict between science and religion; it is also often used to argue that the Catholic Church has opposed science. However, neither point is true. In 1992, Pope John Paul II admitted that the Church had erred in trying and convicting Galileo.

The trial of Galileo was not part of a witch hunt against science. If there was such an effort, who was the next victim after Galileo? The reality was that in Europe, most of the scientific thinkers in Europe held religious beliefs and most were Catholic. A number of Catholic priests were scientists. The Catholic Church would eventually establish a Pontifical Academy of Sciences in 1936.

Who was Jean-Baptiste de La Salle?

De La Salle was recognized as a Roman Catholic saint in 1900. However, his influence on education is so important that he should be better known to all people. De La Salle (1651–1719) was a French priest and pioneer in education. He started the first Catholic schools and organized the Institute of the Brothers of the Christian Schools to help support and train teachers. His group is often called the Christian Brothers.

In a time when most people received no education, De La Salle called for universal free education. He saw the importance of educating children of all classes, particularly the poor. Although he experienced great resistance, he organized his own schools where he stopped the teaching of Latin, replacing it with the language of his students. He saw reading as an essential skill and stressed learning practical skills along with religious instruction. He set up students in classes according to their ability, not age. He also used church Sunday schools for adults to create a Christian Academy so they too could be educated.

Who was Friedrich Schleiermacher?

Friedrich Schleiermacher (1768–1834) was a German biblical scholar, theologian, and philosopher. He tried to answer the criticisms against religion brought by Enlightenment thinkers who emphasized rational thought. Schleiermacher defended the faith of traditional Protestant belief in his most important books: *On Religion: Speeches to Its Cultured Despisers* (1799) and *The Christian Faith* (1821).

Schleiermacher described religious faith as a feeling of absolute dependence on God. We only know God through faith. Religion is the immediate feeling of the eternal and infinite. It is not an intellectual activity. Religion is being conscious of God, but it is also the highest expression of human self-consciousness.

Who was Dietrich Bonhoeffer?

Dietrich Bonhoeffer (1906–1945) was an important German theologian and writer who studied in America before returning to Berlin as a teacher. He opposed Adolf Hitler and the Nazis and their efforts to control churches, and he worked to organize underground

> ## Who was Thérèse of Lisieux?
>
> St. Thérèse of Lisieux (1873–1897) led an uneventful life as a Catholic sister of the order of Discalced Carmelites in France. She lived a very devoted life of simplicity, dedicated to the love of Christ. She wrote her autobiography: *The Story of a Soul (L'histoire d'une âme)*. Thérèse died at age twenty-four of tuberculosis. After her death, she became a very popular Catholic saint and was called "The Little Flower."

seminaries. Bonhoeffer also opposed Hitler's euthanasia program against unwanted people and opposed the Nazi treatment of Jews. In 1937, he published his most important work, *The Cost of Discipleship*. Bonhoeffer joined the plot to assassinate Hitler. When the plot failed, he was arrested by the Gestapo in April 1943 and hanged in 1945.

Who was Albert Schweitzer?

Albert Schweitzer (1875–1965) was a French-German physician, theologian, humanitarian, and much more. In 1906 he wrote *The Quest of the Historical Jesus*. Schweitzer, rejecting the work of writers such as Albrecht Ritschl and Adolph von Harnack, argued that Jesus had to be understood in his own historical and religious context with its background in Jewish eschatology. Eschatology is the religious view that God is going to soon act in history. Schweitzer earned a medical degree and, in 1913, he established the Albert Schweitzer Hospital in West Africa. He won the 1952 Nobel Peace Prize for his philosophy of "Reverence for Life" and for his hospital. Schweitzer was internationally respected.

Who was Karl Barth?

A Swiss Reformed theologian, Karl Barth (1886–1968) is seen by some as the greatest Protestant theologian of the twentieth century. He was even featured on the cover of *Time* magazine in 1962. His two most important works are *The Epistle to the Romans* and *Church Dogmatics*. The thirteen-volume *Church Dogmatics* runs eight thousand pages. It addresses four topics: Revelation, God, creation, and atonement.

Although he grew up in Switzerland, he became a professor of theology in Germany. He became a leader of the Confessing Church in Germany that opposed Adolf Hitler. The church resisted Nazi attempts to control churches. In 1934, Barth led the writing of the Barmen Declaration that rejected Nazi influence on German Christianity. When he refused to swear allegiance to Hitler, he had to resign his position in Germany and moved to Switzerland to teach.

Who was Mother Teresa?

Mother Teresa (1910–1997) was born Anjezë Gonxhe Bojaxhiu in Albania. In 1928, she joined the Sisters of Loreto in Ireland to become a missionary. She went to India in

1929 and became a teacher in Calcutta, where she took the name of Thérèse of Lisieux, although she used the Spanish spelling. She took her solemn vows in 1937. After almost twenty years of teaching, she left to begin working with the poor in 1948. She adopted a new habit of a white, cotton sari with blue trim.

She created the Missionaries of Charity, an order of Catholic sisters, which then set up homes for the dying, soup kitchens, medical dispensaries, orphanages, and schools. Mother Teresa became internationally known for her work with the poor and dying. In 1979, she won the Nobel Peace Prize. She was a vocal opponent of abortion.

She was criticized by some for the conditions in her homes for the dying. Also, as was later revealed in her letters, she had great doubts about God's existence and for many years did not feel the presence of God. She was canonized as a saint in 2016.

Winner of the Nobel Peace Prize in 1979, Mother Teresa was the founder of the Missionaries of Charity. Interestingly, she confessed that she doubted the existence of God.

Who was John Paul II?

John Paul II (1920–2005) was born Karol Józef Wojtyła in Poland and became pope in 1978. During his long reign as pope, he traveled extensively, creating an internal presence for the papacy. He played a role in ending communism, first in Poland and then in the rest of Europe. He improved the Catholic Church's relations with other Christian denominations and also with non-Christian religions. A progressive on many social issues, John Paul II typically took conservative positions on moral issues and church doctrine. He opposed capital punishment and opposed the American invasion of Iraq. He supported the theory of evolution. On the other hand, he reaffirmed the Catholic teaching that it is wrong for married couples to use artificial birth control and that women cannot be ordained.

John Paul II wrote extensively. He created a record number of Catholic saints. Under his leadership, a revised *Code of Canon Law* was released in 1983. The *Code* provides the rules and policies for how the Catholic Church is run. He also oversaw the creation of the 1992 *Catechism of the Catholic Church* detailing Catholic teachings. (The Catechism can be found online if you are interested in exploring it: http://www.vatican.va/archive/ccc_css/archive/catechism/ccc_toc.htm.) He has been criticized for not acting quickly enough on the priest sex abuse crisis and for corruption in the Vatican Bank. His supporters want him to be called "John Paul II the Great." He was canonized as a saint in 2014.

CHRISTIAN HISTORY IN AMERICA: 1492 TO THE PRESENT

Why is the story of Christianity in America so important?

Christianity was completely transformed in America. Although some of the colonies had official religions supported by their governments, by the time of the ratification of the U.S. Constitution in 1788, many Americans were beginning to embrace the idea of religious freedom. In the ensuing centuries, many different Christian groups evolved, creating a unique diversity of Christianity, each competing for members. Christianity became an incredibly rich and multifaceted tradition in America, and then, these American-influenced versions of Christianity spread around the world.

What follows is a look at some of the most important people and movements as well as some of the more interesting Christian figures. However, keep in mind that because so much happened in the Christian world in America, not everyone who was important is covered nor is every group and denomination unique to America covered. There are simply too many significant figures and too many denominations.

What was the role of religion in the Civil War?

Most Christians today believe that slavery is very wrong. However, in the 1800s, many Christians supported slavery and supported the Confederacy in the war. In general, Christians from the North supported the Union and opposed slavery, while Christians from the South supported the Confederacy and slavery. Many abolitionists who fought slavery were motivated by their Christian faith. Irish Catholic units fought on both sides. The Methodists split into northern and southern denominations. After the war, many members of the Ku Klux Klan claimed to be Christians as they terrorized freed slaves. A burning cross was a common KKK symbol.

CHRISTOPHER COLUMBUS
AND THE SPANISH INFLUENCE

What were the religious ideas of Columbus?

Christopher Columbus (1451–1506) is famous for sailing to the New World in 1492. He made three more journeys. He also had a great interest in speculation about the End of the World and wrote the *Book of Prophecies* between 1501 and 1502. He predicted that Christianity would be spread over the entire globe, the Garden of Eden would be found, a final Crusade would take back the Holy Land from the Muslims, and a Last World Emperor would be chosen. Columbus had in mind Ferdinand and Isabella of Spain for this role. This emperor would lead the Crusade to free Jerusalem so that Jesus could return there.

What was the religious impact of the arrival of the Spanish?

When Europeans arrived in the New World, they brought Christianity with them. The Spanish conquered Mexico, all of Central and South America, and large areas of North America, including what would later become Florida, Texas, New Mexico, Arizona, and California. Two well-known Spanish missionaries were Eusebio Kino and Junípero Serra.

Who were Eusebio Kino and Junípero Serra?

Eusebio Kino (1645–1711) was a Jesuit priest sent to the area of Northern Mexico and Arizona. In addition to missionary work converting the Native Americas, he drew maps, explored, and wrote diaries. He set up many missions, including San Xavier del Bac, near what would later become Tucson, Arizona.

The Franciscan priest Junípero Serra (1713–1784) established a string of twenty-one missions up and down the California coast. The missions, named for Catholic saints, eventually became cities such as San Francisco, Santa Barbara, Santa Clara, and San Diego (St. James).

Assessments of the legacy of the missions are very mixed. Although the native people were taught trades and skills and protected from the Spanish outside the walls, the Indians were forced to give up

A statue of the Spanish friar Junípero Serra stands by one of the many missions he founded, Mission San Diego de Alcalá. He established twenty-one missions in California.

their traditional cultures and were not free to leave the mission. People debate whether their lives were a kind of servitude—not unusual for the time—or closer to slavery.

THE BRITISH AND FRENCH

Where were the British?

The British established colonies along the Eastern Seaboard from Georgia in the South to Massachusetts in the North, which included the land that would eventually become Maine. Since most of the immigrants from Britain were Protestants, most of the colonies were Protestant. For example, the Anglican Church was the official religion in Virginia. Maryland was established as a Catholic colony. However, Protestants eventually took control and took away the religious freedom of the Catholics. The colony of Pennsylvania was set up by a Quaker, William Penn.

What about the French?

The French took the land north of the British colonies, which became Canada, and the land around the Great Lakes. The most famous missionary was a Jesuit, Isaac Jogues (1607–1646), who was killed by the Mohawks.

Who were the Shakers?

The Shakers were started by Mother Ann Lee (1736–1784). She grew up in England and had visions as a child. She married and gave birth to four children, who all died at birth. She began to think that the root of all evil was sexual intercourse, and she saw sex as the

---

Who was Roger Williams?

Most Americans do not know much about Roger Williams (1603–1683), yet he was one of the first figures to speak and write about values that most Americans today hold: religious freedom, opposition to slavery, separation of church and state, and fair treatment of Native Americans. In his time, he espoused religious freedom and was widely condemned because most of the colonies had official religions that were supported by the government. In many places, people were required by law to attend specific churches.

Williams was expelled from the Massachusetts Bay colony (later Boston) by Puritan leaders because of his "new and dangerous ideas." He founded the First Baptist Church in America in Providence. The colony of Rhode Island was formed by Williams in 1644, the same year he published *The Bloudy Tenent of Persecution, for Cause of Conscience, Discussed in a Conference between Truth and Peace,* a treatise calling for religious freedom ("Bloudy" means "Bloody").

Original Sin of Eden. She formed a group called the Shaking Quakers or Shakers. In 1774, nine members came to America, where they expected Christ to appear. They formed the "United Brethren of Believers in Christ's Second Coming." They lived as families of celibates, which meant no marriage or sex.

The Shakers saw God as mother-father. God was ambisexual. They believed that Jesus was the fullest male manifestation of the Divine principle and that Mother Ann Lee was the fullest female manifestation. Jesus was the first appearance of the Divine and Mother Ann Lee the second. With this second coming, marriage was rejected. The Shakers believed they were restoring the New Testament church.

The Shakers eventually built nineteen communities from Maine to Kentucky. Many of the buildings of these communities still stand. Men and women lived in separate dormitories, and they entered the meetinghouse through separate doors. The motto of the Shakers was "Hands to work and hearts to God." The Shakers emphasized hard work and high-quality craftsmanship with simplicity of design. Shaker furniture is highly prized today.

The Shakers wrote and sang many songs, including their most famous song, "Simple Gifts." This well-known piece has even been sung at presidential inaugurations. The melody is used in Aaron Copeland's famous symphonic composition *Appalachian Spring*. The song was composed by Elder Joseph Brackett in 1848 in Alfred, Maine. Here are the lyrics:

'Tis' the gift to be simple, 'tis the gift to be free.
'Tis the gift to come down where we ought to be,
And when we find ourselves in the place just right,
'Twill be in the valley of love and delight.
When true simplicity is gained,
To bow and to bend we shan't be ashamed,
To turn, turn will be our delight,
Till by turning, turning we come 'round right.

Shaker services included ritual dance.

The Shaker communities began fading out after the Civil War. Their handmade items could not compete with manufactured items. Also, one of their sources for new members was to take in orphans. Many states passed laws to prevent the practice. Only the Sabbath Lake Shaker community in Maine exists, and it has only a few members.

THE GREAT AWAKENINGS

What was the First Great Awakening?

The First Great Awakening was a period of Christian revivalism in the American Colonies and Britain that lasted from 1726 to 1760, ending just before the Revolutionary War. In addition to John Wesley, two leaders were George Whitefield and Jonathan Edwards.

Jonathan Edwards (1703–1758) was an American preacher and theologian. He was a Congregationalist, which means he was part of the Puritan tradition. He emphasized human sinfulness and the need for repentance. His most famous sermon was "Sinners in the Hands of an Angry God." Here is a sample:

> The bow of God's wrath is bent, and the arrow made ready on the string, and justice bends the arrow at your heart, and strains the bow, and it is nothing but the mere pleasure of God, and that of an angry God, without any promise or obligation at all, that keeps the arrow one moment from being made drunk with your blood.
>
> —"Sinners in the Hands of an Angry God,"
> from DigitalCommons@University of Nebraska

George Whitefield (1714–1770) was an English minister. His last name is typically pronounced "WIT-field." He became a famous preacher in England and the American colonies. In his career, he was heard by perhaps ten million people. He was known for the rhetoric and drama of his preaching. However, he also supported slavery. When first set up, the colony of Georgia did not allow slavery. Whitefield campaigned for legalizing slavery in Georgia.

What was the Second Great Awakening (1790–1840)?

The Second Great Awakening was a series of religious revivals in America after the Revolutionary War and prior to the Civil War. One important preacher of the movement was Charles Grandison Finney (1792–1875). He called for the abolition of slavery and equal education for women and African Americans. He was known for the drama and theatrics of his preaching. One feature of the Second Great Awakening was religious revivals called "camp meetings," which would often last for several days. People would come from the surrounding towns and camp out as they listened to various preachers.

THE MORMONS

Who was Joseph Smith?

Joseph Smith (1805–1844) founded Mormonism, which became the Church of Jesus Christ of Latter-day Saints (the LDS Church). He claimed to have had several visions, including one with the angel Moroni who directed him to find buried golden plates. In 1830 Smith published what he claimed was a translation of the plates as *The Book of Mormon*. According to Smith, the plates had been written by descendants of the ancient tribes of Israel who had come to North America in Ancient Times. (Most historians do not believe that descendants of ancient Israel made it to the New World.)

Smith attracted followers and his church began growing, although it encountered opposition: first in Kirtland, Ohio; then in Independence, Missouri; and finally in Nauvoo, Illinois. Smith and others destroyed a printing press that had attacked Smith's power and the practice of polygamy. He was arrested in Carthage, Illinois, where a mob broke into the jail and killed him. After this event, the Mormons moved west to Salt Lake City under the leadership of Brigham Young.

Although Mormon belief has some similarities to the ideas of mainline Christians, there are also significant differences, especially regarding the nature of God. Mormons believe in God the Father; Jesus Christ, his Son; and the Holy Ghost. However, they believe that both the Father and the Son have perfect bodies of flesh and bone. They do not believe in the Trinity. Humans are seen as God's spirit children.

Mormons believe *The Book of Mormon* is equal to the Bible. They practice immersion baptism, confirmation, and the

The founder of the Church of Jesus Christ of Latter-day Saints, Joseph Smith, told an unusual story of how he was inspired to establish a new religion based on golden plates given to him by the angel Moroni in 1823.

Lord's Supper. Mormons call their rituals "ordinances." They have built magnificent temples across the country for their rituals. Once dedicated, Mormon temples are not open to non-Mormons. The PBS *American Experience* documentary *The Mormons* provides an excellent overview of Mormon history, belief, and practice.

Did Mormons practice polygamy?

Polygamy was first practiced by Joseph Smith and then practiced publicly from 1852 until 1890, when the practice was stopped by the LDS church. Today, there are Mormon fundamentalist groups, not connected to the LDS church, that continue the practice.

MARY BAKER EDDY
AND CHRISTIAN SCIENTISTS

Who was Mary Baker Eddy?

Mary Baker Eddy (1821–1910) founded the Church of Christ, Scientist. She grew up in a strong and harsh religious environment with an image of a punishing God. She had many health problems and misfortunes. Her first husband died after only six months of marriage. Her second husband abandoned her.

She began studying the ideas of Phineas Quimby, a famous healer. In the winter of 1866, Eddy fell on an icy sidewalk and injured her back. Bedridden, she read the Bible story in which Jesus healed the paralytic by telling him to "pick up your mat and walk" (John 5:8). She had a miraculous healing as she understood that illness was a not physical reality but rather a false belief. She came to see sickness as an illusion.

In the next years, Eddy further developed her thinking and wrote *Science and Health with Key to the Scriptures* (first published in 1875). She created the Christian Science movement and in 1879 founded the Church of Christ, Scientist. Her use of the term "science" is different from the modern definition of science as built on evidence and repeatable experiments. She uses the term to mean a rational analysis and explanation. She married her third husband, Asa Gilbert Eddy, in 1877.

Mary Baker Eddy had an epiphany while recovering from a fall. Concluding that the physical world is an illusion, she founded the Church of Christ, Scientist.

What are the principal beliefs of Christian Science?

Christian Scientists believe that God is Mind, and God is infinite; hence all is Mind. Humans are perfect spiritual ideas of the divine mind and thus are not material bodies. The physical senses are the source of all false beliefs. Reality is purely spiritual, and the material world is an illusion.

Jesus proved that the material world is an illusion. Jesus did not have a real body, which means he did not die on the cross. The Crucifixion was all an illusion, which was proved when his disciples later saw Jesus alive.

Christian Science services have readings from both the Bible and *Science and Health*. At services, no sermon or homily is allowed. No one else's ideas, such as might be brought up in a homily, are permitted.

What is the Christian Science view on illness?

According to Christian Scientists, sickness is a mental error. We believe that sickness is real, so we are sick. Here is a simple illustration to explain this view. Have you ever been so stressed that you felt bad physically? Then you found out that what you were worried about was not a problem after all, and suddenly, you felt better. Your physical discomfort was caused by a mental error. You thought there was a problem when there was not. Christian Scientists see all illnesses in a similar way. It is your mind that creates illness.

Do Christian Scientists refuse all medicine?

Christian Scientists hold different views on the use of medical care. The church does not forbid all medical care but rather insists that prayer works best when medicine is not used.

Is the Christian Science Church the same as the Church of Scientology?

No, they are totally different. Scientology was created by L. Ron Hubbard (1911–1986), who developed his teachings in his book *Dianetics: The Modern Science of Mental Health*. The Church of Scientology was organized in the 1950s.

THE UNITY CHURCH, UNITARIANS, AND UNIVERSALISTS

What is the Unity Church?

The Unity Church was created in 1889 by Charles Fillmore (1854–1948) and his wife, Myrtle Fillmore (1845–1931). They were part of the New Thought movement, which believed that divinity dwells within each person. However, our mental states shape our lives. The New Thought movement encouraged positive mental states that emphasize the divinity within ourselves and others. The Fillmores promoted "positive practical Christianity."

The principles of the Unity Church hold that God is present everywhere and that humans are spiritual beings created in God's image. However, humans create their lives through their thinking. Thus, affirmative prayer and positive thinking connect one to God. Furthermore, spiritual principles must be lived out.

Is the Unity Church the same as the Unitarian Church?

No. Although they are often confused, they are two separate denominations.

Who are the Unitarians?

The Unitarians have a long history. The first Unitarian church was formed in England in 1784. The movement soon came to America, and there were Unitarian congregations in New England by 1800. Unitarians reject the idea of the Trinity. Their name comes from their belief that God is a Unity, not a Trinity. Unitarians hold that Jesus is a man who was a model and moral teacher but not a divine being.

Who are the Universalists?

Universalists reject the idea that God would send people to Hell to suffer for eternity. They believe that ultimately God's love and mercy will redeem everyone, and everyone will eventually go to Heaven. Thus, salvation is universal.

In 1866, the denomination known as the Universalist General Convention was formed. In 1942, it changed its name to the Universalist Church of America.

Who are the Unitarian Universalists?

In 1961, the Unitarians and the Universalists in America merged as the Unitarian Universalist Association. Individual congregations have a fair amount of independence in the Unitarian Universalist Association.

What are Unitarian Universalists like?

Unitarian Universalists hold Sunday services like most churches that include music, readings, and teachings. Members of Unitarian Universalist congregations hold a wide range of beliefs since they do not believe in creeds with detailed doctrine. People who have left other denominations because they found them to be rigid in their doctrine often find the freedom of thought in the Unitarian Universalist Church to be a welcome relief.

The Unitarian Universalists have a common set of values as stated in their *Principles and Purposes*. Here is a sample:

We, the member congregations of the Unitarian Universalist Association, covenant to affirm and promote;

The inherent worth and dignity of every person;

Justice, equity, and compassion in human relations;

Acceptance of one another and encouragement to spiritual growth in our congregations;

A free and responsible search for truth and meaning;

The right of conscience and the use of the democratic process within our congregations and in society at large;

Are Unitarian Universalists Christians?

Although both Unitarians and Universalists originally came from Christian denominations, today most Unitarian Universalists are not Christians, nor would they identify themselves as Christians. Although they often respect Jesus as a human teacher, they hold no religious beliefs about him. However, since Unitarian Universalists have no defined doctrine of what to believe and what not to believe, some members might hold religious beliefs about Jesus.

The goal of world community with peace, liberty, and justice for all;

Respect for the interdependent web of all existence, of which we are a part.

—Unitarian Universalist Association

JEHOVAH'S WITNESSES AND THE SOCIAL GOSPEL MOVEMENT

Who are the Jehovah's Witnesses?

The Jehovah's Witnesses were founded by Charles Taze Russell (1852–1916). After a leadership fight upon the death of Russell, Joseph Franklin Rutherford (1869–1942) took over. Jehovah's Witnesses are best known for going door to door telling people about their faith. They often give out literature such as *The Watchtower* and *Awake!* Due to such missionary efforts, the Jehovah's Witnesses are growing in numbers. They call their churches "Kingdom Halls."

Jehovah's Witnesses do not believe in the Trinity, and they put their emphasis on God. Witnesses believe that Jesus alone was directly created by God. Everything else was created through Christ. They see the Holy Spirit as God's active force and not a person.

Jehovah's Witnesses believe we are living in the last days and that the present world order is under the control of Satan. Jesus Christ will return and destroy all governments. After the final battle of Armageddon, only 144,000 will go to Heaven while a new society of true worshippers will live forever on Earth.

The Jehovah's Witnesses do not believe in Hell. They also do not believe that humans have immortal souls. Thus, when people die, they cease to exist. That is the end of bad people. As for good and holy people who die, God will re-create them from memory in paradise.

Jehovah's Witnesses do not participate in religious and public holidays. They do not vote and will not recite the Pledge of Allegiance, as they see all governments as under the control of Satan.

A minister from Pittsburgh, Charles Taze Russell founded the Bible Student Movement and wrote books and pamphlets that formed the basis of what would be called the Jehovah's Witnesses in 1931, fifteen years after his death.

264

Witnesses hold traditional moral values and reject sex outside of marriage, homosexuality, and abortion. Also, based on several texts in the Bible, they do not allow blood transfusions.

What is the Social Gospel movement?

Two Protestant thinkers led the Social Gospel movement: Washington Gladden (1836–1918) and Walter Rauschenbusch (1861–1918). They took a new look at the gospels and emphasized the social message of Jesus. Gladden wrote the book *The Christian Way: Whither It Leads and How to Go On* (1877).

Walter Rauschenbusch was a Lutheran minister. He had been at a wealthy parish but was reassigned to a poor church in a part of New York City called "Hell's Kitchen." He looked at the Bible and noticed that in the synoptic gospels, the main theme of Jesus was the Kingdom of God. Many Christians thought this referred to Heaven when one died or to one's inner spiritual life. Rauschenbusch looked at the gospels and realized that Jesus talked about the Kingdom of God as being in the present. It was about how we treat others. For Jesus, the Kingdom of God was about loving enemies, feeding the hungry, clothing the naked, and healing the sick. The Kingdom of God rejected wealth.

Rauschenbusch worked out his ideas in three books: *Christianity and the Social Crisis* (1907), *A Theology of the Social Gospel* (1912), and *Christianizing the Social Gospel* (1912). He responded to those Christians who only saw morality as involving individual actions such as being sexually responsible, not telling lies, and not stealing. Such people often saw alcoholism as a personal moral issue, not part of larger social issues.

Rauschenbusch saw the big sins as being social: exploitation of the poor, poverty, slums, sweatshops, and lack of health care for the poor. He rejected so much preaching of salvation as focusing on the individual: "Me and Jesus." Salvation was solidaristic: Christians needed to be in solidarity with the poor and needy. Rauschenbusch wanted to redeem economic, social, and political institutions. He saw the Kingdom of God as something to be created in this world.

PENTECOSTALISM

What is Pentecostalism?

Pentecostalism is based on a key story at the beginning of the Acts of the Apostles in the New Testament.

> When the time for Pentecost was fulfilled, they were all in one place together. And suddenly there came from the sky a noise like a strong driving wind, and it filled the entire house in which they were. Then there appeared to them tongues as of fire, which parted and came to rest on each one of them. And they were all filled with the Holy Spirit and began to speak in different tongues, as the Spirit enabled them to proclaim.

Now there were devout Jews from every nation under Heaven staying in Jerusalem. At this sound, they gathered in a large crowd, but they were confused because each one heard them speaking in his own language. They were astounded, and in amazement they asked, "Are not all these people who are speaking Galileans? Then how does each of us hear them in his own native language? (Acts 2:1–8)

Why is this story so important, and what does it mean?

In the story, the followers of Jesus are gathered in an upper room. In Christian art, thirteen people are usually shown: Mary, the mother of Jesus; eleven of the original twelve apostles (the Apostle Judas had killed himself); and Matthias, the man chosen as the replacement for Judas.

According to the story, the Holy Spirit descended on those present: "Then there appeared to them tongues as of fire, which parted and came to rest on each one of them." This event is called Pentecost, named after the Jewish Pentecost. Filled with the Holy Spirit and emboldened, they go out to preach the message of Jesus. For many Christians, this event marks the beginning of the Christian church.

The detail in the story that the apostles were able to speak in different tongues has been understood differently by different Christians. Some Christians understand it as merely symbolic, that Christianity would be preached around the world in many different languages. Others understand it as symbolically undoing the punishment in the

A 1742 painting by Jean II Restout presents a romanticized interpretation of the Pentecost in which the Holy Spirit descended upon the apostles and Mary, inspiring them to begin a mission of preaching about Jesus—the beginning of the Christian Church.

> ## I have never heard of the COGIC church. What is it?
>
> COGIC stands for the Church of God in Christ. It is the fifth-largest Christian denomination in America. It began in 1907 under the leadership of Bishop Charles Harrison Mason. It is considered a Pentecostal Holiness Church, which means it combines both the Pentecostal tradition with the holiness tradition. The denomination has over twelve thousand churches in the United States, made up largely of African Americans.

Tower of Babel story in the Book of Genesis, where God gives people different languages to separate them. Other Christians understand the story as a miracle that happened to these first followers of Jesus.

However, those Christians called Pentecostals believe that speaking in foreign tongues was not just for the early followers of Jesus but is for all followers of Jesus. Pentecostals insist that all Christians should experience being filled with the Holy Spirit and be able to express it in signs such as speaking in tongues.

What is speaking in tongues?

Speaking in tongues, which is sometimes called "glossolalia," is described in several places in the New Testament as a gift of the Holy Spirit. Paul in 1 Corinthians, Chapters 12–14, gives a detailed discussion of various gifts of the spirit, including speaking in tongues. Pentecostals today regularly pray in tongues at their services. For Pentecostals, having an experience of being filled with the Holy Spirit is an important and essential step in faith. Also, many Pentecostals find being filled with the Holy Spirit to be a powerful emotional experience.

Do they actually speak in foreign languages?

Typically, speaking or praying in tongues is not an actual language. It is closer to babbling with no language structure. (Many examples can be found on YouTube.)

Are there other gifts of the Holy Spirit?

Pentecostals also experience other gifts, such as interpretation of the message of those praying in tongues, prophecy, and healing. Some people are "slain in the Spirit," where they are so overwhelmed that they fall to the ground."

What are some Pentecostal churches?

Pentecostals include the United Pentecostals, the Assembly of God churches, and COGIC: the Church of God in Christ.

THE SCOPES TRIAL

What was the Scopes Trial?

A key moment in the fight over evolution was the 1925 Scopes Trial in Dayton, Tennessee. It was often called the "Scopes Monkey Trial." A teacher, John Scopes, was tried for breaking the Tennessee law against teaching evolution. He was found guilty, but the decision was later thrown out in an appeals court on a technicality. The one-week trial was the media event of the time.

National figure William Jennings Bryan came to Dayton to help the prosecuting team. Bryan had run for president three times on the Democratic ticket and had served as secretary of state under Woodrow Wilson from 1912 to 1915. Famous Chicago attorney Clarence Darrow joined the defense team. When the judge refused to let Darrow bring in expert witnesses to defend evolution, Darrow pulled a surprise move and called Bryan to take the stand to defend a literal reading of the Bible. Darrow tried to find inconsistencies in Bryan's explanations.

What about the play and the movie *Inherit the Wind*?

The play *Inherit the Wind,* written by Jerome Lawrence and Robert Edwin Lee (not to be confused with the Confederate general Robert Edward Lee), was based on the trial and first performed in 1955. It was made into the classic black-and-white 1960 movie with actors Spencer Tracy, Fredric March, Gene Kelly, Dick York, and Harry Morgan. The movie has some great performances and dramatic scenes. The movie follows the play very closely. However, the play has numerous inaccuracies. In the actual trial, John Scopes never went to jail. He was not burned in effigy by a hostile town. He did not have a girlfriend, who was brought in as a witness at the trial. William Jennings Bryan did not die in the courtroom. It turns out the play, although built around the actual Scopes trial, was more of a commentary on the controversial McCarthy trials against communism going on in the 1950s.

OTHER IMPORTANT FIGURES

Who was Father Marquette?

Père Jacques Marquette (1637–1675) is important for his journey exploring the Mississippi River in 1673 with Louis Jolliet. They were the first Europeans to travel the northern part of the Mississippi. Many things are named after him, including Marquette University in Milwaukee and several parks. *Père* means "father" in French. Sometimes, people mistakenly refer to him as "Pierre Marquette." The town of Joliet, Illinois, is named for Louis Jolliet.

Who was Kateri Tekakwitha?

Kateri Tekakwitha (1656–1680) was a famous Native American convert to Catholicism, known as the "Lily of the Mohawks." She belonged to the Mohawks, one of five tribes of the Iroquois Nation. She caught smallpox when she was four, which left her with scars on her face and nearly blind. She was given the name Tekakwitha, which means "The One Who Walks Groping for Her Way." She became Catholic at about age twenty. However, she was estranged from her village for refusing to work on Sunday. She was very religious, very devout, and helped the poor and sick with such tasks as bringing firewood to those who could not gather it. She practiced extreme mortification, such as fasting, praying for long periods without sleep, and causing physical pain to her body. She died at the age of twenty-four. She was canonized a saint in 2012.

Who was Billy Sunday?

Billy Sunday (1862–1935) was one of the most popular evangelists in his time. Sunday grew up in poverty, then had an eight-year career in major league baseball, where he was known for his base running. He converted to Christianity and left baseball to become a preacher. He preached against alcohol and played a role in bringing about Prohibition.

He began traveling from city to city and became famous for his tent revivals. In time, he would preach in temporary, wooden buildings called tabernacles. He used the language of common people, including slang, and was known for wild gestures. He was also known for his sayings, such as "Going to church doesn't make you a Christian any more than going to a garage makes you an automobile," "Lord save us from off-handed, flabby-cheeked,

brittle-boned, weak-kneed, thin-skinned, pliable, plastic, spineless, effeminate, ossified, three-karat Christianity," and "Sinners cannot find God for the same reason that criminals cannot find a policeman: They aren't looking!"

Who was Daniel Lord?

Daniel Lord, S.J. (1888–1955), although largely forgotten today, was one of the most influential Roman Catholic figures in the twentieth century. He headed the popular Catholic Sodality movement and edited its magazine, *The Queen's Work*. Lord wrote 230 pamphlets, covering the entire scope of Catholic faith and life, including the sacraments, marriage and divorce, apologetics, and catechetics. Pamphlet titles included: *The Church Is Out of Date* (1935), *Atheism Doesn't Make Sense* (1936), *Your Partner in Marriage* (1936), *The Church Is a Failure?* (1939), *Why Be a Wallflower?* (1940), *So We Abol-*

A former professional baseball player, Billy Sunday became a hugely popular evangelist in the early decades of the twentieth century.

ished the Chaperone (1941), *In-Laws Aren't Funny* (1948), and *God Bless the Newlyweds* (1949). Daniel Lord sold over twenty-five million pamphlets.

Lord also wrote and produced seventy plays and pageants. His 1951 tribute to Detroit, *City of Freedom*, had a cast of one thousand and was seen by over 150,000 people. Lord influenced hundreds of young men and women to choose religious vocations. Lord served as technical adviser for the 1927 film *The King of Kings*. He also wrote the controversial Motion Picture Production Code of 1930.

Who was Thomas Merton?

Thomas Merton (1915–1968) was an American Catholic monk who had great influence through his many writings. Born in France, his mother died when he was six, and his father died when he was nine. Relatives set up a trust fund to support him.

He went to Cambridge University in England. However, when he had an illegitimate son, his grandparents sent him to Columbia University in New York. He quickly became interested in literature, jazz, smoking, and liquor. He joined a communist student group. (There were many communist groups in the United States in the 1930s. Most were made of sincere people calling for a more just society in the wake of the Depression.)

Graduating in 1938, he found something missing in his life, so he investigated the Catholic Church, where he found what he was looking for. He joined the Church and then became a monk. In 1941, he entered a Trappist monastery, the Abbey of Gethsemane near Bardstown, Kentucky.

At the monastery, Merton started writing. In 1948, he published his biography, *The Seven Storey Mountain*, which became a bestseller. (He used an old English spelling of story.) The title of the book is based on the mountain of Purgatory found in Dante's *Divine Comedy*. Here are the opening words:

> On the last day of January 1915, under the sign of the Water Bearer, in a year of a great war, and down in the shadow of some French mountains on the borders of Spain, I came into the world. Free by nature, in the image of God, I was nevertheless the prisoner of my own violence and my own selfishness, in the image of the world into which I was born. That world was the picture of Hell, full of men like myself, loving God and yet hating Him: born to love Him, living instead in fear and hopeless self-contradictory hungers.

> Not many hundreds of miles away from the house where I was born, they were picking up the men who rotted in the rainy ditches among the dead horses and the ruined seventy-fives, in a forest of trees without branches along the river Marne. [Merton was born during World War I during the Battle of the Marne in France.]

At the monastery, he wrote books on meditation, such as *New Seeds of Contemplation*. One book, *Conjectures of a Guilty Bystander*, criticized the nuclear bombing of Hiroshima. He also wrote *My Argument with the Gestapo*. Merton became well known for his opposition to racism, racial violence, and the Vietnam War. In his last years, he began exploring Buddhist meditation.

Who was Martin Luther King Jr.?

Martin Luther King Jr. (1929–1968) was an African American Baptist minister who became the most visible leader of the civil rights movement, which fought for equal rights for all American citizens. (King was named after his father, Martin Luther King Sr. Both are named in remembrance of Martin Luther.) At the time, great discrimination existed toward African Americans. They could legally be denied jobs, housing, the ability to vote, access to education, entrance to public universities, access to restaurants, and equal access to many public spaces.

A Baptist minister by profession, Martin Luther King Jr. is best remembered for his commanding role in the civil rights movement of the late 1960s. Here is a photo of King giving his famous "I Have a Dream" speech in 1963.

In 1955, King led the Montgomery, Alabama, bus boycott. African Americans boycotted the buses because they were required to sit in the back. King, inspired by the teachings and example of Mahatma Gandhi, called for nonviolent resistance and civil disobedience. He led the 1963 March on Washington at which he gave his famous "I Have a Dream" speech. He won the 1964 Nobel Peace Prize. In 1968, King launched the Poor People's Campaign to draw attention to the extent of poverty in America. King also opposed American militarism and the Vietnam War. He was assassinated in 1968.

Martin Luther King's "I Have a Dream" speech can be found on YouTube. It runs about seventeen minutes. It is one of the most important speeches in American history. His last speech, called the "I've Been to the Mountaintop" speech, which he gave the evening before he was assassinated, is also on YouTube. The last three minutes are very powerful.

Who was Fulton Sheen?

Fulton Sheen (1895–1979) was a Roman Catholic bishop who became famous for his radio and then television broadcasts. He hosted *The Catholic Hour* on NBC radio from 1930 to 1950. He moved to television for his show *Life Is Worth Living*, which ran from 1951 to 1957. At the height of the show's popularity, Sheen ran afoul of the powerful Cardinal Francis Spellman of New York. Spellman had Sheen reassigned to Rochester, New York, and *Life Is Worth Living* ended. Sheen later did a syndicated show, *The Fulton Sheen Program* (1961–1968). He is seen by many as one of the first televangelists. (Many of his shows can be seen on YouTube.)

Is actor Martin Sheen related to Fulton Sheen?

No. However, Martin Sheen did take his last name from Fulton Sheen. He was born Ramón Gerard Antonio Estévez, but as a struggling actor, he felt his name might be a hindrance, so he changed his name to Martin Sheen.

Who was Dorothy Day?

Dorothy Day (1897–1980) was a well-known Catholic writer and activist who fought for social justice and the rights of the poor and needy. In her early career, she worked as a journalist and joined the Socialist movement. She became interested in the Catholic faith and became Catholic in 1927. With Peter Maurin, she founded the Catholic Worker movement in 1933 with its newspaper, the *Catholic Worker*. The newspaper is still being published, and numerous Catholic Worker houses exist today. She wrote her autobiography, *The Long Loneliness*, in 1952.

Who was Billy Graham?

Billy Graham (1918–2018) was one of the most famous and influential evangelists. He would preach at well-organized, large-scale crusades across the country that would last for several days. His crusades would end with an altar call, when he would invite people to come forward and "accept Jesus as their personal Savior." Over three million people responded to his invitation. Graham was friends with several presidents and was known internationally. The best way to appreciate him is to watch several samples of his preaching on YouTube.

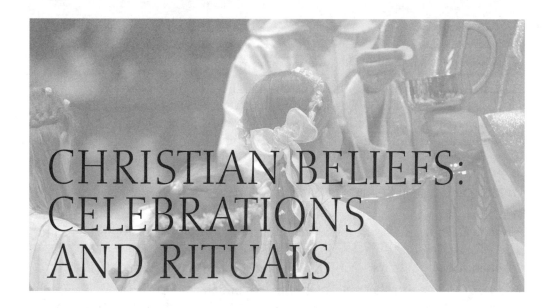

CHRISTIAN BELIEFS: CELEBRATIONS AND RITUALS

THE CALENDAR

What does Jesus have to do with the way our years are numbered?

The years after Jesus' birth are labeled A.D. This book, for example, is being written in the year 2018 A.D. The A.D. is an abbreviation for the Latin words *Anno Domini,* which means "Year of Our Lord." For instance, 2018 is supposed to be the 2018th year from the birth of Jesus. Year 1 A.D. is the supposed year of the birth of Jesus.

This system comes from a Christian monk named Dionysius Exiguus, who lived around the year we call 500 A.D. in what today is Syria. (Christianity was then the main religion in that region of the world.) In the time of Dionysius, the years were dated using the Roman system of counting from the year the city of Rome began. The year we call 753 B.C. was year 1 of the Roman calendar. (Romans used the label "AUC" for their years, which is Latin for *ab urbe condita*, meaning "from the founding of the city.")

Dionysius was a Christian monk and thought the most important event in history was the coming of Jesus, so he put the birth of Jesus as Year 1. However, very likely, Dionysius was off by a few years. Probably, Jesus was born four to six years earlier. A typical range given for the possible birth year of Jesus is 6–4 B.C. (This puts one in the strange position of saying, "Jesus was born 4–6 years Before Christ.") However, keep in mind that this range is our best guess as to the birth of Jesus.

Doesn't A.D. mean "After Death"?

Many people think that A.D. means "After Death." It is an easy mistake to make because B.C. means "Before Christ." However, A.D. means *Anno Domini* and counts from the birth of Jesus. If it counted from the death of Jesus, there would be no label for the years that Jesus lived.

What about C.E. and B.C.E.? What do those terms mean?

The terms *Anno Domini*—Year of our Lord—and "Before Christ" are based on titles for Jesus: Lord and Christ. Only Christians believe that Jesus is the Lord and Christ. Non-Christians wanted a different set of labels so C.E. and B.C.E. were created. C.E. means "Common Era" and B.C.E. means "Before the Common Era." The year numbers are still the same, but now they can be labeled with non-Christian labels if desired.

What is the Christian liturgical calendar?

Many Christians follow a special liturgical calendar for remembering different events from the life of Jesus. For many Christians, the two most important events in the liturgical calendar are Christmas and Easter. Christmas and Easter, along with other dates, are often called "holy days." Our English word "holiday" comes from "holy day."

Keep in mind that there is a wide range of opinion among Christians about celebrating these various religious holy days. In some traditions, these religious feasts are very important. Many Christians just celebrate some of them. In other Christian traditions, such celebrations are rejected. Some Christians even see the honoring of holy days as idolatrous.

When does the liturgical year begin?

The Christian liturgical year begins with Advent. Advent is the four Sundays before Christmas and is a time of anticipation of the celebration of the birth of Jesus at Christmas. The actual dates of the four Sundays vary from year to year. Also, the last week of Advent varies in length.

What is an Advent wreath?

Many Christians have an Advent wreath to celebrate the four Sundays of Advent. The wreath is made of three purple candles and one pink (or rose-colored) candle. Many Christian churches display an Advent wreath, and many Christians have one in their home. On the first Sunday of Advent, a purple candle is lit. On the second Sunday, two purple candles are lit. On the third Sunday, two purple candles and the pink candle are lit. The third Sunday is called Gaudete Sunday. *Gaudete* is the Latin word for "rejoice." On the fourth Sunday, all candles are lit. Advent is followed by Christmas.

Why is Christmas on December 25?

The birth of Jesus is described in the Gospels of Matthew and Luke, but neither gospel gives an indication of what time of year the birth of Jesus occurred. About three hundred years later, as Christianity spread throughout the Roman world, Christians took an existing Roman feast of the sun celebrated on December 25 and changed it into a celebration of the birth of Jesus. (December 25 had been the Roman feast of the sun because it is near the Winter Solstice, the shortest day of the year, which is on either December 21 or 22.)

We celebrate Christmas on December 25 not because that is the date Jesus was born, but, rather, because the early Church decided the celebration should coincide with a traditional Roman feast. The Christmas tree came about later; the tree was a tradition of a pagan winter solstice practice that was added to the Christian holiday.

Why does Easter move around each year?

Easter moves around because it is celebrated on the first Sunday after the first full moon of spring. This is a little complicated. Spring begins with the Spring Equinox (also called the Vernal Equinox), which is March 19, 20, or 21. Easter has to come after the first full moon after the equinox, and Easter falls on the next Sunday after the equinox.

There was a debate for several centuries among early Christians before they decided on the formula of celebrating Easter on the first Sunday after the first full moon of spring. Christians of the Orthodox tradition use a different formula for setting the date of Easter.

Why is the date for Easter each year based on this complicated formula?

In the Gospels of Matthew, Mark, and Luke, Jesus held his "Last Supper" on a Thursday night. Jesus was celebrating the Jewish Passover, which is usually on the first full moon of spring. (The Gospel of John describes the Passover as being on Friday.) Jesus was crucified the next day, a Friday. According to the gospels, Jesus rose from the dead on Sunday. Thus, Christians today celebrate the Resurrection of Jesus on the first Sunday after the first full moon after the first day of spring (the Spring Equinox).

275

If you are interested, you can go online and find the Spring Equinox for the current year, which will be March 19, 20, or 21. Look up the dates of the full moons in March and April and find the first full moon after the equinox. The Sunday after the equinox will be Easter.

What is Holy Week?

Christians call the week before Easter "Holy Week." It starts with Palm Sunday, which remembers the gospel story when Jesus entered Jerusalem and was greeted by people waving palms. Later in the week, the days are called Holy Thursday (night of the Last Supper), Good Friday (the day Jesus was crucified), Holy Saturday, and then Easter.

What is the origin of the word "Easter"?

The English word "Easter" came from an Old English word that was the name of a month in spring named after an Old English goddess known as Ēostre.

Why do people put chocolate rabbits and eggs in their Easter baskets?

Easter traditions include some non-Christian symbols. In ancient times, many cultures celebrated fertility rituals in spring. The rabbit was a symbol of fertility because rabbits are so prolific. Pigs were also seen as fertility symbols. This influenced the custom of having a ham on Easter Sunday. The egg is a symbol of new life because a young chick emerges from its shell. Christians later saw this as symbolic of the Resurrection of Jesus.

Many Christians have chocolate rabbits, hard-boiled eggs, and ham on Easter and are unaware or ignore the pre-Christian roots of these symbols. However, some Christians understand the pagan roots of the symbols and avoid using them at Easter. Other Christians avoid celebrating Easter because of the pagan elements involved.

What is Lent?

According to the Gospels of Matthew, Mark, and Luke, after his baptism, Jesus spent forty days in prayer in the desert before he began his public ministry. The forty days symbolized the forty years the Hebrews wandered in the desert after they left Egypt in the Exodus. The forty days of Lent are a time for Christians to put more emphasis on prayer and religious devotion to prepare for the celebration of Easter and the events leading up to Easter.

At the beginning of Lent, priests smear ashes on the faithfuls' foreheads in the shape of a cross, reminding them of their mortality and to pray and repent.

How is the forty days of Lent calculated?

Lent is forty days counted back from Easter but without counting Sundays. It begins with Ash Wednesday.

What is Ash Wednesday?

Many Christians begin Lent by going to church on Ash Wednesday. During the service, the priest or minister makes a cross on each person's forehead with ashes and says, "Remember that you are dust, and unto dust you shall return." (A Catholic priest can also say, "Turn away from sin and be faithful to the gospel" or "Repent and believe in the Gospel.") This passage is from the third chapter of Genesis, where God tells Adam and Eve that they now have to face death. The purpose of this Ash Wednesday tradition is to remind Christians that they will not live forever and to remind them to devote more time to prayer and repentance. (Repentance is being aware of one's sinfulness and asking God for forgiveness.)

Where do they get the ashes for Ash Wednesday?

Christian ministers save some palms from the celebration of Palm Sunday to be used the following year for Ash Wednesday. The palms are burned to create the ashes.

Why do some Christian churches hold fish fries in Lent?

Hundreds of years ago, many Catholics ate no meat during Lent. By the twentieth century, the rule for Catholics had changed to no meat on Friday. Fish was the usual alternative. Many Catholic churches held fish fries on the Fridays in Lent as church fundraisers.

If you have never been to a church fish fry, check one out. Typically, the food is good, and the prices are reasonable. Bring your appetite; you do not have to be a church member to attend.

What is Ascension Thursday?

Two important religious celebrations follow Easter. According to the New Testament's Acts of the Apostles, forty days after his Resurrection, Jesus ascended into Heaven. Many Christians celebrate this event as Ascension Thursday. It is the fortieth day after Easter. (In counting the forty days of Lent, Sundays are skipped. For the forty days between Easter and Ascension Thursday, Sundays are counted.)

What is Pentecost Sunday?

In the Jewish tradition, Pentecost, called Shavuot, is celebrated fifty days after the first day of Passover. On Shavuot, Jews celebrate God giving the Law to Moses. Acts of the apostles describes the followers of Jesus gathered together in an upper room on the Jewish feast of Pentecost. (This was after Jesus ascended to Heaven.) According to the story in Acts, the Apostles of Jesus received the Holy Spirit. (Mary, the mother of Jesus, was also there.) "Divided tongues, as of fire, appeared among them, and a tongue rested on each of them. All of them were filled with the Holy Spirit and began to speak in other languages, as the Spirit gave them ability" (Acts 2:3–4, NRSV). Christians recall this event on Pentecost Sunday, which is fifty days after Easter.

The number 50 is not a typical symbolic number in the Bible as are the numbers 7, 12, and 40, so why is Pentecost fifty days after Easter? The Jewish Pentecost, called Shavuot, is also called the Feast of Weeks. It is held seven weeks after Passover. Seven weeks of seven days is forty-nine days. Pentecost is held on the next day, the fiftieth day. The word "Pentecost" is based on the Greek word *pente* for five.

What is the Annunciation?

Some Christians also celebrate the Annunciation, which recalls the story in the Gospel of Luke when the Angel Gabriel appeared to Mary and told her that she would bear a child named Jesus. The Annunciation is celebrated on March 25, nine months before the birth of Jesus at Christmas. It is called the "Annunciation" because Gabriel announces to Mary that she will bear the child Jesus. The scene of Gabriel appearing to Mary has been a popular subject in many paintings, particularly during the Renaissance.

What about the birth of John the Baptist?

Some Christians celebrate the birth of John the Baptist. In the Gospel of Luke, after the appearance of Gabriel, Mary visited her cousin Elizabeth, who was six months pregnant with John the Baptist. Christian tradition designated June 24—three months after the Annunciation—as the feast of the birth of John the Baptist.

What is "Ordinary Time"?

For those Christians who follow the liturgical calendar, there are blocks of time that are not part of Advent, Christmas, Lent, Holy Week, or the weeks after Easter. These periods are called "Ordinary Time."

What about feast days for saints?

Some Christians honor saints by dedicating days to them. St. Francis of Assisi is honored on October 4. St. Valentine, an early Christian martyr, is remembered on February 14. However, his feast day has become a day to send cards, flowers, or candy to someone you love. The feast of St. Blaise is celebrated on February 3. Some churches bless the throats of their members on this day. There are saints designated for every day of the calendar year.

What is Mardi Gras?

Mardi Gras is the well-known celebration on the last day before Lent, although for most people, Mardi Gras has nothing to do with religion. In fact, many people celebrate it in unreligious ways. Hundreds of years ago, the forty days of Lent meant not eating meat during Lent. In those days, people had lots of fat on their meat, so, people would eat up all the meat and fat in their homes before Lent. (Very likely, most meat available at that time of the year was bacon.) "Mardi Gras" is French for "Fat Tuesday," so called because you ate meat and the fat with it.

For centuries, Christian cultures in Europe banned theater and other performances. As a result, many places held special celebrations before Lent. In some places in the world, Mardi Gras is called "Carnival." Possibly, this word comes from the Latin words *carne* for "meat" and *levare* for "to take away." Rio de Janeiro, Brazil, holds parades with massive floats and thousands of people in elaborate costumes.

What is the feast of Christ the King?

For many Christians, the liturgical year ends with the feast of Christ the King. This is the last Sunday before Advent.

What is Reformation Sunday?

Many Protestants celebrate Reformation Sunday or Reformation Day to remember when Martin Luther posted his ninety-five theses on the church door in Wittenberg, Germany, on October 31, 1517, and began the Protestant Reformation. Reformation Day is celebrated on October 31. Many Protestant churches choose to celebrate the event as Reformation Sunday, which is the Sunday before October 31 if October 31 does not fall on

Mardi Gras—or Fat Tuesday—celebrations are legendary in New Orleans, Louisiana, where the religious meaning behind the day is often forgotten.

a Sunday. Traditionally, Martin Luther's hymn "A Mighty Fortress Is Our God" is sung on Reformation Sunday.

Are there Christians who do not celebrate special events?

The Jehovah's Witnesses do not celebrate religious holidays such as Christmas and Easter because of all the pagan elements connected to such celebrations. They also see birthday celebrations as having pagan roots. In addition, they will not celebrate cultural and political holidays such as Thanksgiving and Independence Day. They follow the words of Jesus in John's gospel that Christians "do not belong to the world" (John 15:19).

SERVICES AND RITUALS

What does the word "ritual" mean?

In this discussion, the word "ritual" is used broadly to describe any ceremony that is regularly repeated. Some Christians do not use the word for their ceremonies.

Among Christians, there is a great diversity of opinion regarding religious services and rituals. Some denominations have numerous and elaborate services and rituals, while other denominations have a simple religious service and reject any sort of formal ritual.

On the other hand, many Christians find that when they visit the services of other Christian denominations, they often find many similarities. For instance, among those churches that do Communion services, many of the prayers and the order of the service are very similar from one denomination to the next.

What are the most common Christian rituals?

All Christian groups practice some form of baptism and Communion, yet there is a wide variation in the details of how the rituals are performed and great differences between Christian groups on the meaning of these rituals. Before exploring baptism and Communion, it is important to understand the elements of a basic religious service.

What are the elements of a basic religious service?

Regardless of the type of religious service and the style, four elements are used in most Christian services: Bible readings, teachings, prayer, and music. Most Christian services include Bible readings. In some churches, the minister chooses the reading or readings for the particular service. Other churches have assigned readings for each service. Some churches have a lectionary, which is a book of Bible readings selected for each service during the year. For many denominations, the Sunday service includes an Old Testament reading, a psalm, a reading from the epistles, and a reading from the gospels.

Prayer in church can take many forms. It can be silent or spoken out loud. It can be spontaneous prayer or scripted prayer. Sometimes, memorized prayers, such as the

Most Christian church services include a Bible reading, a sermon by the minister, music, and prayer.

Our Father, are recited. Some traditions allow praying in tongues. Prayer can also include periods of silent meditation.

Most Christian services include some kind of teaching, which is often called "preaching." In some Christian traditions, the preaching is the longest part of the service and the most important. Sometimes, the preaching is called a sermon or a homily. Many people use the terms interchangeably, but some see a difference between the two terms. A sermon can be viewed as a theological discussion based on the scripture, whereas a homily is about applying the scripture readings to daily life.

Music in a service can take a wide range of forms from congregational singing to choirs and bands to soloist performances. Many evangelical churches have high-quality rock bands with incredible sound systems. The range of music available includes a Medieval Latin chant called a Gregorian chant.

Why do Christians practice baptism?

Christians are baptized to follow both the example of Jesus and the teachings of Jesus: "Go therefore and make disciples of all nations, baptizing them in the name of the Father and of the Son and of the Holy Spirit, and teaching them to obey everything that I have commanded you" (Matthew 28:19–20, NRSV). Although all Christians recognize baptism, there is a great diversity of practice and understanding of baptism.

Regarding baptism, what are the issues over which Christians disagree?

The three issues are:

281

1. When should someone be baptized?

2. How much water should be used?

3. What does baptism mean?

What are the different views over when someone should be baptized?

Many Christians believe that a person should be baptized only when he or she is old enough to understand what he or she is doing and old enough to make a faith commitment. Such Christians usually baptize people as young adults or as adults.

Other Christians baptize babies, believing that baptism is an important ritual to bring the infant into the Christian community.

Why is the quantity of water required for baptism an issue?

Christians disagree on this element of baptism due to different visions of what happened when John the Baptist baptized Jesus. Did John pour water over the head of Jesus, or did he dunk Jesus in the river Jordan? If one reads the baptism stories in Matthew, Mark, and Luke, one will notice there is not enough detail to answer the question. Due to this lack of specific detail, many Christians have created in their own minds an image of how John baptized Jesus.

Many Christian churches use only a small amount of water for baptism. This has the practical advantage that baptisms can be done by pouring water over the forehead of a child or an adult at a baptismal font, which is simply a bowl on a stand. The adult to be baptized bends over the font and an infant is held over the bowl, so only the head gets wet. A small towel is used to dry the head of the baptismal candidate. Using a small quantity of water makes the whole process simpler.

Other Christians insist on full immersion. A person being baptized needs to go completely underwater. Many churches install baptismal tanks and changing rooms, so people can get out of their street clothes and put on a gown or jumpsuit in order to be baptized. Maintaining such facilities involves extra effort and costs, but many churches believe that full-immersion baptism follows the example of John the Baptist. A few Christians even insist on doing baptisms in an actual river.

What are the different Christian views on the meaning of baptism?

The last issue on which Christians disagree is the meaning of baptism. Some Christians believe that baptism takes away Original Sin, which is the guilt passed down from the first human beings, Adam and Eve. Typically, these Christians also believe that in baptism, a person receives "grace," which is God's love and mercy given freely by God. Other Christians believe that baptism does not do anything to the person; rather, it is a sign of the person's previous acceptance of Jesus and acceptance of salvation.

Christians also disagree on whether baptism is essential for salvation or not. Some Christians believe that baptism is essential and that going to Heaven is impossible with-

What is Original Sin?

Original Sin is the belief that the first humans, Adam and Eve, disobeyed God and committed the first sin—the "original sin." Some Christians, such as Roman Catholics, believe that the guilt of Adam and Eve is passed on to all subsequent human beings. Thus, everyone is born with the guilt of Original Sin. (According to the Catholic teaching, neither Mary, the mother of Jesus, nor Jesus was born with Original Sin.) Christians who believe in Original Sin typically see baptism as the means to remove the guilt of Original Sin.

out baptism. Other Christians see baptism as not absolutely essential, although it is the normal path for salvation, yet other Christians see baptism as unnecessary for salvation. For these Christians, salvation comes from accepting Jesus as one's Lord and Savior. Thus, baptism serves as only a symbol of one's acceptance of Jesus.

What is a christening?

For some Christians, baptism serves as the birth ritual; for other Christians, it is the adulthood ritual. In those traditions that insist on adult baptism, there is often a dedication or naming ceremony for the birth of a child, which is sometimes called a christening. "Christening" is a tricky word since it is used in different ways: either as a label for the dedication of a child without baptism or as another name for the baptism of an infant.

Why do Christians hold Communion services?

Christians hold Communion services in memory of what Jesus did at the Last Supper:

> While they were eating, Jesus took bread, said the blessing, broke it, and giving it to his disciples said, "Take and eat; this is my body." Then he took a cup, gave thanks, and gave it to them, saying, "Drink from it, all of you, for this is my blood of the covenant, which will be shed on behalf of many for the forgiveness of sins."
>
> —Matthew 26:26–28, NRSV (see also Mark 14:22–24 and Luke 22:17–20)

Regarding Communion, what are the issues over which Christians disagree?

The four issues are:

1. What is it called?
2. How often should it be done?
3. What are the details?
4. What is the meaning of Communion?

All Christians have some sort of Communion service, but they give it different names: Communion, the Lord's Supper, Mass, or the Eucharist.

Communion services include the eating of some form of bread and drinking either wine or grape juice in a reenactment of the Last Supper, when Jesus fed bread and wine to the apostles and said that they were his body and blood.

What are different Christian views about the frequency of Communion?

Christian denominations hold different views on the frequency of Communion services that run the gamut from every Sunday to twice a month to once a month to once a year. Catholics are expected to go to Mass every Sunday; however, many Catholics also go to Mass every day. If you drive by a Catholic church early on a weekday, you will see people going to daily Mass.

What are the different views on the details of Communion?

There is great diversity of practice among different denominations over the details of Communion. All Communion services involve either bread and wine or bread and grape juice. Some churches use an actual loaf of bread from which pieces are torn off and given to people. Many other churches use flat wafers called "hosts." The flat wafers are more convenient than a loaf of bread for large congregations.

A number of Christian churches oppose drinking liquor and use grape juice instead. Some churches use a common cup or chalice, and everyone drinks from the chalice. Other churches use small, individual cups. Some churches give the members of the congregation the option of choosing either wine or grape juice.

What are the different views on the meaning of Communion?

Three main positions exist among various Christian groups to describe their understanding of Communion: merely symbolic, spiritual presence, and physical presence (there are other positions, but they are variations on these). As noted above, Communion is based on the words Jesus said over the bread, "This is my body," and the words he said over the wine, "This is my blood." Down through the centuries, Christians have argued over the meaning of these words.

What is the "merely symbolic" position?

In this view, when in the Communion service the bread and wine (or grape juice) are blessed, the action is merely symbolic. The bread is still bread, the wine (or grape juice) is still wine (or grape juice). The bread and wine are simply symbols to remind Christians of what Jesus did by dying on the cross.

What is the "spiritual presence" position?

According to this view, when Christians come together to remember and reenact his Last Supper, Jesus is spiritually present in the community. The bread and wine are not changed. Also, at a Communion service, Jesus is spiritually present in a special way that is different from a service without Communion.

What is the "physical presence" position?

In this view, which is also called "real presence," the bread and wine really become the body and blood of Jesus. This view takes the words of Jesus, "This is my body" and "This is my blood," literally. Even though the bread looks, tastes, and smells like bread and the wine looks, tastes, and smells like wine, somehow at the deepest level—at the essential level—they are changed into the body and blood of Jesus.

Several Christian groups adhere to the belief in the real presence, such as Roman Catholics, Orthodox Christians, Anglicans, Episcopalians, and Lutherans. However, these denominations do not agree on how to explain what happens to the bread and wine in the Communion service.

What is the idea of "rites of passages"?

Anthropologists have long noted that most cultures have rituals to mark key moments in life: birth, adulthood, marriage, and death. These are called "rites of passage" because a person passes from one state to the next. "Rite" is short for "ritual." Christians also mark these key moments. As noted above, baptism can be either the birth ritual or adulthood ritual. In many churches that insist on adult baptism, there is often blessing or naming rituals for babies.

Many Christians use confirmation as the adulthood ritual where a person passes from being a Christian child to a Christian adult. For many Christians, confirmation is done by anointing the confirmand with oil on the forehead.

Most Christian denominations hold marriage ceremonies. Not surprisingly, there is a diversity of practice over how weddings are done and what the meaning of a wedding ceremony is.

Finally, Christians have a wide variety of practices on death services.

Are there other Christian rituals and ceremonies?

This chapter has explored the most important Christian rituals and celebrations but not all of them. Catholic rituals will be covered later. Keep in mind that there are many other ways that Christians celebrate and live out their faith.

CHRISTIAN BELIEFS: THIS LIFE AND THE NEXT

FOUNDATIONS OF CHRISTIAN MORALITY

What are Christian views on morality?

Most Christians see morality as an essential part of living out their Christian faith. For many Christians, moral living is a key to getting to Heaven. However, different Christians hold many different views on all the various moral issues, and there are many disagreements among Christians on these issues.

Is there a difference between Christian morality and Christian ethics?

Most Christians use the terms morality and ethics interchangeably. Both refer to the rules or guides for living life.

What is the source of Christian moral values?

Christians believe that the Bible is the primary source of moral values. Typically, they also believe that these moral values come from God. However, beyond these points, Christians disagree on many things, such as how to interpret many passages in the Bible. They also disagree on which values are timeless principles and which values might be culturally conditioned values of the ancient world that need not be followed today. For example, in Chapter 11 of Paul's letter 1 Corinthians, he calls for women to have their heads covered. Most Christians see this as an ancient cultural value and thus not relevant to the modern world. Are the Old Testament condemnations of homosexuality applicable to today? Christians also disagree on how much freedom they have to decide moral values that are not specifically addressed in the Bible. Lastly, on all the specific moral issues that humans face, you can find Christians with vastly different views.

What about the Ten Commandments?

Most Christians see the Ten Commandments as the foundation of Christian ethics, although they disagree on how to interpret them and even what the list of the Ten Commandments is. Both Protestant and Catholic versions of the Ten Commandments exist. (As to why there are Ten Commandments, one could look on YouTube for "Mel Brooks 10 Commandments" and watch the clip that is 1:11 in length.)

What is the difference between the Protestant and Catholic versions of the Ten Commandments?

The Catholic Ten Commandments do not include "You shall have no graven images or likenesses." Catholics have statues in their churches and do not see them as idolatry. Next, the last commandment about coveting is split into two commandments: "9. You shall not covet your neighbor's wife" and "10. You shall not covet your neighbor's possessions." This changes the numbering for the Commandments in the middle. For example, for Catholics, the "Honor your father and mother" commandment is number 4. In other versions of the Commandments, it is number 5.

Where are the Ten Commandments in the Bible?

The Commandments are found in two places: Exodus 20:1–17 and Deuteronomy 5:6–21. In two different stories, Moses goes up on a mountain and receives the Commandments. There are differences between the two versions. The Exodus version takes place on Mount Sinai, while the Deuteronomy version takes place on Mount Horeb. (If you have never read these important passages, you might find it interesting to do so.)

What are the actual commandments?

The Bible does not call the rules the Ten Commandments nor are they numbered as ten in the biblical text. (Sometimes, they are called the "decalogue.") For some of the rules, it is difficult to figure out where one commandment stops and the next commandment starts. Over the centuries, different lists of the Ten Commandments have developed. Here is a typical Protestant version:

1. I am the Lord your God, you shall have no other gods.
2. You shall have no graven images or likenesses.
3. You shall not take the Lord's name in vain.
4. Keep the Sabbath holy.
5. Honor your father and mother.
6. You shall not kill.
7. You shall not commit adultery.
8. You shall not steal.
9. You shall not bear false witness.
10. You shall not covet your neighbor's wife or possessions.

Here is a typical Catholic version:

1. I am the Lord your God, you shall have no other gods.

2. You shall not take the Lord's name in vain.

3. Keep the Sabbath holy.

4. Honor your father and mother.

5. You shall not kill.

6. You shall not commit adultery.

7. You shall not steal.

8. You shall not bear false witness.

9. You shall not covet your neighbor's wife.

10. You shall not cover your neighbor's possessions.

What do Christians think about the first two commandments?

All Christians recognize the importance of the Ten Commandments, but there are many different views among Christians about how to interpret and follow them. The First Commandment, on one hand, is typically not problematic since most Christians understand the concept of worshipping only one God. On the other hand, Christians have different

The interior of this church in Denmark is a good example of how Protestant churches are bereft of statues and images, unlike Catholic churches, because Protestants believe the Ten Commandments forbid such things.

ideas what the "other gods" might be, especially when the term "gods" is understood metaphorically for such things as wealth, power, fame, and religious institutions.

The commandment against graven images is included in the Protestant Ten Commandments and dropped from the Catholic version. Protestant churches typically do not have statues in their churches. Some have images in their stained-glass windows, but many do not. Catholics, on the other hand, have many statues and images in their churches and do not see them as being false idols.

What do Christians think about the commandment "You shall not take the Lord's name in vain"?

As for the commandment "You shall not take the Lord's name in vain," Christians agree on the importance of treating the various names of the Lord respectfully, such as "God," "Lord," "Jesus," and "Jesus Christ." Christians disagree on whether this commandment forbids other commonly used cuss words and which words are wrong to use.

What do Christians think about the commandment regarding the Sabbath?

Most Christians understand the commandment "Keep the Sabbath holy" to mean that Sunday is a special day to go to church and avoid work. Christians ignore the original meaning of the term "Sabbath," which refers to Saturday. Jews follow the traditional understanding of Sabbath as starting at Friday sundown and ending at Saturday sundown. Christians moved the holy day to Sunday because of the belief that Jesus rose from the dead on a Sunday, the first day of the week. Also, very likely, early Christians wanted to separate themselves from Jewish practices. Some Christians have even reworked the commandment to state "Keep the Lord's day holy." However, one group of Christians, the Seventh-day Adventist Church, goes to church on Saturday, following the original meaning of the word "Sabbath." In the Old Testament/Hebrew Scriptures, Saturday, the Sabbath, is the seventh day of the week.

What about the commandment to "Honor your father and mother"?

All Christians recognize the importance of the commandment "Honor your father and mother," but they often have different views on how to interpret it and apply it. It is worth noting that the commandment itself does not give any specifics.

What do Christians think about the commandment "You shall not kill"?

Christians have the most disagreements over the commandment "You shall not kill." First, it must be clarified that this commandment is about people and not animals. Some Christians, such as the Amish and the Quakers, understand this commandment to ban all types of killing of humans. Their interpretation of this commandment is not based on the Old Testament alone, but rather, they see it through the light of the later teachings of Jesus.

Other Christians interpret this commandment to prohibit murder. Some even write the commandment as "You shall not murder." But what is murder? Although "murder" is a common word, most people have never thought out what the word means. The word is not just a label for the action of killing a human being; rather, the word includes the judgment that a particular act of killing a human being is wrong. Thus, the word "murder" refers to an "unjustified intentional killing" of a human being by another human being.

Suicide does not fit the definition nor does accidentally killing a person since that is not intentional. The word "unjustified" is an essential part of the definition since some people believe that some intentional killing is justified, such as in warfare or in capital punishment.

However, Christians, and people in general, disagree on when intentionally killing a human is justified or unjustified. Most people want to justify some kinds of killing of humans. Here are some examples: police officers acting properly in the line of duty, true self-defense, capital punishment, war, and mercy killing. This is just a sample of cases where some people justify intentionally taking human lives. Christians and others will disagree on what should be on the list and what should not be.

As many Christians have discovered, the Bible does not give detailed answers on many of these ethical questions. The Old Testament/Hebrew Scriptures has stories that justified warfare and capital punishment, yet in the New Testament, Jesus rejected violence.

Also within the Old Testament/Hebrew Scriptures, the commandment does not seem to prohibit all killing. In fact, when Moses came down the mountain from receiving the Ten Commandments, he found the people worshipping a golden calf.

> Moses stood at the gate of the camp and shouted, "Whoever is for the LORD, come to me!" All the Levites then rallied to him, and he told them, "Thus says the LORD, the God of Israel: Each of you put your sword on your hip! Go back and forth through the camp, from gate to gate, and kill your brothers, your friends, your neighbors!" The Levites did as Moses had commanded, and that day about three thousand of the people fell.
>
> —Exodus 32:26–28, NABRE

What about the commandment "You shall not commit adultery"?

As for the commandment "Thou shall not commit adultery," most Christians accept this at its basic level and believe it is wrong for married people to engage in sex other than with their spouses. Also, most Christians believe that it is wrong to have sex with a married person who is not your spouse.

The command applies only to adultery. However, many Christians expand the meaning of this commandment to forbid sex outside of marriage, including premarital sex, although the commandment does not specifically say so. The Bible does not seem to directly address the issue of premarital sex, probably because it was less of an issue when the Bible was written since people were married at such a young age. This is very different from today, when young people who have reached puberty typically have many years ahead of them before getting married and face many temptations.

What about the commandment "You shall not steal"?

All Christians reject the concept of stealing. However, there is a wide of range of views in many cases as to what stealing is and how it should be treated. In the American legal system, there are great inequalities in how stealing is treated. Street crime, such as stealing a purse or a car, is likely to get a serious punishment, while those who commit white-collar theft are rarely caught and often get much milder punishments. The amount of money stolen through embezzlement in workplaces and cheating the government far exceeds the value of street-crime thefts.

What about the commandment "You shall not bear false witness"?

Very likely, this commandment was limited to forbidding bearing false witness in a legal case. Most Christians expand the meaning to forbid telling lies in general.

The commandment about not bearing false witness is likely a dictate against lying in a legal case. Telling the truth all the time might be problematical, such as telling a lie to protect someone from harm.

Many Christians recognize that there are exceptions when telling a lie might be justified, such as if one was a prisoner in war or if one lied to protect someone from being harmed. The bigger problem in society today is that there is far too much falsehood and lying.

What about the last commandment(s) about coveting?

The last commandment for Protestants and the last two for Catholics prohibit coveting. However, what does the word "covet" mean? One definition is "to desire wrongfully"; however, this begs the question of what the difference is between wrongful desire and desire that is not wrongful. What is the boundary? Seeing a married woman as attractive is one thing, but at what point does that turn into wrongful desire? You may appreciate your neighbor's new car and wish you had one like it, but at what point do you start coveting the car?

The point of the commandment (or commandments), which is an important point that Jesus would have supported, is that it is not just one's actions that are wrong but that intentions can be wrong, too. If we have the intentions, even if they do not result in actions, the intentions can be morally wrong. However, it must be added that having wrong desires and not taking action is far less bad than having the wrong desires and then taking action to fulfill them.

Do the Ten Commandments cover all moral issues?

Many Christians note that the Ten Commandments do not cover all moral issues. For example, the Commandments do not forbid slavery. Here is the commandment on the day of rest:

> Remember the sabbath day, and keep it holy. For six days you shall labor and do all your work. But the seventh day is a sabbath to the Lord your God; you shall not do any work—you, your son or your daughter, your male or female slave, your livestock, or the alien resident in your towns. For in six days the Lord made Heaven and earth, the sea, and all that is in them, but rested the seventh day; therefore the Lord blessed the sabbath day and consecrated it.
>
> —Exodus 20:8–11, NRSV

This commandment forbids work on the Sabbath for all people and animals, including children, foreigners, and slaves. Admittedly, this was a huge step forward for servants and slaves in that they also got a day of rest. However, in the Old Testament/Hebrew Scriptures, slavery is an accepted practice. From what we know of ancient customs, very likely, slavery was a requirement to perform a certain amount of work, and this slavery was far less harsh than the slavery of Africans in America, where slaves were seen as property and could be greatly mistreated. However, this still does not diminish the fact that the Bible does not condemn slavery.

This emphasizes the point that many Christians have discovered: the Bible is not a complete and simple guide to answers for all important moral questions. Some Christians disagree, as they find the Bible more than adequate for addressing moral issues. However, those who find the Bible adequate typically have a set of beliefs that fill in the gaps or determine how to interpret certain passages.

What is the biblical concept of "an eye for an eye"?

> But if injury ensues, you shall give life for life, eye for eye, tooth for tooth, hand for hand, foot for foot, burn for burn, wound for wound, stripe for stripe.
>
> —Exodus 21:23–25, NABRE

"An eye for an eye," known as the *lex talionis*, the law of retaliation, is found in the Old Testament/Hebrew Scriptures in Exodus and in Deuteronomy. It is also mentioned in the ancient Babylonian law code of Hammurabi. This ancient moral principle has had great influence over the centuries. It is often cited today as a moral principle. However, "an eye for an eye" is often understood.

In the history of human development, "an eye for an eye" was a step forward because it limited retribution to an equal amount. Thus, if you poked out my eye, I could poke out your eye but I could not kill you. If you broke my arm, I could break your arm but I could not kill you. If you killed someone in my family, my family could kill you, but we could not wipe out your whole family or village. This was progress for humans.

However, in the ancient world, "an eye for eye" typically did not mean retaliating with another injury; instead, it usually meant a money settlement proportionate to the injury. Small injuries required small settlements; large injuries required bigger settlements. The same principle is followed today in lawsuits over injuries and workers' compensation settlements.

In the ancient world, people were smart enough to understand that if you break my arm and I break your arm, then there are two people who cannot work. Even in the case of killings, there would often be cash settlements rather than killing someone in return. This practice became known as paying "blood money." The practice is still around. During the American military action in Afghanistan, there were several times where people were killed, and the U.S. government made a money settlement to the family.

One of the problems with retaliation is that we tend to overvalue injuries to ourselves and undervalue injuries to others. On a simple level, for many people when their feelings are hurt, it is significant; when other people's feelings are hurt, it is insignificant. Thus, we tend to measure injuries differently. The goal in retaliation is to "even the score." But how can that happen if there is no agreed-upon measurement?

There have been a number of retaliation feuds, such as the famous Hatfield/McCoy feud in the 1800s in Kentucky and Virginia. If a Hatfield killed a McCoy, then the McCoy would kill a Hatfield to even the score. However, the Hatfields would not see the score as even and settled. Instead, they would have a need for revenge over the latest killing of a Hatfield, so they would kill another McCoy, which would set up another killing of a Hatfield, and on and on. (I am using the Hatfield/McCoy example in a theoretical way and not getting into the nitty-gritty details of the actual history.)

The Jewish Talmud, which is a set of commentaries on the Jewish Law, contains a discussion of *lex talionis* in which the Torah text is understood to require a money settlement and not physical injury as retaliation.

As described earlier, Jesus totally rejected the concept of "an eye for an eye."

> You have heard that it was said, "An eye for an eye and a tooth for a tooth." But I say to you, Do not resist an evildoer. But if anyone strikes you on the right cheek, turn the other also....

—Matthew 5:38–39, NRSV

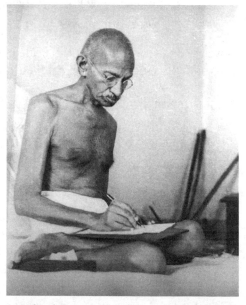

An Indian lawyer who founded a peaceful movement of civil disobedience to free his country from British rule, Mahatma Gandhi didn't believe in the eye-for-an-eye concept, correctly believing, instead, that such attitudes lead to endless war.

294

Lastly, Indian leader Mahatma Gandhi noted: "An eye for an eye will only make the whole world blind." Martin Luther King Jr. repeated this idea: "The old law of an eye for an eye leaves everyone blind." In the musical *Fiddler on the Roof*, Tevye comments: "Very good. That way, the whole world will be blind and toothless."

THE MORALITY OF WAR

What do Christians think about the morality of war?

As with all moral issues, Christians have very diverse views on the morality of war. These views—which also can be found among non-Christians—can be grouped into three categories.

1. *War is wrong. All wars are wrong.* This is the pacifist position. It is held by religious groups, such as the Amish and Quakers. Pacifists often have a great awareness of the horrors of war. The pacifist position is also held by people in other religions—such as some forms of Buddhism—and by many nonreligious people.

2. *Some wars are just.* Many people hold the position that some wars are just and other wars are not just. However, people often hold this position without being able to describe their criteria for determining when war is just and when it is not just. Furthermore, to hold to this position in an honest, moral way, one has to apply the criteria objectively. One has to look at both sides and let one's own side be judged by the same criteria as is used on the other side.

3. *Our side is right.* This is a very common position. Many people believe that if their country is involved in a war, their country is acting in the right. This position makes little attempt to look at both sides or to state objective criteria for justifying a war. Also, many people holding this position make little effort to understand the position or perspective of the other side. It is common for very patriotic people to hold this position.

For those who hold that some wars are just and some are not, what is an example of a set of criteria for judging war?

The best-known criteria for judging the morality of war is called "the Just War Theory." It has a long history going back some two thousand years. There are two parts to the theory: *us ad bellum* (justice in going to war) and *jus in bello* (justice in waging war).

What are the requirements for *jus ad bellum* (justice in going to war)?

Jus ad bellum requires the following:

1. Just cause: Wars can only be waged for a just cause such as true self-defense or to protect the innocent. Wars of aggression, wars to conquer land, wars for economic gain, and wars of revenge would not be just wars. These are not just causes.

2. Comparative justice: This means you have to look at the grievances on both sides. Even if the other side did you wrong, you have to make sure your side has not also done wrong.

3. Competent authority: Is the war being decided by the proper authority? This requirement evolved in the Middle Ages to try to prevent private wars, such as by independent groups of knights.

4. Right intention: If you go to war for a just cause, are you waging the war for that cause? What you cannot do is go to war for a just cause and then use that as an excuse to pursue an unjust goal, such as conquering land.

5. Probability of success: Are you likely to succeed?

6. Last resort: Have other options been exhausted?

7. Proportionality: Is the good to be achieved worth the cost? Humans tend to ignore the true effects and costs of war.

What are the requirements for *jus in bello* (justice in waging war)?

The requirements for *jus in bello* are as follows:

1. Proportionality: In waging the war, is the good to be accomplished worth the damage done?

2. Noncombatant immunity: Nonsoldiers (civilians) should not be directly targeted.

These conditions seem very strict. Is that so?

Yes. Some have pointed out that if the Just War Theory was applied conscientiously, very few wars would be justified. Many of the wars that America has fought over the centuries, such as the Mexican–American War of 1846–1848, did not meet the criteria.

Some thinkers want to add one more requirement for *jus ad bellum*: "Prior innocence." If one side claims that a war is just, that side cannot have helped create the problem over which it is going to war. For example, if a corrupt regime has been supported by another country, that corruption cannot be used later as a justification to go to war by the country that had previously supported the regime.

CAPITAL PUNISHMENT

What are the arguments for capital punishment?

Christians disagree on the morality of capital punishment. Many Christians support it with several arguments. Many cite the biblical text "an eye for an eye" and "a life for a life," despite the fact that Jesus rejected the concept. ("An eye for an eye" is used by some people today as a justification for capital punishment, even though when it was originally used, there were no prisons. Today, the option exists of putting convicted murderers in prison for life.) Such Christians often see capital punishment as a payment of a debt to society. Others see it as balancing the moral order. Some claim that capital punishment is a deterrent, arguing that in the future, those considering murder will hesitate if they know they might be executed for their actions. Proponents of capital punishment also contend that it gives a sense of justice and closure to the family and friends of the murder victim. Finally, they argue that it saves money and frees up prison space.

Executions in the United States are now done using drugs and not by hanging or the electric chair. Sodium thiopental, an anesthetic, was the preferred drug, but the supply has become limited since the primary manufacturer stopped making it, so now pentobarbitol is being used. Christians have been divided on whether or not capital punishment is moral.

What are the arguments against capital punishment?

Christians who oppose capital punishment argue that it does not act as a deterrent since murderers rarely think out the consequences of their actions. Also, those societies with the lowest murder rates do not use it. In fact, most countries in the world have abolished it. The only countries that still have capital punishment are often countries with bad civil rights records.

Furthermore, capital punishment does not save money. Life in prison is far cheaper. Capital punishment also distracts attention from trying to solve some of the underlying problems that lead people to commit murder. Also, capital punishment has not been carried out fairly. African Americans, poor people, and those with limited education get executed at disproportionately higher rates. Opponents argue that capital punishment is about revenge, something that goes against the teachings of Jesus.

HOMOSEXUALITY AND
SAME-SEX MARRIAGE

What is the Christian view on homosexuality?

Christians have very different views on the morality of homosexuality and related questions, such as the morality of same-sex marriage. Attitudes have changed in the last several decades. Not long ago, most Christians saw homosexual acts as immoral and homosexuality as a disorder. Just as cultural attitudes have changed for many people, so too have many Christians rethought their views.

On one side are those who insist that all homosexual acts are immoral and that homosexuality itself is a type of disorder, moral flaw, or character flaw. Some Christians even claim that homosexuality is something that can be overcome or cured and people can move from being homosexuals to heterosexuals. (The mainline scientific view is that a homosexual orientation can rarely be changed.)

A middle position holds that homosexual acts are immoral but that homosexuality itself is not a disorder. Christians who hold this view would typically argue that homosexuals are morally required to not act on their desires and should refrain from sexual activity.

A third position has developed among a number of Christians that homosexuality is not a disorder nor is there something fundamentally immoral about homosexual acts. Christians in this group often also have more relaxed views about when heterosexual acts would be immoral or not. Christians in this third group often accept same-sex marriage and often allow such marriages in their churches.

What are the Bible texts that speak of homosexuality?

Three important passages on homosexuality are often cited:

What is the story of Sodom and Gomorrah?

The story of Sodom and Gomorrah is found in Chapter 19 of the Book of Genesis. In the story, Lot, the nephew of Abraham, is sitting at the gate of Sodom where he lives. Two angels arrive, although it is unclear whether or not he knows they are angels. Following the hospitality customs of the time, Lot welcomes them into his home to feed them and give them a place to stay. That evening, the men of town come to Lot's house demanding the visitors: "Bring them out to us that we may have intimacies with them." Lot refuses, even offering his own daughters as alternatives. According to the custom of the time, one was required to protect strangers above one's interests. Finally, the visitors cause the men of the town to be blinded and then help Lot, his wife, and daughters escape. Sodom is destroyed along with the nearby town of Gomorrah.

This story has a long history of being used to argue that homosexuality is morally wrong. In fact, the word "sodomy" comes from this story. Many people have noted that perhaps the big crime of the men of Sodom was their desire to abuse strangers in a culture that demanded hospitality to travelers. Others point out that this story is about gang rape of angelic beings and may not be relevant to the discussion of morality of sexual acts between consenting adults of the same sex.

You shall not lie with a male as with a woman; it is an abomination.

—Leviticus 18:22, NRSV

If a man lies with a male as with a woman, both of them have committed an abomination; they shall be put to death; their blood is upon them.

—Leviticus 20:13, NRSV

For this reason God gave them up to degrading passions. Their women exchanged natural intercourse for unnatural, and in the same way also the men, giving up natural intercourse with women, were consumed with passion for one another. Men committed shameless acts with men and received in their own persons the due penalty for their error.

—Romans 1:26–27, NRSV

Christians who oppose homosexuality see these prohibitions as still binding today. Other Christians see these texts as products of their time and not binding. They would also note the detail about putting homosexuals to death to emphasize the point that these rules were from an ancient time and not applicable today.

What are Christian views on same-sex marriage?

Christians are divided on it. Many Christians oppose same-sex marriage. Other Christians accept it as part of the culture but do not perform same-sex marriages in their churches. Yet other Christians embrace it and allow same-sex marriage ceremonies in their churches.

It should be noted that same-sex marriage is a very new thing. For most of human history, with only a few exceptions, human cultures have insisted on marriage as between a man and woman. The change of attitudes for many people and the legalization of same-sex marriage have come very quickly.

What is the Christian definition of marriage?

Today, Christians often argue over the definition of marriage. Most agree that marriage should take place between two adults. Marriage between children, or an adult and child, would be wrong. Some Christians insist that marriage can only

Depending on the church, sometimes same-sex marriages are accepted and wedding ceremonies are performed, and sometimes a church will reject them. For this reason, same-sex couples may feel it is easier to go to a city hall to get married.

take place between a man and woman. Others accept a broader definition that can also include two men or two women.

What is the big question about marriage?

The broader question on which Christians disagree is: "Who defines what is a proper marriage: God or humans?" Is marriage an institution created by God, or is marriage an institution created by humans? Some Christians insist that God created marriage as an unchangeable institution between a man and a woman. They often cite this passage in Genesis:

> So the LORD God cast a deep sleep on the man, and while he was asleep, he took out one of his ribs and closed up its place with flesh. The LORD God then built the rib that he had taken from the man into a woman. When he brought her to the man, the man said: "This one, at last, is bone of my bones and flesh of my flesh; this one shall be called 'woman,' for out of man this one has been taken." That is why a man leaves his father and mother and clings to his wife, and the two of them become one body.
>
> —Genesis 2:21–24, NABRE

Other Christians believe that marriage has been created or shaped by human culture and, thus, it can change.

ABORTION

What are the different Christian views on abortion?

Christians hold different views on the morality of abortion from strong pro-life advocates, opposing most or even all abortions, to the strong pro-choice advocates believing in the right of women to decide for themselves. Also, many Christians are indifferent on the issue.

What is the moral issue involved?

Actually, there are several issues involved. When does the fetus become a human being? Does the fetus have rights? What are the rights of a woman in deciding for herself whether to have an abortion or not? What are the special cases that would justify an abortion?

When does a fetus become a human being?

There is no agreement over when a fetus becomes a human being. Everyone agrees that the egg and the sperm are not human beings and that a born baby is, so when in the nine months between conception and birth does the fetus become a human being? Many pro-life Christians believe the fetus becomes a human life at the moment of conception.

Some pro-life Christians oppose scientific research using human embryos, believing them to be human beings. Some Christians add the belief that a human soul enters at the moment of conception. Many pro-life Christians support their position with this passage from Jeremiah: "Before I formed you in the womb I knew you, and before you were born I consecrated you; I appointed you a prophet to the nations" (1:5, NRSV).

From a legal perspective, the fetus becomes a human being with legal rights at birth. The one exception to this is that in some states, if someone kills a pregnant woman and the fetus also dies, the killer can be charged with two murders.

Other Christians do not believe that the embryo, and then the fetus in the early stages, is a human being. Many different answers are given as to when it becomes human.

What is the pro-choice position?

Pro-choice Christians focus more on the rights of women in determining whether or not to have an abortion. Given that there is no agreement on when the fetus becomes a human, the decision should be left up to the woman.

Many Christians are against legal abortion as they believe that life begins at conception and, therefore, abortion is murder.

How can we reduce the number of abortions?

The fight between those who oppose abortion and those who support a woman's right to choose is very intense. The issue is being constantly fought over in state legislatures and in the courts. Both sides agree, however, on the goal of reducing the number of abortions. Many pro-choice advocates are very active in promoting sex education and making contraception more available to reduce the number of unwanted pregnancies.

Are there special circumstances that would justify an abortion?

Many Christians and others accept abortion under certain conditions, such as if the pregnancy resulted from a rape or from incest. Many people accept abortion if it is necessary to save the life of the mother. A few strict pro-lifers reject abortion even to save the life of the mother.

What about teaching abstinence?

Many pro-lifers oppose the teaching of sex education to young people and insist on teaching young people to abstain from sex until marriage. However, studies have shown that teaching abstinence may get young people to delay having sex for a while, but when they do become active, they often lack knowledge about contraception, so teaching abstinence does not lower the rates for unwanted pregnancies.

MISCELLANEOUS TOPICS ON MORALITY

What are the seven deadly sins?

Somewhere in the early centuries of Christianity, a list of seven deadly sins developed: pride, greed, lust, envy, gluttony, wrath, and sloth. Wrath is anger, and sloth is laziness. Most sins or wrongdoings of people fit under one of these seven categories.

However, it might be better to call these the "seven deadly vices" rather than the "seven deadly sins." A sin is an immoral action. A vice is the tendency in a person to do immoral actions. So, for example, greed is the tendency in a person that leads him or her to steal something. The opposite of vices is virtues. Virtues, such as honesty and responsibility, are tendencies that lead a person to act morally.

What are venial and mortal sins?

In the Middle Ages, a distinction developed in Roman Catholic thinking between venial sins and mortal sins. A venial sin is less serious than a mortal sin. Stealing a loaf of bread is minor compared to killing someone. The big distinction between these two sins is the understanding of what the punishment is if one died without having gone to confession to be forgiven of the sin. An unforgiven mortal sin meant the person would go to Hell. An unforgiven venial sin meant the person would go to Purgatory. A mortal sin separates a person from God's saving grace.

What are moral absolutes?

Moral absolutes are rules that prohibit certain actions as always being wrong without any exceptions. However, there are few moral rules that are absolutes. A few opponents of abortion believe that it is always wrong and, therefore, treat it as a moral absolute. However, most opponents of abortion will allow an exception if an abortion is necessary to save the life of a pregnant woman.

One could state that murder is always wrong. However, as defined above, murder is "unjustified intentional killing," so to say "unjustified intentional killing is always wrong" is a tautology and not a helpful moral principle. Most people believe stealing and telling lies are wrong yet can easily think of exceptions when stealing or telling a lie might be moral, such as stealing food if one is starving.

Can you think of a moral prohibition that has no exceptions? For example, most people, except pacifists, believe that there are situations when killing people should be allowed. One of the few moral absolutes is that it is always wrong to sexually abuse children. Can you think of other examples of moral absolutes?

MORTALITY AND IMMORTALITY

What do the words "mortal" and "immortal" mean?

Two words need to be defined: "mortal" and "immortal." Something that is mortal will someday die. All animals and humans are mortal and will die. "Im-" is a prefix meaning "not," so the word "immortal" means to "not die." Christians believe that God is immortal and will live forever. Many Christians believe in immortal angels. Many Christians also believe in an immortal devil and immortal demons.

What is the Christian belief in an immortal soul?

Many Christians believe that humans have a mortal body that will die but also an immortal soul. A typical Christian view is that when a person's body dies, his or her soul leaves the body. The person's soul is judged and then goes to Heaven to be with God for those who are worthy or goes to Hell to be punished for those who die with unforgiven sin or who lack religious faith.

What is the origin of the concept of an immortal soul in a mortal body?

Belief in an immortal soul in a mortal body can be found in a few places in the New Testament. "And do not be afraid of those who kill the body but cannot kill the soul; rather,

303

be afraid of the one who can destroy both soul and body in Gehenna" (Matthew 10:18). However, this concept seems to be influenced by Greek philosophy. It does not match the older Hebrew concept of the whole person as one entity. The Hebrew word, נפש (nephesh) which is sometimes translated as "soul," actually means "living being."

How does the resurrection of the body fit with the idea of an immortal soul?

Many Christians believe in both the idea of an immortal soul and the idea of the resurrection of the body. Many Christians hold to both beliefs without ever trying to think out how the ideas fit together. For some Christians, the immortal soul goes to Heaven when the person dies. Then, at some point, the soul is joined with a resurrected body. Since the Bible gives no details, there are different views on this, and many Christians do not give it much thought.

Many Christians have unclear ideas of what the resurrected body will be like. Most Christians do not believe the actual molecules of their bodies will be constituted into a body in Heaven. Some say it will be a "spiritual body," but what does that mean?

What kind of body will one have: the healthy body one had at age twenty-five or the body one had at seventy-five when one was overweight with arthritis and diabetes? What about an amputee? Most Christians assume that God will re-create an ideal body in Heaven.

HEAVEN AND HELL

Why do Christians believe in Heaven and Hell?

Most Christians believe in Heaven and Hell. Heaven is seen by many as the final reward for believers who have lived moral lives. In Heaven, one will live forever and be in the presence of God. There will be no suffering in Heaven. Some Christians emphasize the importance of faith to get to Heaven. True faith leads to Heaven; the wrong faith, or inadequate faith, leads to Hell. For many Christians, Heaven is the ultimate reward for living morally, and Hell is the ultimate punishment for not living morally. Hell is seen as a place of eternal punishment for those who have disobeyed God's commandments, lack religious faith, or both.

Over the centuries, Christians have done much speculation about the nature of Heaven and Hell. Dante's *Divine Comedy* is a famous example. Many artists have used their imagination to create visual images of Heaven and Hell. Numerous episodes of *The Simpsons* TV show explore ideas about Heaven and Hell. The 1991 movie *Bill & Ted's Bogus Journey* presents a clever take on the afterlife.

Is Heaven up and Hell down?

In the ancient world, Heaven was believed to be up above in the clouds, in the Heavens. Many images of Heaven depict those in Heaven as being on clouds. Hell was seen as

A painting in the New St. George's Church in Bucharest, Romania, depicts Hell as a place of eternal torture and misery. There are some Christians, however, who believe Hell is not an eternal punishment.

being below the earth. The concept evolved from earlier notions of an underworld. Many ancient people literally believed in a Heaven up there and a Hell down below. Today, many Christian people still imagine Heaven as up and Hell as down, yet they know that the Earth is round and has at its center a core of dense, molten rock. Rocket ships have gone far out into the solar system. Telescopes peer at light coming from billions of miles away. However, no one has come up with an alternate way to imagine Heaven and Hell. One answer is to say that Heaven and Hell are realms of spiritual existence, so they do not have locations.

What did Jesus say about Hell?

In several passages in the gospels, Jesus mentions a place of punishment for the wicked:

> The Son of Man will send his angels, and they will collect out of his kingdom all who cause others to sin and all evildoers. They will throw them into the fiery furnace, where there will be wailing and grinding of teeth. Then the righteous will shine like the sun in the kingdom of their Father. Whoever has ears ought to hear.
>
> —Matthew 13:41–43, NABRE

If your hand causes you to sin, cut it off. It is better for you to enter into life maimed than with two hands to go into Gehenna, into the unquenchable fire. And if your foot

305

causes you to sin, cut it off. It is better for you to enter into life crippled than with two feet to be thrown into Gehenna. And if your eye causes you to sin, pluck it out. Better for you to enter into the kingdom of God with one eye than with two eyes to be thrown into Gehenna, where "their worm does not die, and the fire is not quenched."

—Mark 9:43–48, NABRE

What is Gehenna?

Gehenna was the trash dump just outside the walls of Jerusalem that was constantly burning. Jesus uses it to symbolize the place of punishment in the afterlife.

What will Heaven be like?

For Christians, the ultimate goal is to get to Heaven when they die. The Bible says very little about Heaven. In only a couple of parables does Jesus describe anything about it: the Parable of the Sheep and Goats and the Parable of Lazarus and the Rich Man (Matthew 25:31–46 and Luke 16:19–31). Most of the teachings of Jesus, especially in the synoptic gospels, are about this life. Jesus says little about the afterlife.

As Christians imagine Heaven, they often think of several aspects. In Heaven, one will have self-awareness, memory, and relationships. Perhaps this is stating the obvious, but sometimes, it is important to explore the obvious. The typical Christian view is very different from the Hindu concept of moksha, as understood in Hindu philosophy, in which the soul is liberated after death from the cycle of rebirth. There is no self-awareness or memory for the soul. Such things are attachments that one has to let go of to achieve moksha.

As most Christians imagine it, when you get to Heaven, you will know who you are, and you will remember what happened in your life. Also, you will continue the relationships, such as with people you love, who are also in Heaven with you. Many Christians also imagine that once in Heaven, a person will still be aware of what is happening on earth.

Are there Christians who do not believe in Hell?

Most Christians believe in the concept of an eternal Hell as a place for punishment for sinners or for those who do not hold Christian belief. However, some Christians ques-

When is the Final Judgment?

Many Christians believe that there will be final judgment of the good people and evil people at the End of Time, yet many Christians also imagine that when people die, they go immediately to Heaven or Hell. Many Christians hold both ideas, yet make no attempt to explain how they fit together. However, one answer is to note that this is a problem of time: judgment now when one dies or judgment later at the End of Time, yet, many think that the afterlife is eternal and there is no time; therefore, concepts of "now" versus "later" do not apply.

tion how a loving God can send humans to be punished eternally. Some Christians believe Hell is not permanent and that eventually, God will redeem everyone. They believe that no one can ultimately resist the love of God. These people are often called "Universalists" because they believe that salvation is universal.

Those Christians who believe in Hell think it is an essential concept for having a moral order. Fear of Hell is an important motivation for keeping people in line. Those Christians who do not believe in Hell note that considering human history, the fear of Hell has not done a great job keeping people in line.

It is also worth noting that fear of punishment is often a very ineffective motivation. The United States has more people in prison and on parole than any other country in the world. The United States also has a higher percentage of its population in jail, yet crime still continues. Also, as some point out, people who act morally do so less for fear of punishment but more because they believe acting morally is the right thing to do.

The Jehovah's Witnesses do not believe in Hell. They also do not believe that humans have immortal souls. Thus, when people die, they cease to exist. That is the end of bad people. As for good and holy people who die, God will re-create them from memory in paradise.

WHO GETS INTO HEAVEN?

What is the Christian belief about who gets into Heaven?

Among Christians, there is a great diversity of opinion over who gets to Heaven and how difficult it is to get to Heaven. Christians also disagree over what the requirements are to get to Heaven. There are three basic positions on these issues: exclusivism, inclusivism, and pluralism. The three positions are described below. However, keep in mind that there are variations on these positions and that different Christians may understand the terms in different ways.

What is the exclusivist position?

An exclusivist Christian holds that only those who are true Christians will get to Heaven. Even those who never even heard of the teachings of Christianity about Jesus will go to Hell. For many exclusivists, the vast majority of humanity will not go to Heaven. Protestant reformer John Calvin held such a view that only a select few were predestined for Heaven. Everyone else would go to Hell. Christians who hold to exclusivism often cite the Gospel of John and Paul's letter to the Romans:

> Jesus said to him, "I am the way, and the truth, and the life. No one comes to the Father except through me."

—John 14:6, NRSV   307

For God so loved the world that he gave his only Son, so that everyone who believes in him may not perish but may have eternal life. Indeed, God did not send the Son into the world to condemn the world, but in order that the world might be saved through him. Those who believe in him are not condemned; but those who do not believe are condemned already, because they have not believed in the name of the only Son of God.

—John 3:16–18, NRSV

Everyone who calls on the name of the Lord shall be saved.

—Romans 10:13, NRSV

Some Christians who hold to exclusivism would defend the position by arguing that all people deserve damnation for their sins. Although Christians who accept Jesus are forgiven and can go to Heaven, those who are not Christian and who will not go to Heaven are only getting the punishment they deserve for their sins.

What is the inclusivist position?

The Christian inclusivist position holds that although faith in Jesus is the normal path to salvation, other people, such as non-Christians who are moral people, will also go to Heaven. For these Christians, moral living and being a good person are the keys to salvation. Inclusivist Christians reject the idea that a loving God would send the majority of people to Hell. Thus, Buddhists, Hindus, Jews, Muslims, members of other traditions, and even agnostics and atheists who are good, moral people will get to Heaven. Inclusivism is held by many Christians, although they may not know the label for their beliefs.

One attempt to think out the position of inclusivism was worked out by Catholic theologian Karl Rahner (1904–1984), who proposed the concept of an "anonymous Christian" who could go to Heaven. Although such a person was not a believing Christian, if the person lived out the values of Jesus, that person would go to Heaven. This idea is supported by a Roman Catholic teaching from the Second Vatican Council that those "who through no fault of their own do not know the Gospel of Christ or His Church, but who nevertheless seek God with a sincere heart, and moved by grace, try in their actions to do His will as they know it through the dictates of their conscience—those too may achieve eternal salvation" (*Lumen gentium*, 16).

Can anyone enter Heaven, according to Christian beliefs? Some feel you must believe Jesus is your Lord and Savior, while others believe that any good person can go to Heaven, even if they are not Christians.

308

What is the pluralist position?

Christian pluralists hold that there is more than one path to God. Other religions can be valid ways to get to Heaven. This idea is shared by some other religions, such as the Vedanta tradition, one of the schools of Hinduism, which quotes: "Truth is one, sages call it by various names" from the *Rig Veda*. Many Christian pluralists believe that God also works through other religions. They reject the notion that all other religions are wrong and mistaken. Some pluralists, who start out as Christians, move beyond traditional Christian ways of thinking about God and what happens after death. Not surprisingly, Christian traditionalists see Christian pluralists as selling out the essential and unique nature of Jesus and his teachings.

Many pluralists would admit that some religions have done wrong and immoral things. Thus, the belief that there are many paths to God is not blanket approval of all religious beliefs and practices. The religion of the ISIS or Aztec belief in human sacrifice can be condemned as invalid paths to God.

What about accepting Jesus as one's Lord and Savior?

For many Christians, accepting Jesus as one's Lord and Savior is essential for salvation. This is an act of faith in the belief that Jesus died for human sin. These Christians often speak of "being saved." Many can remember that exact moment and date when they were saved. Many found such an acceptance of Jesus as a powerful, emotional experience. Often, people come to accept Jesus after an awareness of their sins and the guilt they feel about them.

However, many other Christians do not see such an act of accepting Jesus as Lord and Savior in this way as essential. These Christians see the normal Christian life as having belief and faith in what Jesus did, but a specific dramatic moment of stating it is

What are the requirements to get to Heaven?

A great diversity of views exists among Christians on the requirements to get to Heaven. Many Protestants believe that salvation comes from faith in the death and Resurrection of Jesus. Although good works, such as acts of charity and moral living, flow from such faith, good works and moral living do not earn salvation. However, according to many Protestants, if one did have faith but then committed terrible sins and did not seek God's forgiveness, one could lose salvation.

Other Christians believe that salvation requires both faith and good works. Good works include moral living and acts of charity to help those in need. Even if one has religious faith, one can lose salvation by committing serious sin. However, if a person asks God for forgiveness of serious sin, then salvation is possible. If the person is never repentant for his or her sins, then salvation is lost.

not necessary. In fact, many Christians assert their faith in what Jesus did every time they recite the Nicene Creed. Many denominations recite the Creed every Sunday. Furthermore, the beliefs of the Creed are restated at baptisms and confirmations.

Do Christians believe that one has to have a conversion experience?

Many Christians believe in the essential nature of having a conversion experience. To be a true Christian, one must come to the point of recognizing one's own sinfulness and need for Jesus. Even if one grows up in a Christian church, at some point, an emotional conversion experience is necessary.

Other Christians do not believe that everyone must have a conversion experience. Many Christians instead believe in raising children in a Christian community where their faith is nurtured from infancy onward. Such Christians often baptize infants and provide religious education either through Christian schools or through Sunday School and Vacation Bible School (VBS). In such denominations, many people simply grow up as Christians. Many of these people never go down the path of serious sin that requires a conversion experience.

Can you know for sure if you are going to Heaven or not?

There is disagreement among Christians over whether or not one can be certain about going to Heaven. Some Christians insist that true Christians can know for certain. Others hold the opposite: that such certainty is not possible, although one has hope of getting to Heaven.

CHRISTIAN BELIEFS: ANGELS, THE DEVIL, AND THE END TIMES

ANGELS

What are angels?

Christians see angels as beings who were created by God. Angels are often described as not having physical bodies; hence, they are noncorporeal. ("Noncorporeal" comes from *corpus,* the Latin word for body.) Most Christians who believe in angels do not think much about how to describe them. However, some religious thinkers describe angels as having free will and an intellect. This means that they are aware, know what they are doing, and can make choices for good or bad.

I have heard of angels and archangels. Are there other kinds of angels?

In Christian tradition, a list of nine different ranks of angels is often cited:

First Sphere
    Seraphim
    Cherubim
    Thrones
Second Sphere
    Dominions or Lordships
    Virtues or Strongholds
    Powers or Authorities
Third Sphere
    Principalities or Rulers
    Archangels
    Angels

This list was created by an early Christian writer called Pseudo-Dionysius the Areopagite, who probably lived in the 400s or early 500s. He described nine ranks of angels in his book *The Celestial Hierarchy*. He went through the Bible and tried to organize all the references to angels, thus creating his system of three spheres and nine ranks.

Who are the archangels?

Gabriel, Raphael, and Michael are the three best-known archangels. Catholics and Eastern Orthodox Christians often call them St. Gabriel, St. Raphael, and St. Michael.

Gabriel appears in the Old Testament/Hebrew Scriptures Book of Daniel in Chapters 8 and 9. Gabriel then appears in the Gospel of Luke announcing to Zachariah that he will have a son named John and then announcing to Mary that she will give birth to Jesus.

Michael is mentioned three times in the Book of Daniel. Michael is also mentioned in the New Testament in the Epistle of Jude and the Book of Revelation (Daniel 10:13, 10:21, 12:1; Jude 1:9; Revelation 12:7–9). Raphael is only mentioned in the Book of Tobit, which is part of the Catholic Old Testament but not part of the Protestant Old Testament.

In the Eastern Orthodox Christian tradition, other archangels are honored: Uriel, Selaphiel, Jegudiel, Barachiel, and sometimes Jeremiel.

Why do all of the archangel names end in "el"?

The Hebrew word "El" is one of the names of God. El as the name for God also appears in other ancient Mediterranean languages. Each of the archangel names has a meaning. Michael means "Who is like God?", Gabriel means "Might of God," and Raphael means "God heals."

Why are angels important?

There has been great interest in angels by many religious people down through the centuries. Angels are important parts of traditional religions such as Judaism, Christianity, and Islam. According to Muslims, it is the angel Gabriel, called Jibril, who appeared to the prophet Muhammad and gave him messages that would eventually become the Islamic holy book, the Qu'ran.

Many people believe that angels are active in their lives, helping and guiding them. For some people, angels are the en-

Archangels such as Michael are chief angels who rank just above regular angels. They often serve as messengers of God (painting of Archangel Michael, St. Peter's Church, Tel Aviv, Israel).

How have angels been portrayed in the media?

Angels appear in popular movies such as *Angels in the Outfield* and TV shows such as *Touched by an Angel*. There are also numerous cultural references to angels, such as the Blue Angels Navy flying team, the Hells Angels motorcycle gang, and Los Angeles, which is Spanish for "the angels."

Angels are frequent characters in all kinds of novels, movies, and animation. They are depicted in many different ways. In fact, trying to understand the use of angel imagery becomes confusing because of the countless and varied representations of angels as both good and bad. People have used their imaginations to take the concept of angels in many different directions.

tire focus of their religious belief. Many Christians believe in guardian angels. A guardian angel is an individual angel watching out for a particular person.

Angels are an important image in Christian art. The angels Gabriel and Raphael show up in a number of famous paintings. The scene, called the Annunciation, where the Angel Gabriel appears to Mary to announce the Incarnation, has been painted by many famous painters. Cemeteries, particularly older ones, often have many angel statues, especially marking the graves of young children who died.

What is the prayer the Angelus?

The Angelus is a set of Catholic devotional prayers built around the scene of Gabriel appearing to Mary. The prayer includes the lines "The Angel of the Lord declared unto Mary, and she conceived of the Holy Ghost" and "Behold the handmaid of the Lord. Be it done unto me according to thy word." The Angelus includes three repetitions of the Catholic prayer the Hail Mary.

What is some interesting trivia involving angels?

Harpo Marx of the famous Marx Brothers comedy team is known for playing the harp. He also composed several pieces, including "Guardian Angels" in 1945. Gerda Beilenson wrote the lyrics. A recording by the famous Mario Lanza can be found on YouTube. (Several other songs have the same title.) Here are the lyrics:

Guardian angels around my bed,
Joining me in my prayers.
They hush the shadows when they dance about,
They shoo away the bears.
Guardian angels to comfort me,
If I wake in the night.
They gather all my dreams,
Their halos are my light.

They dry my tears,
If I should weep.
They tuck me in,
They rouse me from my sleep.

Guardian angels around my bed,
Standing by till I rise.
There's one with shining wings that holds my hand,
And shows me Paradise.

THE DEVIL

What is the Devil?

The Devil is an important concept in Christianity. Sometimes, the Devil is called Satan. The history of the development of the idea of the Devil is extremely complicated and confusing.

The word "devil" is not found in the Old Testament/Hebrew Scriptures, but it shows up over fifty times in the New Testament. The word "Satan" appears over fifty times in the Christian Bible, including fifteen times in the Old Testament/Hebrew Scriptures, mostly in the Book of Job. However, in the Bible, Satan is not a clearly defined figure. In the Book of Job, his role is closer to a prosecuting attorney than the source of all evil. In the Book of Genesis, it is a snake that tempts Adam and Eve; the Devil is not mentioned there. Satan is mentioned frequently in the New Testament, but there is no description given of Satan.

Do most Christians have similar ideas about the Devil?

No. Christians have very diverse views about the Devil and the Devil's significance. Some Christians believe that there is no Devil. In their view of a loving God who rules the universe, there is no room for a Devil.

Many Christians ignore the concept of the Devil in their faith life. Typically, they do not deny the existence of the Devil but see the concept as irrelevant for explaining evil in the world. For these Christians, evil is caused by bad choices made by humans.

Satan is never described in the Bible, so the images we have of a devil with horns were adopted from pagan ideas of how demons look.

However, there are also religious people who see the Devil as active in the world around them. When something bad happens, they see it as the work of the Devil. The Devil is seen as the cause of everything bad from global wars to a flat tire.

The Devil has been used as a character in many countless legends and stories down through the centuries. An old German legend tells the story of Faust, who sold his soul to the Devil in exchange for unlimited knowledge. There have been several music compositions and operas based on the story. A legend follows that the great blues singer and guitar player Robert Johnson (1911–1938) sold his soul to the Devil at a crossroads in order to get his ability to play the blues. In the musical *Damn Yankees!,* a man trades his soul so he can become a great baseball player to help his team, the Washington Senators, defeat the New York Yankees.

What are demons?

Today, many people see demons as helpers of the Devil. Ancient people often believed that demons were the cause of misfortunes and illnesses. They had no science to explain viruses and afflictions such as epilepsy. For example, if someone had an epileptic seizure, it was seen as being caused by a demon. This made perfect sense to ancient people.

Did God create a bad Devil?

Most Christians do not believe that God could have created a creature that was fundamentally evil. Therefore, they need another explanation of how the Devil got to be bad. The most common explanation tells how the Devil was originally an angel who was good yet chose to rebel against God. The Devil was not created bad but, rather, became bad by his own choices and actions.

Many Christians believe that originally, God created the angels, who were all good. However, before God created the earth, some angels went bad and, led by Satan, rebelled. A great battle took place in Heaven, and the good angels, led by Michael the archangel, defeated the bad angels. The bad angels were banished to Hell, with Satan becoming the Devil and the other bad angels becoming the demons who help him.

Many Christians accept this story because it helps fit a lot of pieces together about the origins of the Devil and demons. However, none of this is described in the Old Testament. Much of the story comes from writings that did not make it into the Bible, such as the Book of Enoch. There are references to the story in the Book of Revelation but not the full story.

What about possession and exorcisms?

Among Christians, there is a wide range of belief about whether people can be possessed by the Devil or demons. Those Christians who believe in possession also believe in performing exorcisms. An exorcism is a praying to drive a demon out of a person. In some denominations, exorcisms are commonly done. For some Christians, illnesses and psychological problems are seen as the results of possession. Many other Christians do not believe in demonic possession.

The name Lucifer, which means "the light," has a very long and complicated history in the religions of the Mideast. In some parts of this history, Lucifer is not a bad figure. The word "Lucifer" also refers to the planet Venus, which is often called the Morning Star. At some point, the term became a common name for the Devil.

Who is Beelzebub?

Beelzebub is one of several names that has been used for the Devil, although there is disagreement among scholars over the origin of these words and what they might mean. During the period of the Old Testament/Hebrew Scriptures, the rival religion was the Canaanite religion that worshiped the god Ba'al. The word "Ba'al" actually meant "Lord." It was used as a title for the gods and a name for Ba'al, the son of the god Dagan.

Beelzebub (*Ba'al Zebŭb*), which literally means "Lord of the flies," was either a title for the Canaanite God or some sort of insulting Hebrew pun on the Canaanite title "Lord of Lord," meant to offend the Canaanites. (Beelzebub is also rendered as Beelzebul, which could be "Lord of the dung.") The title of Beelzebub was the inspiration for the title of William Golding's 1964 novel *Lord of the Flies*.

THE APOCALYPSE AND THE ANTICHRIST

What is the Book of Revelation about?

The final book of the Christian New Testament is the Book of Revelation. The Greek word for "revelation" is "apocalypse." To many, the Book of Revelation is a complicated and confusing reading without an obvious or clear meaning. Over the centuries, Christians have argued over the meaning of the book. It is possible that even the early Christians who first read the book were confused by it. The Book of Revelation and other such writings are often called "apocalyptic literature." Such literature has the style of weird imagery and symbolic elements.

The author of Revelation was a man named John of Patmos. However, this is a different man named John than John the Apostle. Also, the writer of Revelation did not write either the Gospel of John or the Epistles of John.

Down through the centuries, there have been many different and sometimes wild speculations about the meaning of the Book of Revelation. However, the book may actually have a very simple meaning. Written around the year 100 C.E., its purpose was to give encouragement to Christians in Asia Minor (Turkey today) who were experiencing harassment and persecution from the Romans. Also, the book promises punishment for the persecutors. The Book of Revelation is filled with symbols, but all of the symbols in the writing can be explained by references to Asia Minor at the end of the first century.

For example, the Beast in Revelation symbolizes both the Devil and the Roman Empire, which the writer saw as in league with each other. Revelation describes how one cannot buy or sell without the "mark of the Beast." The simplest explanation is that this refers to Roman coins, which had an image of the emperor as a god. Devout Christians saw such an image as idolatrous. There has been much speculation about the symbolic number 666, which represents the Beast. Very likely, this is code for the name of the emperor Nero Caesar, the first emperor to persecute Christians.

In Chapter 6 of Revelation, four horsemen appear that are the colors of white, red, black, and green. The first horseman represents the Parthians, an enemy that the Romans could not defeat. The second horseman represents war and bloodshed;

A painting of John of Patmos (c. 1489) by Hieronymous Bosch.

hence, his color is red. The next horseman carries a scale to weigh food as a voice declares, "A ration of wheat costs a day's pay" (a lot of money). This black horseman represents famine. Finally, the pale green horseman represents sickness and death. Some readers of Revelation imagine that these horsemen are symbols for predicting future events. However, the horsemen represent the normal things of history: enemies, war and bloodshed, famine, disease, and death.

Down through the centuries, some people have claimed that the strange, weird symbolism in the Book of Revelation can be used to understand current events or predict future events. Often, Revelation is used to predict the End of the World (the End Times) and the Second Coming of Jesus. Such predictions are being made today. Just search the Internet for "Prophecies of Revelation today" or "Prophecies of the End Times" and look for websites talking about current events and people. (Be aware that some of these websites attack other Christians, and do not take these websites seriously.) The Christian denomination known as the Jehovah's Witnesses have been greatly influenced by the Book of Revelation. They believe we are now living in the End Times.

Over the centuries, the Book of Revelation has been used to make predictions. So far, all the predictions made have been wrong. One striking example is the Münster Rebellion from 1534 to 1535. A group of fanatical Christians, believing they lived in the End Times, took over the city of Münster in Germany. The rebellion came to a tragic end. In

America, preacher William Miller predicted that the Second Coming of Jesus would take place on October 22, 1844. His followers waited, and nothing happened. They called the event "The Great Disappointment." David Koresh, leader of the Branch Davidians in Waco, Texas, preached to his followers about the coming End Times. In 1993, his group came to a tragic end.

The middle of the Book of Revelation builds up to a great battle. The idea of a final battle between good and evil came to Christianity from Zoroastrianism. Revelation names the place of the battle as Armageddon. In ancient Israel, many battles were fought at a fort called Har Megiddo. The fort guarded a key trade route that any army trying to take over the region had to control. Har Megiddo became synonymous with many battles, so it became the name of the final battle: Armageddon.

Several references to a thousand-year period appear in the Book of Revelation, such as:

> Then I saw an angel coming down from Heaven, holding in his hand the key to the bottomless pit and a great chain. He seized the dragon, that ancient serpent, who is the Devil and Satan, and bound him for a thousand years, and threw him into the pit, and locked and sealed it over him, so that he would deceive the nations no more, until the thousand years were ended. After that he must be let out for a little while.
>
> —Revelation 20:1–3, NRSV

Over the centuries, many people have tried to figure out when the thousand years start. A thousand years is a millennium. The plural is "millennia." Thus, speculation about the End Times and when the thousand years would take place has called "millennialism." There is disagreement over whether the thousand years is yet to come or has already happened. As a result, there are "premillennialists" and "postmillennialists."

One concept that some people link with such apocalyptic views is the idea of the Rapture. The Rapture is the belief that when the End Times come, all holy people will be taken directly to Heaven. The rest, those "left behind," will suffer through the End Times. The *Left Behind* series of sixteen popular novels by Tim LaHaye and Jerry B. Jenkins is based on this concept. Years ago, a bumper sticker read: "In case of Rapture, this car will be empty."

The idea of the Rapture is based on a passage in Matthew 24:40–41: "Two men will be out in the field; one will be taken, and one will be left. Two women will be grinding at the mill; one will be taken, and one will be left." However, it is possible that this passage was not about the far future but rather a prediction or reference to those caught up in the Roman destruction of Jerusalem and its environs around 70 C.E.

What or who is the Antichrist in the Book of Revelation?

The word "Antichrist" is not mentioned in the Book of Revelation. The term is found in the two Epistles of John (not the Gospel of John), although it is not clearly defined. The

Antichrist opposes Christianity and Christians. Over the centuries, Christians have argued over who the Antichrist might be. For example, since the time of Martin Luther to the present, some Protestants have identified the Roman Catholic pope as the Antichrist. Some Christians predict that a present or future Antichrist will persecute Christians. An online search will show current figures identified as the Antichrist. Do not take these too seriously. Someone always tags the current U.S. president as the Antichrist.

In the Book of Revelation, a beast is described that many Christians equate with the Antichrist. The number 666 is given as the symbol for this figure. As mentioned above, the simplest explanation of 666 is that it refers to the Roman Emperor Nero, the first emperor to persecute Christians. This means that the Book of Revelation when it was written was not talking about the future; rather, it was interpreting current events in Asia Minor around the year 100 C.E.

The message of the Book of Revelation seems very different from the teachings of Jesus. Is that true?

Yes, many Christians find the image of Jesus in the gospels to be very different from the image of Jesus in the Book of Revelation. This is why many Christians simply ignore the Book of Revelation. A number of early Christian writers argued for leaving the book out of the New Testament. They lost the argument.

If you are interested, you should read the Book of Revelation and decide if you can decipher what it means. Probably, you will discover that the meaning of the book is not at all obvious. Then if you read something or hear someone who claims to have the Book of Revelation figured out, you can take it with a grain of salt.

In the Appendix of this book, there is a helpful, chapter-by-chapter guide for reading the Book of Revelation.

THE CATHOLIC CHURCH

Why is there a chapter devoted just to the Roman Catholic Church in this book?

Because it is the largest Christian church, the Roman Catholic Church deserves a closer look. This chapter is written to explain Catholic practices to non-Catholics in a straightforward way. Some Catholics may fault this chapter for a lack of nuance.

CATHOLIC CHURCH STRUCTURE

What is the Catholic Church structure with priests, bishops, cardinals, and the pope?

To outsiders, the Catholic Church structure with its pope, cardinals, bishops, and priests seems difficult to understand. The Catholic Church is built on a hierarchical organizational model with many decisions made at higher levels and then passed down. The simplest way to understand the Roman Catholic structure is to see it as an organization with six different levels:

1. Pope
2. Bishops, Archbishops, Cardinals (To keep this description simple, these three roles are combined as one level. There are other ways to describe the Catholic hierarchy.)
3. Priests
4. Deacons
5. Religious
6. Laity

However, note that many of these terms, such as "bishop," "archbishop," "priest," "deacon," and "laity," are also used by non-Catholic Christians.

For Catholics, levels 1, 2, 3, and 4 are called the clergy, and all are ordained as deacons or priests. Some go on to be bishops, archbishops, cardinals, and the pope.

The ordinary people in the pews are called "the laity," or "laypeople." The laity, level 6, make up the congregation, and they are not ordained.

Level 5 is made up of the religious who live the religious life. The religious are women who are sisters and nuns and men who are monks and brothers. The religious make three vows or promises: celibacy or chastity, poverty, and obedience. The words "celibacy" and "chastity" mean the same thing: to not be married and to not have sex. Typically, "celibacy" is the name of the vow for men, and "chastity" is the name of the vow for women. Poverty is the promise to not own anything. Religious women are not ordained and cannot perform sacraments, such as saying Mass. Many religious men are only monks or brothers and are not ordained. However, some religious men, in addition to taking vows, go on to be ordained as priests.

What is the role of the Roman Catholic deacon?

The word "deacon" is found in the New Testament. Originally, the deacons were charged with helping the poor and widows. In the Roman Catholic Church today, there are two types of deacons: transitional and permanent. A transitional deacon is a man on his way to becoming a priest who is in his last year of training. He becomes a deacon in a ceremony called "ordination," when he is ordained.

A permanent deacon is also ordained, but he will not become a priest. He can perform baptisms and weddings, but he cannot say Mass or hear confessions. You can pick out a deacon at church because the cloth around his neck, called a stole, is worn on an angle.

What is the role of the Roman Catholic priest?

The priest is the local minister. His congregation is usually a parish. A priest is ordained by a bishop. Ordination means that a priest can perform the sacraments: baptism, reconciliation, Mass, confirmation, marriage, and anointing of the sick. (Although priests can perform confirmation, it is usually done by the local bishop.)

The Roman Catholic faith is built around Mass, so the role of the priest is very important. The Catholic teaching is that only unmarried men can become priests (there is an exception if a man was a Protestant minister, who was married, who then decided to become a Catholic

Deacons in the Catholic Church can perform a number of services, but this varies depending on whether they are eventually going to enter the priesthood or not.

priest). Women cannot become priests. Furthermore, one has to be a priest to be a bishop, cardinal, or pope.

One more term needs to be explained: the title of "Monsignor." It is a detail that adds confusion. Basically, it is a title of honor to a priest, usually as recognition of years of service.

What is the role of the Roman Catholic bishop?

The bishop is the local leader of the Catholic Church. The word "bishop" is found in the New Testament. The Greek word is επίσκοπος, (epískopos), which means "supervisor." The adjective for a bishop is "episcopal." For example, the bishop lives in the episcopal residence.

The priests in a specific area work for the bishop of that area. However, it gets a little complicated since there are three variations on being a bishop: bishop, archbishop, and cardinal.

The territory of a Catholic bishop is called a "diocese." There are almost two hundred dioceses in the United States and about twenty-five hundred in the world. A large diocese in a large city is called an "archdiocese," and the bishop is called an "archbishop." Archbishops often have assistant bishops called "auxiliary bishops."

Some bishops and archbishops get the honorary title of "cardinal." The main duty of a cardinal is to elect the pope. Cardinals wear outfits that are all red. (Red birds in North America were named cardinals after the red outfits of cardinals.) At present, there are about 180 Catholic cardinals in the world.

What is the role of the Roman Catholic pope?

At the top of the Catholic Church is the pope. The pope is also the bishop of Rome. He lives in Rome in an area known as Vatican City. Vatican City is an area of 270 acres in Rome; it is an independent country.

The Roman Catholic theory of the pope is as follows: Jesus chose the Apostle Peter to be the first leader of his Church. Many years after Jesus, Peter went to Rome. He became the first bishop of Rome, where he died for his faith. When the next bishop of Rome was chosen, he inherited the authority that Jesus had given to Peter. With each subsequent bishop of Rome, the authority was passed on. (Historians have raised a number of questions over whether or not the history of the pope is as simple as described here.) This authority has been passed down through the centuries until 2013, when it was passed on to Pope Francis. The pope is called the Vicar of Christ, which means "the representative of Christ." The pope has great authority in the Roman Catholic Church. He picks all the bishops, and he makes the final decisions on Church teachings.

Who is Pope Francis?

Jorge Mario Bergoglio (1936–) became pope in 2013. He is the first pope to use the name Francis, and he is the first Jesuit to become pope. Bergoglio had been an archbishop and

Named pope in 2013, Pope Francis has introduced some more liberal thinking to the Catholic Church, including views about homosexuality, the role of women in the Church, the importance of the environment, and even saying that the pope's authority is not absolute.

then a cardinal in Argentina. Pope Francis has promoted Catholic social teachings and has shown a concern for the poor. He has attacked consumerism and climate change. Many Catholic traditionalists oppose a number of his positions. The most pressing challenge Pope Francis faces is dealing with the priest sex abuse scandal.

What is the big question?

The big question is a theological one. Is the institution of the Roman Catholic Church something created by God, or is it a human creation? In other words, is the structure of pope, bishops, and priests something that God wants, or is it something that human beings created over time? Catholic traditionalists insist that the Catholic structure is God's will present on earth. Protestants, nonreligious people, and even some Catholics see the Catholic structure as a human creation. What do you think?

CATHOLIC SACRAMENTS

What are the important Catholic rituals?

The Catholic Church has an extensive set of rituals. The most important are seven sacraments at the heart of Catholic practice. A sacrament is defined as a "visible sign instituted by Christ that gives grace." The word "grace" lacks a precise definition, but it includes the idea of God's presence, love, and mercy. The seven Catholic sacraments are baptism, reconciliation, Eucharist, confirmation, marriage, holy orders, and anointing of the sick.

What is the Catholic sacrament of baptism?

Most Catholics are baptized as infants; however, converts are baptized as adults. A Catholic baptism is usually done by pouring water over the forehead of the person. In Catholic thought, baptism does three things. It brings the person into the Christian community, it imparts grace, and it takes away the guilt of Original Sin. Original Sin is the guilt of sin with which all humans are born.

What is the Catholic sacrament of reconciliation?

Until the 1960s, this sacrament was called "confession" or "penance." It emphasized human sinfulness. After Vatican II (1962–1965), it was revised to emphasize the idea of being reconciled to God.

In the sacrament of reconciliation, a person meets with the priest in a small room called a confessional and describes the sins that he or she has committed and then the priest absolves the person. To absolve is to forgive. The priest speaks these words: "I absolve you from your sins in the name of the Father and of the Son and of the Holy Spirit."

Many non-Catholics have inaccurate ideas about the sacrament of reconciliation. It is not meant to give one a "blank slate" to go out and sin again. In the sacrament, a person is required to show true regret for his or her wrongdoings and show an intention to avoid repeating the sin. The regret is called "contrition." Also, a person is forgiven of his or her sins not because of the power or goodness of the priest. The actual forgiveness comes from God, with the priest speaking the words of forgiveness.

Catholics today have two options for confession. They can meet face to face with a priest, or they can use an old-style confessional.

In an old-style confessional, the priest sits in the center booth. A person going to confession goes in and kneels on either side. He or she talks through a screen. The person cannot see the priest, and the priest cannot see the person. The old-style confessional sometimes shows up in movies since it makes for a more dramatic scene.

What is the Catholic sacrament of the Eucharist?

The Eucharist is central to Roman Catholic belief and practice. It is also called "Mass" or "Communion," and it is modeled on the Last Supper of Jesus. The Sunday Mass involves prayer, music, three scripture readings, and a psalm.

The central part of Mass is the Consecration. During the Consecration, the priest prays over the bread and wine. According to Catholic belief, by the power of Jesus, the bread and wine are transformed into the body and blood of Jesus. The bread and wine still look, feel, and taste like bread and wine, but Catholics believe that at the deepest level, these things have become the body and blood of Jesus. Catholics at Mass then receive the bread and wine.

The belief that the bread and wine become the body and blood of Jesus is central to Catholic belief. One attempt to explain the transformation is the term "transubstantiation." This word means that the essence of the bread becomes the essence of the body of Jesus even though the look, taste, and feel of the bread remain the same. The essence of the wine becomes the essence of the blood of Jesus.

Catholics are expected to go to Mass every Sunday, but they can go every day if they want.

What is the Catholic sacrament of confirmation?

In confirmation, the faith of a baptized person is confirmed, and for a young person, he or she becomes a Christian adult. The promises made at the person's baptism are restated. If a person was baptized as an infant, confirmation represents coming of age in the Catholic Church. The sacrament unites one with Christ and increases the gifts of the Holy Spirit. The sacrament also bonds one more closely to the church.

Confirmation is usually done by the local bishop, but a priest can also do it. It is commonly done at Catholic schools in the seventh and eighth grades. In the ceremony, the bishop lays his hand on the head of each candidate for confirmation. Then the bishop dips his thumb in blessed oil and makes a sign of the cross on person's forehead. Anointing with oil is an important Christian symbol with roots in the Bible.

One of the goals of confirmation is to allow young people to have some connection to the local bishop. By doing confirmation with seventh and eighth graders in Catholic schools, it requires that the bishop be available every other year. Catholic grade schools are usually connected to a parish. Catholic high schools often are not. If they were to wait on confirmation until high school, the parish might lose track of some of the students.

What is the Catholic sacrament of marriage?

All Christians have a marriage ritual, but for Catholics, marriage is a sacrament. The sacrament takes place when the man and woman say their vows.

For Catholics, if a true sacrament of marriage has taken place and the marriage later fails, neither person is allowed to remarry in the Catholic Church. However, some Catholics who get divorced later get an annulment. An annulment says that a valid sacrament of marriage did not take place. After receiving an annulment, one can remarry in the Catholic Church.

What is the Catholic sacrament of holy orders?

Holy orders is the ritual where a man becomes a priest. It is also called "ordination." The main part of the ritual is the laying on of hands by the bishop. The custom of "laying on of hands" to pass on authority goes back to the New Testament.

The kneeling men are becoming priests. The bishop has a pointed hat, called a mitre. It looks just like the top of the bishop chess piece. "Mitre" means "angle." Carpenters use a mitre box or mitre saw to cut angles on pieces of wood.

For Catholics, only men can become priests.

What is the Catholic sacrament of anointing of the sick?

The older version of this ritual was called last rites or extreme unction. "Last rites" meant it was the last ritual or ceremony for someone who was dying. The sacrament was mostly used for dying people.

After Vatican II, the emphasis of the sacrament changed so that it can be used for all seriously ill people and can include prayers for healing. The key part of the ritual is an anointing of the sick or dying person with oil. It can also include the sacrament of reconciliation and receiving of Communion.

Ordination, or the sacrament of holy orders, is the ritual in which a bishop lays hands on a candidate and officially makes him a priest.

CATHOLIC TEACHINGS ON MARY

What are the important Catholic teachings on Mary?

Mary, the mother of Jesus, plays an important role in the Catholic religion. Many churches, such as Notre Dame (which means "Our Lady"), are named for Mary. Most Catholic churches have statues of Mary, and the Catholic Church has several important teachings about Mary and her role. Many other Christians disagree with the Catholic emphasis on Mary and the Catholic teachings about Mary. Five Catholic teachings about Mary are important: the perpetual virginity of Mary, the Immaculate Conception, the Assumption of Mary, praying to Mary, and appearances of Mary. Lastly, an interesting detail can be seen on many statues of Mary.

What is the Catholic teaching on the perpetual virginity of Mary?

According to the Catholic teaching, Mary was a virgin when she gave birth to Jesus and remained a virgin throughout her life. Catholics speak of Mary as the "Blessed Virgin

Mary." Here is a key quote from the Gospel of Matthew: "He [Joseph] had no relations with her until she bore a son, and he named him Jesus" (1:25, NABRE). For many non-Catholic Christians, the word "until" implies that Joseph and Mary later had relations. This would explain the handful of references to the "brothers of Jesus" in the gospels.

However, according to Roman the Catholic teaching, Mary remained a virgin. This is called the "perpetual virginity" of Mary. According to this view, the word "brother" could actually refer to "cousins." Some even suggest that Joseph was a widower with children from a previous marriage.

What is the Catholic belief of the Immaculate Conception?

The second teaching on Mary is the Roman Catholic doctrine of the Immaculate Conception. Most Protestants reject this concept. Immaculate Conception refers not to the conception of Jesus but to the conception of Mary. According to tradition, the parents of Mary were Joachim and Anna. In this teaching, Mary was conceived in the normal biological way, but she did not receive the guilt of Original Sin.

In the Catholic teaching, Adam and Eve sinned and disobeyed God. This was the Original Sin. The guilt of this sin is passed to everyone—except Mary. She was born without Original Sin. She was conceived immaculately—without the stain of Original Sin. Mary had to be sinless to carry Jesus—who was human and divine—within her for nine months.

Again, this is a Roman Catholic teaching. Joachim and Anna are not found in the gospels. Immaculate Conception is a Catholic teaching, yet a number of Catholics are confused on the teaching and think it refers to the conception of Jesus.

What is the Catholic teaching on praying to Mary?

Praying to Mary is part of Roman Catholic tradition, although there are many Catholics who do not do it. In the Catholic teaching, Mary plays a significant role as an intercessor, taking the prayers of people to Jesus. For many Catholics, praying to Mary is an important and rich part of their faith.

What is the Catholic teaching on the Assumption of Mary?

Another Catholic teaching is that Mary was taken bodily up into Heaven. Her body was not buried. It did not decay. This teaching is called the Assumption of Mary, and it is celebrated on August 15. What is not clear is whether or not Mary died before being taken

While it might seem like adding another intermediary unnecessarily to the practice of prayer, many Catholics pray to the Virgin Mary instead of directly to Jesus or God.

into Heaven. This belief is also held by Orthodox Christians and some other churches. It is sometimes referred to as the "Dormition of Mary." "Dormition" means "sleeping." However, this term does not answer the question of whether she died or not.

What is the Catholic teaching on reported appearances of Mary in modern times?

The Catholic Church has recognized the claims of some that Mary appeared to them. Two of the most famous appearances were in southern France in a town called Lourdes in 1858 to Bernadette Soubirous and in Portugal in a town called Fatima in 1917 to several children. Although important parts of Catholic tradition, many Catholics do not see such appearances as meaningful to their own religious faith.

Medjugorje is a small town in the country of Bosnia and Herzegovina. In 1981, six children claimed that Mary appeared to them. Several of them claim that Mary has continued to appear to them. Medjugorje became a popular pilgrimage site, although the Catholic Church has never officially certified the apparitions.

OTHER CATHOLIC TOPICS

Do Catholics still have relics, such as pieces of the bones of saints, in their churches?

In some religious traditions, relics were very important in the past, although they are not as important today. Modern people find it hard to understand the importance of relics. If, for example, one wants to connect with John Lennon of the Beatles, who died in 1980, it is easy. All of his music is available online. His movies *A Hard Day's Night* and *Help!* are also readily available. There are hundreds of photos of him. In fact, it is easier to find copies of all of his music now than when he was alive.

Why are there snakes on some statues of Mary?

Often, the snake has an apple in its mouth. The snake on the statues represents the snake in the Genesis story that tempted Eve and Adam to eat the forbidden fruit. (Note that in the original story, the snake is not called the Devil or Satan, and the type of fruit is not named.) God then curses the snake: "I will put enmity between you and the woman, and between your offspring and hers; they will strike at your head, while you strike at their heel" (Genesis 3:15, NABRE).

Later, Catholics would interpret this passage as applying to Mary. The idea would be that she gave birth to Jesus, who died to save humans from the penalty of sin and to save them from the Devil, who is represented in Genesis by the snake. That is why you see a snake with an apple under the feet of Mary in so many statues.

But imagine a world before modern technology such as photography and recording. Paintings were mostly available only for the wealthy, so how could you connect with someone holy who had died? You could visit the person's grave or where he or she lived, but what if you could see a tiny piece of the person's bone? What if you could see an artifact from the life of Jesus, such as his Crown of Thorns or a piece of the cross or the head of John the Baptist? In the Middle Ages, visiting such relics was extremely popular among Christians. We know now that many of the older relics were not authentic, but at the time, many people put great faith in them.

Also, in the Middle Ages, many people believed that the relics of holy people had special power. People thought that getting close to the relics would get them closer to God. Their image of God was of a divine being who was harsh and judgmental. The saints and Mary seemed more approachable.

People traveled long distances to visit relics in the hopes of being healed of sickness and disease. Medical treatments were no better than folklore, so for many people, miracles seemed to be the only hope of getting better. Some shrines were noted for their reputations of healing people who had prayed to the relics there.

When Martin Luther came along in the 1500s, he ended the practice for Protestant Christians of praying to saints, Mary, and relics. Catholics continued the practices, however. In Europe, many older Catholic churches and cathedrals have museums attached to them with displays of the relics in elaborate containers called "reliquaries." Although many of the relics in the Middle Ages were not authentic, relics from the last several hundred years tend to be authentic and typically have documentation.

Today, most Catholics have little interest in the relics of saints, so those older churches that have relics keep them put away. Most Catholics probably do not even know whether or not their church has any relics.

What is the Catholic teaching on saints?

The word "saint" is a common term among Christians. The word "saint" derives from the Latin word for "holy": *sanctus*. However, different Christians use the word in different ways. For many Christians, the word "saint" refers to someone who has gone to Heaven or to someone on the way to Heaven. A holy person who is still alive might be called a saint but not in a canonized way. For many Christians, this is the only proper use of the word.

However, for other Christians, such as Roman Catholics, there are officially designated figures called "saints." When the word is used as a person's title, it is capitalized. The Catholic Church has by far designated the most saints. The most famous saint is Francis of Assisi. The process where a holy person is designated to be on the official list of saints is called "canonization." The official list is called a "canon."

In the Roman Catholic tradition, saints are believed to be in Heaven, so praying to saints is allowed. Catholic Churches have saint statues in them. However, many other Christian groups reject the Catholic practice of having statues of saints and of praying to saints.

What is a rosary?

A rosary is a string of beads used for prayer. Many Catholics find praying the rosary to be a very meaningful faith experience. Other Catholics rarely pray the rosary. The circle part of the rosary consists of five sets of ten beads. Each set of ten beads is called a "decade." In between each bead is a separate single bead on which is said the prayer Glory Be to the Father to end one decade and an Our Father to begin the next decade. The Catholic prayer Hail Mary is said on each of the ten beads.

Usually a string of beads, but sometimes knots could be used, a rosary is a helpful way of keeping track of how many prayers one has said.

The cross and the first five beads are used to start the rosary. A person begins with a prayer: "O Lord, open my lips; O God, come to my aid; O Lord, make haste to help me." Then the Apostles' Creed is said while holding the crucifix. The Lord's Prayer is said on the first bead; three Hail Marys follow, and then a Glory Be to the Father.

What is the prayer Glory Be to the Father?

Glory be to the Father, and to the Son, and to the Holy Ghost; as it was in the beginning, is now, and ever shall be: world without end. Amen.

Some English versions replace "shall" with "will." This prayer is also called the "Gloria" or "Gloria Patri."

What is the prayer Hail Mary?

Hail Mary, full of grace, the Lord is with thee; blessed art thou among women, and blessed is the fruit of thy womb, Jesus. Holy Mary, Mother of God, pray for us sinners, now and at the hour of our death. Amen.

The first sentence of the prayer is based on two lines taken from the Gospel of Luke. When the Angel Gabriel appears to Mary, he addresses her with: "Hail, favored one! The Lord is with you" (Luke 1:28, NABRE). When Mary goes to visit Elizabeth, Elizabeth greets her with: "Most blessed are you among women, and blessed is the fruit of your womb" (Luke 1:42, NABRE). Typically, Protestants do not pray to Mary and do not use the Hail Mary prayer.

Some Catholics will pray fifteen rosaries over a period of time. Each rosary is then dedicated to a specific event in the life of Mary or Jesus. Often, the person praying tries to imagine that particular event. The events in the life of Mary are broken into three sets called "mysteries."

331

Joyful Mysteries

- The Annunciation (when the Angel Gabriel appeared to Mary)
- The Visitation (when Mary, pregnant with Jesus, visited Elizabeth, pregnant with John the Baptist)
- The Nativity
- The Presentation of Jesus at the Temple
- The Finding of Jesus in the Temple

Sorrowful Mysteries

- The Agony in the Garden
- The Scourging at the Pillar
- The Crowning with Thorns
- The Carrying of the Cross
- The Crucifixion and Death of Our Lord

Glorious Mysteries

- The Resurrection
- The Ascension
- The Descent of the Holy Spirit
- The Assumption of Mary
- The Coronation of the Virgin Mary (in Heaven)

What are the Stations of the Cross?

Most Catholic churches have the fourteen Stations of the Cross. These are images of the steps of the Crucifixion of Jesus starting with Jesus being condemned by Pontius Pilate and ending with Jesus being placed in the tomb. The images can be paintings or ceramic or wooden statues. In small churches, the stations may be about a foot in height. In large churches, each station can be several feet in height. (Do an online image search of "Stations of the Cross" to see some examples.) Stations can also be built outdoors.

To do the Stations of the Cross, a Catholic stops before each station and prays as he or she remembers in detail the Crucifixion of Jesus. The stations are based on details in the gospels, such as Simon helping Jesus to carry his cross and Jesus meeting the women of Jerusalem, but also details from later Christian tradition such as the station of Veronica wiping the face of Jesus. Here are the fourteen stations:

1. Pilate condemns Jesus to die
2. Jesus accepts his cross
3. Jesus falls for the first time
4. Jesus meets his mother, Mary
5. Simon helps carry the cross

6. Veronica wipes the face of Jesus

7. Jesus falls for the second time

8. Jesus meets the women of Jerusalem

9. Jesus falls for the third time

10. Jesus is stripped of his clothes

11. Jesus is nailed to the cross

12. Jesus dies on the cross

13. Jesus is taken down from the cross

14. Jesus is placed in the tomb

The stations go back to the Middle Ages and were originally places marked in Jerusalem along the path Jesus very likely took while carrying his cross to the place of the Crucifixion. The stations are also called the "Way of the Cross." In Jerusalem, the path Jesus took is called the *Via Dolorosa*, which is Latin for the "Way of Sorrows." Many people today go to Jerusalem to walk the same path.

CHRISTIAN CULTURE: ART AND ARCHITECTURE

PAINTINGS AND SCULPTURE

What did Jesus actually look like?

We do not know what Jesus looked like. Because he was from the Mediterranean region, he might have had olive-colored skin and dark hair. However, there is no way to know for sure. Jewish men at the time typically wore beards, so we assume Jesus had a beard, even though there is no way to verify this detail.

So how do painters know how to depict Jesus?

Since they actually do not know, they have used their imaginations. What Christian painters have tended to do down through the centuries is to paint Jesus to look like the people around them. Since so many paintings of Jesus were done in Europe, he often looks very European and very Caucasian.

How important has Christianity been for the development of art?

The Christian faith has been a great inspiration for art. This can be especially seen in European paintings from the 1400s through the 1600s. There is an immense amount of very beautiful Christian art. The religious images by Michelangelo, da Vinci, and Caravaggio are among the most famous paintings in the world.

The key to exploring this art is to simply look at the photographs of the paintings and sculptures. Luckily, such photos are available online. For reading this section, you need to move to a computer or get out your tablet or iPhone, so you can look up images of this incredible art. Someday, you may see this artwork in person.

Listed below are some important examples of Christian art. (This is a survey of a few examples of the more important European artists to provide an introduction to Christian art. Many other important figures, such as Bernini, Rembrandt, and Velasquez, have been left out. There is much more art to explore online for those who are interested. Also, there are other examples of Christian art created outside of Europe.) Do not feel obligated to look at every piece of art listed. This is an exploration, so feel free to move around the list. Also, as you look at images online, you might find other interesting paintings and sculptures.

Images of these artworks can be found by doing an online image search using the name of the artist and keywords from the name of the piece of art. The Web Gallery of Art (wga.hu) is a great resource with images of all the artworks for countless artists. The search tool is at the bottom of the page.

Are there any suggestions for exploring this art?

If you walked into an art museum, you could go into the first room and look at every painting in that room and then go on to the next room and look at every painting in order and then go on to the next room. However, you would not complete many of the rooms in the museum, and before long, you would be tired and overwhelmed. Instead, imagine yourself browsing through a museum trying to find pieces of art that you find interesting. In a similar way, browse the list below and look for those artworks that you find interesting. You do not have to look at everything. You can also come back later and look at other pieces of art.

As you pull up images of these famous artworks, give each image a moment or two. Look at the image. Look at the detail in the image. Is there a religious message being presented? What is going on in the image? How do you feel as you look at it? These pieces of art are famous because people find that they are interesting and that they stir the emotions. See if you can find what other people over the centuries have found interesting in these artworks.

Who is Giotto?

Giotto di Bondone (1267–1337) was an Italian painter active at the beginning of the Renaissance. His name is pronounced JAW-tow. Do an online search for two of his frescoes: *Nativity* and *Lamentation*.

What is the famous painting of the Holy Trinity in Florence, Italy?

An important painting is *The Trinity* (1425) in the church of Santa Maria Novella in Florence, Italy, by Masaccio (1401–1428). (Search "Masaccio Trinity.") God the Father is at the top, holding the cross. The white dove between God the Father and Jesus on the cross is the Holy Spirit. Look carefully as the dove at first glance looks like a collar on the tunic of God the father. Standing by the cross are Mary on the left side of the painting and John on the right. The kneeling figures on the far left and far right are the patrons who donated the money for the paintings. At the bottom is a skeleton with an Italian caption that translates as: "I once was what you are and what I am you also will be."

Masaccio also painted *The Tribute Money*, which depicts this scene from the Gospel of Matthew:

> When they came to Capernaum, the collectors of the temple tax approached Peter and said, "Doesn't your teacher pay the temple tax?" "Yes," he said. When he came into the house, before he had time to speak, Jesus asked him, "What is your opinion, Simon? From whom do the kings of the earth take tolls or census tax? From their subjects or from foreigners?" When he said, "From foreigners," Jesus said to him, "Then the subjects are exempt. But that we may not offend them, go to the sea, drop in a hook, and take the first fish that comes up. Open its mouth and you will find a coin worth twice the temple tax. Give that to them for me and for you."

—Matthew 17:24–27, NABRE

The painting depicts three different scenes. In the center, the tax collector confronts Jesus and his disciples. On the left of the painting, Peter is getting the coin from the fish, and on the right, he is paying the tax.

The 1425 painting of *The Holy Trinity* by Italian painter Masaccio is one of the most famous artworks in the world concerning this Christian theme.

Notice how Masaccio uses halos in this painting. Jesus and his disciples all have them, indicating that they are holy. However, he paints flat halos, as was done in the past, rather than halos that are positioned more naturally, as if they were hats. Also note the building on the right. Masaccio is using the recently developed techniques of perspective to create a feeling of depth in the painting. Also, note how the positions and poses of the figures have a very natural feel.

Masaccio also created the dramatic fresco *The Expulsion from the Garden of Eden*, which shows an angel driving Adam and Eve from the Garden of Eden.

Who was Rogier van der Weyden?

Rogier van der Weyden (1399–1464) was from the area that today is Belgium. Find his 1435 painting *The Descent from the Cross*. Notice how the position of Mary parallels the position of Jesus.

Next, find his *Beaune Altarpiece* in the Hospices de Beaune. It was painted on six oak panels that fold out. Enlarge *The Last Judgment*. At the bottom of the painting, the dead are rising up from their graves. Michael the Archangel stands below Jesus and weighs the souls of the dead. Those whose souls are heavy with sin are condemned to Hell. Look closely at the torment and anguish of those on the right side of the painting who are going to Hell. On the left side are those who are going to Heaven. This scene was painted in a hospice for dying, poor people. This altarpiece was at the end of the room, so the dying could see it from their beds.

Tell me about Leonardo da Vinci.

Leonardo da Vinci (1452–1519) was a genius interested in all things: science, music, mathematics, engineering, anatomy, and much more. He is the model of a Renaissance Man. He created several beautiful and important religious paintings, such as:

- *John the Baptist* (c. 1513–1516)
- *Annunciation* (1475–1480)
- *The Virgin and Child with St. Anne* (c. 1503). According to some Christians, St. Anne was the mother of Jesus. Notice that the infant Jesus holds a lamb. Many Christians refer to Jesus as the Lamb of God.
- *Virgin of the Rocks* (1483–1486). Mary is the central figure. The infant John the Baptist is on the left side of the painting, and an angel sits behind Jesus on the right. This was painted between 1483 and 1486. There are two versions of this painting. You want the one in the Louvre.

Leonardo's most important painting is *The Last Supper*, which is the most reproduced religious painting in history. As discussed earlier, the painting is of Jesus and his Twelve Apostles. Mary Magdalene is not in the painting. From left to right as one looks at the painting, the figures are Bartholomew; James the Lesser, son of Alphaeus; Andrew; Judas Iscariot, with dark hair and a beard holding his money bag; Peter, with white hair and a beard; John the evangelist; Jesus; Thomas; James the Greater; Philip; Matthew; Jude/Thaddaeus; and Simon the Zealot. Judas has also knocked over the salt shaker, a sign of bad luck. Da Vinci left a notebook identifying all the figures.

Tell me about Raphael.

Raphael (Raffaello Sanzio da Urbino; 1483–1520) was another Italian painter and architect of the Renaissance. Among his numerous paintings of Christian figures, three are important to view:

- *Resurrection of Christ* (1499–1502)
- *The Madonna of the Meadow* (c. 1506)
- *Transfiguration* (1520)

Be sure and check out Raphael's dazzling *Transfiguration*. Blow it up on your screen.

You have mentioned the names of Leonardo, Michelangelo, and Raphael. Aren't these the names of three of the Teenage Mutant Ninja Turtles?

Yes. Donatello, the fourth Turtle, was named for an important Renaissance sculptor. The creators of the Teenage Mutant Ninja Turtles named them after four famous Renaissance artists.

Who was Albrecht Dürer?

Albrecht Dürer (1471–1528) was an influential artist. Do an online search for "Durer woodcuts." In his woodcuts, Dürer carved an image in a block of wood. This block was used for printing multiple copies of the image. The block was covered with ink and then a sheet of paper was pressed against it. When the paper was removed, it had the carved image printed on it. Dürer created some of the first mass-produced art. His prints of the *Apocalypse* series (1498), based on the Book of Revelation, were very popular in his time. Take a look at his *Four Horsemen of the Apocalypse* (search "Dürer four horsemen").

Although the image printed from the block was black ink on white paper, color was added to many of these images. A cut-out stencil was made for all the parts of the image that were blue. A painter painted all the blue parts. Another stencil was created for all the red parts, which were then painted. Other stencils were used for other colors. Since the stencils could be reused over and over, multiple color copies could be made. This was one of the first attempts at color printing of multiple copies.

Dürer also did etchings. Instead of carving a wood block, etchings were done by scratching on a copper plate. The finished copper plate was covered with ink, and paper was pressed against it to print an image on the paper. Etchings allow much more detail. Search "Dürer etchings" to see examples. His most famous etchings are *Knight, Death, and the Devil* (1513) and *Saint Jerome in His Study* (1514).

Around 1508, Dürer did a pen and ink drawing that is called *Praying Hands*. This image has been widely copied and also imitated in other paintings and sculptures, such as the thirty-two-foot-tall version in Webb City, Missouri. Dürer also did beautiful watercolors of animals.

Who was Matthias Grünewald?

The German painter Matthias Grünewald (c. 1470–1528) is best remembered for his

Albrecht Dürer was famous for his woodcuts and etchings, many of which had religious themes, such as this 1415 work *Knight, Death, and the Devil*.

339

Isenheim Altarpiece. The altarpiece has a number of different panels that originally could be flipped to produce a number of different scenes. Search "Isenheim crucifixion" to find an online image of the Crucifixion. Mary Magdalene is the kneeling figure. The woman in white is Mary, the mother of Jesus, who is being held by John, one of the disciples of Jesus. Look at some detailed images of the hands and torso of Jesus.

The painting is filled with symbolism. The figure on the right is John the Baptist. He was dead by the time of Jesus' Crucifixion; however, in the gospels, he pointed the way to Jesus. Notice that the right hand of John the Baptist points to Jesus. The lamb symbolizes Jesus. Just as lambs were slain as sacrifices for sin, so Jesus was sacrificed for human sin. Notice that the blood of the lamb is flowing into the cup. Many Christians believe that the cup of wine at Mass becomes the blood of Jesus.

Now search "Isenheim Anthony" for images of the two panels *Visit of Saint Anthony to Saint Paul the Hermit* and *Saint Anthony Tormented by Demons*. Be sure to find a large image, so you can see clearly the demons tormenting St. Anthony. Be sure and check out the small demons on the destroyed building in the background. Grünewald created some amazing and bizarre imagery that could easily fit in a science fiction movie today.

What can you tell me about Michelangelo?

Michelangelo Buonarroti (1475–1564) lived in the cities of Florence and Rome in Italy during a period called the Renaissance. The Renaissance was a period of great creativity and art based on a renewed interest in themes and artistic imagery from the older Roman and Greek cultures. One of the most famous works of Michelangelo is his paintings on the ceiling and walls of the Sistine Chapel in Rome, completed between 1508 and 1512. Today, the chapel is part of the Vatican complex in Rome, which is the headquarters of the Roman Catholic Church.

The Sistine Chapel ceiling looks complicated, but it takes just a moment to figure out all the images. Open this link (https://www.wga.hu/tours/sistina/index1.html) to explore the Sistine Chapel ceiling. Simply click on different places to get close-up views.

In the center are nine scenes from the first chapters of the book of Genesis:

- *The Separation of Light from Darkness*
- *Creation of the Sun, Moon, and Planets*
- *Separation of the Earth from the Waters*
- *Creation of Adam* (this painting is one of the most famous images of Christian art)
- *Creation of Eve*
- *The Fall and Expulsion from the Garden*
- *Sacrifice of Noah*
- *The Deluge* (the Flood)
- *The Drunkenness of Noah*

Michelangelo spent four years painting the walls and ceiling of the Sistine Chapel at the Vatican. Given the massive amount of work evident here, four years was actually amazingly quick!

There are four triangle paintings called "spandrels" on each side of the ceiling. Within the triangles are people from the Bible who are ancestors of Jesus.

Between the triangles are seated figures. These seated figures alternate between biblical prophets, such as Isaiah and Jeremiah, and figures such as the Cumaean Sibyl and the Persian Sibyl. There are seven prophets and five sibyls. The sibyls are characters from pagan literature who were believed to have powers to predict the future.

Another important painting of Michelangelo in the Sistine Chapel is *The Last Judgment*. It is forty-eight feet tall and forty-four feet wide. Jesus is in the center, coming in triumph and judgment. The person to the right of Jesus holding his skin is St. Bartholomew, who was skinned alive.

What was Michelangelo's technique in painting the Sistine Chapel?

The Sistine Chapel ceiling and walls are fresco paintings. Fresco was a common technique for painting on walls. Oil paints did not come until later, and acrylic paints are very recent.

To create a fresco, the artist starts with a wall with a new layer of plaster. Many people today do not know what plaster is since most houses and buildings are built using drywall on interior walls. Before drywall, the interior walls of buildings and homes were covered with plaster, a paste made of lime, gypsum, or cement. The plaster paste could be smoothed out on the wall or textured, and it would dry to be very hard and durable.

Fresco is a technique for painting on walls while the plaster is still fresh. "Fresco" means "fresh." In fresco painting, pigment, which is colored powder, is mixed with fresh plaster and then painted on. Fresco painting requires careful planning since the artist needs to complete one area of the painting each day; it is very hard to come back the next day and mix the exact same color to match the color of the previous day.

Did Michelangelo lie on this back while painting the Sistine Chapel ceiling?

He did not. The Sistine Chapel was kept in use during the several years of the painting of the ceiling. Michelangelo designed frames along the side walls that held a platform for painting. This platform could be moved along the ceiling as he worked on each part of the painting.

What are the famous sculptures of Michelangelo?

Although he painted the Sistine Chapel, Michelangelo considered himself a sculptor. In fact, Pope Julius II bullied him into painting the chapel, which is why he signed it "Michelangelo—Sculptor."

Michelangelo created several pieces based on biblical figures that are considered some of the greatest sculptures of all time: *Moses*, *David*, and the *Pietà*, which depicts Mary holding the dead body of Jesus. Be sure and look up these images since these statues are so important.

Michelangelo depicts Moses as a powerful figure with muscular arms. The horns on his head are due to a mistranslation of the Bible text of that time that actually refers to rays of light on the head of Moses.

Michelangelo's *David* might be the most famous sculpture in the world. The statue is eighteen feet tall—three times the height of a six-foot-tall person! This statue is a curious representation of the biblical story of David presented in the style of an ancient Greek or Roman nude statue. The story of David in the Bible says nothing about him facing Goliath in his birthday suit.

Who was Caravaggio?

The paintings of Caravaggio (Michelangelo Merisi da Caravaggio; 1571–1610) are particularly interesting. He wanted to portray the biblical stories with great drama. He designed his scenes and posed the figures in such a way as to increase the dramatic impact. He also used a technique called *chiaroscuro*, which involved contrasting very bright parts of the painting with very dark backgrounds.

Another technique of Caravaggio was to paint the gospel stories with the characters dressed as if they were people living in the time of Caravaggio. This can be most clearly seen in his painting *The Calling of St. Matthew*. The figures at the table are dressed in fashionable outfits from around the year 1600. They are not wearing clothes from the time of Jesus. Caravaggio wanted the viewers of his time to feel that they were part of the story.

Here are some of Caravaggio's most important paintings:

- *The Calling of Saint Matthew* (1599–1600)
- *The Conversion on the Way to Damascus* (1601)
- *The Crucifixion of Saint Peter* (1601)
- *The Supper at Emmaus* (1601)
- *The Incredulity of Saint Thomas* (1601–1602)
- *Ecce Homo* (c. 1605): *Ecce Homo* is Latin for "Behold the Man," the words spoken by Pilate at the trial of Jesus.
- *The Beheading of St. John the Baptist* (1608)
- *The Raising of Lazarus* (1609)
- *David with the Head of Goliath* (c. 1610): Caravaggio used his own face for the face of Goliath.

Who was El Greco?

El Greco (1541–1614) was a famous painter who lived in Spain. He was called "El Greco" because the Spaniards could not pronounce his name, Doménikos Theotokópoulos. He was born on the island of Crete in the Mediterranean and then studied art in Venice. He moved to Toledo, Spain, where he produced his most famous works. His paintings are known for their ghostly quality and his depictions of stretched-out human figures with

343

gray-colored skin. Do an online image search for "El Greco Saint" and see which saints pop up, such as *St. John the Baptist* and *St. Francis Meditating on Death*.

Who was painter Henry Ossawa Tanner, and what are his most noteworthy pieces?

Henry Ossawa Tanner (1859–1937) was the first African American painter to gain international attention. He painted a wide range of subjects, including many beautiful biblical scenes. Here are the most important ones:

- *Daniel in the Lion's Den* (1895)
- *The Annunciation* (1898)*
- *The Good Shepherd* (1903)
- *Return of the Holy Women* (1904)
- *Christ and His Mother Studying the Scripture* (1909)
- *The Holy Family* (1910)
- *Destruction of Sodom and Gomorrah* (1920)
- *Moses in the Bulrushes* (1921)*
- *Flight into Egypt* (1923)*

Be sure and at least check out the three marked with an asterisk. Also, check out *The Thankful Poor* (1894).

Who was Warner Sallman?

Do an online image search of "paintings by Warner Sallman." Warner Sallman (1892–1968) is not considered one of the great artists of all time; however, his images have been widely reproduced and are instantly recognizable by many people.

Henry Ossawa Tanner's *Daniel in the Lion's Den* (1895).

Are there some modern painters who created Christian art?

Most modern art has rejected the emphasis on religion of much older art. Modern art has tended to explore the human condition or to explore art itself. Some modern pieces of modern art have no meaning. For example, some paintings are simply interesting images on canvas. However, there are some examples of modern religious art, such as several paintings by Spanish painter Salvador Dalí.

Salvador Dalí (1904–1989) is known for his often bizarre, surrealistic paintings. "Surreal" is the opposite of real. Some of Dalí's paintings remind people of bad dreams. Many of his paintings are hard to decipher. However, his religious paintings are very accessible. Here are four paintings to view with an online image search:

- *Christ of St. John of the Cross* (1951)

- *Crucifixion* (*Corpus Hypercubus*) (1954)

- *Sacrament of the Last Supper* (1955)

- *Santiago El Grande* (St. James the Greater) (1957)

There are two interesting Dalí religious paintings that are a little more difficult to figure out: *Madonna of Port Lligat* (there are two versions, painted in 1949 and 1950) and *Assumpta Corpuscularia Lapislazulina* (a depiction of the Assumption of Mary, painted in 1952).

ARCHITECTURE

How has Christianity impacted architecture?

Christianity has had an immense impact on architecture. Thousands of impressive and magnificent cathedrals exist. For many people, the medieval cathedrals in the Gothic style, such as Notre Dame in Paris, are some of most glorious Christian buildings. Because so many interesting cathedrals exist, this chapter will only mention a handful for you to explore online. For each of these examples, find online images of the exteriors and interiors.

What is the Hagia Sophia?

The Hagia Sophia was built as a magnificent Orthodox Christian church with a massive dome. The words "Hagia Sophia" mean "holy wisdom." Built by Emperor Justinian I, it was completed in 537 C.E. For a thousand years, it was the largest church in the world. It stands today in the city of Istanbul in modern Turkey, although at the time it was built, the city was called Constantinople. In the year 1453, the region was conquered by the Muslim Ottoman Turks, and the Hagia Sophia was converted into a mosque. Four towers, called "minarets," were added. Five times a day, men called "muezzins" would go to the top of the towers to call Muslims to prayer. In 1935, the Hagia Sophia became a museum and is visited by many tourists each year.

What are the Gothic cathedrals?

About a hundred Gothic cathedrals were built in Europe in the Middle Ages. The Gothic style includes pointed arches, extensive use of stained glass, and flying buttresses to support the wall. The Gothic movement began with the Church of St. Denis outside of Paris. The leader of this church, Abbot Suger (1081–1151), had been influenced by the writings of an early Christian monk called Pseudo-Dionysius, who saw light as God's essence. Suger wanted to open the church walls to include lots of window space for colorful, stained-glass windows. The trick was to design buttresses in the walls to hold up the roof and ceiling of the cathedral. The buttresses held the weight, which meant the walls could be opened up for glass. Do an image search for "St. Denis Paris" and then a search for "flying buttresses." Two of the most famous Gothic cathedrals are Notre Dame in Paris and Chartres Cathedral in Chartres, France. Take a look at them online. Today, these cathedrals are still used as places of worship, but they are also popular tourist destinations. An American example of a Gothic church is St. Patrick's Cathedral in New York, completed in 1879.

What do I need to know about St. Peter's Basilica in Rome?

St. Peter's Basilica in Rome is the largest church in the world. The church itself and St. Peter's Square in front of it were designed by famous Renaissance architects Donato Bramante, Michelangelo, Carlo Maderno, and Gian Lorenzo Bernini. For many Catholics, it is one of the holiest places on earth. Tradition holds that it was built on the burial site of St. Peter the Apostle.

What do the words "cathedral" and "basilica" mean?

The word "cathedral" comes from the word "cathedra," which means "throne" or "seat." Every cathedral has a chair in the front for the bishop of the diocese, so a cathedral is the bishop's church. The word "basilica" is used for a specific style for a large church. Although St. Peter's in Rome is the church of the pope, it is not a cathedral, even though the pope is the bishop of Rome. The pope's cathedral is a different church in Rome: St. John Lateran.

Are cathedrals being built today?

Because of their cost, large cathedrals are not often built today. However, one exception is the Sagrada Familia, an immense cathedral being built in Barcelona, Spain. Named for the Holy Family of Jesus, construction began in 1882 and still continues today, fol-

The immense Sagrada Familia is still under construction in Barcelona, Spain. Very few new cathedrals have been built in recent decades, mostly because of the prohibitive expense.

347

lowing the designs of architect Antoni Gaudí (1852–1926). Explore online images of the Sagrada Familia. However, to get the feel for the massive size of the Sagrada Familia, you will need to see it for yourself in Barcelona.

What is the Crystal Cathedral?

The Crystal Cathedral in Orange County, California, was completed in 1980. It was built by Reverend Robert H. Schuller, who became famous through his *Hour of Power* radio broadcast. At its completion, the Crystal Cathedral was claimed to be the largest glass building in the world. It is made of glass, not crystal, and it is not a cathedral in the technical sense of being the seat of a bishop. The church has one of the largest organs in the world. Eventually, the church had to declare bankruptcy. The building was sold to the Roman Catholic Diocese of Orange. It is currently being restored.

What is a megachurch?

A megachurch is a Protestant Christian church having an attendance of over two thousand people each week. The largest U.S. megachurch is the Lakewood Church in Houston, Texas, with over forty thousand members. The largest in the world is the Yoido Full Gospel Church in Seoul, South Korea, which has almost five hundred thousand members.

Typically, megachurches are not architecturally impressive. For many such churches, the emphasis is on creating a functional space for large congregations. They typically use high-tech media, and often, services are broadcast on television. Do an online search for "megachurch" to see what they look like.

Are there any other suggestions for exploring other interesting churches?

Are there any interesting churches in your neighborhood or in the city where you live? Are there any churches in nearby cities? Many people enjoy exploring other churches. One trick is to show up before or after services to look around. Another trick is to call the church office and say you want to see the church. Most churches are glad to show off their churches, and many will have someone meet you to explain the history and the details of their churches.

When you travel to other cities, think about visiting churches. In some older cities, you can see the church steeples on the skyline. Just drive to the steeples. Or do an online search of churches in a particular city and see which ones you would like to visit.

What do Christians think about their church buildings?

Different Christian groups have different ideas about their buildings. For some Christians, the church building is simply a functional space in which to hold services. For such Christians, convenience and comfort are important, and often, there is a lack of religious decoration and art. For other Christians, church buildings provide sacred space, a special place with a very different feel and look to it. Often, their church buildings include religious art such as statues and stained-glass windows.

The Roman Catholic Church is one denomination that sees a church as sacred space. People are expected to be quiet in the church before and after services. Catholics often genuflect as they take their seats in the pews. To genuflect is to go down on one knee as a sign of respect for God. People are expected to show a reverential attitude when in the church. Using cell phones and texting are discouraged. Catholics typically believe that God is especially present when the Eucharist is being kept in the tabernacle in the front of the church. A red candle is kept lit in the front of the church, indicating the presence of the Eucharist. Often, Catholics feel that God is present in the church even if no one is in the building. Because the church is a special place, Catholics avoid using the space for nonreligious events.

In addition to religious reasons for creating a sacred space, there are practical reasons. Such spaces provide a quiet and inspiring place to pray, think, or meditate. Even when other people are in the church and a service is not going on, one can pray quietly. Today, many people desperately need such a place. Our modern world is filled with lots of distracting noise. Notice the many restaurants and bars with numerous television screens. Next time you are in an airport, see if you can find a quiet place without a TV blaring. It is harder than you think.

Other Christians, such as many Protestant denominations, have very different attitudes regarding church buildings. They believe that God is not present in the building but rather in the people who come together to worship. Talking and conversing before and after the service is fine and is often encouraged as a way to build community. The Quakers, also known as the Religious Society of Friends, do not have churches. Instead, they gather in meetinghouses.

What are the problems of big church buildings?

Big church buildings cost lots of money to build and lots of money to maintain. Many pastors spend much of their time and energy dealing with the physical aspects of the building. When churches also have schools, the problems are compounded. For many Christian communities, much of the money donated in the collection goes to the building. There is an old saying about the five "L"s, which are the five biggest worries of a pastor: lights, leaks, locks, lawns, and lawsuits.

In a number of large U.S. cities that have vast abandoned areas, many magnificent churches stand empty and unused. In many cases, these buildings did not even get one hundred years of use. Do an online image search for "abandoned churches" with the name of a large city such as Philadelphia, Cincinnati, Detroit, Chicago, Boston, or St. Louis.

At the other end of the spectrum are storefront churches that can be found in less affluent or poor areas. These small churches use inexpensive spaces. If the congregation moves or disbands, there is no large church building to be abandoned. Do an online image search for "storefront church."

CHRISTIAN CULTURE: MUSIC

What is the difference between religious and secular music?

Throughout Christian history and into the present, most congregations have rules about which music styles are appropriate for religious services and which are not. Sacred music is allowed. Nonreligious music, often called "secular music" or "profane music," is not allowed. In the Renaissance, there were a number of fights over what music in a popular style could be used or not used in church services. Similar views hold today. For example, a common rule at a number of churches is that at weddings, popular love songs cannot be used.

Some evangelical churches have Christian rock music, which is based on popular musical styles. Although the music is based on the sound of rock music, actual rock music cannot be used. Playing songs of the Rolling Stones would not be allowed, though playing music that sounds like the Rolling Stones with Christian lyrics is acceptable.

Why is music important for Christians?

Although a few Christian groups down through the centuries have rejected religious music as a distraction, most Christians see music as an important part of Christian life and worship. Christians often find good church music to be inspiring and uplifting. However, many people have also experienced church music that was boring and tedious. Sometimes, this is due to the lack of quality in the music and the performance. More often, it is simply a matter of musical tastes. People have different tastes in music, and their tastes often change over time. Since music can stir the emotions, different people are stirred by different music. Occasionally, people will change churches to find music they like. Many churches work hard on creating great music that the congregation will enjoy because they know that good music helps keep people coming.

THE EARLY CENTURIES

What about music in the early centuries of Christianity?

Music has been part of Christianity from the very beginning, as shown in three New Testament passages. The Gospel of Matthew describes Jesus and his Twelve Apostles after the Last Supper: "When they had sung the hymn, they went out to the Mount of Olives" (Matthew 26:30, NRSV). In his letter to the Colossians, Paul states: "Let the word of Christ dwell in you richly; teach and admonish one another in all wisdom; and with gratitude in your hearts sing psalms, hymns, and spiritual songs to God" (Colossians 3:16, NRSV). The Book of Ephesians states: "Be filled with the Spirit, as you sing psalms and hymns and spiritual songs among yourselves, singing and making melody to the Lord in your hearts, giving thanks to God the Father at all times and for everything in the name of our Lord Jesus Christ" (Ephesians 5:18–20, NRSV).

From the beginning, Christians used music in their religious services. In part, they followed the older Jewish customs of setting the Psalms to music. As noted earlier, several psalms even mention the instruments used. Some Christians imagined that angels sang in choirs in praise of God. Others believed that Christians singing on earth were joined by such Heavenly choirs.

We do not know much about how this early Christian music sounded. However, it is possible that ancient melodies have survived into the present, yet we are unaware of their origins. However, as the centuries passed, a music style developed by monks did get written down. Called Gregorian chant, it has survived and is still sung today.

What is Gregorian chant?

If you are unfamiliar with Gregorian chant, you should pull up some samples on YouTube before reading the description that follows. For some people, Gregorian chant is an acquired taste, which means they have to spend some time with it in order to learn to like it. If you are new to Gregorian chant, you might try listening to short selections at several different times.

Many people find Gregorian chant very soothing. Many people find it provides a nice background for meditation and prayer. It also sounds very religious, especially when the recording is done in a church building with lots of resonance. Other people find it to be good background music for work and study.

Gregorian chant is a music style used for prayers and chanting the Psalms that goes back at least to the 700s C.E. and was based on earlier music forms. It gets its name from Pope Gregory I, who died in 604 C.E. Gregory encouraged the development of the liturgy and collected various chants for liturgical use. Although his name is attached to this style of music, many of the individual pieces of Gregorian chant were created in the centuries following Gregory.

Gregorian chant is monophonic, which means that only one melody is sung at a time. Even if there are numerous singers, they all sing the same note. This is different from polyphonic music, where singers sing different melodies that are interwoven. It is also different from singing harmony, where the singers sing different notes of the same chord while singing the same word.

Gregorian chant typically has no instrumental accompaniment. It is sung a cappella, usually by a choir, although sometimes by a soloist. Gregorian chant does have a rhythm, but the rhythm can be very subtle. There is no instrument, such as a drum, to emphasize the beat. It is the exact opposite of rock and hip-hop music, where the beat, emphasized by the drum and bass, predominates. Because Gregorian chant is monophonic with no instruments, it is a very simple style of music, yet it can be emotionally powerful.

Why do most churches have organs?

The organ has played an immense role in Christian music down through the centuries. Electronic and pipe organs are still used today in many churches. One of the reasons for the popularity of the organ was its ability to fill large spaces with full-volume music that only needed one musician and someone to pump the bellows. Also, organs could produce a wide range of sounds. Today with electronic organs, they can reproduce the sound of all musical instruments.

The organ is surprisingly old. In the 200s B.C.E., a Greek, Ctesibius of Alexandria, created the water organ. Other organs developed based on blowing air through pipes to create different pitches. In time, different types of pipes of both metal and wood were used to give the organ more varied sounds. A keyboard was developed to select the pipes for different notes. "Stops" were added, which were buttons to pull to select different sets of pipes with different sounds. Up until the development of electric pumps, someone had to pump the organ bellows by hand to create enough air pressure to make the sound of the organ.

In the 1800s, the reed organ or harmonium became popular. The reed organ used the same principle as a harmonica, in which air is blown over reeds to produce music. On a reed organ, the musician played the keyboard and at the same time moved foot pedals to blow air over the reeds. The reed organ was significantly smaller and cheaper than the pipe organ.

A common fixture in most Christian churches is an organ, which is a favorite instrument because it more easily fills the entire large room with sound. This was helpful back in the days before electronics.

The electric organ appeared in the 1930s. The most famous was the Hammond organ with a Leslie speaker. Speakers made it easy to produce lots of volume. For many years, a common setup in African American Baptist churches was to have both an organ—usually the Hammond organ with the Leslie speaker—and a piano providing the music. A sample of this traditional organ and piano can be heard and seen in the background of Mahalia Jackson singing "Joshua Fit the Battle of Jericho," which can be viewed on YouTube.

Digital keyboards started appearing in the 1970s. These are very common in churches today because they can produce both the piano and the organ sound and also the sound of hundreds of other musical instruments.

FAMOUS HYMNS, REQUIEMS, AND MASSES

What hymn did Martin Luther write?

A very famous and powerful Protestant hymn was written around 1527 by Martin Luther: "A Mighty Fortress Is Our God" (in German, "Ein feste Burg ist unser Gott"). Here is the first verse:

> A mighty fortress is our God,
> A bulwark never failing:
> Our helper He, amid the flood
> Of mortal ills prevailing.
> For still our ancient foe
> Doth seek to work his woe;
> His craft and power are great,
> And armed with cruel hate,
> On earth is not his equal.

Who was Charles Wesley?

John Wesley (1703–1791), the founder of Methodism, had a brother named Charles Wesley (1707–1788). Charles never left the Anglican Church to join the Methodist Church, but he helped John by creating over six thousand hymns. Charles Wesley helped promote congregational singing—the idea that everyone in the church should sing along—a new concept at the time. For most of his hymns, Charles just wrote the lyrics, which he put to existing popular tunes. He wanted church singing to be lively and enjoyable. Some of his better-known hymns are "Christ the Lord Is Risen Today," "Come Thou Long Expected Jesus," and "Hark! The Herald Angels Sing."

Is it true that "Amazing Grace" was written by a slave trader?

"Amazing Grace," published in 1779, was written by John Newton, an Anglican clergyman. As a young man, he was conscripted into the British Navy. Then he became involved in the slave trade. As a sailor, he was known for his crude and obscene language. (He used language far worse than a sailor's typical crude language.) During a terrible storm at sea, he cried out to God for mercy and had a spiritual conversion. He continued to work as a slave trader until he decided to study for the ministry and was ordained in 1764. He wrote the words "Amazing Grace" for a sermon in 1773. Originally written to be read, the words were put to a number of existing

Arthur Sullivan—better known for his amusing operettas written with W. S. Gilbert—penned "Onward, Christian Soldiers."

melodies until the tune "New Britain" became the most frequent version. "Amazing Grace" is one of most popular Christian hymns and one of the most recognizable songs. It is often played at funerals, especially when a bagpipe is used. The famous first verse is:

> Amazing grace! How sweet the sound
> That saved a wretch like me.
> I once was lost, but now am found,
> Was blind but now I see.

Later, another verse was added to the song:

> When we've been there ten thousand years,
> Bright shining as the sun,
> We've no less days to sing God's praise,
> Than when we first begun.

What is the song "Onward, Christian Soldiers"?

This hymn was written in 1871 by Arthur Sullivan (1842–1900), who is best known for the fourteen operettas he wrote with W. S. Gilbert (1836–1911), including *H.M.S. Pinafore*, *The Pirates of Penzance*, and *The Mikado*. "Onward, Christian Soldiers" became popular with the Salvation Army.

> Onward, Christian soldiers, marching as to war,
> With the cross of Jesus going on before.
> Christ, the royal Master, leads against the foe;
> Forward into battle see His banners go!

What is a requiem?

A requiem is a Mass said for someone who has died. In a musical requiem, the parts of the Catholic Latin Mass are set to music. The most famous example is Mozart's "Requiem in D Minor, K. 626," composed in 1791. Wolfgang Amadeus Mozart (1756–1791) died before finishing it, so another composer completed it. Mozart's requiem is filled with very powerful music. Check it out on YouTube if you are interested. Two moving parts are "Dies Irae" (Day of Wrath) and "Lacrimosa." Lacrimosa means "tears." Mozart's "Dies Irae" is based on an old Latin hymn. Several dozen composers, from Johannes Brahms to Stephen Sondheim, have also quoted the melody of the original Latin hymn in their compositions. Another famous requiem is by Gabriel Fauré.

What are some examples of musical settings of the Catholic Mass?

During the Middle Ages, the Catholic Latin Mass developed. Over the centuries, many composers have set to music the text of several of the prayers: the Kyrie ("Lord have mercy! …"), the Gloria ("Glory to God in the Highest …"), the Credo ("I believe …"—the text of the Nicene Creed), the Sanctus ("Holy, Holy, Holy …), and the Agnus Dei ("Lamb of God who takes away the sin of the world, have mercy on us").

Many musical versions were created by famous composers such as "Mass in B Minor" by Johann Sebastian Bach (1685–1750) and "Mass in C Major" by Ludwig van Beethoven (1770–1827). Modern Mass composers include Igor Stravinsky, Leonard Bernstein, and jazz composer Dave Brubeck, who created "Mass to Hope." In the late 1960s, the rock band Electric Prunes recorded "Mass in F Minor." In recent years, famous movie composer Ennio Morricone, known best for the music for classic Clint Eastwood westerns such as *The Good, the Bad, and the Ugly*, wrote a Mass for Pope Francis in 2015.

What are the prayers of the Catholic Mass?

The title of the Kyrie, also called the "Kyrie eleison," is based on the Greek words used in this prayer. Although the rest of Mass is in Latin, this prayer is in Greek. In English, this prayer is:

Lord, have mercy.
Christ, have mercy.
Lord, have mercy.

There are several different English translations of the Gloria. Here is one example:

Glory to God in the highest and peace to his people on earth. Lord God, Heavenly King, Almighty God and Father, we worship you, we give you thanks, we praise you for your glory. Lord Jesus Christ, only Son of the Father, Lord God, Lamb of God, you take away the sin of the world: have mercy on us; You are seated at the right hand of the Father: receive our prayer. For you alone are the Holy One, you alone are the Lord, you alone are the Most High, Jesus Christ, with the Holy Spirit, in the glory of God the Father. Amen.

The Credo is based on the Nicene Creed. The English text of the Sanctus is:

Holy, holy, holy Lord, God of power and might, Heaven and earth are full of your glory. Hosanna in the highest. Blessed is he who comes in the name of the Lord. Hosanna in the highest.

Sanctus is the Latin word for "holy." The English words "saint" and "sanctify" are based on this Latin root. The prayer is based on two Bible passages. The first is a description by the prophet Isaiah, who had a vision of being taken before the throne of God:

In the year King Uzziah died, I saw the Lord seated on a high and lofty throne, with the train of his garment filling the temple. Seraphim were stationed above; each of them had six wings: with two they covered their faces, with two they covered their feet, and with two they hovered. One cried out to the other: "Holy, holy, holy is the LORD of hosts! All the earth is filled with his glory!"

—Isaiah 6:1–3, NABRE

Seraphim are the class of angels closest to the throne of God.

The second passage is from the Gospel of Matthew when Jesus is entering Jerusalem: "The crowds preceding him and those following kept crying out and saying: 'Hosanna to the Son of David; blessed is he who comes in the name of the Lord; hosanna in the highest'" (Matthew 21:9, NABRE).

Here is prayer the Agnus Dei in Latin and English:

Agnus Dei, qui tollis peccata mundi, miserere nobis.
Agnus Dei, qui tollis peccata mundi, miserere nobis.
Agnus Dei, qui tollis peccata mundi, dona nobis pacem.
Lamb of God, who takes away the sins of the world, have mercy upon us.
Lamb of God, who takes away the sins of the world, have mercy upon us.
Lamb of God, who takes away the sins of the world, grant us peace.

I have often heard the famous musical piece the "Hallelujah Chorus." Who wrote it?

A very important piece of Christian music is the *Messiah*, composed in 1741 by George Frideric Handel (1685–1759). Although Handel was born in Germany, he had moved to London, where his career flourished.

Handel's *Messiah* is an oratorio, which means it is a sung piece performed by an orchestra, a chorus, and four singers—a base, a tenor, an alto, and a soprano. The piece uses every possible combination of singers and orchestra. Today, the piece is often performed with larger orchestras and choruses than Handel had originally used. The complete piece takes about two hours and twenty minutes to perform.

The best-known part of the *Messiah* is the "Hallelujah Chorus." Most people instantly recognize the piece. One can listen to the entire oratorio or selected pieces such as the "Hallelujah Chorus" on YouTube.

GOSPEL AND POPULAR MUSIC

Who was Thomas A. Dorsey?

Thomas A. Dorsey (1899–1993) is known as "the father of black gospel music."

Can you tell me more about Thomas A. Dorsey, the gospel music writer?

Thomas Dorsey grew up in Georgia; as a young man, he went to Chicago, where he became a blues pianist who recorded under the name Georgia Tom. He married Nettie Rainey, the daughter of Ma Rainey, who led the popular jazz band Ma Rainey and the Wild Cats. In 1932, Nettie died in childbirth. The newborn son died the next day. Thomas Dorsey poured his grief into writing the song "Take My Hand, Precious Lord."

Dorsey became the choir director at the Pilgrim Baptist Church and the Ebenezer Baptist Church, both in Chicago. The Ebenezer Baptist Church on the south side of Chicago was originally built as a Jewish synagogue called the Isaiah Temple. One choir member during Dorsey's leadership was Mahalia Jackson, who would become, according to some, "the greatest gospel singer." Elias McDaniel, who would later become famous as Bo Diddley, played trombone at the church.

Dorsey created his own publishing firm, Dorsey House of Music, for black gospel music. He wrote other gospel songs, including "Peace in the Valley." Both "Take My Hand, Precious Lord" and "Peace in the Valley" were recorded by a wide range of artists, including Elvis Presley and Johnny Cash. In fact, Elvis sang "Peace in the Valley" in 1957 on one of his famous TV appearances on *The Ed Sullivan Show*. Thomas A. Dorsey was the first African American elected to the Nashville Songwriters Hall of Fame.

Who was Mahalia Jackson?

Mahalia Jackson (1911–1972), one of the most popular and influential gospel singers, is often called "the queen of gospel." Others call her "the world's greatest gospel singer." Her thirty albums and singles sold many millions of copies. She was also a civil rights activist. She could have become very rich by recording the blues in the tradition of Bessie Smith, but Jackson did not want to sing such worldly music, preferring to serve God with gospel music.

Wasn't Tommy Dorsey a bandleader and not a gospel music composer?

There are two important musical figures with the same name. Thomas A. Dorsey was an African American gospel music writer. Tommy Dorsey (1905–1956) was a Caucasian who played the trombone and led a very popular big band. His brother, Jimmy Dorsey (1904–1957), had his own popular band.

The simplest way to learn about Mahalia Jackson is to listen to her music on YouTube. Some of her greatest hits are "Take My Hand, Precious Lord" and "Joshua Fit the Battle of Jericho." In the latter, she pronounces Joshua as "Joshee" and "Joshway." In some of the black-and-white videos of her television appearances, if you listen closely and look in the background, you can see the traditional instruments for African American gospel music—a piano and a Hammond organ with Leslie speakers.

"The Queen of Gospel," Mahalia Jackson was also active in the civil rights movement.

Explain the different beat of African American gospel music.

Most contemporary music has a 4/4 rhythm of four beats to each measure. Typically, beats 1 and 3 are stressed. In African American gospel music, beats 2 and 4 are usually emphasized. It might take you a little practice to learn to clap to it. However, once you get the feel of it, you will discover that emphasizing the 2 and 4 beats gives the music a special power and drive.

Elvis Presley was a rock and roll star. What does he have to do with Christian music?

Elvis Presley (1935–1977) was one of the key figures in the development of rock and roll. He also made thirty-one movies. He sold countless records, and he and his music were—and remain—extremely popular. However, he also recorded several albums of gospel music that sold quite well. In particular, he helped popularize the song "How Great Thou Art." Today, there are even groups of Christians who came to religious faith by listening to Elvis's gospel records.

As a child, Elvis was exposed to the Assembly of God Church and to gospel music. He listened to gospel music on the radio. As his career developed, Elvis rarely went to church. He read the Bible, but he also read a wide range of spiritual literature. Much of it was non-Christian, such as Kahlil Gibran's *The Prophet* (published in 1923) and *Autobiography of a Yogi* by Paramahansa Yogananda (published in 1946).

In many ways, Elvis did not live a Christian lifestyle. He had liaisons with many women during his early career. Although Elvis was married to Priscilla Presley from 1967 to 1973, he continued to have relationships with other women. Early in his career, Elvis also began abusing a wide range of prescription drugs such as uppers and downers. Late in his career, he was taking vast quantities of prescription drugs. Ironically,

359

Elvis was very opposed to street drugs and even went to Washington, D.C., to talk to President Richard Nixon to help him get a badge from the Drug Enforcement Agency. The photo of Nixon and Elvis in the Oval Office is one of the most requested photos from the Library of Congress. Very likely, Elvis was high on prescription drugs at the time of the encounter. In the end, at age forty-two, Elvis died because of his misuse of prescription drugs.

However, despite all this, many people today still find his gospel music to be beautiful and inspiring. Check it out for yourself by either getting a CD of one of his albums or going on YouTube to sample some of his gospel music. His "How Great Thou Art" from his concerts in 1972 and 1977 are considered classic Elvis performances.

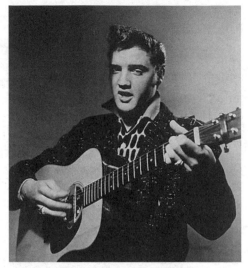

Although known as the "King of Rock 'n' Roll," Elvis Presley recorded numerous gospel music albums. Indeed, Elvis's groundbreaking style was heavily influenced by gospel music.

Who are some important figures in gospel and Christian music?

Exploring the world of gospel and Christian rock is beyond the scope of this book because there are so many important and popular composers, singers, vocal quartets, and bands. To get an overview of all the important figures in gospel music, check out the Web page for the Gospel Music Hall of Fame.

What is the best-known Christian music?

Christmas songs are some of the best-known Christian music. However, there are two types of Christmas songs: secular or nonreligious songs such as "Jingle Bells," "Frosty the Snowman," "The Twelve Days of Christmas," "Rudolph the Red-Nosed Reindeer," and "The Christmas Song," and religious Christmas songs such as "Silent Night," "The First Noel," "Hark! The Herald Angels Sing," "Angels We Have Heard on High," and "Adeste Fideles." These songs are very popular and very well known. Many people can sing these songs from memory.

Often, these religious Christmas songs are called Christmas carols. Christmas caroling is the practice of going from house to house singing Christmas songs and sometimes raising money for charity.

I heard a beautiful piece of music called the "Ave Maria." What is the piece?

The "Ave Maria" is the Latin version of the Catholic prayer "Hail Mary." The most famous version of the "Ave Maria" is the one written by German composer Franz Schubert (1797–1828). He originally wrote it in 1825 as "Ellen's Third Song," a setting of Walter

Who was the Singing Nun?

The Singing Nun was Jeanne-Paule Marie "Jeannine" Deckers (1933–1985), who lived in Belgium. As a Catholic sister known as Soeur Sourire ("Sister Smile"), she sang, played guitar, and wrote songs. Her 1961 song "Dominique" became an international hit, selling almost two million copies. She appeared on the popular American TV show *The Ed Sullivan Show* in 1964. A film, loosely based on her life, *The Singing Nun*, starring Debbie Reynolds, was released in 1965.

Deckers left the convent and had little success with other recordings. Eventually, the Belgian government claimed she owed $63,000 in taxes for the income on "Dominique." She had little money since the profits had gone to the producer and the convent where she lived. In serious financial trouble, she tried a disco version of "Dominique," which failed to raise money. Due to her financial problems, she and her partner, Annie Pécher, committed suicide in 1985. Her music is available on YouTube.

Scott's poem "The Lady of the Lake." Eventually, the Latin words of the Catholic "Ave Maria" prayer were put to his music to create this well-known hymn to Mary, the mother of Jesus. The other famous version is the "Ave Maria" of French composer Charles Gounod (1818–1893), published in 1853. Gounod wrote a melody set against Johann Sebastian Bach's "Prelude No. 1 in C Major." Both versions of the "Ave Maria" can be heard on YouTube.

CHRISTIAN CULTURE: MOVIES AND MUSICALS

MOVIES ABOUT THE OLD TESTAMENT

What are some classic movies based on the Old Testament?

Three Old Testament movies are important: *The Ten Commandments* (1923), *The Green Pastures* (1936), and *The Ten Commandments* (1956).

What was the first significant Old Testament movie?

The soon-to-be-famous Hollywood producer Cecil B. DeMille (1881–1959) created the classic silent film *The Ten Commandments* in 1923—with amazing special effects for its time—to tell the story of Moses receiving the Ten Commandments. As Daniel Lord, S.J., wrote in his *The Glorious Ten Commandments* in 1944:

> Then upon the film Mr. DeMille produced a modern miracle of the Red Sea. Audiences sat aghast as the waters opened, the Israelites walked through, and then the sea flooded back over the Egyptian hosts. A favorite dinner-table discussion of those days was how Mr. DeMille had produced what seemed to be a duplicate of Jehovah's amazing miracle.

> Yet when Moses walked up the Mount, I forgot all that had gone before. In spirit I was on Mount Sinai at the tremendous moment of history when God handed to the sons of men His great Ten Commandments and hedged them round with strong stone walls symbolized in the Tables of the Law.

The film had two parts: in Part 1, Moses received the Commandments; in Part 2, modern people broke them.

What was the second version of *The Ten Commandments*?

Cecil B. DeMille redid his 1923 film in 1956 with sound, Technicolor, and even greater special effects, for which the movie won the Academy Award. Watch the scene of the crossing of the Red Sea, and you will see why. This epic film, which runs four hours, stars Charlton Heston as Moses and Yul Brynner as the pharaoh Rameses II. The story describes the life of Moses, the Exodus when Moses led the Hebrews out of Egypt, and Moses receiving the Ten Commandments.

What is the movie *The Green Pastures* about?

This film has an entirely African American cast, one of only six such feature films made by Hollywood in this era. Rex Ingram plays De Lawd (God) and Adam. Noah is played by Eddie "Rochester" Anderson, who would later become famous for his work with comedian Jack Benny. *The Green Pastures* begins with a preacher explaining the Bible to children. As he tells the stories of Noah and Adam, the stories come alive in a rural African American setting.

The Green Pastures has been criticized by some for using stereotypical images of African Americans. Check out several of the clips on YouTube, or watch the entire movie and decide for yourself.

What are some more recent movies based on the Old Testament?

An animated feature, *The Prince of Egypt* (1998) is a DreamWorks version of the story of Moses with an all-star cast doing the voices, including Val Kilmer as the voice of Moses and Ralph Fiennes as the voice of Rameses. More recently is the film *Exodus: Gods and Kings*. Ridley Scott directed this epic drama, starring Christian Bale as Moses and Joel Edgerton.

MOVIES ABOUT JESUS

What is the earliest major film about Jesus?

After producing the first version of *The Ten Commandments*, Cecil B. DeMille produced *The King of Kings* (1927). Although it is a silent film, the movie is another must-see classic. Long and short versions of the movie were created. The long version is worth the extra time. The film provides an opportunity to see how silent films could be just as entertaining and powerful as later "talkie" movies. Most of the film is black and white, except the opening sequence with Mary Magdalene and the Resurrection scene, which are in Technicolor.

Several things stand out in the movie, such as when Jesus first appears on the screen eighteen minutes into the film. (You will have to watch the movie to find out how he appears.) Another great scene is the driving out of the seven demons from Mary Magdalene: lust, greed, pride, gluttony, indolence, envy, and anger.

The scene of the temptation of Jesus by the Devil is particularly well done and effective. The earthquake scene at the Crucifixion is totally over-the-top with the bad guys getting their due. Apparently, God the Father did not listen to the admonition of Jesus: "Forgive them, for they know not what they do."

A St. Louis Jesuit priest, Daniel Lord, served as technical adviser for the movie. He encouraged DeMille to reduce the footage on Mary Magdalene at the beginning. DeMille was famous for salacious scenes of scantily clad women.

Are there many movies about Jesus and his followers?

As the most important figure in human history, it is not surprising that Jesus has been portrayed in movies. A number of important films depict the life of Jesus. There

Director Cecil B. DeMille filmed some classic movies about the Bible, including *The Ten Commandments* and *The King of Kings*.

are also several musicals about Jesus. Hollywood has made a number of classic movies about the Old Testament. Movies have also been made about contemporaries of Jesus. The stories of Christian heroes and saints have been made into movies. A surprising number of movies about Catholic priests and nuns have also been made.

All of these movies are still worth seeing and available. The trailers for most of these films can be found on YouTube if you want to get a quick feel for the films. The plots of these movies are only briefly described below so as to not give away the stories.

What is the issue of the doves in *The King of Kings?*

In the movie, DeMille begins a long cinematic tradition of having doves fly away during the Cleansing of the Temple scene. It makes for great cinematography! The doves reappear after the Resurrection. However, Jesus did not release doves in the gospels. This seemingly trivial point is important because some mistakenly argue that Jesus destroyed property when cleansing the Temple. Jesus only turned over the chairs of the dove sellers; the cages were left intact.

Was there a remake of *The King of Kings*?

Cecil B. DeMille died in 1959, so the 1961 version of *The King of Kings* is not a remake of the 1927 film. It stars Jeffrey Hunter as Jesus. The script takes liberties with the original gospel story.

What star-studded epic failed at the box office?

The film *The Greatest Story Ever Told* (1965) has an all-star cast, including Max von Sydow as Jesus, Dorothy McGuire as the Virgin Mary, Charlton Heston as John the Baptist, and Claude Rains as Herod the Great. The original film ran over four hours. It was cut to two hours and seventeen minutes for general release. Many critics did not like the film, and it did not draw large audiences.

Was the story of Jesus ever done on television?

The television miniseries *Jesus of Nazareth* (1977) was directed by Franco Zeffirelli (1923–) and starred Robert Powell (1944–) as Jesus. The all-star cast includes Academy Award winners Anne Bancroft, Ernest Borgnine, Laurence Olivier, Christopher Plummer, Rod Steiger, James Earl Jones, and Peter Ustinov. *Jesus of Nazareth* covers the entire gospel story from the Nativity of Jesus to the Resurrection. The full version is almost six and a half hours long. Some viewers find it a little slow moving.

What were the two films of the 1980s that took nontraditional looks at Jesus?

The Last Temptation of Christ (1988), directed by Martin Scorsese (1942–), is based on the controversial 1955 novel of the same name, written by Nikos Kazantzakis. The movie stars Willem Dafoe as Jesus, Harvey Keitel as Judas, Barbara Hershey as Mary Magdalene, and David Bowie as Pontius Pilate. The novel and the movie have both been controversial for depicting a Jesus who struggles with his own temptations, including sexual temptations. As the film's disclaimer states, this portrayal of Jesus is not based on the gospels.

Jesus of Montreal (1989) is a French-Canadian film written and directed by Denys Arcand (1941–). It is not exactly about Jesus as depicted in the gospels. It stars Lothaire Bluteau as Daniel. Set in Montreal, Daniel gathers a group of actors to perform a Passion Play about Jesus for a Catholic church. However, Daniel begins exploring nontraditional ideas about Jesus. As the story unfolds, his life begins to parallel the life of Jesus in the gospels. The film is filled with many New Testament allusions.

CHRISTIAN MUSICALS
THAT BECAME MOVIES

What are the musicals about Jesus?

There are three musicals about Jesus: *Jesus Christ Superstar* (1971), *Godspell* (1973), and *Cotton Patch Gospel* (1981).

What is the origin of the musical *Jesus Christ Superstar*?

Jesus Christ Superstar (1971) is a rock opera with music written by Andrew Lloyd Webber (1948–) and lyrics by Tim Rice (1944–). It was originally released as a two-record concept album in 1970. The music is sung through with no spoken dialogue between the numbers. The character of Judas plays a large role in the story.

The rock opera then became a popular Broadway show in 1971. There have been many productions since. A film version was released in 1973. Some fans still prefer the original LP version.

Christians have had different views on *Jesus Christ Superstar*. Some reject it because it does not mesh with their own theology. Many think the divinity of Jesus is understated. Other Christians simply enjoy the music and the story and do not worry about its take on the gospel stories.

What is the musical *Godspell*?

Godspell (1973) is a popular musical composed by Stephen Schwartz (1948–). The title is based on the old English term for the word "gospel," which means "good news." The show first opened off Broadway in 1971. It has had many productions since. *Godspell* is loosely based on the Gospel of Matthew. The show has catchy songs with clever lyrics.

The song "Day by Day" from the show was released as a single and reached number 13 on the Billboard chart in 1972. In 1973, a film version was released that is set in New York.

The musical is sometimes criticized for lacking a Resurrection scene. The show typically ends with Jesus dying and then the cast carrying the body of Jesus over their heads as they walk through the audience. Schwartz's intention was to emphasize the impact of the teachings of Jesus on his followers and their willingness to carry on his ideals, not whether or not he was resurrected.

What is the musical *Cotton Patch Gospel*?

Cotton Patch Gospel (1981) was written by singer Harry Chapin just before his tragic

American composer and lyricist Stephen Schwartz is the creative voice behind the musical *Godspell*.

367

What is the problem involving Judas in movies and musicals about Jesus?

One of the difficulties in reading the gospels is trying to figure out what the motivation of Judas was in betraying Jesus. The gospels, with their focus on Jesus, do not offer a clear explanation of why Judas betrayed Jesus. Ever since, in books, plays, and movies, the character of Judas has been fleshed out to give him a motivation for betraying Jesus. To modern people, brought up on murder mysteries and crime stories, understanding the motivation of the wrongdoer is important to the reader or viewer.

Explaining the motivation of Judas was not seen as necessary by the gospel writers. The entire focus of the gospels is on the character of Jesus, and all other characters, including his followers, play minor roles. When trying to make a movie about Jesus, the tendency is to flesh out these minor characters to make a better story, so typically, Judas is given a motivation for his betrayal of Jesus. The character of Mary Magdalene is often further filled out to make her a character with her own backstory.

In movies about Jesus, various motivations have been given to Judas, including the story that Judas lost his love interest, Mary Magdalene, when she started following Jesus. Another idea used is that Judas wanted to force Jesus's hand by bringing him before the Jewish high council so that Jesus could prove who he was. Yet another idea is that Judas was disappointed in the direction of the mission of Jesus. In particular, Judas resented Jesus reaching out to the poor and lowly instead of the rich and powerful. In his anger, Judas betrayed Jesus.

death in a car accident. It is a musical telling of the Gospel of Matthew set to a southern dialect. It can be performed as a one-man show or with a larger cast. Numerous renditions of the show can be seen on YouTube.

Harry Chapin was a popular singer, best known for his 1974 hit "Cats in the Cradle." He was a humanitarian who fought against hunger in America and across the globe.

What is the musical *The Book of Mormon* about?

The Book of Mormon (2011) is a musical comedy about two young Mormon men who are sent to Africa to do missionary work. The show was written by Robert Lopez, Trey Parker, and Matt Stone. The show has been very popular since its Broadway premiere in 2011. (As of the writing of this book, a movie version of the musical has not been made.)

The musical is named for the sacred text of Mormons, which is called *The Book of Mormon*. Very different from the musical is the 2003 movie *The Book of Mormon, Volume 1: The Journey*, which is based on some of the stories in the actual *Book of Mormon*. Mormons are members of the Church of Jesus Christ of Latter-day Saints.

MOVIES ABOUT
CONTEMPORARIES OF JESUS

What are some important movies about contemporaries of Jesus?

Movies about contemporaries of Jesus are *Ben-Hur*, *Barrabas*, and *Monty Python's Life of Brian*.

What is the film *Ben-Hur*?

There are two versions of this film: a silent version entitled *Ben-Hur: A Tale of the Christ* (1925), starring Ramon Novarro, and a later version entitled simply *Ben-Hur* (1959), starring Charlton Heston. Both are epic movies based on the bestselling 1880 novel *Ben-Hur: A Tale of the Christ*, written by Lew Wallace, who had served as a Union general in the Civil War. The novel tells the story of a Jewish prince, Judah Ben-Hur, who is falsely accused by a Roman official, Messala. Ben-Hur is enslaved. He becomes a galley slave on a ship and then a chariot driver. In both versions of the movie, the dramatic scene of the chariot race is the highlight of the film. Several times in his life, Ben-Hur crosses paths with Jesus. The 1959 version won eleven Academy Awards, including Best Picture, Best Director, Best Actor, Best Costume Design, and Best Cinematography. The 1925 version is also worth seeing.

What is the movie *Barabbas*?

In the gospels, Pontius Pilate is the Roman official who orders the Crucifixion of Jesus. Before deciding to execute Jesus, he offers to free one of the Jewish prisoners, and he

Is the Monty Python movie *Life of Brian* a satire about Jesus?

*L*ife of Brian (1979) is a Monty Python comedy in which Brian lives a life parallel to the life of Jesus. They are born at the same time and, in fact, the Magi come to honor the baby Brian until they realize their mistake, take their gifts back, and head to the stable where Jesus is. One of the classic lines from the movie is the scene where Jesus is giving his Sermon on the Mount and the people listening at a distance hear "Blessed are the peacemakers" as "Blessed are the cheesemakers." The stoning scene is particularly funny.

This movie is not for everyone. The movie is not a satire on Jesus; the actual references to Jesus are in fact very few. Despite this, some Christians took offense at the movie, seeing it as blasphemy. It was banned in Norway and Ireland. Some protestors showed up at movie theaters. Many other Christians saw the movie and understood its quirky Monty Python take on the religious world at the time of Jesus.

The opening graphics of the film are a satire on the graphics from the 1961 film *The King of Kings* and the theme music is a satire on music of James Bond movies.

gives the crowd the choice of Jesus or Barabbas. The Gospel of Mark states: "A man called Barabbas was then in prison along with the rebels who had committed murder in a rebellion" (Mark 15:7). The crowd chooses Barabbas, and Jesus is then crucified.

In 1950, Pär Lagerkvist published his 1950 novel, *Barabbas,* which follows what later happens to Barabbas. Lagerkvist received the 1951 Nobel Prize in literature. In 1953, the Swedish film *Barabbas* was released, starring Ulf Palme. The 1961 version, starring Anthony Quinn, was considered a film classic. Finally, in 2012, a TV movie version was created starring Billy Zane.

MOVIES ABOUT CATHOLIC PRIESTS

Why are there so many movies about Catholic priests?

Quite a few movies have Catholic priests and nuns in title roles. Other movies have Catholic religious as important minor characters. In the twentieth century, the Catholic Church became the largest religious denomination in America. Starting in the late 1930s, Hollywood reached out to this large potential audience. Many non-Catholics were also interested in the world of Catholics as they were portrayed through the Hollywood lens. The following covers the better-known movies about Catholic priests.

What are some movies of the 1930s and 1940s about priests?

There are many classic black-and-white films with Catholic priests as main characters. Here are some important examples:

- *Angels with Dirty Faces* (1938): This is a crime story in which James Cagney (1899–1986) plays gangster Rocky Sullivan. Pat O'Brien plays a Catholic priest, Jerry Connolly, who tries to keep the neighborhood youth from following in Rocky's path.
- *Boys Town* (1938): This movie tells the story of the real-life Father Edward J. Flanagan, who created Boys Town outside of Omaha, Nebraska, to help poor, orphaned, and delinquent boys. It stars Spencer Tracy and Mickey Rooney.
- *Men of Boys Town* (1941): This sequel to *Boys Town* again features Tracy and Rooney.
- *The Fighting 69th* (1940): This movie is set during World War I and is based on actual events involving the famous New York 69th Infantry Regiment. Pat O'Brien plays Father Francis P. Duffy, the chaplain. Duffy Square at the north end of Times Square in New York City is named for Father Duffy.

What are the two movies with Bing Crosby?

Bing Crosby (1903–1977) played a priest in *Going My Way* and its sequel, *The Bells of St. Mary's.*

Going My Way (1944) is a charming movie that tells the story of Father Charles "Chuck" O'Malley, played by singer Bing Crosby, who arrives to rescue the failing St. Dominic's Church, run by the curmudgeonly Father Fitzgibbon, played by Barry Fitzgerald. It won seven Academy Awards, including Best Picture. Crosby won the Academy Award for Best Actor, and Fitzgerald won for Best Supporting Actor. The movie includes several musical numbers.

The Bells of St. Mary's (1945) is the sequel to *Going My Way.* Bing Crosby returns as Father O'Malley to help save a struggling inner-city school run by Sister Mary Benedict, played by Ingrid Bergman. This movie also includes several songs. The record versions of these songs did well on the popular charts, and the movie did extremely well at the box office.

Popular crooner and actor Bing Crosby starred in the movies *Going My Way* and *The Bells of St. Mary's,* feel-good films about a Catholic priest.

What other movies depicting priests were made at this time?

The Miracle of the Bells (1948) is about Bill Dunnigan, played by Fred MacMurray, who has brought the body of the dead movie actress Olga Treskovna (Alida Valli) back to be buried in Coal Town, where she grew up. Frank Sinatra plays Father Paul. Sinatra agreed to do the movie to deflect attention from the questions being raised about the morality of his personal life. Despite this being an atypical role for Sinatra, he plays a convincing Father Paul.

Fighting Father Dunne (1948) tells the true story of Father Peter Dunne, a Catholic priest who set up the News Boys home in St. Louis. It stars Pat O'Brien as Father Dunne. At that time, newspapers were sold by newsboys, who were poor and often abandoned boys or orphans.

What are some important movies about priests in the 1950s and 1960s?

Three interesting films are *The First Legion, On the Waterfront,* and *The Hoodlum Priest.*

What is *The First Legion*?

In 1951, United Artists released the movie *The First Legion* starring Charles Boyer, a story of several Jesuit priests who have their faith restored after several miracles happen. A contemporary Jesuit, Daniel A. Lord, had this to say about the film in *Played by Ear*:

371

The producers wanted to know exactly what a Jesuit house would look like. So they sent their scene supervisors on a tour of important Jesuit houses. They searched for a typical Jesuit recreation room, library, chapel, and private room. After much rubbing of chins and flashing of bulbs and comparing of notes, the scouts reported that none of the Jesuit houses were sufficiently Jesuitical....

So Hollywood tore up the snaps that had been made and drew up designs for their own sets. These turned out to be a cross between Grand Central Station, a Benedictine chapter room, the main room of the First National Bank, tessellated overtones of Metro-Gothic-Mayer.

What are some gritty movies about priests?

An important one is 1954's *On the Waterfront,* which was directed by Elia Kazan (1909–2003). Budd Schulberg (1914–2009) wrote the screenplay, and Leonard Bernstein (1918–1990) composed the music. The movie starred Marlon Brando and Eva Marie Saint. Karl Malden played the character of Father Barry, who is based on the real-life "waterfront priest" Father John M. Corridan, a Jesuit who ran a Catholic labor school in New York. Father Barry encourages the longshoremen, the men who loaded the ships, to stand up to corruption.

This movie won eight Academy Awards, including Best Motion Picture, Best Director, Best Actor, Best Screenplay, and Best Supporting Actress.

Less well known is 1961's *The Hoodlum Priest.* This movie, starring Don Murray, did well at the box office when it was released but has been mostly forgotten. It is based on the true story of Father Dismas Clark, a Jesuit who set up the first halfway house to help men coming out of prison, called Dismas House. Father Clark changed his name from Charles to Dismas because that was the name Christian tradition had given to the Good Thief crucified with Jesus as described in the Gospel of Luke. *The Hoodlum Priest* was filmed on location in St. Louis. Particularly gripping are the last scenes. Father Clark died in 1963; however, in 1965, Frank Sinatra did a famous concert in St. Louis called the *Frank Sinatra Spectacular* to raise money for Dismas House.

What are other movies made about Jesuit priests?

- *Black Robe* (1991), based on the novel of the same name, tells the dramatic story of Jesuit missionary Father Paul Laforgue, who in 1634 is working in the area that later became Quebec. He sets out on a journey to convert the Huron Indians.

- In *The Mission* (1986), set in the 1740s, Jesuit missionaries build a mission in the jungles of Paraguay in South America. The mission is destroyed when Portuguese forces come to enslave the people. The main musical theme, written by famous movie composer Ennio Morricone, has become a popular piece with numerous recordings.

- *Romero* (1989) tells the true story of Archbishop Óscar Romero in El Salvador in Central America. He organized peaceful protests against a brutal military regime that eventually assassinated him in 1980. Raúl Juliá played the role of Romero.

MOVIES ABOUT CATHOLIC NUNS

What movie about a nun stars Audrey Hepburn?

The movie *The Nun's Story* (1959) stars Audrey Hepburn and Peter Finch. It tells the story of Sr. Luke, a Belgian girl who enters the convent. She wants to go to the Belgian Congo to work in a hospital. However, she is first sent to work in a mental hospital and has to deal with the most difficult and violent cases.

What movie about building a chapel won Sidney Poitier an Oscar?

In *Lilies of the Field* (1963), Homer Smith, played by Sidney Poitier, is cajoled by Mother Maria, played by Lilia Skala, into building a chapel. Poitier won an Oscar for Best Actor, the first time an African American won the award.

Which film starred Susan Sarandon as a nun working to help a prison inmate?

Dead Man Walking (1995) stars Susan Sarandon as Sister Helen Prejean and Sean Penn as Matthew Poncelet, who faces the death penalty for murder and rape. The story is based on real-life events. Sister Prejean works to get Matthew's sentence reduced to life in prison and then tries to get him to accept responsibility for what he did.

Which two 1960s films featured singing nuns?

The Sound of Music (1965), starring Julie Andrews, won five Academy Awards, including Best Picture, Best Director, and Best Music. The movie was based on the 1959 Tony Award-winning hit musical *The Sound of Music,* with music written by Richard Rodgers and the lyrics written by Oscar Hammerstein. The musical was inspired by the story of Maria von Trapp (1905–1987) and the Trapp Family Singers.

The scene in the film where the Mother Abbess sings *Climb Every Mountain* is a particularly dramatic and inspiring moment.

The Singing Nun (1965) is loosely based on the life of Jeannine Deckers. Debbie Reynolds plays Sister Ann, who becomes famous by composing and performing the song "Dominque." Ricardo Montalbán plays Father Clementi, and TV variety show host Ed Sullivan appears as himself.

What are some other lighthearted films about Catholic sisters?

Five movies fit this category:

- *The Trouble with Angels* (1966), starring Hayley Mills and Rosalind Russell
- *Where Angels Go, Trouble Follows* (1968), starring Rosalind Russell and Stella Stevens
- *Change of Habit* (1969), with Mary Tyler Moore as Sister Michelle, who is conflicted over her love for Jesus and her love for Dr. John Carpenter, played by Elvis Presley
- *Sister Act* (1992), starring Whoopi Goldberg
- *Sister Act 2: Back in the Habit* (1993), starring Whoopi Goldberg

OTHER CHRISTIAN MOVIES OF NOTE

What are some movies about saints and heroic Christians?

- *The Song of Bernadette* (1943), about St. Bernadette of Lourdes (1844–1879)
- *A Man for All Seasons* (1966), about St. Thomas More (1478–1535)
- *Brother Sun, Sister Moon* (1972), about St. Francis of Assisi (1181–1226)
- *Roses in December* (1982), about the assassination of three Catholic sisters and a lay missionary in El Salvador in December 1980
- *Thérèse* (1986), about St. Thérèse of Lisieux (1873–1897)
- *The Saint of 9/11* (2006), about Father Mychal Judge, a chaplain for the New York Fire Department, who was killed on September 11, 2001

Is there a movie about the early Mormon church?

Brigham Young (1940), starring Tyrone Power, tells the dramatic story of Brigham Young, who led the Mormon pioneers west to Utah in the 1840s.

What movie is concerned with a prominent Presbyterian figure?

A Man Called Peter (1955) tells the true story of Peter Marshall (1902–1949), pastor of the New York Avenue Presbyterian Church in Washington, D.C., and chaplain of the U.S. Senate. Marshall is played by actor Richard Todd.

Is there a film about Martin Luther?

Actually, there are three, all of which were titled *Luther* (1928, 1973, and 2003). The 1928 version was a silent film, the 1973 film starred Stacy Keach, and the 2003 film starred Joseph Fiennes.

What classic horror film concerns priests and exorcisms?

The popular horror movie *The Exorcist* (1973) is based on the 1971 bestselling novel of the same title by William Peter Blatty. In the movie, starring Ellen Burstyn, Linda Blair, and Max von Sydow, two priests attempt to exorcise a demon from a twelve-year-old girl.

Blatty was inspired by the story he had heard while a student at the Jesuit Georgetown University in Washington, D.C., about an exorcism that was conducted in 1949 by Jesuits connected to St. Louis University in St. Louis, Missouri. An exorcism is a series of prayers to drive out a demon possessing a person.

The original *Exorcist* movie was followed by several sequels: *Exorcist II: The Heretic* (1977), *The Exorcist III* (1990), *Exorcist: The Beginning* (2004), and *Dominion: Prequel to the Exorcist* (2005).

Are any movies about Christian monks worth a look?

The documentary *Into Great Silence* (2005), directed by Philip Gröning, explores a monastery of Carthusian monks in the French Alps.

What social satire comments on how Christian values don't always mix with human society?

Heaven's Above (1963) is a fun and intriguing movie starring Peter Sellers that explores what would happen if people were to follow the teachings of Jesus. Sellers plays a reverend whose acts of charity upset the landed gentry of an English town.

375

Are there any other films that touch on religion that are worth seeing?

The 1991 film *Bill and Ted's Bogus Journey* (1991), starring Keanu Reeves, Alex Winter, and George Carlin, gives an interesting depiction of Heaven and Hell.

Mel Brooks's *History of the World, Part I* (1981) has several classic scenes, such as Moses receiving the Ten Commandments and the Last Supper.

The Blues Brothers (1980), with a lively church scene, and its sequel, *Blues Brothers 2000* (1998), with a scene at a tent revival, are worth seeing.

THE MOTION PICTURE
PRODUCTION CODE

What was the Motion Picture Production Code?

In the 1920s, many people were concerned that movies often emphasized sexual irresponsibility, crime, and violence. Hollywood producers and directors knew that these elements often made movies more interesting. As Hollywood producer Jack Warner admitted in Daniel A. Lord's *Played by Ear*, "Whenever my directors are stuck for something to do, they make the heroine take off her clothes."

Many people were upset about movie content, as there was no rating system for movies and children could see any movie shown. Some states and local municipalities started enacting censorship laws. The movie producers did not like such censorship since it varied from place to place, and they feared federal censorship.

FitzGeorge Dinneen, S.J., a pastor in Chicago, led boycotts over film content at local movie theaters. He knew Cardinal George Mundelein, head of the Catholic Church in Chicago. By coincidence, Mundelein had regular lunches with prominent bankers who, because of the 1929 financial collapse, now owned the movie companies. The bankers were also bothered by movie content.

Also concerned about movie content was Martin Quigley, publisher of the *Motion Picture Herald*, a publication for movie theater owners and operators. In discussions with Dinneen, Quigley, and Mundelein, guidelines for movies were written. The code itself was written in Chicago by Daniel Lord (1888–1955), a Jesuit from St. Louis. (The complete story of Daniel Lord can be found at daniellordsj.org) Due to Mundelein's influence, the Hollywood producers agreed to accept the code in the hope of avoiding federal censorship. The code, called the Motion Picture Production Code, was approved by the producers in 1930. In time, the Hays office, named for Will Hays (1979–1954), the chair of the Motion Picture Association of America, became the enforcer and interpreter of the Code. The later impact of the Hays Office is a long, complicated, and controversial story.

Lord's authorship of the Code was kept secret. Although a number of Catholic figures were involved in the creation of the Code and its later enforcement, there was nothing specifically Catholic or even Christian about the code. Many Protestants, Jews, and other people concerned about movie content supported the Code.

Lord was not some sort of moral prude. He got involved because he loved movies and theater. In his lifetime, he wrote over seventy plays, musicals, and pageants. He produced his largest plays with casts of over one thousand actors. Lord was not opposed to dealing with adult topics; he just thought live theater was the better place.

There is a large cross in Illinois on Interstate 70. Is it the largest cross in the world?

The cross stands at the intersection of Interstates 70 and 57 in the town of Effingham. The cross stands 198 feet tall. It is the largest cross in America but ranks seventh worldwide.

The tallest cross in the world is the Holy Cross of the Valley of the Fallen in Spain, which is 500 feet tall. The cross at the Shrine of Valor in the Philippines is 302 feet tall. The Cruz de Tercer Milenio (Cross of the Third Millennium) in Chile is 272 feet tall. There are many other large crosses around the world.

What is the largest statue of Jesus?

There are many large statues of Jesus around the world. The tallest is the 112-foot- (34-meter-) tall Christ of Peace statue in Bolivia. Next comes Christ the King in Poland at 108 feet (33 meters). Christ of Vũng Tàu in Vietnam stands 104 feet (32 meters) tall. Fourth in size, and perhaps the most famous, large Jesus statue is Christ the Redeemer perched on a mountain overlooking Rio de Janeiro, Brazil. It is 98 feet (30 meters) tall.

The Christ of the Ozarks statue in Eureka Springs, Arkansas, reaches 65.5 feet (20 meters). The Ozarks is a region of southern Missouri and northern Arkansas. The grounds of the statue are the site of *The Great Passion Play*, which is an outdoor production of the story of the Crucifixion and Resurrection of Jesus.

Where is "Touchdown Jesus"?

The University of Notre Dame in northern Indiana built the Theodore Hesburgh Library in 1963 with a large, 134-foot-tall "World of Life" mural on the outside with Jesus at the top with his arms raised. The mural faces the stadium and can be seen from the stadium. Since the raised arms of Jesus match a football referee's signal for a touchdown, the image is often called "Touchdown Jesus."

What was the attitude of Jesus toward women? Did he treat them differently from the surrounding culture?

Jesus never directly addressed the issue of the role of women, so gospel readers have to guess based on how he treated women and a few isolated statements. Jesus did not advocate for the rights of women and women's equality because the concepts of equality and rights are very modern concepts from the last several hundred years. However, given the time and place he lived and his culture, where women were treated very unequally, Jesus in many ways broke down boundaries. For instance,

The largest statue of Jesus Christ in the world is 112 feet (34 meters) tall and stands atop San Pedro Hill in Cochabamba, Bolivia.

women were among his followers and played important roles, although we do not know the exact details. Jesus also taught theology to women, which at the time was groundbreaking, and went against traditional views that theology was for men alone.

What is the Jesus Seminar?

About 150 biblical scholars and researchers met from 1985 to 2006 under the leadership of Robert Funk. They sorted through all the sayings of Jesus in the traditional four gospels as well as other material, such as the Gospel of Thomas, to try to assess what the original sayings and ideas about Jesus were. The seminar published three books: *The Five Gospels* (1993), *The Acts of Jesus* (1998), and *The Gospel of Jesus* (1999). Seminar members were trying to reconstruct the life and teachings of the historical Jesus. In doing so, for example, they saw the sayings of Jesus in the Gospel of Thomas as more authentic than the sayings of Jesus in the Gospel of John. The seminar was criticized by some for both its methods and conclusions. Others found the project both helpful and insightful for understanding Jesus.

Who are Messianic Jews?

Jews typically reject all the religious claims about Jesus that are made by Christians, such as beliefs in the Resurrection, the Incarnation, and the Trinity. Although Jews may recognize that Jesus existed and that he was a religious teacher, they typically reject his teachings. Many Jews believe in the hope for a Messiah to rescue the Jewish people;

however, they reject the idea that Jesus was the Messiah (the Christ). Also, many Jews see a rejection of the Christian claims about Jesus—especially that he is the Messiah—as one of the key boundaries between Christianity and religious Judaism.

However, there is a small group of Jews who accept the religious claims about Jesus. They are called Messianic Jews. These Jews accept that Jesus is the promised Messiah and believe in the Christian beliefs of Incarnation, Resurrection, and Trinity.

Probably, there are over two hundred thousand Messianic Jews in the United States. Messianic Jews retain many of their Jewish customs and rituals. Although most Christians accept Messianic Jews as true Christians, many traditional Jews see Messianic Jews as no longer being true Jews.

What is the Nag Hammadi library?

In 1945, in the Egyptian town of Nag Hammadi, a farmer found a large, sealed jar containing thirteen ancient documents bound in leather that were written in the Coptic language. They were probably buried by Christian monks in the 300s. The most important work in the collection was the only complete copy of the Gospel of Thomas. The other writings were both Christian and Gnostic texts. The findings have greatly increased our knowledge of the religious world in the early centuries of Christianity. Also, for many, the Gospel of Thomas has shed more light on the teachings of Jesus.

What is the Mexican story of Our Lady of Guadalupe?

To understand Roman Catholicism in Mexico, you must know about Our Lady of Guadalupe. The basilica of Our Lady of Guadalupe in Mexico City is one of the most visited Catholic shrines in the world.

The story of Our Lady of Guadalupe is as follows. In 1531, a Mexican peasant, Juan Diego, climbed a hill, where he claimed that Mary, the mother of Jesus, appeared to him several times in December 1531. Speaking his native language of Nahuatl, she asked for a church to be built in her honor.

When Juan Diego told the story to the bishop, Juan de Zumárraga, the bishop did not believe him. When Juan Diego next saw Mary, she told him to take some roses to the bishop. Although it was winter, when roses do not grow, Juan found the roses. He gathered them in his cloak. When Juan presented the roses to the bishop, an image of Mary was left on the cloak. It was a miracle!

What is the Oberammergau Passion Play?

This play depicting the last days of Jesus has been performed on an outdoor stage since 1634 in the town of Oberammergau in Bavaria, Germany. It is performed for several months every ten years with a cast of two thousand. The play is internationally well known.

Following Mary's instructions, a church was built in Mexico City. The first church was started in 1531. It still stands and is called the Old Basilica. A later and much larger church, the New Basilica, was built; it is there where the cloak of Juan Diego with its image of Mary is on display. Countless pilgrims go to see the cloak.

What is the symbolism in the image?

Many link the symbolism of the cloak with this passage in the book of Revelation: "A great sign appeared in the sky, a woman clothed with the sun, with the moon under her feet, and on her head a crown of twelve stars" (Revelation 12:1, NABRE).

Others think the image has Aztec symbolism. Some people even think that this image of Mary is based on the image of the Mexican mother goddess Tonantzin. Tepeyac Hill, where Juan Diego had his visions, is possibly the site of an ancient shrine to Tonantzin.

How important is Our Lady of Guadalupe?

Very important! The image can be found all over Mexico. It is found in homes, churches, shops, and even in buses and taxis. Our Lady of Guadalupe has been a unifying symbol for the very diverse population of Mexico. It was an important symbol during the War for Independence. Our Lady of Guadalupe is sometimes called the "Patroness of the Americas." Many miracles are attributed to Our Lady of Guadalupe.

What is the historical documentation for the Juan Diego story?

The documentation of the story comes from two written sources: *Imagen de la Virgen Maria, Madre de Dios de Guadalupe*, written by Miguel Sánchez in 1648, and *Huei tlamahuiçoltica*, written by Luis Laso de la Vega in 1649. Notice that both sources were written more than one hundred years after 1531, when the story took place. There is no reference to Juan Diego and the miracle in the writings of Bishop Juan de Zumárraga, the bishop in the story.

What is the Prayer of St. Francis?

The famous Prayer of St. Francis was not written by St. Francis of Assisi. The prayer first appeared in print in 1912 in *La Clochette* (The Little Bell), a Catholic spiritual magazine in Paris. Perhaps it was written by Father Esther Bouquerel.

Statues and other images of Our Lady of Guadalupe are very important among Mexican Catholics.

Lord, make me an instrument of your peace.
Where there is hatred, let me bring love.
Where there is offense, let me bring pardon.
Where there is discord, let me bring union.
Where there is error, let me bring truth.
Where there is doubt, let me bring faith.
Where there is despair, let me bring hope.
Where there is darkness, let me bring your light.
Where there is sadness, let me bring joy.
O Master, let me not seek as much
to be consoled as to console,
to be understood as to understand,
to be loved as to love.
For it is in giving that one receives,
it is in self-forgetting that one finds,
it is in pardoning that one is pardoned,
it is in dying that one is raised to eternal life.

Are there really Christians who handle live poisonous snakes in their church services?

There is a small and unusual group of Christians known as "snake handlers." They exist in several small, independent churches mostly in the Appalachian region. They often follow typical Pentecostal practices such as speaking in tongues, but they go further.

This group is inspired by a verse in the Gospel of Mark: "They will pick up snakes in their hands, and if they drink any deadly thing, it will not hurt them; they will lay their hands on the sick, and they will recover" (Mark 16:18, NRSV). They handle poisonous snakes during their church services. Most Christians ignore this passage, but not these churches. They see snake handling as a witness of their faith and a way to demonstrate their trust in God. From time to time, snake handlers get bit, and sometimes, they die. (A bite from a snake will not always kill you. It depends on what kind of snake bites you, how much venom goes in you, and your overall health.)

The vast majority of Christians and Pentecostals see the practice of handling snakes as wrong and not consistent with the true spirit of the gospels. If you are interested in exploring this topic, there are several videos on YouTube, but keep in mind the general advice: "Do not try this at home!"

What are stigmatics?

Stigmatics are people who have the bleeding wounds of Christ on their hands, feet, and sides of their chests. The first recorded case was St. Francis of Assisi (c. 1181–1226). The most famous recent stigmatic was Padre Pio of Pietrelcina (1887–1968) in Italy. Both figures are Roman Catholic saints. There have been a number of stigmatics down through the centuries.

The term "stigmata" refers to the wounds. A person with these wounds is called a stigmatic or a stigmatist. Although stigmatics are found in the Catholic tradition, there is much disagreement about whether these wounds are true miracles that are a sign of devotion or fakes. Typically, Christians outside the Catholic tradition do not accept the authenticity of claims about stigmatics.

What is the Two-Swords Theory that developed in the Middle Ages?

In the stories of the arrest of Jesus, all four gospels refer to there being one or two swords among those around Jesus. As described earlier, the swords fulfilled a prophecy about Jesus being found among brigands. In 1302, Pope Boniface VIII took the gospel references to two swords to create a theory that the Catholic Church under the pope had ultimate control over both religious and secular power, which the Church gave to the political authorities. Religious power is the spiritual sword, and secular power is the temporal sword. Here are the words from his decree, *Unam Sanctum*:

> We are taught by the words of the Gospel that in this Church and under her control there are two swords, the spiritual and the temporal … both of these, i.e., the spiritual and the temporal swords, are under the control of the Church. The first is wielded by the Church; the second is wielded on behalf of the church. The first is wielded by the hands of the priest, the second by the hands of kings and soldiers, but at the wish and by the permission of the priests. Sword must be subordinate to sword, and it is only fitting that the temporal authority should be subject to the spiritual.

It is important to note that Jesus had no interest in either kind of power. In fact, in the Gospels of Matthew and Luke, the lure of political power is a temptation by the Devil. Most kings and rulers ignored such claims by the pope. Most later popes also ignored the theory.

Which Christian church is the true Christian church?

Because there are so many different Christian denominations and churches, it is no surprise that a wide range of answers exist to this question. Typically, Christian groups believe that their denomination or church is part of the true Christian church. The question then is "What about those other Christians who are not part of my denomination or church?"

A number of Christian denominations or churches feel that their group alone represents the true Christian faith and that other groups are not part of the true Christian church. Some groups down through history have even believed that salvation can only be given to members of their church or denomination.

Other Christians have a broader view that the boundaries of the true Christian church are left to God to decide. Christians in this category see many of the other Christian churches as sharing in the true teaching of Christianity. This is a more inclusive view of how the different denominations fit together. Sometimes, Christians with this more inclusive view do see some boundaries such as core Christian beliefs that are the marks of the true Christian church. For example, for those Christians who believe in the Incarnation and Trinity, they would see those denominations and churches that also believe in the Incarnation and Trinity as part of the broader Christian church and those denominations and churches that do not believe in the Incarnation and Trinity as not being part of the broader Christian church. Other Christian groups might make certain beliefs about the Bible the measure of which groups are true Christians or not.

What is the Vatican?

There is an area of Rome, going back to ancient times, known as the Vatican. According to Christian tradition, both Peter and Paul were executed in the first century in this area. By the time of the Roman Emperor Constantine in the 300s, a church had been

St. Peter's Square in Vatican City spreads out in front of St. Peter's Basillica and marks the heart of the city.

built on the site to remember St. Peter and St. Paul. Eventually, the church was referred to as St. Peter's.

In the early Middle Ages, the role of the bishop of Rome became more important. He became the pope, who claimed authority over all the Christian churches in Western Europe. He had several palaces and churches in Rome. The pope's main cathedral was the Church of St. John Lateran. By the Middle Ages, the pope also owned and controlled an area of land that was about one fifth of the size of Italy today. This area was called the Papal States, and the pope was in effect the king of this land. The rest of what would become Italy was broken up into other kingdoms.

By the time of the Renaissance, the popes were very interested in St. Peter's church and other buildings in the Vatican area, such as the Sistine Chapel. Pope Julius II forced Michelangelo to paint the ceiling of the Sistine Chapel.

The old St. Peter's was demolished and rebuilt as the current giant church. It is the largest church in the world. Michelangelo designed the dome of the church.

In the 1600s, the colonnade was added in front of the building. It was designed by famous architect and sculptor Gian Lorenzo Bernini. The area is called St. Peter's Square, although it is actually a circle.

From the Renaissance on, the Vatican complex of buildings was the headquarters for the church. It is where the pope lives today.

In the 1800s in Europe, the movement known as nationalism was very strong. Many people wanted to create independent nations based on their nationality. At the time, Italy was divided. A revolutionary movement developed with the goal of uniting all of Italy and driving out foreigners who controlled some parts of Italy.

By 1870, the Italians had taken all of Italy, except Rome, which they could not take because French soldiers protected the pope. It was at this point that Pope Pius IX called the first Vatican Council, also known as Vatican I. At the same time, German troops had invaded France and were surrounding Paris in the Franco-Prussian War. (Prussia was a kingdom that would become part of the nation of Germany.) Due to the desperate situation in France, the French troops were pulled out of Rome and sent back home. The Italian nationalists then took over most of Rome, except for the complex of buildings of the Vatican where the pope lived.

Although Pope Pius IX complained bitterly about the loss of the Papal States, it freed the him from having to deal with political concerns of the kingdom. The pope could now focus on spiritual issues and Catholic moral teachings. In time, the popes would become internationally recognized moral teachers.

The legal status of the Vatican remained unresolved until 1929, when an agreement, called the Lateran Treaty, was worked out between the Italian government under Benito Mussolini and Pope Pius XI to make the Vatican a separate country within Italy. Thus, Vatican City, at 270 acres, became the smallest country in the world.

What is the importance of Zoroastrianism for Christianity?

Zoroastrianism was the first religion to include the following elements:

- A clearly defined Heaven for good people and a Hell for bad people
- A judgment of the dead to decide who goes to Heaven and Hell
- A resurrection of the dead in Heaven for good people; angels as the assistants of a good God
- A powerful evil being; demons as assistants to the evil being
- A final battle of good against evil at the end of time

All of these ideas entered the Jewish world in the centuries before Jesus and were being debated at the time of Jesus. Some Jews accepted these ideas, and some did not. The Pharisees were open to many of these ideas, particularly the idea of the resurrection of the dead. The Sadducees were not. A passage in the Gospel of Mark states: "Some Sadducees, who say there is no resurrection, came to him and put this question to him …" (Mark 12:18; see also Matthew 22:23 and Luke 20:27).

In the Book of Acts, in Chapter 23, Paul is brought before the Jewish high council, the Sanhedrin. He starts a dispute:

> Paul was aware that some were Sadducees and some Pharisees, so he called out before the Sanhedrin, "My brothers, I am a Pharisee, the son of Pharisees; I am on trial for hope in the resurrection of the dead." When he said this, a dispute broke out between the Pharisees and Sadducees, and the group became divided. For the Sadducees say that there is no resurrection or angels or spirits, while the Pharisees acknowledge all three. A great uproar occurred, and some scribes belonging to the Pharisee party stood up and sharply argued, "We find nothing wrong with this man. Suppose a spirit or an angel has spoken to him?" The dispute was so serious that the commander, afraid that Paul would be torn to pieces by them, ordered his troops to go down and rescue him from their midst and take him into the compound.
>
> —Acts 23:6–10, NABRE

Early Christians embraced all these key ideas of Zoroastrianism. At the time of Jesus, the Jewish world was complex with many groups such as the Sadducees, the Pharisees, and the revolutionaries—later called the Zealots and the Essenes. In the decades after Jesus, there were a number of Jewish revolts that were brutally crushed by the Romans. The temple was destroyed in the year 70 C.E.

The Sadducees were the priestly families who ran the Temple. When the Temple was destroyed, the Sadducees lost their reason to be and faded away. All the revolutionary groups, such as the Zealots, were destroyed by the Romans. The Essenes disappeared, probably also destroyed by the Romans. The only group to survive were the Pharisees, who in time became the rabbis of later Judaism. Thus, many concepts that had first been Zoroastrian ideas, such as angels and the resurrection of the dead, entered Judaism.

Further Reading

Aslan, Reza. *Zealot: The Life and Times of Jesus of Nazareth*. New York: Random House, 2014.

Augustine. *Confessions: A New Translation by Sarah Ruden*. New York: Modern Library, 2017.

Bainton, Roland. *Here I Stand: A Life of Martin Luther*. New York: Abingdon-Cokesbury Press, 1950.

Cross, F. L., and E. A. Livingstone, eds. *The Oxford Dictionary of the Christian Church*. Oxford: Oxford University Press, 1984.

Cunningham, Lawrence S., and John J. Reich. *Culture and Values: A Survey of the Humanities*. Alternate Volume, 6th ed. Belmont, CA: Thompson Wadsworth, 2006.

Fisher, James T. *Catholics in America*. New York: Oxford University Press, 2000.

Gayla, Visalli, ed. *After Jesus—The Triumph of Christianity*. New York: Reader's Digest Association, 1992.

Livingston, James C. *Modern Christian Thought: The Enlightenment and the Nineteenth Century*. 2nd ed. Minneapolis: Fortress Press, 2006.

Lord, Daniel. *Played by Ear: The Autobiography of Daniel A. Lord, S.J.* Chicago: Loyola University Press, 1956.

Mueller, J. J., ed. *Theological Foundations: Concepts and Methods for Understanding Christian Faith*. Winona, MN: Anselm Academic, 2011.

Noll, Mark A. *Protestants in America*. New York: Oxford University Press, 2000.

Peterson, R. Dean. *A Concise History of Christianity*, 2nd ed. Belmont, CA: Wadsworth Publishing, 1999.

Prince, Jennifer R. *The Handy Bible Answer Book*. Detroit, MI: Visible Ink Press, 2014.

Renard, John. *The Handy Religion Answer Book*, 2nd ed. Detroit, MI: Visible Ink Press, 2012.

Westrheim, Margo. *Celebrate! A Look at Calendars and the Ways We Celebrate*. Oxford: One World, 1999.

Index

Note: (ill.) indicates photos and illustrations.

391

illness, Christian Science view on, 261–62
Immaculate Conception, 29, 328
immortality, 303–4
incarnation, 121–23
inclusivist position on Heaven, 308
independent churches, 8
Indulgences, 205–6, 226
Infancy Narratives, 27–28
Inherit the Wind, 268
Innocent III, Pope, 214, 217
Inquisition, 216
"I.N.R.I." on crucifixion sign, 18
Interstate 70 cross (Effingham, IL), 379
Into Great Silence (2005), 375
Ireland, snakes in, 199
Irenaeus, 179
irresistibility of grace, 229
Isabella, Queen, 200, 216, 256
Isaiah, 146–47, 342, 357
Isenheim Altarpiece, 340
Islam, 200
Islamic tradition, 143
Israel, 145

J

Jackson, Mahalia, 354, 358–59, 359 (ill.)
Jairus, 42
James, brother of Jesus, 94, 96 (ill.), 96–97
James I, King, 241
James the Greater (Apostle), 103, 105, 338
James the Lesser (Apostle), 103, 106, 338
Jehovah's Witnesses, 4, 117, 264–65, 280, 307
Jenkins, Jerry B., 318
Jeremiah, 162, 342
Jerome, 197
Jerusalem, 144
Jesuits, 240
Jesus, 131 (ill.). *See also* crucifixion of Jesus
   accepting as one's Lord and Savior, 309–10
   Agony in the Garden, 56
   almsgiving, 86, 86 (ill.)
   anger, 79
   Annas and Caiaphas, 113
   answered questions about, 13
   anti-Semitism in Gospel of John, 25
   apocryphal writings, 12
   Ascension, 62–63, 63 (ill.)
   attitude toward women, 380
   baptism of, 32–35, 33 (ill.), 282
   biblical sources on, 9–11

   birth of, 30 (ill.), 30–32, 273
   brothers of, 94, 96 (ill.), 96–97
   burial of, 60–61
   as the Christ, 118
   Christian tradition, 13
   Cleansing of the Temple, 52–54, 53 (ill.)
   Dead Sea Scrolls, 12
   in definition of Christianity, 1
   description of, 172
   in desert, 35–36
   divorce, 81–82
   driving out demons, 40–42
   driving out demons from Mary Magdalene, 108–9
   early life of, 15–16
   entry into Jerusalem, 50, 51, 51 (ill.)
   Essenes, 21–22
   ethical teachings of, 75–89
   exaggeration, 81
   faith, 68–69
   feeding the multitudes, 43–44, 44 (ill.)
   forgiveness, 88, 89
   Gehenna, 79–80, 80 (ill.)
   Golden Rule, 87–88
   Good Samaritan parable, 70–72, 71 (ill.)
   gospels and lack of details about, 13–15
   healing of bleeding woman, 39–40, 40 (ill.)
   on Hell, 305–6
   "I am" statements, 90–91
   Infancy Narratives, 27–28
   Jewish Law, 78–79
   Jewish sources, 11
   Jewish world of, 20–25
   John (Apostle), 102–3
   John's Gospel vs. synoptics, 155–56
   Joseph, 94–96, 95 (ill.)
   Judas Iscariot, 55, 111–12
   judging others, 87
   Kingdom of God, 66–68
   Kingdom of Heaven, 67
   language spoken by, 14 (ill.), 15
   last days of, 49
   Last Supper, 54–56, 55 (ill.)
   Law of Moses, 78
   left behind in Jerusalem, 153–54
   legend of the dogwood tree, 60
   lepers, 39
   loving one's enemies, 85–86
   as the Messiah, 47–48, 118–20
   Messianic Secret, 52, 119–20
   miracles of, 38–39, 44–45
   miracles over nature, 45–47, 46 (ill.)
   miraculous catch of fish, 45–47, 46 (ill.)

   money, 86–87
   movies about, 364–68, 368
   name of, 13
   nonbiblical sources on, 9, 11
   in paintings, 335, 338
   parables, 69–75
   Pharisees, 21
   political environment during time of, 15
   Pontius Pilate, 112–13, 113 (ill.)
   Prodigal Son parable, 73 (ill.), 73–75
   public ministry of, 16 (ill.), 16–17
   public ministry stories, 37–49
   raising the dead, 42–43
   Redeemer, 132
   relationship to God the Father, 91
   religious faith in God the Father, 68
   religious people around him, 79
   Resurrection, 60–62, 120–21, 122 (ill.)
   retaliation, 83–84
   riding a donkey, 51
   Roman sources, 11
   Sadducees, 21
   Savior, 131–32
   Second Coming of, 169–70
   Sheep and Goats parable, 72
   sources on, 9–13
   sower and the seed parable, 70
   statements about himself, 90–91
   statue, 379, 380 (ill.)
   swearing oaths, 82–83
   and tax collector, 337
   teachings of, 65–66
   Temple (Jerusalem), 22 (ill.), 22–23
   temptations of, 35–37
   Thomas, Gospel of, 13
   Transfiguration, 37–38, 38 (ill.)
   Two Swords, 84–85
   violence, 84
   walking on water, 45–47, 46 (ill.)
   Zacchaeus, 89
   Zealots, 22
Jesus Christ Superstar (1971), 53, 111, 366–67
Jesus of Montreal (1989), 366
Jesus of Nazareth (1977), 366
Jesus Seminar, 380
Jewish Bible, 135–36, 136, 136 (ill.)
Jewish Law, 78–79
Jewish sources, 11
Jews in the Middle Ages, 206-07, 207 (ill.)
Joachim, 114
Joan of Arc, 220
Jogues, Isaac, 257

N